D1201843

Volume 1

Garland Folklore Casebooks

General Editor
Alan Dundes
University of California, Berkeley

THE WISDOM OF MANY
Essays on the Proverb

edited by
Wolfgang Mieder
Alan Dundes

GARLAND PUBLISHING, INC. • NEW YORK & LONDON
1981

Library of Congress Cataloging in Publication Data

Main entry under title:

The Wisdom of many.

(Garland folklore casebooks ; v. 1)
Bibliography: p.
1. Proverbs—History and criticism—Addresses, essays, lectures. I. Mieder, Wolfgang. II. Dundes, Alan. III. Series.
PN6401.W57 398.9 80-8512
ISBN 0-8240-9472-7 AACR2

Printed on acid-free, 250-year-life paper
Manufactured in the United States of America

Folklore Casebook Series

The materials of folklore demonstrate remarkable variation. Each of the cultures which share a particular item of folklore, for example, a myth, a folktale, a custom, a folk belief, has its own special version of that item. Sometimes individuals within a given culture will have their own idiosyncratic variations within the larger culturewide tradition. Students of folklore who study the folklore of only their own group may fail to appreciate the range of variation in folklore. By bringing together different studies of the same item of folklore, I hope to provide a means of demonstrating both the ways in which folklore remains constant across cultures and the ways in which folklore is inevitably localized in different cultural contexts.

With respect to the distribution of an item of folklore, there are two all too common erroneous assumptions. The first assumption is that the item of folklore is peculiar to one culture. Those anthropologists, for example, who are unwilling to be comparative, typically assume or assert that a given folktale is unique to "their" people, meaning the people among whom they have carried out their fieldwork. The critical theoretical point is that one cannot tell whether or how a folktale is really unique to one culture without knowing if the same tale is found in other cultures. Once one has examined other versions of the tale, then and only then can one comment intelligently on just how a particular version of that tale reflects the culturally relative characteristics of a given society.

The second erroneous assumption, equally irritating to professional folklorists, is that a given item of folklore is universal. This is the opposite extreme from the first assumption. Rather than presuming that the item is unique to one culture, the universalist (typically a literary or psychologically oriented student) simply posits the existence of the item in all cultures. Yet the facts do not support this position any more than the other. Most items of folklore have limited areas of distribution. For example, there are Indo-European folktales reported from India to Ireland, but most of these tales are *not* found among Australian aborigines, the peoples of Melanesia and Polynesia, South American Indians, etc. Similarly, there are folktales found in North and South American Indian tradition which are not found in Europe. If one takes the trouble to check the sources cited by universalists, he or she will normally find little if any reference to the traditions of the peoples of New Guinea, native South America, and sub-Saharan Africa among other areas.

One cannot say a priori what the distribution of a particular item of folklore might be. One needs to consult the scholarship devoted to the item before venturing an informed opinion. Chances are great, however, that the item will not be limited to a single culture nor will it be worldwide. One aim of the Folklore Casebook series then is to show by example something about the range and spread of individual items of folklore.

Questions about the geographical distribution of an item of folklore are not the only ones worth asking. Even more important are questions about meaning and interpretation. Far too often, students of folklore simply collect and report. Pure descriptions of data are surely a precondition for serious study, but they do not offer a substitute for significant analysis. Unfortunately, the majority of writings about a particular item of folklore never attempt anything more than mere description. The discipline of folklore began several centuries ago with the collection of antiquities and presumed "survivals" from earlier periods. It was not until the late nineteenth century and especially the twentieth century that the crucial study of how folklore functions in context may be said to have begun. In most cases, the application of sociological, anthropological, psychological and other theories and methods to folkloristic data has yet to be undertaken. One reason for this is that most theorists in the social sciences are just as unaware of the nature of folklore data as folklorists are unaware of the theories and methods of the social sciences. One intent of the Folklore Casebook series is to bring data and theory together—at least for students of folklore.

Folklore has always fascinated members of many academic disciplines, e.g., scholars in classics, comparative literature, Bible studies, psychiatry, sociology, but despite its interdisciplinary appeal, the study of folklore has rarely been interdisciplinary. One can find lip service to the notion of interdisciplinary study, but scholars and their work for the most part tend to be parochial. Anthropologists cite only the work of fellow anthropologists, psychiatrists only the work of other psychiatrists. Similarly, folklorists too are not always open to considering studies of folklore made by nonfolklorists. Accordingly, students who come upon a specific problem in folklore are commonly restricted by the limited disciplinary bias and knowledge of their instructors.

One difficulty in being truly interdisciplinary involves a mechanical problem in locating the previous scholarship devoted to a problem. Folklore studies appear in an incredible and often bewildering variety of books, monographs, and professional periodicals. One needs sometimes to be a virtual bibliographical sleuth to discover what other scholars have said about the subject one has chosen to research. Yet the credo of the true scholar ought to be that he should begin *his* work where other scholars have ended theirs. With this in mind, one other aim of the Folklore Casebook series is to bring together under one cover a representative sampling of the scholarship relevant to a single item or problem. It is hoped that it will encourage students of folklore not to be parochial in outlook but rather to be willing if not anxious to explore all possibilities in investigating the folklore research topic they have selected.

The topics covered in the Folklore Casebook series are of sufficient general interest to have received the critical attention of numerous scholars. Topics such as the evil eye, the flood myth, the bullfight, Christmas, the custom of couvade, or the folktale of Oedipus would be examples of topics appropriate for casebook treatment. In most instances, whole books or monographs have been devoted to the topics. However, for the most part, the selections chosen for the Casebook have been taken from periodicals. Assembling representative essays from a variety of sources seemed to be the best means of achieving the various goals of the Casebook series. Students who wish to explore further the topic of one of the Casebooks would be well advised to consult the book-length treatments available. In each Casebook, the editor will provide some bibliographical references for the student who wishes to go beyond the necessarily limited materials contained in the volume.

The selections included in the casebooks will be presented as they originally appeared, wherever possible. To be sure, essays written in foreign languages will be translated for the casebook, but individual words or phrases in foreign languages may be left untranslated. It is important for students of folklore to be aware of the necessity for learning to read foreign languages. Because the different selections were written independently, it is inevitable that some repetition will occur. Students must realize that such repetition in scholarship is not unusual. In folklore in particular, the repetition of data is often desirable. As indicated above, folklorists are often concerned with the question to what extent is an item of folklore in one culture similar to or different from an apparently comparable item in another culture.

The scholarly apparatus including footnote and bibliographical reference style have also been left intact wherever possible. Differences between the humanities and social sciences exist with respect to reference techniques as any scholar who has had occasion to rewrite or recast an essay to conform to the requirements of another discipline can very well attest. Leaving the footnotes in their original form also serves to demonstrate the partial nature of scholarship. Probably no one scholar ever controls all the relevant data and has read all the books and essays pertaining to his subject. For one thing, few scholars can read all those languages of the world in which germane material has been written. For another, there remains the perennial information retrieval problem which normally precludes even locating all the possible sources. Still granting the unavoidably incomplete nature of most scholarship, the student can still see differences in how well an individual scholar succeeded in finding source materials. Some writers make little or no attempt to consult sources—almost pretending that they are the first to ever contemplate the issue under consideration. Others seem to make a pedantic fetish out of citing esoteric and fugitive sources. In the final analysis, the criteria for the inclusion of an essay in a casebook did not include counting the number of references contained in an author's footnotes. Rather the criteria concerned the clarity of the description of the data and the degree of insight attained in the analysis of the data. It should be understood that not every important essay written about the topic or theme of a casebook could be included. Some essays were simply too long while others may have been superseded by later studies.

Despite limitations, it is hoped that the sampling of scholarship presented in the Folklore Casebook series will assist students of folklore in undertaking research of their own. Whether they are stimulated to continue the study of the particular topic treated in a casebook or whether they use one or more of the essays as a model for the investigation of some other topic, the ultimate goal is the upgrading of the quality of folklore research. As the discipline of folkloristics continues to grow, its success and its achievements will unquestionably depend upon how well future students study the materials of folklore.

Alan Dundes, General Editor
University of California, Berkeley

CONTENTS

Introduction

We have attempted to bring together in one volume what we consider to be representative studies of the proverb. Proverb scholarship is extremely diverse, including as it does research by folklorists, psychologists, linguists, and students of literature among others. Generally speaking, we limited our selections to English-language essays since our primary goal was to illustrate the various approaches employed in paremiology (proverb studies). Essays written in other languages typically cited proverbs in those languages, making it difficult if not impossible to translate them easily.

It is our hope that the book will prove useful as an introduction to modern proverb research techniques. It is intended both for individual scholars and for students enrolled in courses where the proverb is treated.

The twenty essays begin with general overviews and questions of definition. This is followed by discussions of the function and meaning of proverbs in social context. Next we present examples of the proverb in literary contexts ranging from the Bible to Shakespeare. Included also are detailed investigations of individual proverbs. Other essays address the utilization of proverbs in psychological testing, the possible relevance of proverbs to identifying national character, and, finally, the influence of proverbs in the modern world of mass media. Several of the essays contain technical features, e.g., texts in Latin, statistical charts, etc., but the majority should be intelligible enough for the literate reader. In any case, our aim was to present a sampling of scholarship to show the state of the art of studying proverbs. At the end of the volume we have provided a very short, selected bibliography designed to direct readers further into proverb scholarship.

It is unlikely that any two individuals interested in the proverb would necessarily agree upon what essays should be included in a volume such as this. In this case, each paper selected from the hundreds examined had to be acceptable to both of us. Even a cursory glance at the range of periodicals in which these studies originally appeared should attest to our genuine effort to be as eclectic as possible. We wish to thank all of the authors and publishers for their kindness in allowing us to reprint copyrighted materials.

Wolfgang Mieder and Alan Dundes
Berkeley, California 1980

THE WISDOM OF MANY

The Wisdom of Many and the Wit of One

*Archer Taylor**

It is inconceivable to think of having a volume of essays devoted to the proverb without including at least one written by the acknowledged doyen of proverb studies, Archer Taylor. We have deliberately chosen one of his less technical papers in order to show the extraordinary appeal of proverbial materials. The paper was an address given at Swarthmore College in 1962. Readers interested in Professor Taylor's huge corpus of works on the proverb would do well to start with his still classic The Proverb, *first published by Harvard University Press in 1931. A valuable compilation of many of his important papers may be found in Wolfgang Mieder, ed.,* Selected Writings on Proverbs by Archer Taylor, *FFC 216 (Helsinki, 1975). This latter volume also includes a comprehensive bibliography of Archer Taylor's many notes and articles in paremiology.*

A proverb is wise; it belongs to many people; it is ingenious in form and idea; and it was first invented by an individual and applied by him to a particular situation. My title illustrates both the origin and the nature of a proverb. One morning at breakfast Lord John Russell, the English statesman who negotiated the treaty to put an end to the Seven Years War, is said to have defined a proverb by saying it is *One man's wit and all men's wisdom.* Popular use has shifted the order of the elements and their emphasis. A proverb is, in the first place,

*Reprinted from *Swarthmore College Bulletin*, 54 (1962), 4–7.

wisdom—what sort of wisdom we shall see later, and the element of individual invention has subordinate importance.

What is wisdom, which is the first and most significant quality of a proverb? The easiest and surest answer is to look at some samples. For one thing, it is moral advice based on experience. *Honesty is the best policy* is familiar enough and cannot be said too often. *Don't cross your bridges before you come to them* is sound counsel from a traveler's experience. The truth may be bitter and cynical: *Never give a sucker an even break. Money doesn't grow on trees,* and *Them as has gits.* I know very well that the last of these is an aphorism coined by a California poet. Still, we can safely say that *One man's wit* (as Lord John would have it) has become traditional.

A proverb is practical as well as moral wisdom. *Rain before seven, shine before eleven* is a traditional observation about the weather that is more likely to be true in England than in California and thus betrays its foreign origin. Where it was at home it had practical value. *You must eat a peck of dirt before you die* means, as proverbs often do, two things. Either one should not mind too much what has been called "clean dirt" or one will suffer many humiliations during one's life. *An apple a day drives the doctor away* is proverbial medical recommendation, and probably a very sensible one, too.

Every aspect of life yields general advice, that is to say, proverbs. Law gives us *Every man's—or an Englishman's—house is his castle. First come, first served* is an old rule about bringing corn to the mill. *Silence gives consent* and *The king can do no wrong* are legal maxims. Beside these one can name proverbs giving us a kind of law not written down in books: *All's fair in love and war, Hands off is fair play,* and *Don't kick a man when he is down.* Does *Every dog is allowed his first bite* have any standing in court? From the church we have *An honest confession is good for the soul,* and modern psychology tells us how wise this advice is and urges us to put it into practice. In daily life we see that *A new broom sweeps clean, Too many cooks spoil the broth,* and *You can't spoil a rotten egg.* The advice may be ironical: *Bachelors' wives and old maids' children are well taught.* There is sound counsel in *Fish or cut bait* and *Make friends while you are going up, you may need them coming down.* Few proverbs reflect a highly organized social and commercial life: *Business is business, Cut your losses and let your profits run,* and *You never lost money taking a profit.* Here are enough examples of the kinds of wisdom found in proverbs, and we are told *Enough is enough.*

The word "proverb" is used in a limited and a more general sense. It may be an old or a new comment on life and morals, like *Beggars must not be choosers,* which has a long history, and *Poor but proud,* which may not be more than a century old. In either case it sums up a situation. In this we can find another definition of a proverb and one that includes more than statements in the form of full sentences. The summing up may have the shape of traditional combinations of words like *Every Tom, Dick, and Harry,* and *Rag, tag, and bobtail.* It may be a phrase like *From A to Z, Once in a blue moon, When Hec was a pup, Kneehigh to a grasshopper, Age before beauty.* We can at times guess when the phrases were invented. *After us the deluge* foretold the French Revolution, much as *A chicken in every pot* summed up the hope for material prosperity a generation ago. The summing up may be a verbal phrase like *To cut off one's nose to spite one's face, To be on the fence,* and *To be behind the eight ball.* The verbal phrase may be almost always used in the negative: *Not to have sense enough to come in when it rains, To have no more backbone than an eel.*

The number and variety of proverbial phrases are endless. *To have an ace up one's sleeve* and *To have an ace in the hole* come from the card table; *To be left at the post* from the racetrack; *To bark up the wrong tree* from hunting. New phrases are invented or establish themselves in traditional use every day; *To give the show away, To be the milk in the coconut, To be a big wheel.* Worn-out phrases disappear, but we can rarely say why. *To fix his flint for him,* meaning to defeat or humiliate, is, I think, no longer heard, but the much older *To shed crocodile tears* is still in familiar use. Our understanding of a phrase may change when its original meaning has been forgotten. *To lick him into shape* probably now means to beat, but it is a reminiscence of an old belief that a bear cub was born as a lump of shapeless flesh and was literally licked into the shape of a bear by its mother's tongue.

Some phrases contain both verbs and comparisons: *I wouldn't trust him farther than I can throw a bull by the tail, That went over like a lead balloon,* and *He is low enough to crawl under a snake's belly,* or, with a whimsical enlargement, *He is low enough to walk under a snake's belly with a tall hat on.* Finally, proverbial comparisons may sum up a situation. There are traditional literal statements like *As blue as the sky, As cold as ice* and *As black as pitch.* Some of these almost always have moral implications: *As green as grass* rarely refers to color. *As cool as a cucumber* to the temperature of the day, or *As red as a beet* to a dress. The ingenuity of the comparisons is often amusing: *Crooked enough to hide behind a pretzel, As busy as a one-armed paperhanger,* and, with enlargements *As busy as a one-armed paperhanger with the hives,* or ironically, *To take off like a herd of turtles.*

Some proverbs are clearly quotations: Perhaps *Why don't they eat cake?* or *Let them eat cake* may be a familiar quotation. It has been ascribed to Marie Antoinette. English examples of quotations or dialogues having traditional proverbial quality are rare. Bernard Shaw is said to have had the inscription *They say. What do they say? Let them say!* over his fireplace. This is inscribed on the walls of Marischal College at Aberdeen and on a ring picked up in the ruins of Pompeii. Proverbs of this sort are Eastern, not English, in their currency. There is a story about an Irishman who captured a Turk in a battle. The Irishman called out, "I have caught a Turk." The captain replied, "Bring him here." The Irishman answered, "He won't let me." In the Orient this is a proverb in dialogue about a bear.

Proverbs in the form of general observations are not easily recognized as proverbial unless we have heard them applied to particular situations: *It takes two to make a bargain.* One must be familiar with colloquial speech to know whether a remark is or is not proverbial. *God is above all* was accepted as proverbial in Elizabethan England, but one could now easily pass it over. I would claim *You never can tell* to be such a modern proverb. Sayings with metaphorical quality are more easily recognized as proverbial. Someone saw that *You can lead a horse to water, but you can't make him drink,* and drew a lesson from the scene. We have not yet lost the trick of doing this. *Watch your step* is advice borrowed from the steps of a Pullman car or a guard's cry in the subway or a policeman's call at a crossing.

More interesting than these proverbs in which we recognize the scene are those in which it is apparently inexplicable or impossible. *Those in glass houses should not throw stones* cannot be understood literally in English, for there were no houses of glass in Elizabethan times, when the proverb first appears. The explanation that the Duke of Buckingham, a favored counselor of James I, owned a house with many windows that was called a glass house and that the King rebuked the duke's freedom with criticisms by quoting the proverb is ingenious, but not well supported by evidence. Very likely it is a literal translation of a Spanish idiom in which a glass house does mean a house with windows. *When the fox preaches, beware of your geese* must refer to an invented situation, but it does not seem possible to learn when and where someone hit upon it. Stories told to explain the origin of proverbs must be looked on with suspicion.

We are told that *A cat may look at a king* refers to a visit of Emperor Maximilian to the free city of Regensburg. On this occasion he visited the shop of a man making woodcuts. The cat on the workbench, when it was disturbed, rose, stretched, and looked insultingly at the emperor. No doubt courtiers noted and remembered the incident. However, Regensburg was a free city and was visited rarely by the emperor and then only on invitation. We can fix definitely the date of Maximilian's visit, and the proverb was in print some years earlier. Another and perhaps more fantastic explanation is offered for *Before you can say Jack Robinson.* It is supposed to have a French origin. "Jacques" is a name for a servant, and "Robinson" for an umbrella. On seeing rain clouds, one calls, "Jacques! Robinson!" and a servant appears instantly with an umbrella. I cannot be sure about the French scenery of this explanation, but, strange as the facts are, there was a century ago a circus company owned by John Robinson and "Jack Robinson" is—or was—a term used by circus folk for a sudden shower.

Circumstances may popularize a proverb. *Mad as a hatter* had its origin in the fact that hatters used mercury in making felt and were poisoned by it. Their staggering gait and thick speech made it possible to call them "mad." This comparison might not have come into general use but for two accidents. Three candidates for Parliament in the 1830's were hatters. Political opponents called two of them mad with or without good reason, and the third acknowledged publicly that he had been in an insane asylum. This might have been sufficient to establish the comparison in traditional use, but Lewis Carroll's Mad Hatter in *Alice in Wonderland* ensured its acceptance.

Because proverbs are the "wisdom of many," men have often tried to characterize the "many" by choosing examples and drawing inferences from them. One cannot learn much from such studies. Those who have written have not had open minds. They knew—or thought they knew—the answer before they began. The history of proverbs is so confused and so little studied that we can do little in this direction.

We come to the second half of Lord John Russell's definition, that is, "one man's wit." A proverb is an invention of an individual who uses ideas, words, and ways of speaking that are generally familiar. Because he does so, his sayings win acceptance and circulate in tradition. The phrases that accompany proverbs recognize this fact. A user of proverbs is likely to say, "As the Bible, Plato, Shakespeare says," but we may look for it vainly in such places. While the phrase may not be true of the particular proverb, it has a general truth: some one person did say it for the first time. The ascription is not necessarily true and that fact need not trouble us greatly. "Confucius say" was a popular cliché some years ago but does not prove a descent from Confucius or even a Chinese source. "Little Audrey," "my grandfather," "the old feller," and most popular of all, "they" did not necessarily invent the sayings which they are credited, but mention of them stresses the share of the individual in proverbs. Abraham Lincoln seems to have given us, *Don't swap horses when crossing a stream,* and the prizefighter James J. Corbett, *The bigger they come, the harder they fall.*

In one curious variety an ascription to the inventor of the proverb forms part of it and is carried along with it traditionally. The Wellerism, which has its name from Sam Weller's use of many of them in *Pickwick Papers*, is much older than Dickens. We may begin with *"Sour grapes," said the fox and could not reach them* from Aesop's fables. The name of the speaker and usually, but not necessarily, the circumstances are essential parts of a Wellerism. Allusions to a well-known or readily imagined scene represent perhaps the oldest form of the Wellerism. In what are more recent forms as far as the record goes, the words of the speaker are a proverb in its own right and the wit consists in the incongruity of proverb and scene: *"Everyone to his taste," said the farmer and kissed the cow. Everyone to his taste* is a well-established proverb. Still more recent Wellerisms play with puns: *"It won't be long now (or 'That's the end of my tale')," said the monkey when he backed into the lawn mower. "My pop's in that racket," said the cat at the tennis game.* The Wellerism is—or claims to be— the "wit of one," but it is not necessarily historical truth. *"With my looks and your brains," as*

Lillian Russell said to Bernard Shaw, "there's nothing we couldn't do" may not be a record of an actual conversation, but it is no doubt "one man's wit."

A wise Frenchman said, *Style is the man,* and in style rather than content we feel (we cannot put our hands on) the individual. In the days of alliterative poetry, someone coined *Man and mouse, House and home,* and the trick has persisted in tradition. *To rob Peter to pay Paul* and *Handsome is that handsome does* do not reach back to the time of alliterative poetry and have been no doubt invented by an individual. Rhyme makes proverbs and keeps them alive. *Fools' names and fools' faces are often seen in public places* may have been composed by an anonymous folk-poet. Someone first hit on the metaphor in *Bad news travels fast, Necessity knows no law.*

It is hard, indeed impossible, to know what men live by (is this book title now proverbial?) or what makes them click (which is perhaps proverbial and is certainly a cliché). Proverbs give us as clear an idea as we can hope to get about the forces that influence men and the ideals that they hold. Their range is limited to rather commonplace observations, but most of us are rather commonplace, too. In difficult situations men turn to proverbs for answers, and they find them there. In civilizations without writing, proverbs are used in settling disputes, and the man who quotes the proverb best suited to the situation wins. I have heard a judge on the bench say, *Two wrongs don't make a right,* and felt that his comment clarified the situation and prevented it from becoming worse. In a difficult situation we say, with a shrug, *It could be worse, The worst is yet to come.* Such consolation is poor help, but it is help and many have nothing better. *Don't count your chickens before they are hatched* is a good warning to be cautious about *Building castles in the air.* If we are tempted to an unkind or thoughtless act, remember that *The chickens, when hatched, will come home to roost.* By no means have all proverbs a cynical and bitter taste. We are told *Not to look at the hole in the doughnut* and *Everything will come right in the end. Miracles never cease* is still true. *There's gold in them thar hills,* and some of it is in proverbial shape.

Proverbs in Africa

*Ruth Finnegan**

Nowhere in the world is the proverb more popular than in Africa. Fortunately, social anthropologist Ruth Finnegan has written a superb survey of the African proverb as a part of her important volume entitled Oral Literature in Africa. *We are including the greater part of her chapter on the proverb for two reasons. First, it provides the reader with a useful introduction to the considerable African proverb scholarship, and second, it raises many of the critical issues found in proverb studies generally: definition, structure, style, context, function, and meaning. For an entrée into the European scholarship covering these same issues (with extensive bibliographical references), see Lutz Röhrich and Wolfgang Mieder,* Sprichwort *(Stuttgart, 1977).*

I

Proverbs seem to occur almost everywhere in Africa, in apparent contrast with other areas of the world such as aboriginal America and Polynesia. Relatively easy to record, they have been exceedingly popular with collectors. Particularly well represented are proverbs from the Bantu area (especially the Southern Bantu); the Congo and West Africa have also provided many extensive collections. It is

* Reprinted from *Oral Literature in Africa* by Ruth Finnegan (Oxford: Clarendon Press, 1970), pp. 389–418. © Oxford University Press 1970. Reprinted by permission of Oxford University Press and the author.

notable, however, that there are apparently few or no proverbs among the Bushmen of southern Africa and the Nilotic peoples,[1] and few seem to have been recorded in Nilo-Hamitic languages. In other areas proverbs seem universal and in some African languages occur in rich profusion. Four thousand have been published in Rundi, for instance, about 3,000 in Nkundo, and roughly 2,000 in Luba and Hausa. In addition Bascom lists about thirty other African peoples for whom 500 or more proverbs have been recorded.[2] Also many editors say that they doubt whether their collections are complete.

The literary relevance of these short sayings is clear. Proverbs are a rich source of imagery and succinct expression on which more elaborate forms can draw. As Nketia puts it in his comment on Ghanaian proverbs

> The value of the proverb to us in modern Ghana does not lie only in what it reveals of the thoughts of the past. For the poet today or indeed for the speaker who is some sort of an artist in the use of words, the proverb is a model of compressed or forceful language. In addition to drawing on it for its words of wisdom, therefore, he takes interest in its verbal techniques—its selection of words, its use of comparison as a method of statement, and so on. Familiarity with its techniques enables him to create, as it were, his own proverbs. This enables him to avoid hackneyed expressions and give a certain amount of freshness to his speech.
>
> This . . . approach to proverbs which is evident in the speech of people who are regarded as accomplished speakers or poets of a sort makes the proverbs not only a body of short statements built up over the years and which reflect the thought and insight of Ghanaians into problems of life, but also a technique of verbal expression, which is greatly appreciated by the Ghanaian. It is no wonder therefore that the use of proverbs has continued to be a living tradition in Ghana.[3]

In many African cultures a feeling for language, for imagery, and for the expression of abstract ideas through compressed and allusive phraseology comes out particularly clearly in proverbs. The figurative quality of proverbs is especially striking; one of their most noticeable characteristics is their allusive wording, usually in metaphorical form. This also emerges in many of the native words translated as "proverb" and in the general stress often laid on the significance of speaking in symbolic terms. Indeed, this type of figurative expression is sometimes taken so far as to be almost a whole mode of speech in its own right. The Fulani term *mallol* for instance, means not only a proverb but also allusion in general, and is especially used when there is some deep hidden meaning in a proverb different from the obvious one.[4] Similarly with the Kamba term *ndimo*. This does not exactly correspond to our term "proverb" but is its nearest equivalent, and really means a "dark saying" or "metaphorical wording," a sort of secret and allusive language.[5]

The literary significance of proverbs in Africa is also brought out by their close connection with other forms of oral literature. This is sometimes apparent in the local terminology, for proverbs are not always distinguished by a special term from other categories of verbal art. The Nyanja *mwambi*, for instance, refers to story, riddle, or proverb, the Ganda *olugero* means, among other things, a saying, a story, a proverb, and a parable,[6] and the Mongo *bokolo* is used of all poetic expression including fable, proverb, poetry, and allegory.[7] This overlap in terms is fairly common in Bantu languages and also sometimes occurs in West Africa too: the Limba *mboro* refers to story, riddle, and parable as well as to sayings which we might term proverbs, while the Fulani *tindol* can mean not only a popular moral story but also a proverb or maxim.[8]

In some languages (such as Yoruba or Zulu) a distinction does exist in terminology between proverbs and other types of literary expression.[9] But even here there is often a practical connection between proverbs and other forms of oral literature. Chatelain pointed out that Kimbundu proverbs are closely related to anecdotes, so much so that anecdotes are sometimes just illustrations of a proverb, while a proverb is frequently an anecdote in a nutshell.[10] Again, the Nyanja proverb "Pity killed the francolin" is a direct allusion to the story in which the francolin came to the help of a python and was in return eaten by it.[11] Similar connections between story and proverb are mentioned for Azande, Zulu, Ashanti, and many others, and a moralizing story may end with, or imply, a proverb to drive home its point. As well, proverbs frequently appear in songs and poems. The drum proverbs of Ghana or Dahomey are particularly striking examples here. Among other instances we could mention the Nguni saying "The earth does not get fat" (i.e. however many dead it receives the earth is never satiated) which also appears as the central theme and chorus in an impressive Ngoni lament,[12] and the Swahili poem about silence based on the proverb "Much silence has a mighty noise" ("Still waters run deep") but elaborated and drawn out in the verses arising from it.[13] Written forms too sometimes make use of traditional proverbs, as in Muyaka's Swahili poems, and these in turn may give further currency to new or old proverbs.[14] Proverbs are also sometimes connected with riddles[15] or, as among the Liberian Jabo, with praise names.[16] They also frequently occur in general conversation and in oratory to embellish, conceal, or hint. Proverbs, in short, are closely interwoven with other aspects of linguistic and literary behaviour.

As well as these obvious and common ways in which proverbs overlap with other kinds of verbal art, they also appear in certain specialized forms. Their use in the form of "proverb names" is one. Among the Ovimbundu, to give one example, the woman's name *Simbovala* is a shortened form of the proverb "While you mark out a field, Death marks you out in life"—in life you are in the midst of death.[17] Another connection is with bird lore, a form particularly popular among the Southern Bantu. The cries attributed to certain birds can be expressed as a proverb or a song. The hammerkop, for instance, can be referred to as a symbol of vanity either in a brief proverb or in the full song in which he is represented as praising himself at length; the songs here are thus inextricably linked with the proverbs. Proverbs are also sometimes connected with other artistic media; they can be drummed (a characteristic form in some West African societies), sung, as with Lega judicial proverbs,[18] or can appear on the flags of military companies, as among the Fante.[19] Most striking of all is the way the Ashanti associate a certain proverb with one or other of their many "gold-weights"—small brass figures and images originally used to weigh gold dust and worked with great skill and humour. Thus a snake catching a bird represents the proverb "The snake lies upon the ground, but God has given him the hornbill" (that flies in the sky). Another weight depicts two crocodiles with only a single stomach between them, representing "Bellies mixed up, crocodiles mixed up, we have between us only one belly, but if we get anything to eat it passes down our respective gullets"—a famous proverb often cited when one individual in a family tries to seize for himself rather than sharing.[20]

Certain of the direct associations between proverbs and other artistic forms such as metalwork or drumming may be peculiar to certain African societies, but the general association of proverbs and other forms of literature is not after all very surprising. These close connections are perhaps particularly characteristic of an *oral* literature without a clear-cut distinction between written and unwritten forms, but the sort of way in which proverbial expression and other types of literary art (including the art of conversation) mutually enrich and act upon each other is something which is presumably a quality of most cultures. In this sense, then, proverbs in Africa are not so very different from those in any literate culture, in both of which their main impact seems, in fact, to be in an *oral* rather than a written form. In neither case should they be regarded as isolated sayings to be collected in hundreds or thousands on their own, but rather as just one aspect of artistic expression within a whole social and literary context.

The close connection of proverbs with other literary forms raises a difficulty. How, particularly in an oral culture, can we distinguish proverbs from other forms of oral art? or, indeed, from ordinary clichés and idioms, and from such related but different forms as maxims and apothegms?

Most of the published collections ignore this point of definition and by merely entitling their works "Proverbs" often give the misleading impression that these sayings are clearly differentiated from other expressions or that they are in all ways equivalent to our idea of proverbs. Some of the best collections, such as those of Hulstaert, Nyembezi, Doke, or Chatelain, specifically point out this difficulty, but most have little or no discussion of this point.

The exact definition of "proverb" is no easy matter. There is, however, some general agreement as to what constitutes a proverb. It is a saying in more or less fixed form marked by "shortness, sense, and salt" and distinguished by the popular acceptance of the truth tersely expressed in it. Even so general a picture as this contains some useful pointers for the analysis of African proverbs.

First, their form. They are picked out first and most obviously as being short; and secondly by the fact that even where the wording itself is not absolutely fixed, at least the main structural pattern is accepted in the society concerned as an appropriate one for this purpose. This question of form has been well noted by collectors and is pursued further in the following section. It will emerge that, in addition to terseness and relative fixity, most sayings classed as proverbs are also marked by some kind of poetic quality in style or sense, and are in this way set apart in form from more straightforward maxims.

The question of "popular acceptance" is, however, a more difficult one. If one of the marks of a true proverb is its general acceptance as the popular expression of some truth, we are seldom given the data to decide how far this is indeed a characteristic of the sayings included in collections of "proverbs." In many cases presumably the sayings included are proverbs in this full sense. But we have in fact no way of telling whether some of the "proverbs" included are not just the sententious utterance of a single individual on a single occasion which happened to appeal to the investigator.

The sort of terminology involved can sometimes provide a clue to the local attitude to "proverbs." As we have seen, there is sometimes a specialized term, sometimes not. This is not always made clear by collectors. Even more serious is the frequent failure to consider when, how, and by or among whom common proverbs are used.[21] Even where something about the general context is given we are practically never told in detail how a given single proverb was actually used. Yet, as will emerge, this may in fact determine its significance, the way in which it is appreciated locally, even its meaning. This aspect is often crucial, if whether or not some attractive saying is really a "proverb" depends on the local evaluation of it. This question is made more difficult because proverbs often have no specialized occasions for their use. Unlike such forms as riddles and stories they are not normally set apart as suitable for relaxation after, say, the end of the day's work, but are closely involved with speech and action on every sort of occasion (including general conversation). Therefore to differentiate those sayings which are merely idiomatic from those which *the people concerned* consider to have that special flavour which makes it correct to call them proverbs, we need more precise information about context and attitude than we are usually given.

This said, we can in a general way accept most of the published sayings as falling, more or less, within the general category of proverb. But it is worth making these points about the difficulties inherent in differentiating proverbs if it helps to deter yet more facile collections and to encourage more consideration of their context. In the case of proverbs above all, an understanding of this is essential.

II

In discussing the style and structure of African proverbs one of the first things one notices is the poetic form in which many are expressed. This, allied to their figurative mode of expression, serves to some degree to set them apart from everyday speech. This point often does not emerge in collections of translated examples. A more detailed discussion of form in African proverbs is therefore needed here to show these two characteristics more clearly.

The general truth touched on in a proverb can be conveyed in several ways: more or less literally, through a simile, or (most commonly) through a metaphor.

The relatively literal forms of proverbs often contain some allusion or a picturesque form of speech, and among certain peoples at least are marked by some poetic quality such as rhythm. Examples of this type are fairly common. "The dying of the heart is a thing unshared," "If the chief speaks, the people make silent their ears," and the humorous description of a drunkard, "He devoured the Kaffir-beer and it devoured him," are instances from South Africa.[22] Comments on what is considered to be the real nature of people or things often occur in this form, as in the Thonga "The White man has no kin. His kin is money," the Xhosa description of Europeans as "The people who rescue and kill" (i.e. they protect with one hand, destroy with the other),[23] or the witty Akan comment that "An ancient name cannot be cooked and eaten; after all, money is the thing."[24] General advice is also often tendered in this sort of form, as in the Thonga "Dis du mal du chef quand tu quittes son pays" or the humorous Ila injunction to hospitality in the form of "The rump of a visitor is made to sit upon."[25] It is true that several of these (and similar) proverbs may also conceal deeper meanings as well as picturesque language, but in explicit form, in contrast to the clearly figurative, they present the thought in a simple and straightforward way.[26]

More often the proverbs are figurative in one way or another. Direct similes occur fairly often. The Hausa, for example, say that "A chief is like a dust-heap where everyone comes with his rubbish (complaint) and deposits it."[27] Among the Southern Bantu the likening of something to dew melting away in the sun appears in many forms: the Zulu suggest that something is only a passing phase by asserting that "This thing is like the dew which showers down," and the comparison often appears in a more direct and concise form, as with the Thonga "Wealth is dew" or Ndebele "Kingship is dew."[28] Wealth is another stock comparison, as in the Swahili "Wits (are) wealth," or the vivid saying of the Thonga and others that "To bear children is wealth, to dress oneself is (nothing but) colours."[29] Many other examples of these direct comparisons could be cited: the Southern Bantu "To look at a man as at a snake" (i.e. with deadly hatred), or "To marry is to put a snake in one's handbag;"[30] the Ashanti proverbs "Family names are like flowers, they blossom in clusters" or "A wife is like a blanket; when you cover yourself with it, it irritates you, and yet if you cast it aside you feel cold;"[31] and the Xhosa "He is ripe inside, like a water-melon," describing a man who has come to a resolution without yet expressing it publicly (one cannot tell if a water-melon is ripe from the outside).[32]

Most frequent of all, however, and the most adaptable are the proverbs where comparison is evoked metaphorically. In this form proverbs about animals and birds are very common indeed (perhaps particularly in the Bantu areas); here, as in the tales about animals and in certain praise names, a comment is often being made about human life and action through reference to non-human activity. Egotism, for instance, is commented on and satirized in the Sotho " 'I and my rhinoceros' said the tick bird" or the Ndau "The worm in the cattle kraal says 'I am an ox,' " and among the Ila it is said of squanderers "The prodigal cow threw away her own tail."[33] Similarly, generalizations about animals imply a comment on human affairs. Thus the Thonga "The strength of the crocodile is in the water"[34] can comment in various ways, implying from one point of view that a man is strong when his kinsmen help him, from another that a man should stick to his own place and not interfere with others. The importance of self-help is stressed in "No fly catches for another,"[35] while the Zulu generalization "No polecat ever smelt its own stink" alludes picturesquely to man's blindness and self-satisfaction.[36]

Though proverbs about animals are particularly common, generalizations about other everyday things are also used to suggest some related idea about people. The Zulu observe that man is able to manage his own affairs through the metaphor that "There is no grinding stone that got the better of the miller," and the Ndebele remind one that "The maker of a song does not spoil it" when wishing to warn that it is not right to interfere with someone who understands his own business.[37] The Lamba "Metal that is already welded together, how can one unweld it?" can be used in the same sort of way as our "Don't cry over spilt milk," while the Thonga "The nape of the neck does not see" alludes to the way people get out of control when the master of the village is away.[38]

Perhaps even more common than the metaphorical generalization is the form in which a general or abstract idea is conveyed not through any direct generalization at all but through a single concrete situation which provides only one example of the general point. Thus the Thonga "The one who says 'Elephant die! I want to eat! I am on the way' " alludes to the way in which some people are over-impatient instead of taking the time to do the job properly, while a different point of view is suggested in the specific Hausa statement that "The man with deepest eyes can't see the moon till it is fifteen days old"—in other words is so narrowly concentrated that the obvious escapes him.[39] The Zulu express the general idea that people reap the fruit of their own folly by mentioning specific situations: "He ate food and it killed him" and "The won't-be-told man sees by the bloodstain."[40] The frequent effects of over-confidence and officious advice are alluded to in the pointed Nyanja saying "Mr. Had-it-been-I caused the baboons belonging to someone else to escape," while they comment on fools from the specific case of "Mr. Didn't-know" who "took shelter from the rain in the pond."[41] Fools are similarly alluded to in the Ewe "If a boy says he wants to tie water with a string, ask him if he means the water in the pot or the water in the lagoon."[42] This hinting at a general or abstract idea through one concrete case, either direct or itself metaphorical, is a common proverbial form throughout the continent.

Hyperbole and exaggeration are also frequent motifs, often in addition to some of the forms mentioned above. Many instances could be cited, among them the common Bantu saying that "If you are patient, you will see the eyes of the snail," or "The monitor has gone dry," which alludes to the fact that even the monitor, famed for its affection to its young, has come to the end—and that the guest has outstayed his welcome![43] There is the Fulani proverb "You will not see an elephant moving on your own head, only the louse moving on another's;" and the Zulu description of an unblushing and flagrant liar, "He milks also the cows heavy with calf"—he would actually go as far as saying he could milk cows *before* they had calved.[44] Paradox is also occasionally used with the same kind of effect, as in the Hausa comment on the effects of idleness ("The want of work to do makes a man get up early to salute his enemy"), or the cynical Ila remark "He has the kindness of a witch."[45] The quality of being far-fetched and humorous is used for similar effect in the Zulu reference to impossibility. "A goat may beget an ox and a white man sew on a (native) head ring," the Yoruba "He who waits to see a crab wink will tarry long upon the shore," the Nyanja "Little by little the tortoise arrived at the Indian Ocean," or the exaggerated Yoruba equivalent of our idea that one reaps as one sows—"One who excretes on the road, will find flies when he returns."[46]

The allusions of proverbs in the various collections are often not obvious. This is frequently due to our ignorance of the culture, particularly with proverbs which allude to some well-known story or famous individual. A knowledge of the situations in which proverbs are cited may also be an essential part of understanding their implications, and this is complicated further by the fact that the same proverb may often be used, according to the context, to suggest a variety of different truths, or different facets of the same truth, or even its opposite. Some proverbs, furthermore, are obscure even to local individuals or groups. We cannot, then, expect African proverbs to be crystal-clear or to be able to grasp in each case the modes through which they figuratively or picturesquely suggest certain truths. However, it does seem that the main ways in which these are expressed are the ones already mentioned: by a straight, relatively literal statement; by similes; by various types of metaphor (often comparisons with animals or with one particular case suggesting a generalization); and by hyperbole and paradox.

Having considered some of the general forms in which proverbs appear, we can now look at the detailed stylistic devices which these mainly figurative sayings employ to make their points effectively. Unlike stories and songs, the *performance* does not generally seem to be of importance. Rather, proverbs rely for their effect on the aptness with which they are used in a particular situation and—the point considered here—on the style and form of words in which they appear.[47]

Proverbs are generally marked by terseness of expression, by a form different from that of ordinary speech, and by a figurative mode of expression abounding in metaphor. The first two characteristics can be treated together here with illustrations from the Bantu group of languages. There are no *general* rules for the formation of Bantu proverbs and particular peoples have their own favourite forms, but certain common patterns are apparent. Pithiness and economy are always noticeable in proverbs, but in the Bantu languages this can be achieved particularly effectively through the system of concord. The subject noun, for example, can be omitted as in "It is worked while still fresh" (i.e. "Make hay while the sun shines"), where the concord makes clear that "it" refers to "clay."[48] Economy of wording is also often achieved through elision: not only are whole words left out (often for the sake of rhythm) but vowels are frequently elided, especially the final vowel of a word.[49] The terse expression grammatically possible in Bantu can be illustrated from a Tswana proverb, "Young birds will always open their mouths, even to those who come to kill them," which in the original is only three words.[50] Furthermore, proverbs are often quoted in abbreviated forms; in Bantu languages these are almost always preferred to more drawn-out forms.[51]

The actual wording may take the form of a simple positive or negative proposition, as in the Swahili "The goat-eater pays a cow" (i.e. sow the wind and reap the whirlwind), or the Zulu "He has no chest" (he can't keep secrets), or of various types of simple rhythmic balanced propositions (e.g. the Lamba *muŋanda yācitāla, ubwālwa ŵulasasa,* "In the house of wrangling, beer becomes bitter," where there is exact balance in the two parts, each with three followed by four syllables). Double propositions in which the second portion is explanatory are also common, as in the Lamba "A male is a millipede, he is not driven away with one driving (only)" (a man does not take a single refusal from a girl). Negative axioms also occur and are a particularly popular form in Xhosa and Zulu: "There is no elephant burdened with its own trunk" (a comparison which occurs widely with various connotations, among them the idea that a mother does not feel her baby's weight), "There is no partridge (that) scratches for another" (everyone for himself), "There is no sun (which) sets without its affairs" (every day has its own troubles). Contrast propositions are a particularly striking and economical form and may be presented in either of two ways: by a direct parallel between the two portions of the proverb, as in the Lamba "The body went, the heart did not go" (*umuŵili waya, umutima taw̄ile*), or by cross parallelism (chiasmus), as in the Lamba proverb "One morsel of food does not break a company, what breaks a company is the mouth" (*akalyo kamo takotoŵa—citenje, icitoŵe'citenje kanwa*). Another common form is reduplication, with repeated words or syllables. This usually comes at the beginning, as in the Swahili "Hurry, hurry, has no blessing" (*haraka, haraka, haina baraka*) or the Ganda "Splutter, splutter isn't fire" (*bugu-bugu simuliro*).[52]

Among the Bantu, as elsewhere, the use of quoted words attributed to some actual or fictional person is another device for giving point and sometimes authority to a proverbial saying, the form sometimes known as "wellerism."[53] This may be humorous as with the Ganda " 'I'll die for a big thing,' says the biting ant on the big toe,"[54] but is usually more serious. There are also miscellaneous patterns of fairly frequent occurrence such as the widespread "If . . . then . . ." formula, the proverbs opening with "It is better," particularly popular among the Thonga, the frequent Lamba form "As for you . . .," the Zulu negative axioms opening "There is no . . ." or "There is not . . .," the Nyanja use of special diminutive prefixes (*ka-* and *ti-*),[55] and the "slang" form in Tumbuka-Kamanga proverbs of *cha-*, referring to the typical behaviour of some animal or thing.[56] Another form that occurs occasionally is the rhetorical question, as in the Karanga "The swallower of old cows, is he choked with the bone of a calf?" (a chief who settles big cases is not likely to be overcome by a small one).[57] Although not mentioned by Doke a further formal element in the proverbs of certain peoples is that of tones (e.g. in Luba proverbs[58]), and rhyme, in parts of East Africa.[59]

The wording of Bantu proverbs seems to be relatively fixed in outline so that these general patterns are maintained, or recalled, in their various citations. Minor variations, however, not infrequently occur. A proverb may appear in the singular or plural, with various verb tenses, or in the first, second, or third persons.[60] The forms also sometimes vary from place to place. Two sets of Ndebele proverbs, for instance, collected about a hundred miles from each other, differed slightly in form though they were clearly the "same" proverbs,[61] and over wider areas there may be similar variations due to differences in dialect.[62] As mentioned already there are sometimes two forms, the full and the abbreviated, the second being the one normally cited. Sometimes the saying is cut down even further and merely referred to in one word, a phenomenon particularly common in one-word personal names. Thus among the Ovimbundu a woman may be called *Sukuapanga* ("God willed") from the proverb "God willed; Death unwilled" (*Suku wa panga; Kulunga wa pangulula*), or *Mbundu* from a proverb about customs differing: "The mist of the coast (is) the rain of the upland" (*Ombundu yokombaka ombela yokonano*).[63] A similar tendency is noted among the Ganda who often prefer to leave a proverb to be completed by the hearer: names are sometimes the first word of a proverb, and even the title of a book appears as just *"Atanayita"* (from the proverb *Atanayita atenda nyina okufumba*— "The untravelled man praises his mother's cooking").[64] Thus on any particular occasion the actual form of a proverb may vary according to whether it is abbreviated, merely referred to, or cast in one or other of various grammatical forms. But the basic patterns which mark Bantu proverbs tend to recur and be recalled in their various citations.

Bantu proverbs, then, are noted for special patterns which in many cases give a poetic flavour to the saying. They use various devices to express the thought succinctly and sometimes rhythmically, or even in what Chatelain calls "blank versification."[65] The effectiveness is heightened by the fact that often, though not always, there are archaic or unusual words and picturesque phrasing.

Similar tendencies probably also occur in many non-Bantu proverbs, although no such detailed synthesis as Doke's has been published for any other language group. There is widespread evidence of balanced propositions. Yoruba proverbs, for instance, are said often to come in couplets with antithesis between the two lines, noun answering to noun and verb to verb: "Ordinary people are as common as grass, / But good people are dearer than the eye," or "Today is the elder brother of tomorrow, / And a heavy dew is the elder brother of rain," while repetition also occurs effectively in the form "Quick loving a woman means quick not loving a woman."[66] Parallelism and chiasmus also occur as in the Baule praise of mutual help, "Gauche lave droite, droite lave gauche,"[67] and rhythm may also be evident. Fulani proverbs use assonance, special grammatical forms such as subjectless verbs or the subjunctive without specific time reference, and parallel phrasing as in "An old man does what men don't like, but he does not do what men don't know" (i.e. his actions may be unpopular, but they cannot be unnoticed).[68] Related forms sometimes employ elaborate and studied expression; particularly good examples of these are the neat Fulani epigrams cited by Arnott or the long and complex Akan "drum proverbs."[69]

In proverbs the actual performance as distinct from apt citation and picturesque form is not usually significant. Nevertheless, it is sometimes of interest, perhaps particularly where the words themselves are not so elaborately stylized as in Bantu proverbs. Thus in Limba, where proverbs are not highly developed in any fixed form and there is little stress on rhythm or balance, I was told that in the saying mocking unjustified self-importance ("Do not walk like a European while wearing a loin-cloth"), part of its attractiveness lay in the way it was said, with a pause before the last word and the emphasizing of the idea of the loin-cloth by the long-drawn-out way in which it was pronounced. Herzog says of the Jabo that proverbs are uttered in a much more rhythmic way than would be the case with the corresponding words in ordinary speech.[70] Also a more studied and rhetorical utterance is likely when, as so often in West African societies, proverbs are used in formal speeches before law courts. It is possible then that where the poetic quality of a proverb is not so evident in its verbal content, this is sometimes compensated for by the manner or the context in which it is said.

The question, therefore, of the actual style of proverbs appears to demand further research. Whatever the details, however, it is clear that *some* sort of heightened speech, in one form or another, is commonly used in proverbs: and that this serves to set them apart from ordinary speech.

III

Since proverbs can refer to practically any situation, it would be impossible to give any comprehensive account of the content of African proverbs. Something of their variety can be gathered from the headings under which they are classed in many collections (in terms either of explicit content or implied allusion), for these headings include every aspect of human affairs. Categories of the manifest content include such headings as "Animals" (subdivided into, for instance, "dangerous," "game," and "domestic"), "Birds," "Insects," "Mice, rats, and others," "Strangers, Europeans, and

Europe," "War, fighting, guns, and weapons," and innumerable others; while classifications in terms of the latent reference range from "Man and woman," "Efficiency and its conditions," "Home life," "Life and death," and "Passage of time" to "Conceit," "Power," "Cunning," and, of course, "Miscellaneous."

Since the actual import depends on the context of use, it is in fact impossible to give any definitive treatment of the allusive content of proverbs without a study of their situations; this material is not usually included in the published collections. A few general points, however, may be worth mentioning briefly and tentatively.

It could perhaps be said that though abstractions in the sense of generalizations are an essential aspect of proverbs, abstract notions are little considered in their own right (except perhaps in some of the more religiously orientated sayings of the Islamic peoples). The stress is rather on comments about human affairs; thus the Thonga "The heart of a man is a sea" and the picturesque Yoruba saying about the mind confronted with a difficult problem ("As the leper's hand struggles to grip the needle") exemplify the exception rather than the rule.[71] It is noteworthy also that in most Bantu proverbs there are few references to religion; this contrasts with West Africa where the topic is fairly frequent, particularly among Muslim peoples such as the Hausa and Fulani. This may perhaps be connected with the significance of the ancestor cult in many Bantu societies, so that the equivalent of this sort of allusion is made in terms of *human* experience and activity without reference to a transcendent god or specialist religious activity.

There are very many proverbs about authority, government oppression, or the burden of power. Some examples are the Akan suggestion that a king's sons do not need to be taught violence ("No one teaches a leopard's cub how to spring"), or the frequent reminders that even power must bow sometimes, which the Hausa express by "Even the Niger has an island" and the Yoruba by "The river carries away an elderly person who does not know his weight."[72] The Thonga saying "The centipede's legs are strengthened by a hundred rings" alludes to the chief's dependence on the number of his subjects, while through "Authority is the tail of a waterrat" they bring out the way power can slip away from its possessor;[73] many other comments on the nature and consequences of power could be cited. Death is another favourite topic, for "Death has many petticoats" and "There is no hillside without a grave."[74] The inexorability of death is often stressed—"There is no ragwort that blooms and does not wither" and "Death has the key to open the miser's chest"—and resignation and the fact that no one after all is indispensable are also brought out: "Even there where no cock is crowing, it becomes light."[75] The conflicts inherent in marriage are very frequently satirized ("Two wives are two pots full of poison," according to the Kikuyu), and self-importance is often picked on—as in the Kikuyu "Knowing too much is like being ignorant," the Southern Bantu "No cleverest fellow ever licked his own back," or the Nyanja " 'Watch me' was carried off by a crocodile" (the man plunged in vaingloriously instead of patiently waiting for the boat).[76] But a list of popular topics could be prolonged almost indefinitely.

Something has already been said about the sorts of comparisons which appear explicitly in the proverbs. Very often these are to animals or birds, not because Africans have some mystical closeness to nature but because many live in relatively rural and sparsely populated areas where the animal world impinges closely on their lives. But in fact almost anything of which people have experience—not excluding problems of modern government—can appear directly in their proverbs. It is often impossible to grasp the point or attraction of a given proverb without some knowledge of the cultural background and of what the thing mentioned means to those who utter it. Thus the effectiveness of the Zulu saying that "No proud girl ever had the better of the skin-skirt" is lost to us unless we know that it is customary for only married women to wear skin-skirts and that the proverb therefore refers to the tonic effect of marriage on "proud cheeky girls."[77] Similarly the image in the Xhosa likening of a woman to "a mimosa tree that yields gum all day long" arises from the Xhosa fondness for chewing gum, and the picture in the Mongo proverb "La marche pendant les eaux hautes, c'est celui qui marche devant qui est intelligent" fits their swampy surroundings where the one in front warns those behind of holes and obstacles underwater.[78] Among pastoral people as preoccupied with cattle as are many of the Southern and Eastern Bantu it is not surprising to find very many proverbs referring to cattle. There is, for example, the warning "Don't throw away the milk-pails" (your last hope), the common description of a liar ("He milks even cows which are in calf"), and the comment on people's sensitivity and interdependence in terms of cattle, "It licks the one which licks it, it kicks the one which kicks it."[79] The interests of each society tend to be reflected in the sort of images through which their proverbs are expressed—like the Ashanti experience of gold ("Wisdom is not gold-dust that it should be tied up and put away"), or the Fulani interest in rank in "Les vêtements cachent le corps mais ne cachent pas la généalogie"—even a rich and well-dressed man of servile origin will still only be a slave: appearances are not everything.[80]

Similar comparisons sometimes occur over a wide area, often in nearly the same words. This may be partly due to cultural contact between peoples in the present or past. Many Hausa and Fulani proverbs, for instance, are near identical in overt meaning and translation, and the same applies to the Kru and Jabo of Southern Liberia and many others. The Bantu languages provide many examples of this, the more striking owing to their similarity in language as well as sentiment. Thus very similar proverbs are mentioned in many collections from different Bantu societies—"The eye crosses a full river" (usually referring to man's ambition), "The buttocks rubbing together do not lack sweat" (friction between those who live together), and "The sweat of a dog ends in its hair" (a poor man must swallow his wrath or, alternatively, hard work and effort are not always appreciated). Doke gives a detailed example of the way a proverb can take slightly different forms in the many languages in which it occurs (this one is the equivalent of our pot calling the kettle black): the Ila have "The baboons laughed about one another's overhanging brows," Tswana "A monkey doesn't see its own hollow eyes," Kimbundu "The monkey does not notice his tail," Nyanja "Baboons laugh at one another's buttocks," Swahili "The ape sees not his own hinder parts, he sees his neighbour's."[81] The comparisons, then, are close. But the actual application and interpretation may vary from society to society, whatever the wording.

The range of comparisons and applications, then, is enormous. References to the animal world seem particularly frequent everywhere, but they are by no means the only analogies. These include everything with which a given people is preoccupied, and the extent to which any single sphere is stressed depends, as one would expect, on the culture and experience of a particular society.

IV

So far we have been considering the content and formal characteristics of proverbs in Africa. However, it is particularly true of proverbs whose use and application depends so crucially on their context that no full understanding can be reached without some knowledge of the occasions and purposes of their actual use. To consider the myriad different occasions (and hence meanings) would manifestly be impossible—as a Fante elder put it, "There is no proverb without the situation"[82]—but some comments should be made about the main contexts of proverbs and the functions they fulfil.

There are two themes that one encounters particularly in any discussion of the uses and contexts of proverbs. First, there is the sense of detachment and generalization inherent in proverbs. The speaker stands back, as it were, from the heat of the actual situation and draws attention, for himself or others, to its wider implications. And secondly, there is the oblique and allusive nature of expression through proverbs which makes it possible to use them in a variety of effective ways.

Perhaps most often mentioned is their use in oratory, particularly in law cases or disputes. In this situation proverbs are often used by one or other of the parties to get at his opponent or try to make out a good case for himself by drawing some analogy through the image in a proverb. Among the Anang Ibibio, for instance, proverbs are often skillfully introduced into speeches at the crucial moment and are influential in the actual decisions reached.[83] In one Anang law case, the plaintiff managed to stir up antagonism towards the accused (a chronic thief) by alluding to his past record and untrustworthy reputation. He did this by quoting the proverb "If a dog plucks palm fruits from a cluster, he does not fear a porcupine": if a dog can deal with the sharp needles of the palm fruit, he is likely to be able to face even the porcupine's prickles; similarly a thief will not be afraid to steal again. In this case, however, the thief's guilt was not in fact clear. As part of his defence he on his side used a proverb which was influential in winning over the judge to acquit him, hinting at the way in which he alone had no sympathizers and supporters—"A single partridge flying through the bush leaves no path."[84]

Counsellors and judges also use proverbs to comment obliquely on the conduct of those involved, often with implied advice or rebuke.

A number of these have been recorded among the Nyanja, for whom the court is *the* place for the use of proverbial wit and wisdom and who often refer to such cases in metaphors drawn from hunting. As they put it, " 'Quietly—quietly' doesn't kill game (that which) kills game is 'there it is! there it is' "—unless, that is, those who bring the case explain what it is all about, they cannot expect to win any more than a hunt can be successful without noisy beaters driving the game into the net; what is more, the judge should be quiet and listen like the guard at the net. People are rebuked for their wrong behaviour in court and reminded allusively that what they are doing falls into some general category they too disapprove of. Telling lies, for instance, only makes matters worse: an animal caught in a net only entangles itself further with wild struggles, and so a man is told in court that "It is patience which gets you out of the net." Again, those who try to excuse themselves before the court by saying that what they did was only a small thing may be reminded that "The thing which upsets the porridge-pot is a small piece of *tsekera* grass."[85]

In court and elsewhere there are also frequent occasions for using a proverb to smooth over a disagreement or bring a dispute to a close. According to the Yoruba proverb, "A counsellor who understands proverbs soon sets matters right,"[86] and a difficult law case is often ended by the public citation of an apt proverb which performs much the same generalizing function as citing legal precedents in other societies. Some of these might be classed as juridical axioms and maxims, but many in fact succeed just because the attempt at reconciliation is oblique and through an analogy rather than a straightforward injunction. The contenders are not only brought to view the dispute in a wider perspective (and thus be more ready to come to terms), but this is conveyed in a tactful and allusive way. Among the Limba, for instance, an elder in court tries to persuade one party to a dispute not to be angry with someone younger by reminding them that one "does not shoot the chimpanzee for its ugliness"; i.e. one should not go to extremes in punishing a child, however bad, any more than one actually kills a chimpanzee because it is ugly. In pronouncing his decision the president of an Anang court frequently used the proverb "If you visit the home of the toads, stoop" to remind those involved that one should conform to the divine moral law, and the Yoruba make the similar point that once a dispute has been brought to an end it should then be regarded as finally settled—

"When the face is washed you finish at the chin."[87] In a less formal context, the Kikuyu bring an interminable and profitless discussion to an end by asking the question, agreed to be unanswerable, "When new clothes are sewn, where do the old ones go?"[88]

More or less formalized law cases, then, provide many opportunities for proverbs. However, they also occur in less formal situations for giving ordinary advice. Here too their oblique and tactful nature makes them particularly effective. Many examples of this could be given. In Lamba culture, for instance, the young are warned in such terms as "Your mouth will turn into a knife and cut off your lips" or "You will let the mouse rot in the trap" (i.e. let the opportunity pass),[89] and among the Tetela the proverb "The palm-tree grows in the tall grass" may be used as a gentle hint to parents that it is best to leave a child alone and to let him play and get dirty—he will grow up.[90] The Oron miser who, with some polite excuse, refuses a request, particularly for money, is told obliquely that the asker knows quite well that he does not really want to do it: "The child who refuses to go an errand says he does not know the way."[91]

This function of proverbs to advise, rebuke, or shame another into complaisance has been particularly well described for the Ila of Zambia.[92] A man may be reminded that, as we would put it, Rome was not built in a day—"One day is not sufficient to rot an elephant"—or that pride and contempt of authority are not admired since "We do not like the pride of a hen's egg": eggs in a nest are all equal, so one of them should not be proud. Practical as well as ethical advice is given: "If you eat with one chief only, it is because you have no feet," for you should get what you can out of all of them. Ridicule and mockery in proverbs are also effective. As Smith writes of Ila proverbs, wit has a utilitarian aim; laughter is never far away, and because of their susceptibility to ridicule the Ila, like many others, can sometimes be laughed out of a thing more effectively than deterred by argument or force. Thus Pharisees are mocked as those who "spurn the frog but drink the water": they are the kind of people who object to finding a frog in their drinking water but are perfectly happy to drink once the frog has been removed. Another pressure is through irony, assuming that what *ought* to be done *is* always done; the quickest way to gain hospitality among the Ila is to quote "The rump of a visitor is made to sit upon."[93] Indeed, any kind of satirical or penetrating comment on behaviour may be made in the form of a proverb and used to warn or advise or bring someone to his senses. He is reminded of the general implications of his action—and the fact that the reminder is cast in apparently innocent and irrelevant terms may make it all the more effective.

There is another aspect of proverbs which is connected with their use for comment or persuasion and which sometimes appears in a specialized and extreme form. This is their oblique and suggestive character. The speaker wishes to convey something, but in such a way that later on he can deny that he actually stated what was implied, or so that only some among his listeners may understand the point. This type of suggestiveness is developed to a particularly high degree in the Zande *sanza* in which a kind of malicious double-talk is used to convey a meaning other than the obvious sense. Again, the Nyanja have a special term which can be translated as "speaking by opposites" by which they make deliberate mis-statements with an esoteric intention—the older people and *cognoscenti* can understand, but not other listeners.[94] Similarly among the Thonga a proverb may be used with an apparently clear meaning but in practice a completely different intention,[95] while the Kamba *ndimo*, "dark saying," is a kind of secret language.[96]

Irony or sarcasm as a way of getting at someone is, of course, widespread in many forms, but the proverb is a particularly good way of conveying this. This kind of implicit attack on another, already mentioned in the context of a formal law case, sometimes takes more unusual forms. An example is the elliptical language of names. Through this people can refer to another's fault while at the same time avoiding any direct commitment. Thus, among the Karanga, a dog may be called by the proverbial name "Things which change from day to day" in allusion to a capricious wife, or a flirtatious woman may be called "All eyes" as a reproof since she has eyes for all personable males; similarly a dog's name may be "Home-wrecker," given him by a suspicious husband to warn off his wife's lover.[97]

Certain themes seem to be present in the various contexts of proverbs we have discussed so far. Though proverbs can occur in very many different kinds of contexts, they seem to be particularly important in situations where there is both conflict and, at the same time, some obligation that this conflict should not take on too open and personal a form. Such conflict can occur in many different ways—there may be competition for scarce resources, there may be a stress, as among the Zulu or Ibo, on the idea of personal achievement or, as among the Azande, on the significance of hierarchy, with the competitiveness for advancement and notice so closely connected with these; in all these situations there may also be an idea that the conflict involved should not be allowed to become extreme and explicit. It can be seen how the veiled and metaphorical language of proverbs is particularly relevant in such contexts.[98] Indeed, proverbs may also be specially suitable even in everyday situations of advice or instruction where the hidden tensions that are sometimes inherent in such relationships are controlled through the use of elliptical, proverbial speech. Even in cases of overt and institutionalized conflict—for example, the law cases in the more highly organized African states—proverbs play a part in formalizing and controlling the conflicts involved. In some Western societies, there are provisions in the legal system for minimizing personal clashes involved in lawsuits while at the same time making it possible for each side to present their case effectively by the relative impersonality of the written word, and by the institution of counsels for each of the two parties who, as well as forwarding their clients' interests, impose a kind of veil which prevents direct confrontation. It seems that in certain non-literate African societies the use of proverbs may fulfil something of the same function.

Proverbs, then may be a particularly suitable form of communication in situations and relationships of potential or latent conflict. This aspect may perhaps serve to throw some light on the fact that whereas some peoples make great use of proverbs, among others, for instance the Nuer, they seem to be of little or no importance.[99] For it may be that it is precisely those societies in which there is marked latent conflict, or in which there is particular need to regulate formalized conflicts, that proverbs play an especially large part.

Collectors and commentators frequently mention the use of proverbs in education. Although the details are often not made very clear, it seems that there are several different senses in which proverbs can fulfil educational functions. Sometimes proverbs (and other verbal forms like riddles) are used in a quite specific way in societies which lay great stress on initiation ceremonies. The initiates may be instructed in the proverbs and aphorisms current in the society, just as they are also often taught dances, songs, and other skills. Among the Chaga, for instance, proverbs play an important part in formal instruction during initiation ceremonies and are highly valued;[100] "the Chaga," it is said, "have four big possessions: land, cattle, water and proverbs."[101] This sort of formal instruction may have a certain esoteric intention; the members of the group versed in these proverbs are now, by their very knowledge, marked off from those who have not yet reached this stage. In addition, in a non-literate society instruction through proverbs provides a means for relatively formal education and transmission of cultural traditions. Proverbs with their implicit generalized import are clearly a suitable and succinct form in which to verbalize socially prescribed actions and attitudes.

Proverbs, then, are sometimes used quite formally and consciously as a vehicle to achieve the ends, and in the same sort of contexts, that we associate with formal education. However, when collectors comment on the educational function of proverbs they do not necessarily intend to convey such a specific role as that described above, one which certainly does not occur in every African society. What they often seem to be describing is the *general* educative role of proverbs. Now proverbs often imply some general comment on the way people do, or should, or should not behave. It is clear that the conveying of a people's experience and expectations can be performed in a particularly effective way through the use of proverbs. But proverbs are in practice cited in a whole variety of situations, and only in some of them does there seem to be any intentionally educational purpose. The manifest aim may in fact be to get at an opponent, to defy a superior in a polite and oblique way, to make an effective and unanswerable point in a speech, etc.—yet at the same time the latent function is performed of transmitting a certain view of the world, a way of interpreting and analysing people and experience, and recognition of certain situations. Among the Ibo, for instance, proverbs fulfil this aim incidentally even though the explicit occasion is that of a dance. As the masked dancer progresses, he has proverbs and aphorisms called out before him, and, as Green writes, "the chanting in front of the masked figure of these utterances is a way of steeping the members of the society in the traditional values of their culture."[102] Other quasi-educational results which may come from the frequent use of proverbs seem only incidental, not really distinguishable in kind from the general socialization and education undergone by people just because and in that they are members of a particular society.

In between these two extremes there is the kind of situation in which, without any specific formal occasion for their use, proverbs are yet consciously used from time to time with the intention of instructing or giving advice. Thus we are told of proverbs in many societies[103] that they are used for "instruction" or "child-rearing." Most authors, however, do not give details of the actual situations of such usage. It is true that the generalizatons implicit in many proverbs make them suitable vehicles for this sort of instruction; but the occasions we are told about suggest that what in fact is often being done is to convey the applicability of a proverb to a particular *situation* rather than to teach any actual generalization implied or stated in the proverb. This too is of course a type of education. But it is perhaps not quite that implied by the frequent references to the "educational purpose" of these proverbs.[104]

Besides these relatively utilitarian aspects of proverbs it is clear that there is also what might be called a purely literary aspect. That this view is not just that of the outside observer is clear from the overlap in terminology already mentioned between proverbs and such unquestionably literary genres as stories, parables, or riddles. In the case of certain peoples, indeed, their proverbs (sometimes together with their riddles) appear to be the richest or most interesting part of their oral literature.[105] Of the proverbs in many African societies we are told that they are consciously used not only to make effective points but also to embellish their speeches in a way admired and appreciated by their audiences. It is part of the art of an accomplished orator to adorn his rhetoric with apt and appealing proverbs. The Anang Ibibio reputation for eloquence largely arises from their skilful use of proverbs, and a Zulu orator who can quote aptly, readily, and profusely is particularly admired.[106] Proverbs are also used to add colour to everyday conversation. This aspect seems to be very widespread indeed and in some cases at least to be an art cultivated to a very high degree. Thus among the Mongo, proverbs are said to be continually cited; among the Zulu, someone who did not know their proverbs would be lost in the allusiveness of their conversation; while among the Bambara, proverbs are honoured to such an extent that they tend to use a proverb every two or three phrases even in everyday conversation.[107] The Akan allude to the subtlety in proverbs by their saying "When a fool is told a proverb, the meaning of it has to be explained to him," and as Nyembezi writes of the Zulu, in words also applicable to many other African cultures, proverbs are essential to life and language: "Without them, the language would be but a skeleton without flesh, a body without soul."[108]

This literary use of proverbs in ordinary speech is sometimes taken further and shades into more elaborate forms like the Akan drum proverbs, Fulani epigrams, or Zulu bird songs. Unlike many other prose forms, proverbs are not normally used specifically for entertainment but are more involved in everyday situtations. However, we do hear occasionally of contests in proverb telling. Among the Fante proverbs are recited as entertainment both at casual gatherings in the evening and at ceremonies and celebrations with a panel of judges to decide between the contestants, while Lestrade writes of the South African Bantu that proverbs are sometimes used in a regular game similar to that of riddle asking—interpretations of proverbs are exchanged and the players "buy" a new proverb and its interpretation in exchange for one they know.[109] In all these contexts the proverb is a vehicle particularly suited to give depth and elegance through its allusive, figurative, and poetic mode of expression.

Proverbs, finally, are often said to represent a people's philosophy. In proverbs the whole range of human experience can be commented on and analysed, generalizations and principles expressed in a graphic and concise form, and the wider implications of specific situations brought to mind. This aspect has always appealed particularly to collectors. Some editors have taken it rather far and suggested that proverbs make up "tribal law"[110] or illustrate every belief and prescribed piece of behaviour in a direct and literal way. This is to miss the flexibility and situational aspect that is so striking a characteristic of African proverbs. As has been pointed out by several authorities, the same proverb may be used in a whole range of situations with different applications and meanings. Furthermore, as has frequently been noticed, the occurrence of "contradictory" proverbs is widespread; thus the Southern Bantu stress both the unruliness *and* indispensability of a man's tongue: "The mouth has no lid to cover it," yet "The tongue is man's tail-switch to drive away the flies";[111] and many other such examples could be cited. If interpreted as literal injunctions or evaluations, clearly there is contradiction. Instead they might be regarded as a way of summing up what is recognized as only one facet of the truth, to be used as and when it applies or appeals; then it is possible to appreciate more fully the flexible and subtle way in which, through a whole series of overtones and depths of meaning, proverbs represent "the soul of a people."

In relation to the question of the occasions and functions of proverbs something should be said about the people who cite or listen to proverbs. There is not much evidence on this, but clearly the details vary from society to society. Sometimes the proverbs are potentially known to everyone and free for all to use on suitable occasions. The actual use, of course, depends on the occasion: thus where proverbs are most common in law cases and men are the chief litigants, proverbs are seldom used by women; and proverbs giving advice are most naturally used by elder people. In other societies there seem to be certain proverbs which are reserved for use only by older people and would not be cited in the presence of youths or uncircumcised adults. Sometimes proverbs as tools in argument are reserved for the elderly alone; thus of the Fon Herskovits tells us that "one limiting principle governs their use. The young may not presume to press a point with their seniors by using proverbs."[112] Among the Nyanja proverbs are sometimes used with a definitely esoteric intention,[113] and we may guess that in societies with a fairly high degree of specialization, particularly with regard to religious and artistic affairs, there is likely to be a group who are particularly conversant with the allusions and possibilities inherent in proverbs. The situation described of the Mongo is very likely typical of many societies: that whereas some proverbs are used by the whole population and known very widely, others are rare or reserved for certain specialists.[114] But this whole subject is obscure and the evidence scanty.

There is also the question of individual authorship and originality. Since one of the characteristics of a proverb is that it should be accepted by the community as a whole, the scope for individual initiative is clearly limited. However, the fact that there is a certain amount of variation in form and the great range of varied situations to which proverbs can be applied with greater or lesser aptness and insight give some opening for individual contributions. There is a certain amount of evidence about the way new proverbs are coined by individuals and later taken up by the community. As Nyembezi points out about the Zulu, there are no special people with the job of evolving proverbs, but new ones nevertheless arise through individuals; and we are told elsewhere that many Zulu proverbs were first uttered by famous men or by bards or jesters before the king or at a beer-drink and were then taken up and popularized by others.[115] It is common for proverbs to be attributed to well-known historical personages; this is often conventional but in some cases may be justified. Similarly new proverbs are mentioned as being taken by individuals from various outside sources, or arising from individual inventiveness and poetic imagination within the framework of the conventional forms and functions in any given society.[116]

We can, then, sum up the various ways in which proverbs are used in African societies by saying that they really occur on *all* occasions when language is used for communication either as art or as a tool—i.e. on every sort of occasion imaginable. In particular societies there may be certain rules or tendencies about the sorts of occasions on which they are most frequent or suitable, or the classes of people who should use them. Some people may use proverbs in a particularly sophisticated way as the basis for more elaborate forms of literature, while others stress the useful aspect of proverb-citing or their more literary and artistic purpose. But they are above all used as a form of formalized conflict and its resolution, as an oblique and allusive way of communication, as a form of expression with a certain educational relevance, as an artistic activity in its own right, or as all these at once.

Notes

1. C.M. Doke, "A Preliminary Investigation into the State of the Native Languages of South Africa," *Bantu Studies* 7, 1933, p. 6; Evans-Pritchard 1963*b*, p. 109.
2. Bascom 1964, pp. 16–17; cf. Doke 1947, pp. 115–17; Whitting 1940.
3. J.H. Nketia, "Folklore of Ghana," *The Ghanaian* I, 1958, p. 21.
4. Gaden 1931, p. vi.
5. Lindblom iii, 1934, p. 28.
6. Doke 1947, p. 102.
7. Hulstaert 1958, p. 6.
8. Gaden 1931, p. vi.
9. There are also several cases where there are both a general term, covering both proverbs and other types of verbal art, and, in addition, a more precise term referring to proverbs only.
10. Chatelain 1894, p. 21.
11. Gray 1944, p. 102.
12. See M. Read, "Songs of the Ngoni People," *Bantu Studies*, 11 (1937), 16.

13. Taylor 1891, pp. 32–3.
14. Doke 1947, p. 105.
15. E.g. the Anang "proverb-riddles" discussed by Messenger 1960.
16. Herzog 1936, p. 12.
17. Ennis 1945, p. 3.
18. A.E. Meeussen, "Aktiespreuken bij de Lega," *Kongo-Overzee* 25, 1959, p. 73.
19. Christensen 1958, p. 240.
20. R.S. Rattray, *Ashanti*, Oxford, 1923, pp. 312–13. Cf. also D. Paulme, "Les poids-proverbes de la Côte-d'Ivoire au Musée de l'Homme," *J. Soc. Africanistes* 11, 1941; M.W. Plass, *African Miniatures, the Goldweights of the Ashanti*, London, 1967.
21. A point well made in Arewa and Dundes 1964; cf. also Evans-Pritchard 1963*a*.
22. McLaren 1917, pp. 343, 338, 341.
23. Junod 1938, p. 49; Theal 1886, p. 199.
24. Rattray 1916, p. 118.
25. H.P. Junod, *Quelques Proverbes Thonga*, Lausanne, 1931, no. 56; Smith and Dale ii, 1920, p. 312.
26. In these straightforward forms the veiling or allusiveness characteristic of so much proverbial expression is sometimes in fact achieved by devices other than direct imagery. Abbreviation is one common way (e.g. in the Ovimbundu proverb-names); another is to express the proverb in some medium other than verbal utterance, with drums, for instance, or through gold-weights (Ashanti).
27. Tremearne 1913, p. 62.
28. J. Stuart and D. Malcolm, *Zulu Proverbs and Popular Sayings*, Durban, [1949], p. 70; Junod 1938, p. 49; K.D. Leaver and C.L.S. Nyembezi, "Proverbs Collected from the Amandebele," *Afr. Studies* 5, 1946, p. 137.
29. W.E. Taylor 1891, p. 2; Junod and Jaques 1936, no. 450.
30. McLaren 1917, p. 336; Junod 1938, p. 50.
31. Rattray 1916, pp. 125, 139.
32. Theal 1886, p. 194.
33. McLaren 1917, p. 334; E.B. Jones, Ndau proverbs (manuscripts in Doke Collection, University College Library, Salisbury, S. Rhodesia); Smith and Dale ii, 1920, p. 316.
34. Junod 1938, p. 47.
35. McLaren 1917, p. 340.
36. F. Mayr, "Zulu Proverbs," *Anthropos* 7, 1912, p. 958.
37. Stuart and Malcolm, op. cit., p. 17; N. Jones, "Sindebele Proverbs," *Nada* 3, 1925, p. 66.
38. Doke 1934, p. 361; Junod and Jaques 1936, no. 352.
39. Junod and Jaques 1936, no. 2; Whitting 1940, p. 3.
40. O. Ripp, Newspaper cuttings on Zulu proverbs, 1930 (Doke Collection, University College Library, Salisbury, S. Rhodesia); Dunning 1946.
41. Gray 1944, pp. 112, 117.
42. Ellis 1890, p. 260.
43. Werner 1906, p. 212; McLaren 1917, p. 335.

44. Whitting 1940, p. 160; Nyembezi 1954, p. 40.
45. Whitting 1940, p. 121; Smith and Dale ii, 1920, p. 323.
46. J.G. Stuhardt, "A Collection of Zulu Proverbs," *Nada* 8, 1930, p. 69; Ellis 1894, p. 237; Gray 1944, p. 110; Gbadamosi and Beier 1959, p. 60.
47. On form and style the best discussion is that by Doke (1947) on Bantu proverbs, and his account is followed closely here.
48. Doke 1947, p. 106.
49. Nyembezi 1954, pp. 13 ff.
50. A. Werner, *J. Afr. Soc.* 16, 1917, p. 184.
51. Doke in *Afr. Studies* 18, 1959, p. 150.
52. Examples quoted from Doke 1947, pp. 106–10.
53. For some non-Bantu "wellerisms" see A. Dundes, "Some Yoruba Wellerisms, Dialogue Proverbs and Tongue-twisters," *Folklore* 75, 1964.
54. Doke 1947, p. 110.
55. Gray 1944, p. 102.
56. T. Cullen Young, *Notes on the Customs and Folk-lore of the Tumbuka-Kamanga Peoples*, Livingstonia, 1931, p. 266.
57. C.J. Bisset, "Some Chikaranga Proverbs," *Nada* 11, 1933, p. 98.
58. Van Avermaet 1955, pp. 3 ff.
59. See e.g. J. Knappert, "Rhyming Swahili Proverbs," *Afr. u. Übersee* 49, 1966; for some non-Bantu rhyming proverbs see H.C. Jackson, "Sudan Proverbs," *Sudan Notes* 2, 1919.
60. This, incidentally, makes the alphabetical classification adopted by some collectors an unsatisfactory one.
61. W.R. Benzies and H.M.G. Jackson, "Proverbs from the Matabele," *Nada* 2, 1924; G. Taylor and N. Jones, "Sindebele Proverbs," *Nada* 3, 1925.
62. Hulstaert 1958, p. 8.
63. Ennis 1945, p. 3.
64. R.A. Snoxall, "Ganda Literature," *Afr. Studies* I, 1942, p. 59; M.B. Nsimbi, "Baganda Traditional Personal Names," *Uganda J.* 14, 1950, pp. 204–5.
65. Chatelain 1894, p. 22.
66. Ellis 1894, p. 238.
67. G. Effimbra, *Manuel de baoulė*, Paris, [1952], p. 289.
68. Arnott 1957, p. 389.
69. Nketia 1958.
70. Herzog 1936, p. 8.
71. Junod and Jaques 1936, no. 803; Gbadamosi and Beier 1959, p. 60.
72. Rattray 1916, p. 63; Whitting 1940, p. 5; Gbadamosi and Beier 1959, p. 61.
73. Junod and Jaques, no. 107.
74. McLaren 1917, p. 344.
75. Ibid., p. 343; Rattray 1916, p. 51; Ripp, op. cit.
76. G. Barra, *1000 Kikuyu Proverbs,* London, 2nd ed., 1960, pp. 2, 40; McLaren 1917, p. 341; Gray 1944, p. 112.
77. Nyembezi 1954, p. 11.
78. McLaren 1917, p. 333; Hulstaert 1958, p. 412.
79. Ripp, op. cit.; Nyembezi 1954, p. 6.

80. Rattray 1916, p. 154; Gaden 1931, p. 103.

81. Doke 1934, p. 360.

82. Christensen 1958, p. 232; and cf. the story about the Akan attitude to proverbs cited in Evans-Pritchard 1963, p. 7.

83. See the article by Messenger 1959.

84. Ibid., pp. 68–9.

85. Gray 1944, pp. 107, 108.

86. Ellis 1894, p. 218.

87. Messenger 1959, p. 70; Ellis 1894, p. 231.

88. M.S. Stevenson, "Specimens of Kikuyu Proverbs," *Festschrift Meinhof*, Glückstadt, 1927, p. 246. On judicial proverbs, see also A.E. Meeussen, "Aktie-spreuken bij de Lega," *Kongo-Overzee* 25, 1959; E. Van Goethem, "Proverbes Judiciaires des Mongo," *Aequatoria* 10, 1947; I. Schapera, "Tswana Legal Maxims," *Africa* 36, 1966.

89. Doke 1934, p. 361.

90. E.B. Stilz, Otetela proverbs, Wombo Nyama, 1939 (manuscripts in Doke Collection, University College Library, Salisbury, S. Rhodesia).

91. Simmons 1960, p. 135 (slightly expanded to make the literal English translation intelligible).

92. Smith and Dale ii, 1920, pp. 311 ff.

93. Ibid., p. 312.

94. Gray 1944, p. 102.

95. Junod and Jaques 1936 (foreword).

96. Lindblom iii, 1934, p. 28.

97. N.A. Hunt, "Some Notes on the Naming of Dogs in Chikaranga," *Nada* 29, 1952.

98. Proverbs are not, of course, the only way of dealing with such situations and relationships in non-literate societies. There are also, for instance, witchcraft beliefs and accusations; the use of veiled political and satirical songs; or joking relationships. In this last form, the opposite means is, in a sense, being chosen: proverbs may deal with conflict by smoothing it over; joking resolves it by exaggerating the hostility involved and thus, in its way, resolving it.

99. A point raised by Evans-Pritchard in 1963*b*, p. 109 and, so far as I know, nowhere satisfactorily discussed.

100. O.F. Raum, *Chaga Childhood*, London, 1940, pp. 217, 333–4.

101. Ibid., p. 217.

102. Green 1948, p. 840.

103. E.g. Zulu, Lamba, Ila, Nyanja, Kuanyama Ambo, Fante, Anang Ibibio.

104. Straight generalizations and aphorisms are sometimes included in collections of proverbs and these may be used to instruct in some general sense; but further study may show that several of these satisfy neither the criterion of being a generally accepted truth, nor that of involving allusive, figurative, or otherwise picturesque expression; they are thus strictly only marginal to the analysis of proverbs and of oral literature in general.

105. For example the Fang (Tardy 1933, p. 282) and the Anang Ibibio (Messenger 1959, p. 64).

106. Messenger 1959, p. 64; Vilakazi 1945, ch. 10.

107. Hulstaert 1958, p. 5; J. Stuart and D. Malcolm, *Zulu Proverbs and Popular Sayings*, Durban, [1949] (intro.); Travélé 1923, p. 35.

108. Rattray 1916, p. 152; Nyembezi 1954, p. 44.

109. Christensen 1958, p. 239; Lestrade 1937, pp. 293–4.

110. E.g. G. Barra, *1000 Kikuyu Proverbs*, London, 2nd ed., 1960 (foreword).

111. McLaren 1917, p. 341.

112. Herskovits 1958, p. 57.

113. Gray 1944, p. 102.

114. Hulstaert 1958, p. 5.

115. Nyembezi 1954, p. xi; Ripp, op. cit.

116. Cf. Herzog 1936, p. 7; Hulstaert 1958, pp. 5–6.

Bibliography

Arewa, E.O., and Dundes, A., "Proverbs and the Ethnography of Speaking Folklore," *American Anthropologist* 66.6, pt. 2 (1964).

Arnott, D.W., "Proverbial Lore and Word-play of the Fulani," *Africa* 27 (1957).

Bascom, W.R., "Folklore Research in Africa," *Journal of American Folklore* 77 (1964).

Chatelain, H., *Folk-tales of Angola* (Memoir of the American Folklore Society, 1), Boston and New York, 1894.

Christensen, J.B., "The Role of Proverbs in Fante Culture," *Africa* 28 (1958).

Doke, C.M., "A Preliminary Investigation into the State of the Native Languages of South Africa with Suggestions as to Research and the Development of Literature," *Bantu Studies* 7 (1933).

——— "Lamba Literature," *Africa* 7 (1934).

——— "Bantu Wisdom-lore," *African Studies* 6 (1947).

Ellis, A.B., *The Ewe-speaking Peoples of the Slave Coast of West Africa*, London, 1890.

——— *The Yoruba-speaking Peoples of the Slave Coast of West Africa*, London, 1894.

Ennis, E.L., "Women's Names among the Ovimbundu of Angola," *African Studies* 4 (1945).

Evans-Pritchard, E.E. "Meaning in Zande Proverbs," *Man* 63 (Jan. 1963) (1963a).

——— "Sixty-one Zande Proverbs," *Man* 63 (July 1963) (1963b)

Gaden, H., "Proverbes et Maximes Peuls et Toucouleurs," *Travaux et Memoires de l'Institut d'Ethnologie* 16 (1931).

Gbadamosi, B., and Beier, U., *Yoruba Poetry*, Ibadan, [1959].

Gray, E., "Some Proverbs of the Nyanja People," *African Studies* 3 (1944).
Green, M.M., "The Unwritten Literature of the Igbo-speaking People of South-Eastern Nigeria," *Bulletin of the School of Oriental and African Studies* 12 (1948).
Herskovits, M.J., and Herskovits, F.S., *Dahomean Narrative*, Evanston, 1958.
Herzog, G., and Blooah, C.G., *Jabo Proverbs from Liberia*, London, 1936.
Hulstaert, G., *Proverbes Mongo, Musée Royal du Congo Belge. Annales (Sciences de l'Homme, Linguistique).* Tervuren. 15 (1958).
Junod, H.P., *Bantu Heritage*, Johannesburg, [1938].
Junod, H.P., and Jaques, A.A., *The Wisdom of the Tsonga-Shangaan People*, Pretoria, 1936.
Lestrade, G.P., "Traditional Literature" (in I. Schapera (ed.), *The Bantu-speaking Tribes of South Africa*, London, 1937).
Lindblom, K.G., *Kamba Folklore*, 3 vols. Uppsala, 1928–35.
McLaren, J., "The Wit and Wisdom of the Bantu, as Illustrated in Their Proverbial Sayings," *South African Journal of Science* 14 (1917).
Messenger, J.C., "The Role of Proverbs in a Nigerian Judicial System," *Southwestern Journal of Anthropology* 15 (1959).
——— "Anang Proverb-Riddles," *Journal of American Folklore* 73 (1960).
Nketia, J.H.K., "Drum Proverbs," Voices of Ghana, Accra (Ministry of Information and Broadcasting, 1958).
Nyembezi, C.L.S., *Zulu Proverbs*, Johannesburg, 1954.
Rattray, R.S., *Ashanti Proverbs: The Primitive Ethics of a Savage People*, Oxford, 1916.
Simmons, D.C., "Oron Proverbs," *African Studies* 19 (1960).
Smith, E.W., and Dale, A.M., *The Ila-speaking Peoples of Northern Rhodesia*, 2 vols., London, 1920.
Tardy, L., "Contribution à l'Étude du Folklore Bantou. Les Fables, Devinettes et Proverbes Fãng," *Anthropos* 28 (1933).
Taylor, W.E., *African Aphorisms or Saws from Swahililand*, London, 1924 [1st ed. 1891].
Theal, G.M., *Kaffir Folk-lore: A Selection from the Traditional Tales Current among the People Living on the Eastern Border of the Cape Colony*, London, 1886.
Travélé, M., *Proverbes et Contes Bambara et Malinké, Accompagnés d'une Traduction Française et Précédés d'un Abrégé de Droit Coutumier Bambara et Malinké*, Paris, 1923.
Tremearne, A.J.N., *Hausa Superstitions and Customs: An Introduction to the Folk-lore and the Folk*, London, 1913.
Van Avermaet, E., "Langage Rythmé des Baluba," *Aequatoria* 28 (1955).
Vilakazi, B.W., "The Oral and Written Literature in Nguni," (unpub. D. Litt. thesis), University of the Witwatersrand (1945).

Werner, A., *The Native Tribes of British Central Africa*, London, 1906.
——— "Swahili Poetry," *Bulletin of the School of Oriental Studies* 1 (1917–20).
Whitting, C.E.J., *Hausa and Fulani Proverbs*, Lagos, 1940.

On the Structure of the Proverb

*Alan Dundes**

One of the problems which has plagued proverb scholars is that of definition. The magnitude of the problem is evident if one turns to Bartlett Jere Whiting's "The Nature of the Proverb," Harvard Studies and Notes in Philology and Literature, *14 (1932), 273–307. A relatively new means of tackling the definition question involves the use of structuralism. The following essay must be considered tentative inasmuch as it is based almost exclusively upon Anglo-American proverb data. However, recent scholarship in Finland and in the Soviet Union by proverb scholars Matti Kuusi and G.L. Permyakov respectively is in a similar vein. See, for example, Matti Kuusi,* Towards an International Type-System of Proverbs, *FFC 211 (Helsinki, 1972) and G.L. Permyakov,* From Proverb to Folk-Tale: Notes on the general theory of cliché *(Moscow, 1979).*

The study of the proverb has fascinated a great many scholars from a variety of disciplines and this may account for the vast bibliography of works devoted to the proverb.[1] Most of the scholarship—as opposed to mere reportorial collection—has tended to be historical in emphasis. Commonly the goal is to discover proverb cognates among peoples with related languages or to propose possible places and times of origin for individual proverbs.

*Reprinted from *Proverbium* 25 (1975), 961–973.

In the twentieth century, thanks in part to the influence of the social sciences, there has been a shift away from purely literary and historical studies of proverbs.[2] There have been detailed field investigations of the concrete contexts in which specific proverbs are uttered[3] and it has been suggested that there may be laws or, rather, principles of usage governing the decision-making process which results in the citation of one proverb rather than another, or rather than no proverb.[4] With regard to content analysis, there have been attempts to correlate proverb content with national character and to extrapolate worldview from proverbs.[5] In the area of 'applied folklore' there have been a number of interesting practical uses of proverbs. Proverb reasoning tests have been devised as a means of attempting to measure various mental skills. (In these tests, individuals are presented with a given proverb and then asked to select the one proverb of a list of five which most nearly resembles the initial proverb.) Other proverb tests allegedly serve as diagnostic tools in the identification of possible schizophrenics. The assumption underlying the tests is that schizophrenics are unable to read metaphorical proverbs as metaphors but only as literal statements.[6]

In view of the considerable attention which the proverb has continued to receive, it comes as something of a surprise to learn that the proverb has never been adequately defined. Archer Taylor begins his important book on the proverb with the following defeatist statement: "The definition of a proverb is too difficult to repay the undertaking. An incommunicable quality tells us this sentence is proverbial and that one is not. Hence no definition will enable us to identify positively a sentence as proverbial." When asked about this pessimistic statement, Professor Taylor remarked that in a way his whole book constituted a definition of the proverb.[7] B.J. Whiting, another leading literary scholar, takes more or less the same stance: "To offer a brief yet workable definition of a proverb, especially with the proverbial phrase included, is well nigh impossible." Moreover, he goes on to claim that definitions are not really needed anyway. "Happily, no definition is really necessary, since all of us know what a proverb is."[8] Now it may well be that all of us do know what a proverb is, but it seems incredible that if this is so, someone could not articulate this supposedly common knowledge. I submit that a definition of the proverb genre, even a most tentative definition, should be useful to any form of proverb research, be it a historical investigation of a single proverb or be it a search for national character traits in an extensive proverb corpus from a single culture.

The proverb may best be defined in structural terms. Purely functional definitions are inadequate inasmuch as other genres of folklore may share the same function(s) as proverbs. For instance, most functional definitions of proverbs make mention of 'summing up a situation' or 'recommending a course of action.' Clearly gestures and narrative exempla among other genres of folklore may involve the same functional criteria. This is not to demean the genuine utility of functional considerations, but only to affirm the necessity for internal rather than external formal definitional criteria. The critical question is thus not what a proverb does, but what a proverb is.

Another reason for attempting a structural analysis of the proverb is that it would represent a valuable test case for the structural analysis of folklore generally. If it is truly possible to analyze the structure of the genres of oral literature, then it ought to be possible to analyze the structure of proverbs in particular. All of the general theoretical problems associated with structural analysis are relevant to the proverb. These problems include: the nature of the basic or minimum structural units, the persistent question of if and where the continuum is or can be meaningfully segmented, and the inevitable controversy as to whether the units of analysis are really in the data (God's truth) or are only a heuristic device found exclusively in the mind of the analyst (Hocus-Pocus).[9] The great advantage of using proverbs rather than folktales, myths, or ballads is obviously the relative simplicity of the genre. It makes sense therefore to attack the crucial theoretical questions of structural analysis by focusing upon a simple proverb rather than a complex myth.

In the past we find there have been several discussions which have been concerned with proverb structure. In 1947, Kimmerle attempted to devise a classification of folk sayings which included proverbs. However, her schema was closely tied to linguistic and syntactic formulas. Not all of her seventeen categories were relevant to proverbs and the use of such grammatical distinctions as the presence of a predicate noun or predicate adjective or direct object suggests that her analysis was more of a surface structure than deep structure, to employ the Chomsky metaphor.[10] While it is true that it is possible to "parse" proverbs, so to speak, it is highly questionable whether parts of speech per se can significantly illuminate the structure of proverbs. It is not that there isn't linguistic structure. To the extent that proverbs are composed of words, there would have to be linguistic structure involved. The question is rather whether there are underlying patterns of 'folkloristic structure' as opposed to 'linguistic structure' which may be isolated.[11]

One problem which arises with respect to isolating possible folkloristic structures which may underlie proverbs has to do with whether one is analyzing proverb image, proverb message, or proverb architectural formula.[12] For example, there appear to be a finite number of proverb compositional or architectural formulas. There is "Better . . . . than . . . . " (e.g., Better late than never, Better safe than sorry, Better bend than break). Other common proverb formulas include: "A . . . . is a . . . . " (e.g., A bargain is a bargain); " . . . .(s) never . . . . " (e.g., Barking dogs never bite); " . . . . or . . . . " (e.g., do or die); and the Wellerism " . . . . , said the . . . . (as he . . . .)" (e.g., "I see" said the blind man as he picked up his hammer and saw).[13]

Proverb formulas appear to be relatively independent of image and to a lesser extent message. "Better late than never" does not mean the same as the Italian proverb "Better a mouse in the mouth of a cat than a man in the hands of a lawyer." There is, to be sure, a commonality of semantic message to the extent that in both cases, the first item, let us call it 'A,' is deemed better than the second item 'B.' But the messages are quite different. In one, an individual may be urged *not to go* to a lawyer, in the other, an individual is urged *to go* (somewhere)—even though it is late. Since 'not going' is not the same as 'going,' the message would appear to be distinct from the overall formula 'Better . . . . than . . . . .'

Finnish proverb scholar Kuusi also observes that the message or referential aspect of proverbs is not tied to the image employed.[14] That is to say that the same or similar message may be communicated by different images. The proverb "He who is bitten by a snake fears even a rope" is in terms of semantic import quite similar to the French proverb "A scalded cat fears even cold water" and both proverbs are similar in message to the Greek proverb "Whoever is burned on hot squash blows on the cold yogurt." The images differ; the messages do not. The question then with respect to structural analysis is: precisely what is it that is being analyzed? The Turkish proverb "You cannot make a stallion out of donkey by cropping its ears" has a similar message to "You can't make a silk purse out of a sow's ear," yet the images are different. What exactly should be subjected to structural analysis? The image, or the underlying formula: 'you can't make a . . . . out of a . . . . ' which is seemingly independent of any one specific image? I believe it should be the underlying frame or formula rather than the image. Different proverb images are rather like different Aarne-Thompson tale types. The point is that differences in content do not necessarily mean that there are correlative differences in underlying structure. As Propp's syntagmatic model may underlie different Aarne-Thompson tale types and as Lévi-Strauss's paradigmatic model may underlie many different South American Indian myths, so the would-be analyst of proverbs should seek a syntagmatic or paradigmatic model for proverbs.[15]

A recent ambitious attempt to bare the nature of proverbs tends to concentrate upon content rather than form. Initially stimulated by working with a collection of Samoan proverbs, G.B. Milner has suggested that proverbs might be defined as traditional sayings consisting of quadripartite structure.[16] According to Milner's theory, the four quarters (minor segments) of a proverb are grouped into 'halves' (major segments) which "match and balance each other." The opening half Milner terms the 'head' while the second half is labelled the 'tail.'

Milner then examines the word or words in each quarter and determines whether it or they have a plus or minus value. Thus in the proverb "soon ripe, soon rotten" the values are assigned by Milner as follows:

+	+	
soon	ripe	(which means that the head is +)
+	−	
soon	rotten	(which means that the tail is −)

Within each half of a saying, Milner argues, the two quarters may both be plus (as in "soon ripe") or both be minus or they may be opposites (as in "soon rotten"). If both quarters are plus or both quarters are minus, the meaning of the whole half is considered to be positive. If the quarters are opposites, the whole half is considered to be negative. By this reasoning, any proverb consists of a positive or negative 'head' followed by a positive or negative 'tail.' Having established this general scheme, Milner can assign any individual proverb to one of sixteen possible classes. These sixteen are reduced to four main classes (each consisting of four subclasses). Class A has a positive head and a positive tail; Class B has a negative head and positive tail; Class C has a positive head and negative tail; and Class D has a negative head and a negative tail. Within each main class, there are four different means of achieving the end. For example, in Class A, the four quarters may be of any of the following schemes: ++++; ----; ++--; --++. The other main classes are similarly broken down into subclasses.[17]

Unfortunately, there are several difficulties with Milner's scheme, though these difficulties in no way minimize the novelty of Milner's analysis. For one thing, Milner's analysis seems to have no other end than that of classification. It is not clear what the advantage is of being able to assign a given proverb to one of Milner's sixteen classes. Another problem arises from Milner's assumption of the logical priority of his basic quadripartite proverb structure. From this assumption, Milner is led to speculate that any proverbs not possessing four 'quarters' must be mere survivals from an earlier fuller form. In his words, "... it is likely that a very large number of tripartite, bipartite and unipartite idioms current today, were once quadripartite, and have been eroded by the familiarity of usage."[18] This is not only a form of throwing away empirical data that doesn't fit a theory, but is itself a 'survival' of English survival theory in which it is invariably assumed that the full, original form in the past has evolved or rather devolved through time suffering such ravages of attrition that only a fragment remains.[19] Milner's hint that the fundamental quadripartite structure of proverbs may ultimately be related to the 'fourness' of the Jungian mandala is also extremely speculative. But there are other theoretical difficulties.

One issue recognized by Milner himself is the subjective nature of the assignment of plus and minus values to the four quarters. And he does give two contrasting analyses of the same proverb, "Rolling stones gather no moss." The Scottish and English interpretations of the meaning of the proverb necessitate different value assignments. In England, the stones refer to the stones in a brook and these stones rarely move. Moss is considered to be wealth, prosperity, etc. Hence the Milner formulation for the English meaning of the proverb is:

−	+	
Rolling	stones	(the head is −)
gather	no moss	(the tail is −)
+	(− +)	
	−	

In Scotland, however, the stones are thought to be the cylindrical stones of an old fashioned roller. Such stones must not be idle or else moss (lichen) will grow on them. In the Scottish context, then, rolling is plus, stones are plus and no-moss is plus.

+	+	
Rolling	stones	(the head is +)
gather	no moss	(the tail is +)
+	(− −)	
	+	

Thus though the proverb continues to manifest a four part structure, the English and Scottish meanings involve different plus-minus patterns. (One wonders also if given this variability whether one could make such plus or minus assignments without close consultation with informants. If this is so, then one could not by definition make such assignments just by looking at the text alone.)

But Milner doesn't see the subjectivity of some of his other examples. For instance, he makes the following analysis of the proverb "England has mild winters but hard summers."

	+	+	
(England has)	mild	winters	(the head is +)
but	hard	summers	(the tail is −)
	−	+	

Milner places the proverb in his Class C (Positive head; Negative tail). However, it seems to me that one could very well argue that the value to be assigned to "winters" should be 'minus,' not 'plus.' And the point here is not simply that Milner mislabelled one of his quarters, but rather that he is the victim of a much too atomistic analysis. For whatever the structural units of a proverb may be, they cannot be defined apart from their relationship to the rest of the proverb. Milner's error lies in trying to assign plus or minus values to each of the quarters as though the other three quarters were not present. Just so there is no mistake, let me quote Milner's own views in his own words: "Within each half, the two quarters have *independent* value which modify and affect each other (*but do not modify the quarters of the other half*)."[20] My point is that one cannot understand the structural significance of "winters" in the proverb "England has mild winters but hard summers" without taking "summers" into account. Clearly, "winters" and "summers" are in opposition (just as "mild" and "hard" are in opposition). This is, in my view, a fundamental weakness in Milner's scheme of analysis. Whether one favors syntagmatic or paradigmatic structural analysis, one cannot define any structural element in total isolation from the whole syntagmatic sequence or the whole paradigm.

My own approach to proverb structure assumes that there is a close relationship between proverb structure and riddle structure. While there is no doubt that there are important functional differences between these two genres, e.g., riddles confuse while proverbs clarify, I believe that structurally speaking there are major similarities. First of all, both proverb and riddle depend upon 'topic-comment' constructions.[21] A minimum proverb or riddle consists of one descriptive element, that is to say, one unit composed of one topic and one comment. It is true that in riddles the referent of the descriptive element is to be guessed whereas in proverbs the referent is presumably known to both the speaker and the addressee(s). And that is one of the principal differences between proverbs and riddles.

Several scholars have drawn attention to the similarity of my previous structural definitions of proverb and riddle, arguing that if the only difference is that in the riddle "the referent of the descriptive element(s) is to be guessed," this is not a structural difference.[22] I think that it is a structural difference, especially in the case of oppositional riddles inasmuch as the answer (referent) provides the means of resolving the apparent opposition. In proverbs which are oppositional, the opposition normally remains unresolved. The initial situation which stimulated the utterance of the proverb in the first place may or may not resolve the opposition delineated in the proverb. In oppositional riddles, the answer always resolves the opposition. One reason for this is that frequently the oppositions in riddles are only pseudo or pretended oppositions. In oppositional proverbs, the oppositions are genuine ones and are not to be easily resolved if indeed they can be resolved at all.

Other folklorists have previously observed the similarities in the construction of proverbs and riddles. The Russian folklorist Sokolov cites an example: "Nothing hurts it, but it groans all the time."[23] If the text is used as a proverb, it refers to a hypocrite and a beggar. If used as a riddle, it refers to a swine. Sokolov is incorrect, however, when he contends it is only by means of a single change of intonation that a proverb is transformed into a riddle. It is obviously not intonation per se which is the critical causal factor. Instead, it is the context in which the text is cited. If the text is being used to refer to a hypocrite known to both the speaker and the audience, the text functions as a proverb. If the speaker wishes to test an adressee, then he may state the text as a question using an appropriate interrogatory intonation pattern. The context or rhetorical intention of the speaker determines the intonation pattern *and* the genre distinction. The intonation is a concomitant feature, a signal or indicator of the genre, but hardly a 'cause' of the genre.

The double life of a text as both proverb and riddle is apparently not that uncommon. In a Burmese example, we find the same phenomenon.[24] The text: "The one who does not know about it may walk over it; the one who knows about it will dig it up and eat it." As a riddle, the referent (answer) is a potato or any crop which grows underground. As a proverb, the statement is applied in many different situations where someone is ignorant of something valuable which is not readily apparent but which is close at hand. If such texts can be employed as both proverbs and riddles, then it should not be surprising to discover that the structures of proverbs and riddles are similar. It is also interesting in this connection to remark that in cultural areas where proverbs seem to be absent or scanty, riddles appear to be likewise. Among North and South American Indians, there are relatively few proverbs and riddles. One wonders if there is any culture which has the one genre without the other. Structurally speaking, one is tempted to argue that the existence of one makes the presence of the other logically possible.

As there are non-oppositional riddles, so there are non-oppositional proverbs. Those proverbs which consist of a single descriptive element, e.g., money talks, would be examples of non-oppositional proverbs. Note that with the minimum structural definition of a proverb as one descriptive element (consisting of one topic and one comment), it is theoretically impossible to have a one word proverb. According to this definition, one would have to have at least two words to have a proverb. There are traditional one word items of folk speech, but these would not be proverbs.[25]

Before discussing the nature of oppositional proverbs, it might be well to consider for a moment the proverb with respect to what linguist Kenneth Pike has termed "identificational-contrastive" features.[26] In such linguistic units as the phoneme and the morpheme, the sub-units or allo-units demonstrate a combination of both identificational and contrastive features. Thus, for example, two allophones of the English phoneme /p/ as manifested in "pit" and "tip" share common articulatory characteristics (identificational) but differ with regard to aspiration (contrastive). Initial "p" in English is aspirate whereas final "p" in English is inaspirate. (This is in contrast to the French phoneme /p/ where, for example, initial "p" is normally inaspirate). I am not concerned with the validity of the identificational-contrastive distinction in linguistics so much as seeing it as a means to analyze proverb structure. I believe that multi-descriptive element proverbs are composed of analogous identificational-contrastive features. Some proverbs are primarily identificational; some are primarily contrastive; and some are combinations or composites of identificational and contrastive features.

The reason I refer to multi-descriptive element proverbs is that proverbs which consist of just one descriptive element cannot be oppositional. English examples of one descriptive element proverbs include: money talks, opposites attract, and time flies. One descriptive element proverbs cannot be said to be as common as multi-descriptive element proverbs. Nevertheless, they do exist and consequently any definition of the proverb must take them into account.

I should also like to raise briefly the question of metaphor and its relationship to proverb structure. In a previous analysis of riddle structure, it was pointed out that nonoppositional riddles could be either literal or metaphorical.[27] In other words, the structure of riddles did not depend upon whether the riddle was a literal or metaphorical description. The same seems to be true of proverbs. Just as nonoppositional riddles may be either literal or metaphorical so nonoppositional proverbs may be either literal or metaphorical. Representative literal nonoppositional English proverbs include: Honesty is the best policy; The customer is always right; Haste makes waste; Virtue is its own reward; Experience is the best teacher;

Discretion is the better part of valor. Some scholars may prefer to call literal proverbs by some other term, e.g., aphorism, but structurally speaking, literal proverbs appear to be similar to metaphorical proverbs.

If we imagine an axis, one end of which represents identificational features and the other end of which represents contrastive features, then what I have previously termed the "equational proverb" falls close to the identificational end.[28] Moreover, if the equation consists explicitly of an identity as in "A bargain is a bargain," "Business is business," "Let bygones be bygones," "Boys will be boys" or "Enough is enough," then there are virtually no contrastive or oppositional features. Generally equational proverbs of the form A = B are identificational rather than contrastive. Examples of equational proverbs include: Time is money; Seeing is believing, and many of the literal nonoppositional proverbs mentioned above. Proverbs of the form "He who A is B" seem to be transformations of the basic A = B formula. "He who laughs last laughs best" suggests that 'laughing last' = 'laughing best.' Similarly, "He who hesitates is lost" implies that 'hesitating' = 'losing.' In much the same fashion, proverbs with the formula "Where there's an A, there's a B," would appear to be another transformation of the basic equational formula. "Where there's life, there's hope" tends to argue that 'life' = 'hope.' "Where there's smoke, there's fire" would be reduced to 'smoke' = 'fire.' "Where there's a will, there's a way" might be rendered as 'will' = 'way.' (In the last two examples, there is a postulated equivalence of cause and effect. In the first, an effect, smoke, is presumed to mean its cause, fire. In the second, will is assumed to causally lead to a way. But whether cause = effect or effect = cause, the equational structure is maintained.)

Another transformation of the equational structure consists of a series of two or more descriptive elements. These descriptive elements are often linked by a repetition of either the topic or comment: "Many men, many minds"; "First come, first served." I believe that either of these series could be written in normal equational form with no loss of meaning; many men = many minds; first come = first served. Interestingly enough, it is usually the *first* term of two in a nonoppositional series or equation which is identical, e.g., Monkey see, monkey do; coffee boiled is coffee spoiled; a friend in need is a friend in deed (indeed); handsome is as handsome does; a penny saved is a penny earned; nothing ventured, nothing gained; out of sight, out of mind. Occasionally, there are series which are more coordinate or conjunctional than equational. Examples are "Live and learn," "Live and let live," "Laugh and grow fat" and "Love 'em and leave 'em."

Let us now turn to oppositional proverbs. There seem to be a number of different forms of opposition which are found in proverbs. One of the simplest is negation.[29] Negation in this sense denies an identificational equation. "Two wrongs don't make a right." Here we have the basic formula $A \neq B$. The opposition is strengthened by 'two' $\neq$ 'one' and by 'wrong' $\neq$ 'right.' Similarly, "One swallow does not make a summer," 'swallow' $\neq$ 'summer.' Presumably, many swallows do indicate that summer has arrived, thus the 'one' is implicitly contrasted with 'many.' I suggest that all the proverbs based on formulas that 'A is less than B' or 'A is greater than B' (which would include all the proverbs with the familiar formula Better . . . . . . than . . . . . .) are contrastive rather than identificational proverbs. "Hindsight is better than foresight." Hindsight certainly does not equal foresight. Rather the two entities are contrasted. And this is the point really: all proverbs are potentially propositions which compare and/or contrast. Comparing originally referred to finding similarities or identificational features in common; contrasting referred to delineating differences. Other examples of A is greater than B include "His eyes are bigger than his belly" and "Fingers were made before forks."

In investigating the nature of the oppositions found in proverbs, one is tempted to see a certain parallel to the types of oppositions found in oppositional riddles. In a previous study, three types of opposition in English riddles were distinguished: antithetical contradictive, privational contradictive, and causal contradictive.[30] Each of the three types can be produced by either affirmation or negation. Accordingly, antithetical contradiction in riddles can come from statements that $A = B$; $A \neq B$ (which incidentally is a beautiful illustration of the combination of identificational and contrastive features) or via affirmation: $A = B$; $A = C$ (where $B \neq C$).[31]

Antithetical contradiction might be said to be analogous to complementary distribution in linguistics theory. If you have A, then you can't have B; if you have B, you can't have A. (When /p/ occurs initially in English, you will automatically have the aspirate p allophone and never the inaspirate allophone. If /p/ occurs at the end of an English word, you will automatically have inaspirate p, never aspirate p—unless you wish to signal great stress or emphasis in asking a thief to 'stop!').

There seem to be proverbs which demonstrate such complementary distribution. "You can't have your cake and eat it too." If you have your cake, you obviously can't have eaten it. If you eat it, then you no longer have it. 'Having your cake' is thus mutually exclusive with 'eating it.'

This form of oppositional proverb is evidently of considerable antiquity, judging from its occurrence in Sumer. Consider the following Sumerian text:[32]

> The poor man is better dead than alive
> If he has bread, he has no salt,
> If he has salt, he has no bread,
> If he has meat, he has no lamb,
> If he has a lamb, he has no meat.

Having both meat (dead) and the lamb (alive) is just as impossible as having one's cake and eating it too. Another Sumerian illustration:

> Who builds like a lord, lives like a slave;
> Who builds like a slave, lives like a lord.[33]

Evidently, building like a lord and living like a lord are in complementary distribution; they cannot co-occur.

Complementary distribution, it should be noted, can occur even if there is no explicit signal of negation. In the well known international proverb "When the cat's away, the mice will play" there is an opposition between presence and absence in addition to the obvious contrast between cat and mice (which also entails 'one' versus 'many'). If cats are present, then mice are absent; if cats are absent, then mice are present. Cats and mice, according to the proverb are thus in complementary distribution and cannot co-occur.

Although one can have opposition without explicit negation, it is more common to have opposition produced through overt negation. It is important to realize that the negation need not be limited to the verb as in $A \neq B$. Either A or B can be negative (as non-A or non-B). In this respect, Milner was on the right track in attempting to assign plus and minus values to constituent elements of proverbs. However, I would argue that the negation is, more often than not, explicit and therefore one does not need to employ subjective value judgments to determine whether or not negation is a factor. Consider the proverb "No news is good news." Here the negation occurs in the first descriptive element. There is opposition insofar as there is a question as to how no news can be 'news' at all, much less good news. But clearly the absence of news may be good news. Thus as in the cat and mice proverb 'absence' = 'presence.'

It would appear that negation occurs more often in the second or final descriptive element of multi-descriptive element proverbs. For example, consider "Rolling stones gather no moss." The negative is the 'no' in "no moss." Yet the negation is presumably caused by the comment in the first descriptive element, namely "rolling." If we consider the proverb as "stones which roll are stones which gather no moss," then it is the act of rolling which rules out the accumulation of moss. If a stone rolls, it can't have moss; if a stone has moss, it can't have rolled. Notice that this analysis holds regardless of whether moss is deemed a good thing or a bad thing. Structure is more or less independent of meaning although to be sure there will always be conscious or unconscious meanings attached to any given structure. In the same way, it is the 'barking' in "Barking dogs never bite" which precludes biting. The negative equation might be written 'barking dogs are not biting dogs.' Although the proverb is normally understood metaphorically, it is perfectly true, physically speaking, that it is impossible for a dog to bark and bite at the same time. Thus 'barking' and 'biting' may be said to be in complementary distribution insofar as they are mutually exclusive activities. One is tempted to generalize that there seems to be a formulaic pattern ....s never .... in which the presence of the initial factor means the absence of the last. It is 'watching' which prevents boiling (in "A watched pot never boils"); it is "too many" which negates the broth (in "Too many cooks spoil the broth") and it is the "dead" which precludes taletelling (in "Dead men tell no tales").[34]

There are other examples of oppositional proverbs which contain oppositions remarkably similar to the antithetical contradictions of riddles. "A straight stick is crooked in the water" ('straight' = 'crooked'). A most interesting German proverb in this connection is "He who rules, must hear and be deaf, see and be blind." 'Seeing and being blind' is surely reminiscent of riddle oppositional structure. (Cf. What has eyes and cannot see? A potato.) There are also proverb analogues for privational contradiction where a logical part or attribute of an object is denied. "The mob has many heads but no brains" would be a proverb of this type. (This is quite similar to the riddle for a match: "It has a head, but can't think").

There are even proverb parallels for causal contradictives where normal effects or consequences are denied. There are, of course, numerous non-oppositional causal proverbs in which A simply causes B, e.g., Practice makes perfect; Haste makes waste; Familiarity breeds contempt. Ideally, the effect should be parallel to the cause: "As you sow, so shall you reap." However, in oppositional causal proverbs, the cause is denied or deemed impossible. "You can lead a horse to water but you can't make him drink." If one leads a horse to water, one might expect the horse to drink or possibly that one could force him to drink. The opposition results from the contrast of what "can" be done and what "can't" be done. One "can" lead a horse to water but one "can't" make him drink. Again, there is an obvious riddle parallel, "What goes to the branch (stream) and drinks and doesn't drink? (Cow and bell)." Other causal contradictive proverbs include: you can't make a silk purse out of a sow's ear; one can't be in two places at the same time; you can't get blood from a turnip. In these and other proverbs, A cannot produce or yield B.

Still another form of causal opposition occurring in proverbs plays upon the possibility of having the normal effect being illogically placed before the cause. The proverb seemingly reverses the usual chronological priority of actions A and B in "Don't lock the barn door after the horse has been stolen," "Don't set the cart before the horse," "Don't count your chickens before they are hatched," "Catch the bear before you sell its skin."

In attempting to distinguish between identificational versus contrastive features in proverbs or between nonoppositional and oppositional proverbs, one needs to bear in mind that not all proverbs fall neatly into just one category. As has already been suggested, some proverbs contain both identificational *and* contrastive features. Westermarck noted some years ago in his brilliant introductory essay on the nature of the proverbs he had collected in Morocco that in some proverbs there is a tendency to have two or more parallel assertions while in others there is a predilection for antithesis and contrast. With respect to the latter, he even went so far as to indicate that subjects could be contrasted, predicates could be contrasted, or both subjects and predicates could be contrasted.[35] I agree with Westermarck's observations except that I would employ the terminology of 'topic' and 'comment' in place of his subject and predicate, and I would underline his suggestion that parallel and contrastive features may occur in one and the same proverb. I would also speculate that the phenomenon of simultaneous identificational/contrastive features might be a characteristic of proverbs in all cultures where the genre is found.

Perhaps the most common means of building opposition in proverbs is to utilize one or more of a number of traditional semantic contrastive pairs. In English these include:

one	versus	two
few		many
young		old
old		new
little		great
near		far
weak		strong
worst		best
easy		hard
always		never
good		bad
black		white
before		after
today		tomorrow

It should be made clear that this is only a partial list. It should also be noted that no one member of any of these pairs is always superior. In the "one" versus "two" sometimes "one" is preferred, sometimes "two." For example, in many of the 'A is greater than B' proverbs, one can find 'One A is better than two B's' (e.g., "One hour's sleep before midnight is better than two after") but one can also find 'Two A's are better than one' as in 'Two heads are better than one.' (Then again, sometimes 'one' = 'two' as in "A bird in the hand is worth two in the bush" though of course it is the contrast between "in the hand" and "in the bush" which balances the numerical inequity.)

In causal proverbs, the obvious contrast between cause and effect is heightened by the use of such pairs. For example, "A little spark kindles a great fire" has not only the contrast between spark and fire but also "little" and "great." The same opposition is found in "Great oaks from little acorns grow." A different pair is employed in "A black hen will lay a white egg," but the opposition principle is the same.

In some proverbs, there are both oppositional and non-oppositional features. For example, there is an equational proverb: "The longest way round is the shortest way found." There is an equation which implies an identificational feature, but the equation involves "longest" = "shortest" which is clearly oppositional. Consider "One man's meat is another man's poison" in which "meat" (life) = "poison" (death). Or "An ounce of prevention is worth a pound of cure" in which "ounce" = "pound." The equational structure provides a frame suggesting identification, but the content within this frame contains contrastive features. Another example is "Easy come, easy go." 'Coming' and 'going' are in opposition, but the two instances of 'easy' constitute an identity. The same sort of combination occurs in "Win a few; lose a few." One could say that in such proverbs there is not only the opposition between members of a contrasting semantic pair (e.g., coming-going, winning-losing) but also the opposition caused by having both an identity and a contrast in the same proverb!

Less ambiguous are the multi-descriptive element proverbs in which *both* topics *and* comments are members of contrastive pairs. Here are some examples: "The spirit is willing but the flesh is weak" (spirit/flesh; willing/weak); "United we stand, divided we fall" (united/divided; stand/fall); "Man proposes but God disposes" (man/God; proposes/disposes); "Last hired, first fired" (last/first; hired/fired); "Here today, gone tomorrow" (present/absent; today/tomorrow); "Jack of all trades and master of none" (Jack/master; all/none); "Penny wise and pound foolish" (penny/pound; wise/foolish). In a proverb like "Many are called but few are chosen," it is clear that 'many' are opposed to 'few' and that 'being called' ≠ 'being chosen.'

From this we can see that there does seem to be a continuum from non-opposition to opposition. One can have a set of topic-comment constructions which are parallel or in series and are not in opposition: "Many men, many minds"; "First come, first served." One can have a set in which either the topic or the comment is parallel or identical with the remaining element in opposition "Easy come, easy go." Finally, one can have a set in which both topics and comments are in opposition: "Last hired, first fired."

One of the most striking contrasts between terms in series and terms in opposition is provided by the difference between proverbs of the form "Live and learn" on the one hand and proverbs of the form

"Do or die" on the other. There is no opposition or contradiction between living and learning. On the contrary, to live is to learn. Living = learning. But 'doing' and 'dying' are in opposition. If one does not do, one dies. If one dies, one cannot do. The same is true for "sink or swim," "put up or shut up," "fish or cut bait," "shape up or ship out," "publish or perish," etc. In alternative structure proverbs, the terms are normally in complementary distribution, that is, they are mutually exclusive. And as has already been noted, complementary distribution in proverbs represents one of the strongest forms of opposition.

In summary then, the proverb appears to be a traditional propositional statement consisting of at least one descriptive element, a descriptive element consisting of a topic and a comment. This means that proverbs must have at least two words. Proverbs which contain a single descriptive element are non-oppositional. Proverbs with two or more descriptive elements may be either oppositional or non-oppositional. "Like father, like son" would be an example of a multi-descriptive element proverb which was non-oppositional; "Man works from sun to sun but woman's work is never done" would be an example of a multi-descriptive element proverb which is oppositional (man/woman; finite work/infinite or endless work). Non-oppositional multi-descriptive element proverbs emphasize identificational features, often in the form of an equation or a series of equal terms; oppositional proverbs emphasize contrastive features, often in the form of negation or a series of terms in complementary distribution. Some proverbs contain both identificational and contrastive features. The means of producing opposition in proverbs is strikingly similar to the means of producing opposition in riddles. However, whereas the oppositions in riddles are resolved by the answer, the oppositional proverb is itself an answer to a proverb-evoking situation, and the opposition is posed, not resolved. In this sense, proverbs only state problems in contrast to riddles which solve them.

The above analysis is most tentative and needs to be empirically tested with proverb materials from a variety of cultures. To the extent that the proverb is a cross-cultural genre of folklore, there should be a cross-culturally valid definition of the proverb. One research possibility resulting from the above analysis concerns the discernment of oicotypes.[36] Do all cultures which have proverbs have the same proverb structural types? For example, which cultures have equational proverbs consisting of perfect identities as "Enough is enough"?

There are also possible oicotypes of content. Do all cultures which have proverbs have contrastive pairs emphasizing time and quantity, for example?

It may well be that the foregoing discussion is based upon too limited a sample and that close analysis of proverbs from Asian and African cultures will require considerable revision of the distinctions outlined above. It is also likely that insofar as proverbs are traditional propositions, they should properly be studied by scholars with expertise in symbolic logic and related disciplines. However, for the time being, I am encouraged to find some confirmation of the importance of oppositional structure in proverbs as found in two famous "definitions" of proverbs. One is Cervantes' suggestion that proverbs are "short sentences drawn from long experience." And equally supportive as 'short' versus 'long' is the beautiful definition attributed to Lord Russell which suggests that proverbs are: "the wisdom of many, the wit of one."[37]

Notes

1. For an entry into proverb scholarship, see Wilfrid Bonser and T.A. Stephens, *Proverb Literature: A Bibliography of Works Relating to Proverbs* (London, 1930) and Otto E. Moll, *Sprichwörterbibliographie* (Frankfurt, 1958).

2. For an excellent survey of recent proverb studies, see Matti Kuusi, *Parömiologische Betrachtungen*, Folklore Fellows Communications 172 (Helsinki 1957).

3. An exemplary field investigation of the proverb is Mathilde Hain, *Sprichwort und Volkssprache: eine volkskundlich-soziologische Dorfuntersuchung,* Giessener Beiträge zur deutschen Philologie 95 (Giessen, 1951).

4. For a discussion of the proverb with respect to communication rules, see E. Ojo Arewa and Alan Dundes, "Proverbs and the Ethnography of Speaking Folklore," *American Anthropologist*, 66, (6) Part 2 (1964), 70–85.

5. For a discussion of proverbs and national character, see Joseph Raymond, "Attitudes and Cultural Patterns in Spanish Proverbs," *The Americas*, 11 (1954), 55–77; for proverbs and worldview, see D.B. Shimkin and Pedro Sanjuan, "Culture and World View: A Method of Analysis Applied to Rural Russia," *American Anthropologist*, 55 (1953), 329–348.

6. See Donald R. Gorham, "Use of the Proverbs Test for Differentiating Schizophrenics from Normals," *Journal of Consulting Psychology*, 30 (1956), 435–440; and Clyde M. Elmore and Donald R. Gorham, "Measuring the Impairment of the Abstracting Function with the Proverb Test," *Journal of Clinical Psychology*, 13 (1957), 263–266. The difficulty in interpreting metaphor as metaphor may also be

related to certain forms of aphasia, see Roman Jakobson and Morris Halle, *Fundamentals of Language* (The Hague, 1965), p. 69. For another practical use of proverbs, see Franziska Baumgarten, "A Proverb Test for Attitude Measurement," *Personnel Psychology*, 5 (1952), 249–261.

7. Archer Taylor, *The Proverb* (Hatboro, Pennsylvania, 1962). Professor Taylor's remark was a personal communication to the author.

8. Professor Whiting's comments were made in "Proverbs and Proverbial Sayings: Introduction," in *The Frank C. Brown Collection of North Carolina Folklore*, Vol. I (Durham, North Carolina, 1952), p. 331. Whiting has even made a survey of previous definitions of the proverb but his own definition leaves much to be desired, e.g., "It is usually short but need not be; it is usually true, but need not be." See B.J. Whiting, "The Nature of the Proverb," *Harvard University Studies and Notes in Philology and Literature* 14 (1932), 273–307. Whiting does suggest that true proverbs be distinguished from proverbial phrases or what I would term "folk metaphors." This is a thorny question. However, I would agree that true proverbs can be distinguished from proverbial comparisons or folk similes. Structurally, they do not appear to be transformationally equivalent. The proverb "Love is blind" does not occur as a folk simile "as blind as love." By the same token, the folk simile "as blind as a bat" does not occur as "A bat is blind."

9. For a discussion of the God's truth versus the Hocus-Pocus positions with respect to the reality of structure in folklore, see Alan Dundes, *The Morphology of North American Indian Folktales*, Folklore Fellows Communications 195 (Helsinki, 1964), p. 57.

10. Marjorie M. Kimmerle, "A Method of Collecting and Classifying Folk Sayings," *Western Folklore*, 6 (1947), 351–366. I believe that Noam Chomsky's search for "deep structure" as opposed to surface structure is intellectually similar to Freud's interest in the latent content as opposed to the manifest content and to Jung's interest in archetypes. In the same way, Lévi-Strauss tries to isolate the paradigmatic structure which underlies syntagmatic structures. See Alan Dundes, "Introduction to the Second Edition," Vladimir Propp, *Morphology of the Folktale* (Austin, Texas, 1968), p. VII, for a discussion of this point. Chomsky, Jung, and Lévi-Strauss are all looking for universals in the form of 'deep structure,' 'archetype' and a binary oppositional paradigm.

11. For a discussion of the distinction between 'folkloristic structure' and 'linguistic structure,' see Robert A. Georges and Alan Dundes, "Toward a Structural Definition of the Riddle," *Journal of American Folklore*, 76 (1963), p. 117, nn. 15, 18.

12. These three aspects of proverbs have been well differentiated by Matti Kuusi. See his "Ein Vorschlag für die Terminologie der parömiologischen Strukturanalyse," *Proverbium*, 5 (1966), 97–104. See also Siegfried Neumann, "Zur Terminologie der parömiologischen Strukturanalyse," *Proverbium*, 6 (1966), 130.

13. In the tripartite structure of the Wellerism, the third portion appears to be structurally optional rather than obligatory. Thus one can have Wellerisms of the form: . . . said the . . . See Archer Taylor, *The Proverb*, pp. 214–215. On the other hand, the third portion is usually present as it is this section which puts the first portion—the quotation or proverb—in a new and often humorous light.

14. Kuusi, p. 98.

15. For a discussion of the distinction between syntagmatic and paradigmatic structures, see Alan Dundes, "Introduction to the Second Edition," Vladimir Propp, *Morphology of the Folktale*, pp. XI–XIII.

16. G.B. Milner, "What is a Proverb?" *New Society*, 332 (6 February 1969), 199–202. A shorter statement of Milner's scheme is his "Quadripartite Structures," *Proverbium*, 14 (1969), 379–383. A fuller account is "De l'armature des locutions proverbiales: Essai de taxonomie sémantique," *L'homme*, 9 (1969) 49–70.

17. Milner, "What is a Proverb?" pp. 200–201.

18. Milner, p. 202.

19. For a discussion of this theoretical position, see Alan Dundes, "The Devolutionary Premise in Folklore Theory," *Journal of the Folklore Institute*, 6 (1969), 5–19.

20. Milner, p. 200. The emphasis is mine.

21. For a discussion of topic-comment constructions, see Alan Dundes, "Trends in Content Analysis, A Review Article," *Midwest Folklore*, 12 (1962), 37, or Georges and Dundes, "Toward a Structural Definition of the Riddle," 113.

22. One such scholar is Charles T. Scott in his "Some Approaches to the Study of the Riddle," *Studies in Language, Literature, and Culture of the Middle Ages and Later*, ed. E. Bagby Atwood and Archibald A. Hill (Austin, Texas, 1969), pp. 110–127, see esp. p. 124. The criticism is also contained in Scott's *Persian and Arabic Riddles: A Language-Centered Approach to Genre Definition*, Publications of the Research Center in Anthropology, Folklore, and Linguistics, Indiana University, 39 (Baltimore, 1965). The same criticism was made independently by Bertel Nathhorst in his "Genre, Form and Structure in Oral Tradition," *Temenos*, 3 (1968), 128–135.

23. Y.M. Sokolov, *Russian Folklore* (New York, 1950), p. 285.

24. Alan Dundes, "Texture, Text, and Context," *Southern Folklore Quarterly*, 28 (1964), 262.

25. This brings up two points with respect to Milner's analysis. First of all, if "Money talks" is a bona fide proverb, then must we assume that it was once part of a larger quadripartite proverb? I would say that although there are proverbs with what Milner terms quadripartite structure, it would be wrong to claim that all proverbs have or had this one structure. The basic unit of proverbs seems to me to be a topic-comment construction and Milner's quadripartite structure is essentially a doubling of the basic structure. The second point concerns Milner's reference to "unipartite idioms." I doubt that there is a one word proverb. Milner's one example is really an allusion to a proverb rather than a proverb per se. If there are truly unipartite proverbs, I should like to see some examples.

26. Kenneth L. Pike, *Language in Relation to a Unified Theory of the Structure of Human Behavior*, Part I (Glendale, California, 1954), p. 83.

27. Georges and Dundes, p. 113.

28. Alan Dundes, "Trends in Content Analysis," pp. 37–38. In this initial discussion of the equational proverb, I failed to make any mention of oppositional proverbs.

29. The relationship of negation to equation is not altogether clear. In folktales, for example, Propp noted that "A command often plays the role of an interdiction," Propp,

p. 27. 'Keep your eyes closed' would be a command; 'Don't open your eyes' would be an interdiction. I found the same difficulty in defining disequilibrium in American Indian narratives. A flood could be construed as too much water or too little land! See Dundes, *The Morphology of North American Indian Folktales*, pp. 61–64. Similarly, riddle oppositions can be produced by affirmation or by negation. The role of negation in folkloristic structure should be the subject of a separate investigation.

30. Georges and Dundes, p. 114.

31. Ibid.

32. Samuel Noah Kramer, *History Begins at Sumer* (New York, 1959), p. 121.

33. Kramer, p. 125. Milner in "Quadripartite Structures," *Proverbium*, 14 (1969), 382, gives a number of examples in which the order of words in the first half is inverted in the second half, e.g., Those who speak don't know; those who know don't speak. He claims this type of formula AB/BA is quite widespread, occurring, for instance, in Chinese and African proverbs.

34. The initial factor seems to be equally crucial in equational proverbs. In "The early bird catches the worm" it is the 'earliness' which = the worm. In "A new broom sweeps clean," it is the newness which = cleanliness.

35. Edward Westermarck, *Wit and Wisdom in Morocco: A Study of Native Proverbs* (London, 1930), pp. 5–6.

36. For a discussion of the concept of oicotype, see Alan Dundes, ed., *The Study of Folklore* (Englewood Cliffs, 1965), pp. 219–220, and Laurits Bødker, *Folk Literature (Germanic)*, International Dictionary of Regional European Ethnology and Folklore, Vol. II (Copenhagen, 1965), p. 220.

37. I wish to thank the members of an informal seminar on structural analysis who met weekly during the Winter Quarter of 1970. I am especially indebted to Angie Berry, Rob Hanford, Bess Hawes, Dr. William Hendricks, Bill Herzog, Sharon Heuga, Toni Ihara, Ed Kahn, Mellie Lopez, Gail Schow, Barbara Vogl, Fred Walden, and Marcia Walerstein for their stimulating suggestions.

Towards a Structural Analysis of Yiddish Proverbs

*Beatrice Silverman-Weinreich**

Most formalistic considerations of the proverb genre tend to analyze linguistic, textural features rather than structural ones. The term "structure" in such studies often refers to grammatical patterns as well as to textural attributes, for example, assonance, alliteration, meter, and rhyme. In the following detailed account of the formal characteristics of the Yiddish proverb, we find a praiseworthy concern for the most important recurring poetic and stylistic elements.

For other representative examples of what is essentially a language-centered approach to the proverb, see Iwan Klimenko, Das russische Sprichwort. Formen und konstruktive Eigentümlichkeiten. *(Bern, 1946); Fatma M. Mahgoub,* A Linguistic Study of Cairene Proverbs *(The Hague, 1968); John Mark Thompson,* The Form and Function of Proverbs in Ancient Israel *(The Hague, 1974); Werner Koller,* Redensarten. Linguistische Aspekte, Vorkommensanalysen, Sprachspiel *(Tübingen, 1977); and Gerhard Peukes,* Untersuchungen zum Sprichwort im Deutschen *(Berlin, 1977).*

The Yiddish proverb[1] *men ken dem yam mit a kendl nit oysshepn* [M 620][2] "one can't drain the ocean with a ladle" is an apposite introduction to the present paper. For a veritable ocean of Yiddish

*Reprinted from *Yivo Annual of Jewish Social Science*, 17 (1978), 1–20.

proverbs have been assembled by such collectors as Bernshteyn, Tendlau, Bastomski, Landau, Lehman, Pirozhnikov, Prilutski, Mark, Beem, and Eynhorn—and in the format of a dozen pages I certainly won't be able to "drain the ocean." What I would humbly undertake here is to pinpoint a number of research problems and advance a few hypotheses on the structural analysis and study of Yiddish proverbs. Before turning to these tasks, a brief review of what has been done to date is perhaps in order.

1. As stated above, there is no dearth of raw data. Moreover, collectors could undoubtedly still turn up many hitherto unrecorded Yiddish proverbs, a worthwhile task in itself, to be sure. For the purposes of this paper, however, let's limit ourselves to the proverbs that have already been collected and published, and see to what extent this material has been analyzed, what the avenues of approach have been, and what can still be done with the material. To begin with, what research tools are available to the scholar? Unfortunately, we still lack a systematic, critical evaluation of the collections, of the biases of the collectors, their methods of collecting, and the classification systems they used. Vaynig's endeavor in this direction is not entirely satisfactory.[3] We also lack a bibliography that covers both the main collections and proverbs that turn up in relatively inaccessible newspapers and magazines like *Globus*, *Ost und West*, etc., or scattered throughout YIVO's publication, *Yidishe shprakh*. If we turn to the studies themselves, to the monographs on Yiddish proverbs, unfortunately we cannot say that much has been accomplished here either.

Previous research has been limited largely to two main approaches: (a) attempts at determining the Jewish and non-Jewish sources of individual Yiddish proverbs, and (b) attempts at extracting the "philosophy of life" which they allegedly reflect.

2. *The genetic approach* (a) is perhaps especially attractive in the case of Yiddish proverbs precisely because the sources are so diverse.

2.1. In the first place we have the older Jewish (Biblical, Talmudic and Midrashic) proverbs that reached Yiddish-speakers: a) through direct contact with the written Hebrew-Aramaic sources (which were often translated and adapted into Yiddish) or via the related edifying literature (*muser-sforim*) originally written in Yiddish; and b) through oral transmission of such older literary sources by itinerant Jewish preachers (*magidim*), or scholars, or other popular transmission channels. A proverb like *ver es grobt a grub far yenem, falt in im aleyn arayn* "whoever digs a pit for another, will himself fall into it" can easily be traced back to *koreh shakhat bah yipol* "whoever digs a pit will fall into it" (Proverbs 26:27) or to *bor karah vayakhperehu vayipol* "he has dug a pit and hollowed it out and has fallen into the pit which he has made" (Psalms 7:16). While it may be tempting to link the Yiddish proverb: *a mentsh trakht un got lakht* "man thinks and God laughs" [= Man proposes and God disposes] to the German proverb *Der Mensch denkt und Gott lenkt*, the Yiddish proverb (and the German one, as well) can of course also be traced directly to the older Biblical proverb *lev adam yekhashev darko va'adoshem yakhin tsa'ado* "a man's heart devises his way, but the Lord directs his steps" (Proverbs 16:9).

2.2. In the second instance, there are some Yiddish proverbs that apparently are indeed based on non-Jewish popular or literary sources. *Afn ganef brent dos hitl* "the cap burns on the thief" [=the thief's cap blazons his guilt] may well be based on an identical co-territorial Russian proverb *na vore shapka gorit*, which is the climax of a Russian folktale.[4] *A kats meg oykh kukn afn keyser* "a cat may also look at the emperor" may be a borrowing from the German *Darf doch die Katze den Kaiser ansehen*, which according to one theory[5] is related to a visit paid to the shop of Hieronymus Resch, the maker of woodcuts, by Emperor Maximilian I in 1517: A cat was supposedly lying on a worktable and would not budge, staring at the Emperor suspiciously.

2.3. In addition to Yiddish proverbs that are based on older Jewish proverbial sources, and those that are reshaped, translated borrowings from a co-territorial language, we find a third category of purely Yiddish-language proverbs, i.e., of new coinages created during the East-European era and within the Yiddish-speaking community per se. The sources again are either popular or literary (older and modern Yiddish literature in this case). In an interview for the *Language and Culture Atlas of Ashkenazic Jewry*[6] an informant from Rostik, Bukowina, provided this local proverb: *bay eyner iz di mamelige biter, bay der tsveyter iz dos shterntikhl shiter* "one [poor Jewish] woman complains that her *mamelige* [a pudding made of corn flour, a staple food popular especially in Rumania] is bitter, and the other [wealthier] one complains that her *shterntikhl* [Ashkenazic Jewish woman's traditional headcovering] is sparsely embroidered [with pearls]." This proverb clearly belongs in this third category. Yudel Mark recorded the following saying in Lithuania or Latvia: *in gan-eydn iz nito keyn ort far meshulokhim* [M 696] "in paradise there's no room for *meshulokhim* [fund-raisers in the employ of traditional East European Jewish organizations]." Bernshteyn collected the following gem: *az got vil shtrofn an amorets leygt er im a loshn-koydesh vort in moyl arayn* [A 117] "If God wants to punish an unlearned man, he puts a learned Hebrew word into his mouth" [i.e., the man gives away his lack of learning by his mis-use and/or mis-pronunciation of the learned term].

The collectors themselves frequently ventured a "guess" at the origins of some of their proverbs, as can be seen from their annotations. In addition to such attempts by collectors, there are a few studies like Leybl Toybes' and Khaim-Shlomo Samet's.[7]

The genetic study of proverbs of course bristles with difficulties. The origins of a particular orally circulating proverb are often obscure and one can seldom, if ever, be certain of having ascertained *the* true literary or other source or sources. Precisely because proverbs are so short—as short as a motif in folk-tale analysis—it is perforce difficult to uncover their history. This is not to question the validity of the genetic approach; such studies can be fascinating and I wish we had many solidly based and methodologically rigorous monographs.

3. As for the romantic topic of extracting a "Jewish philosophy of life" from the corpus of collected Yiddish proverbs, I am much less certain how worthwhile this approach is.[8] To begin with there is the thorny problem of how to treat the "philosophy" reflected in items of folklore with known international currency. It can be argued that one could and perhaps must include such universal proverbs in the corpus of each ethnic group's folklore that shares them, and view them as representative of each such individual ethnic group's "philosophy of life" (and a large number of Indo-European proverbs *are* current among many different ethnic groups all over Europe). That problem aside, we're still, however, faced with meeting the important objection that each culture seems to have proverbs expressing diametrically opposed values, attitudes, moral principles, and rules for living. Take, for example, the following proverb-pairs: the laudatory *a yidishe neshome ken men nit shatsn* "a Jewish soul is inestimable" and the ironical and humorous *mit a yidn iz nor gut kugl tsu esn* "the only good thing one Jew can do together with another is to eat *kugl* [=a kind of pudding]"; or the pairs *gelt iz blote* "money is mud" and

af gelt shteyt di velt "the world rests on money"; or *an oylem iz a goylem* "people are fools" as opposed to *an oylem iz nisht keyn goylem* "people are not fools." These are of course antitheses—and could it be otherwise? A culture's fund of proverbs, as represented in standard collections, is not a delimited and consistent philosophical system devised by an individual, but at best a summation of many moods of several generations in different regions. The matter must be approached very carefully.

4. A third, safer approach has been completely overlooked: *the study of the formal structure*—the "morphology" as it were—of Yiddish proverbs and of the poetic taste that has shaped them. No matter what historical complexities or philosophical contradictions the study of a proverb may lead to, we can be reasonably certain that its structure is an instance of the taste of those that employ the proverb at a given moment and in a given place. It is to the formal aspects of Yiddish proverbs that I want in fact to devote the bulk of this study. I should add that some of what follows is probably applicable to proverbs in other European languages, as well as to American-English proverbs.

4.1. The first step in a formal study of the corpus of Yiddish proverbs is that rather formidable one of defining the word proverb (*vertl/shprikhvort/glaykhvort/veltsvertl*) clearly; i.e. to differentiate it from related forms like idiomatic expressions (*idyomen* or *redn-sartn*), *maymrekhazal* "sayings of the sages," *farshteynerte frazes* "proverbial apothegms," and similar proverbial truisms and platitudes. Archer Taylor, America's foremost paremiologist, perhaps wisely refused to define *proverb*: "An incommunicable quality tells us this sentence is proverbial and that one is not."[9] In his monumental work on German proverbs, Friedrich Seiler gives every possible example of functional criteria and stylistic devices but he ends by floundering in the sea of definienda and cannot arrive at an internally consistent definition to cover every proverb.[10]

It nevertheless remains sorely tempting to at least try to find a satisfactory solution to this problem. If we say that every proverb is a short, simple, and didactic sentence, a usual definition, we must be able to answer such questions: "How 'short' is 'short'? Short in relation to what? What shall we call 'simple'?" Even if we agree that a proverb like *gezunt kumt far parnose* (four words) [M630] "good health is more important than employment" is short, simple, and didactic, one wonders whether the following proverb can also rightly be termed "short": *durkhlernen gants shas iz a groyse zakh; durkhlernen eyn mide iz a gresere zakh* (15 words) [M 639] "mastering the entire Talmud is a great achievement; mastering one single virtue is a greater achievement." When we get to the criterion of didactic purpose, one wonders how "didactic" such ironic sayings as these are: *der tsadek falt fun di fis un der roshe halt zikh* [M 665] "the righteous man stumbles and the wicked man stands firmly."

And if all the other stylistic devices that have been attributed to proverbs are examined, like rhyme, alliteration, meter, personification, and paradox, it is not at all difficult to find proverbs lacking this or that device. *A shlekhter sholem iz beser vi a gute krig* [A 54] "a bad peace is better than a good war" does not rhyme; *a nar geyt tsvey mol dort vu a kluger geyt nit keyn eyntsik mol* [A 41] "a fool goes twice where a smart person doesn't go even once" is not in meter; *an aynredenish iz erger vi a krenk* [A 81] "illusory illness is worse than [real] sickness" contains neither metaphor nor personification. Where are we to begin?

In preparing this article, I scrutinized hundreds of Yiddish proverbs to see if I could discern what united them all vis-à-vis mere idiomatic expressions, proverbial apothegms, etc. I had no choice but to go on the assumption that each item in a collection was more than just a one-time improvisation. Many, of course, I recognized as "popular" proverbs, current among Yiddish-speakers today in New York, and have personally heard used as argument markers and intensifiers of conversation. Where a proverb was unknown to me, I nevertheless assumed that what a collector included in his collection was in fact a saying current in some Yiddish-speaking community at the time of collection.

4.2 It would seem that the key to a precise definition of a proverb as a genre apart lies in focusing on its *function* as a starting point. All other criteria lead to contradictions and exceptions.

The function of a proverb is *to point out that a given specific situation or occurrence illustrates an accepted general rule with which the hearer must already be acquainted.* Assume that two people are having a conversation. Saul tells David that a new acquaintance of theirs played a nasty trick on him. Says David: *an alter fraynd iz beser vi naye tsvey* [A 80] "an old friend is better than two new ones." By saying this, David is pointing out to Saul that the situation Saul just described to him illustrates the known general rule that old friends are better than new ones. The proverb in this case has been used descriptively; but it can also function normatively, i.e., to remind one of a rule of behavior appropriate in a given situation. David may also want to remind Saul that since "an old friend is better than two new ones," Saul ought to behave accordingly. As this example shows, the division into descriptive and prescriptive proverbs is not always sharp and we, in fact, do not need it for the following discussion. The main point is still valid, viz., that a proverb points out that a given specific occurrence illustrates an accepted general rule. The hearer supposedly already knows the rule, and the intention of the user of the proverb is to *link situation and rule.*

The proverb can introduce the rule in several ways. It can actually formulate it as in the above example, or it can hint at it allegorically. In the latter case the proverb provides a new example which the hearer must compare with the real situation at hand, and from which he must deduce the common ground—some general rule—applicable to both. *Az di mil hert uftsu moln, hert der milner uftsu tsoln* [B.*s.v.* mill—1] "if the mill stops grinding, the miller stops paying" is generally used allegorically. The hearer must himself surmise what the "mill" stands for and what "paying" stands for.

4.3. To set it apart from ordinary utterances, the proverb, as an indicator of a rule, appears to be cast into certain linguistic molds, and to be characterized by certain formal markers. These markers serve as a kind of oral quotation marks, making the proverb easier to remember and to transmit for those who know it, while intimating to those who do not know it that it *is* a proverb, when heard for the first time.

What follows is based on a structural analysis of some three hundred Yiddish proverbs from diverse sources (Ayalti, Mark, Bernshteyn, and Litvin, in particular). The identification of obligatory and optional formal markers seems to be the logical second step in defining this genre. While my conclusions are admittedly no more than hypotheses that must be tested on a larger sampling, I do not think that a broader analysis will result in many surprises.

4.31. We will begin with *grammatical markers*. The typical Yiddish proverb appears to be a self-contained sentence (or sentences) requiring no larger context than itself. It is a full statement lacking personal pronouns or articles that might refer to previously uttered sentences. There is, in other words, no place for free variables. (Where a personal pronoun does appear in an exceptional proverb—see those on the chart listed under imperatives—it is essentially translatable as the impersonal "one.") Personal names are also avoided, unless they are introduced generically or symbolically, as e.g., in *az khaimke lernt nit, ken nit khaim* "if Khaimke [= the young Khaim] doesn't study, Khaim [=the adult Khaim] won't know" [recorded in 1954 from my grandmother, born in Bar in the Ukraine circa 1865]; *reb nogid fargest az koyrekh iz geven a greserer nogid* [M 650] "Mr. Money-Bags forgets that Korah [a Biblical figure of enormous wealth according to the Talmud] was richer." The first proverb does not refer to a specific person named Khaim and in the second one, Korah is the symbol of a rich man. A similar proverb is one that goes *ver s'iz fun nemerov iz nit fun geberov* [B *s.v. nemerov*] "a person from Nemirov [paronomastic effect: interpretable both as "the city of Nemirov" or as the ad-hoc coinage: "Takers-ville"] is not from Gebirov [an ad-hoc coinage, meaning "Givers-ville"]." Proverbs like these three seem to occur only very rarely. Most proverbs are impersonal: *a krankn fregt men, a gezuntn git men* [A 31] "*one* asks *a* sick person [whether he wants to eat]; *one* gives *a* healthy person [without asking]."

4.311. If the rule-status of the proverb requires the *subject* to be *abstract, generic or symbolic,* this nomic-status of the proverb likewise determines the form of the verb: Universally applicable rules are apparently not expressed in the past tense, and the *main verb* in a Yiddish proverb is therefore usually in the present or future tense (*nomic present* or *nomic future*). In the rare proverbs where the verb has been omitted, it can be understood as a nomic present too: *karg badungen, erlekh batsolt* [A 343] "sharp bargainer, honest payer" is understood as "one who bargains sharply, pays honestly."

The self-containedness of the sentence, its closed form, is the main difference between Yiddish proverbs and idiomatic phrases. In popular idiomatic expressions like *leygn zikh feygelekh in buzem* "to build castles in the air" [literally "to put little birds in one's bosom"], the subject and tense of the verb are free variables and can change from case to case. Thus, one can say: *du leygst zikh feygelekh in buzem, er hot zikh geleygt feygelekh in buzem* etc. "you are building . . . ; he was building . . ." etc. This idiom could easily be converted into a proverb by generalizing it: *feygelekh in buzem tor men zikh nit leygn* "one shouldn't build castles in the air." The boundaries between proverbs and other types of idiomatic expressions are thus quite thin, and one can therefore forgive collectors for having lumped together proverbs and certain types of related expressions in undifferentiated lists. This mixed nature of the collections however led to some later researchers' accepting each item as an "authentic proverb," thus preventing them from arriving at a clear definition of the genre. This study concentrates only on proverbs *strictu senso*, as per our definition.

4.312. The accompanying chart illustrates a number of grammatical patterns that occur in Yiddish proverbs. It is striking that the two grammatical markers just discussed in this paper—the nomic verb and the generic or abstract subject—appear to be valid for proverbs encased in every type of sentence: simple and compound, declarative, interrogative and imperative.

A Sampling of Grammatical Patterns Which Occur in Yiddish Proverbs

Conditional Sentences

az men hot gute skhoyre, hot men nit keyn moyre
"if one has good merchandise, one is not afraid"

az men hot nit tsu entfern, muz men farshvaygn
"if one doesn't have an answer, one must keep quiet"

az men hot nit keyn esreg, darf men keyn pushke nit hobn
"if one doesn't have a citron [a fruit over which blessings are said during the Feast of Booths], one doesn't need a citron-box"

Comparative Sentences

beser mit a klugn tsu farlirn eyder mit a nar tsu gevinen
"better to lose with a wise person than to win with a fool"

beser zikh tsu vintshn eyder yenem tsu sheltn
"better to hope for oneself than to swear at another"

Imperatives (the second person is used generically and can be understood as "one")

hostu—halt, veystu—shvayg, kenstu—tu
"[if] you have [something]—keep [it]; [if] you know—keep silent; [if] you know how to—do"

tsekalupe nit di vund, es vet rinen blut
"don't pick your sore or it will bleed"

gefin dem din, der heter kumt shpeter
"find the law, permission comes later"

freg nit dem royfe, nor dem khoyle
"don't ask the doctor; ask the patient"

Interrogative Sentences (Rhetorical Questions)

az men iz in kaas afn khazn, tor men keyn omeyn nit zogn?
"just because one is angry with the cantor, need one stop saying 'amen'?"

Negatives: <Accusative> + *men* "one" + <Verb>

a falshe matbeye farlirt men nit
"one doesn't lose a counterfeit coin"

a nar ken men nit oysnarn
"a fool can't be cheated"

a yidishe neshome ken men nit shatsn
"one can't treasure a Jewish soul enough"

<Accusative> + *iz* "is" + <Adjective> + *tsu* "to" + <Infinitive> (See also emphatic word order)

a barimer iz gut tsu shlogn
"nobody takes a beating like a braggart" [lit. "a braggart is good to beat up"]

a tserisn gemit iz shver tsu heyln
"a wounded spirit is hard to heal"

Riddle Pattern

a gast iz vi a regn: az er doyert tsu lang, vert er a last
"a guest is like rain: if he stays too long, he becomes a burden"

a vort iz vi a fayl; beyde hobn groys ayl
"a word is like an arrow: both are in a great hurry"

libe iz vi puter: es iz gut tsu broyt
"love is like butter: it goes well with bread"

Some Secondary Grammatical Markers

Parallelism: <Adjective + Noun> *iz beser/erger vi* "is better/worse than" <Adjective + Noun>

a shlekhter sholem iz beser vi a gute krig
"a bad peace is better than a good war"

a beyze tsung iz erger fun a shlekhter hant
"a nasty tongue is worse than a wicked hand"

a shtendiker groshn iz beser vi a zeltener rubl
"a constant penny is better than a rare ruble"

Parallelism: *beser a* "better a" + <Adjective + Noun> *eyder a* "rather than" + <Adjective + Noun>

beser an alter top eyder a nayer sharbn
"better an old pot than a new[ly] broken crock"

beser an ufgekumener gvir eyder an opgekumener oysher
"better [to be] a parvenu than an impoverished has-been"

beser a guter soyne eyder a shlekhter fraynd
"better a good enemy than a bad friend"

Emphatic Word Order Which Separates the Two Most Stressed Elements in the Proverb:

Proverb	Control: Non-Proverb (= Word order in ordinary utterances)
a falshe matbeye farlirt men nit [lit. "a counterfeit coin—one doesn't lose"]	*men farlirt nit a falshe matbeye* "one doesn't lose a counterfeit coin"
a foyln iz gut tsu shikn nokhn malekh-amoves [lit. "a lazybones—is good to send for the angel of death"]	*s'iz gut tsu shikn a foyln nokhn malekh-amoves* "it's good to send a lazybones for the angel of death"

af a mitsve gefinen zikh a sakh balonim [lit. "to [earn] a good deed—there are many eager people"]	*s'gefinen zikh a sakh balonim af a mitsve* "there are many eager people to [earn] a good deed"

Ellipsis of the Verb; Parataxis

karg badungen—erlekh batsolt
"sharply bargained—honestly paid"

a berye—er nemt tsuzamen in eyn glebe di tsig un di kroyt
"an efficient person—in one hand he grabs both the goat and the cabbage"

4.313. The second set of examples in the chart highlights some secondary, i.e., optional grammatical markers. Parallel syntax, in two parts of a proverb is a frequent phenomenon. Where such parallelism is absent, emphatic word order is often found. Ellipsis of the verb or the conjunction also occurs, though not as frequently as the other two secondary features.

4.32. We now turn to *semantic markers* which serve to set proverbs off from their context.

4.321. In defining a proverb, I stated that it can refer to an accepted rule in two ways: directly or allegorically. Proverbs that are used allegorically are immediately set off from ordinary speech by dint of their having nothing to do with the subject of discourse when interpreted literally. Allegory is therefore one of the clearest semantic markers of a proverb.

Metaphors may also appear as a secondary marker in direct proverbs as well. If one says *di neyt* [St. Yid.: *noyt*] *iz afn haldz a keyt* [M 604] "need is a chain around the neck," one is using a proverb whose subject is, indeed, "need." The "chain around the neck" in this case is a metaphor in the predicate, serving to indicate that the subject, "need," is a burden. Thus, in spite of the fact that we find a metaphor contained in it, at the highest level, from the standpoint of the sentence as a whole, the proverb belongs, of course, to the direct category. Quite a few researchers needlessly felt disillusioned with the dual classification into direct vs. allegorical proverbs precisely because they neglected to take into consideration the hierarchical structure of the proverb; the so-called "mixed" forms they felt invalidated this scheme, are not really mixed forms at all.

4.322. Another means of setting proverbs off from their context which often accompanies syntactic parallelism, is semantic parallelism. Outright repetition, synonyms and contrasts occur mainly in compound declarative proverbs. Here is an example of semantic parallelism: *a gutn vet der shenk nit kalye makhn un a shlekhtn vet der bes-medresh nit farrikhtn* [A 20] "the tavern won't ruin the good person and the synagogue won't reform the bad person." Here we have three semantic parallels (in this case, contrasts): *gutn* "good person"—*shlekhtn* "bad person"; *shenk* "tavern"—*bes-medresh* "synagogue"; and *kalye makhn* "to ruin"—*farrikhtn* "to reform." An example of repetition: *a GOY in a hitl iz a GOY, un a YIDENE in hoyzn iz a YIDENE* [M 637] "a non-Jew wearing a cap [to cover his head as do pious Jews] is nevertheless a non-Jew; and a Jewish woman in pants is nevertheless a Jewish woman." An example of a mirror image repetition: *beser a YID on a BORD vi a BORD on a YID* [B *s.v. beser*—7] "better a Jew without a beard than a beard without a Jew" [= it's better to follow the ethical Jewish precepts and not outwardly look like a Jew than to have the outer appearance of a Jew and not follow them]. To sum up, the logical connection between the parallel elements can be: (1) antonymy or contrast (*shenk—bes-medresh*); (2) equality or identity (*goy—goy/yidene—yidene*); (3) synonymy (*gvir—oysher*, in *beser an ufgekumener gvir eyder an opgekumener oysher* [A 176]; or (4) cause and effect (*az der talmid is a voyler iz der rebe oykh a voyler* [A 104] "if the pupil is good then his teacher is also good").

4.323. Paradox, irony, sharp contrasts, surprising comparisons—these are all devices which are apparently often found in Yiddish proverbs. *A shlimazl falt afn rukn un tseklapt zikh di noz* [A 55] "a luckless [clumsy] person falls on his back and hurts his nose"; *a kalike git men gikher vi a talmed-khokhem* [A 33] "a mediocre person [lit. "cripple"] is on the receiving end more often than is a scholar." The astute quality and ingenuity of the thought are emphasized by these devices. Not all proverbs use these means, however. Some direct and some indirect ones manage without surprises of this type.

4.324. Personification is also found, but is apparently a rare device in Yiddish proverbs: *di tsayt brengt vundn un heylt vundn* [M 693] "time brings wounds and heals wounds"; *der dales un di matbeye nekhtikn nit unter eyn dakh* [M 625] "poverty and money don't spend the night under the same roof."

4.325. There is one class of very succinct proverbs, only a few words long, that has none of the above-mentioned semantic markers, i.e., neither parallelism, metaphor, allegory, personification, paradox nor irony. Its only semantic marker consists of operating with two abstractions, or with one generic and one abstract term: *gezunt kumt far parnose* [M 630] "health is more important than income"; *a nar hot kheyres* [A 43] "a fool may take liberties"; *a sod iz keyn brokhe* [A 61] "[to be in on] a secret is no blessing."

4.326. We find, in sum, not one single obligatory semantic marker for proverbs. What this analysis does show, however, is that every proverb must apparently have at least one of these semantic markers. Some kind of clever combination of words seems to be mandatory, but the actual way this is done varies. Some are used more often (metaphor, parallelism, paradox) and some less often (personification).

4.33. We now turn to the last group of markers: *phonic devices*. First let us consider rhyme. It certainly can not be said that all proverbs contain rhyme, but where it occurs, it obviously serves to set the proverb off from ordinary utterances. Rhyme is achieved in several ways. The most frequent pattern in our material appears to be end rhyme. Rhymed words can either (1) split a proverb into two parts, (e.g., *der raykher FETER / hot dem HETER* [M 635] "the rich guy / gets what he wants [lit. rabbinical permission]"); or (2) connect two sentences (e.g., *der mentsh TRAKHT / un got LAKHT* = man proposes / and God disposes [lit. "man thinks / and God laughs")]; or a main clause and subordinate one (e.g., *ven men darf hobn MOYEKH/ helft nit keyn KOYEKH* [A 456] "where brains need to prevail / mere brawn won't avail"). In all of these cases the rhymes underscore binary structure and enhance what grammatical and semantic parallelism prevails. Examples of rarer patterns: *nor in kholem zaynen MERN vi BERN* [M 551] "only in dreams are carrots like bears," where the rhyming words appear consecutively; or instances where two pairs of words rhyme in one proverb (e.g., *GEFIN dem DIN; der HETER kumt SHPETER* "[first] find the law; rabbinical permission comes later").

4.331. A less vivid, but often used, device is assonance, as in *a mentsh zol LEBN shoyn nor fun naygerikeyt VEGN* [A 36] "a man should live if only to satisfy his curiosity." Quite often in nonrhyming proverbs, almost all of the stressed syllables have the same vowel, e.g., *in gan-eydn, iz nitO keyn Ort far meshulOkhim* [M 696] "in paradise there is no room for *meshulokhim* [fund raisers in the employ of traditional Jewish organizations such as *yeshives*]" or *tsekalUpe nit di vUnd; es vet rinen blUt* [M 636] "don't pick your sore or it will bleed."

4.332. A curious phonic device, which produces punning effects, is consonance: *a MLoKHe iz a MLuKHe* "a trade is a kingdom," where the words *mlokhe* and *mlukhe* share the same consonants. Another similar example: *fun a kleyner MiLkHoMe vert a groyse MeHuMe* [A 284] "a petty war turns into a major upheaval."

4.333. Alliteration seems to be little used as a phonic device for differentiating proverbs from ordinary speech. Some examples or quasi-examples: *a Kats Ken oykh Kalye makhn* [A 25] "even a cat can spoil plans"; *di Hun Hert dem Hons droshe un zukht zikh a kerndl prose* [M 644] "the hen listens to the rooster's sermon and [goes about her normal business] looks for a bit of millet." The repetition of /l/ in *az a Leyb shLoft, Loz im shLofn* [A 89] "let a sleeping lion lie" might also be taken as a quasi-alliteration.

4.334. The last phonic device to be discussed is that of metric patterning. Rhyme often, but not always, implies a pattern of stressed and unstressed syllables within a proverb. Absence of rhyme makes meter all the more important as a means of setting a proverb off from ordinary speech. Perfect syllabo-tonic meter is apparently a rare phenomenon in Yiddish: *ale kales zaynen sheyn / ale meysim zaynen frum* [A 75] "all brides are beautiful, all the deceased are devout." On the other hand, the device of an equal number of stresses in two parts of a proverb *is* frequent. It is found in all types of sentences. Most simple declarative sentences have four stresses, in two pairs: *a shēyn pōnem / kōst gēlt* [A 50] "a pretty face costs money"; *a frēmder bīsn / shmēkt zīs* [A 8] "another's morsel smells sweet." Two stresses are found less frequently: *a sōd iz / keyn brōkhe* [A 61] "a secret is no blessing." Compound sentences show from four to ten stresses, divided as follows: 2:2, 3:3, 4:4, or 5:5.

Aside from sharply dividing proverbs into two metrically equal parts, meter sometimes serves to emphasize the parallelism that exists in only certain constituents of proverbs that are not strictly binary in their construction. In proverbs that have the sentence form: . . . *i* . . . *i* . . . " . . . both . . . and . . . " for example, the compared parts (and only they) are often in the same meter: *er hot pakhed/i făr dĭ shēydĭm/, ī fărn dūnĕr* [M 626] "he's afraid/both of the ghosts/and of the thunder." This is also true of comparative sentences, even if the sentence taken as a whole lacks a consistent metric pattern: *ă bēyzĕ tsūng / iz erger fun / ă shlēkhtĕr hānt* [A 22] "a nasty tongue is worse than a wicked hand"; *ăn āltĕr frāynd / iz beser / vĭ nāyĕ tsvēy* [A 80] "an old friend is better than two new ones."

4.335. Let us summarize what we have discovered about phonic devices. While not all proverbs are characterized by a phonic device which sets them off from their context, most of them do have one or more of the following devices: balance of stresses, alliteration, assonance, identifiable metrical pattern. Perhaps extreme brevity should be considered a phonic device too: *blut shvaygt nit* [L 148] "blood [= relatives] does not keep silent"; *khutspe gilt* [A 348] "cheek helps."

4.34. *Every Yiddish proverb then seems to have at least two grammatical markers (nomic verb and generic or abstract subject), one distinctive semantic feature (metaphor, paradox, sharp or surprising contrasts), and generally at least one phonic device as well (rhyme, assonance, consonance, alliteration, meter).*

5. The foregoing discussion was concerned with the structure of single proverbs, i.e., with constituents of and the interrelationships between the various parts of a proverb. However, when a community develops a fund of thousands of proverbs with certain patterns appearing again and again, an unmistakable affinity between one proverb and another naturally emerges too. If a given pattern is well represented, this is per se a stimulus for its becoming productive, a stimulus for the emergence of fresh proverbs in the same pattern. Moreover, it would seem that the diversity of patterns at any one time and place must be sufficient for a proverb not to sound banal; and that the diversity of patterns, on the other hand, must not be so large that a proverb heard for the first time cannot be immediately recognized as a proverb.

The productivity of certain patterns sometimes leads to the emergence of a proverb that is like an echo of an existing one. *Der ayzn iz royt nor der shmid iz nit greyt* "the iron is hot but the blacksmith is not ready" for example, alludes to the well-known proverb *shmid dos ayzn kol-zman es iz heys* "strike while the iron is hot." If someone says *a mlokhe iz a mlukhe* "a trade is a kingdom" his interlocutor may add, as a superclimax (or rather an anti-climax) *nor vu nemt men a minut menukhe?* "but where does one find a minute of peace?" (In another variant, both parts have been recorded together as a single proverb [A 33].) The response to *af morgn vet got zorgn* "God will worry about tomorrow" is sometimes the echo *ober dervayle ver vet borgn?* "but in the meantime who will lend [what's needed]?" There are also cases of a purely structural echo effect, a sort of semantically empty parallelism. The proverb *er hot pakhed i far di sheydim i farn duner* "he's afraid both of the ghosts and of the thunder" is used as if there were some essential semantic contrast between "ghosts" and "thunder" such as that which obtains between *shikh un zokn* "shoes and socks." The contrast between "ghosts" and "thunder" can be viewed as a mere semantic illusion, created by using grammatically tested contrastive patterns found in the large fund of proverbs in a parasitic way.

6. The results of the above analysis point to a wealth of interesting problems for future research.

6.1. The chronology and geography of the various structural patterns mentioned ought to be investigated as thoroughly as possible. A certain pattern may, for example, have been more popular in the south (Southern Yiddish) than in the north.[11] A case in point: where Mark's Northeastern (Lithuanian and Latvian Yiddish) variants of a proverb are in the imperative, Bernshteyn provides Central and Southern Yiddish variants with the verb in the impersonal form of the nomic present [M 684/B 1072; M 680/B 1275]. Is the copious use of the imperative then a regional development among speakers of Northeastern Yiddish? Unfortunately, not all collectors indicated the exact provenience of their material with the same precision as did Mark, Landau (Galicia), Beem (Holland), and Eynhorn (various specified localities); often, however, there are indirect references to geography.

6.2. To gain proper chronological perspective, the paremiologist has at his disposal all of Jewish literature from the earliest times to the present; he should perhaps direct special attention to the edifying literature written in Yiddish dating from the sixteenth to eighteenth centuries.

6.3. Another important field of research is the comparison of Yiddish and German patterns which can be traced back to various periods. It seems, for example, that the omission of the definite article, which is so popular in German (cf. *Guter Gast kommt ungeladen* "a good guest comes uninvited"), is very rare in contemporary Yiddish. We can also surmise, from what we know about Yiddish as compared to German folksongs,[12] that the interval between stressed syllables may well be longer in Yiddish than in German proverbs. Strict iambic meter, often found in German proverbs, is therefore also less prevalent in Yiddish proverbs. Consonance may be found more often in Yiddish, but personification is perhaps less frequent. These hypotheses must, of course, be tested carefully.

6.4. It is also extremely important to compare Yiddish with various Slavic proverbs. It is well-known that East-European Jews have a special affinity for Slavic proverbs. In fact there is a proverb to attest to this: *a goyish vertl iz lehavdl a toyre* "a non-Jewish [e.g. Ukrainian, etc.] proverb, though not of the sacred sphere, is [equal to] an item of traditional [Jewish] learning." It is likely that many Jews in the Ukraine and Byelorussia not only used more Slavic than Yiddish proverbs in their daily speech as argument markers and intensifiers of conversation, but even coined original monolingual and multilingual, serious as well as parodying, proverbs in Ukrainian and Byelorussian (Litvin, p. 123).

6.5. Similarities and differences between Yiddish proverbs and proverbs in other Jewish languages (Hebrew, Judezmo, Parsic, etc.) must of course also be investigated. How do they compare both with respect to content and form? Do they employ the same or other grammatical and semantic stylistic devices and in the same or different proportions than is true for Yiddish proverbs? Are phonic devices used as in Yiddish? Do they refer explicitly to Jewish life and experience in the same proportions? What traditional models from the Hebrew Scriptures, the Talmud, and the Midrash [= the body of post-Talmudic literature of Biblical exegesis] have been preserved in these Jewish languages? Do they also have mixed-language proverbs like the Yiddish *bimokem sheeyn ish iz hering oykh a fish* [A 185] "[Heb.] where there is no man, [Yid.] herring is also a fish" [= in the kingdom of the blind, the one-eyed is king]; or *nye ganvay i nye fastay* "[Slav.] don't [ad-hoc coinage: Yid. verb plus Slavic ending] steal [Slav.] and [Slav.] don't [ad-hoc coinage: Yid. verb plus Slavic ending] fast."

There is, in a word, no lack of suitable research topics. Hopefully, researchers will soon get to some of these tasks.

1977 Postscript

Sixteen years have gone by since I delivered this paper in Jerusalem, and it is gratifying to add this postscript; for since then there have been several important additions to the field.

An index to YIVO's publication, *Yidishe shprakh*, prepared by Dror Leshem and edited by Mordkhe Schaechter which includes the proverbial materials contained therein is in press, and should appear in print this year. Hans Peter Althaus has written an elaborate introduction to a republication of Ignats Bernshteyn's [Ignaz Bernstein] classic 1908 collection of Yiddish proverbs and proverbial expressions.[13] Althaus critically surveys research done in the field (see xvii–xviii for a review of this article) and uses the available sources towards a careful evaluation of Bernshteyn's work as a collector. His introduction is very important for the fine bibliography as well. For bibliography, also see Schwartzbaum.[14] Furman has filled a gap with his recent volume of Yiddish proverbs which reflects geographic areas not covered systematically heretofore: Rumania, Bessarabia, Bukowina, Moldavia, and Transylvania.[15] His volume is all the more welcome because he gives copious examples of contexts for most of the proverbs he has included, something many earlier collectors neglected. Zivy has filled another gap with his collection of Alsatian Yiddish proverbs.[16] David L. Gold, lists some parallel Yiddish and Judezmo proverbs.[17] Sadan does a very scholarly in-depth study of 27 Yiddish sayings and their variants, discussing their origins, and the changes that have occurred in them (both formal and semantic) over time and in different places.[18] Rothstein in his article on the poetics of proverbs, uses an approach close to mine, and cites interesting parallel examples from Russian, Polish and Yiddish proverbs, along with other languages.[19]

The general field of paremiology has also seen some changes. Since 1965 we have the bulletin *Proverbium* devoted to research on this one genre. Abrahams summarizes succinctly several older and more recent approaches to the study of proverbs.[20] On the study of variants within this genre there is the fine article by W. Voigt.[21] In recent years the "ethnography of speaking" approach has become very fashionable. We have articles like Arewa and Dundes' and Seitel's[22] to turn to as models for a future study of the range of social uses and the cultural situations in which Yiddish proverbs are encountered, an important, though neglected vantage point until now.

Sources of Cited Proverbs and Abbreviations

[A]yalti, H.J., *Yiddish Proverbs*, New York, 1949.

Bastomski, Sh., *Baym Kval*, Vilna, 1920.

Beem, H., *Jerösche; jidische spreekwoorden en zegwijzen uit het nederlanse taalgebied*, Assen, 1959.

[B]ernshteyn, I., *Yidishe shprikhverter*, Warsaw, 2nd ed., 1908.

Eynhorn, Sh., *Mishlei-am beyidish*, Tel Aviv, 1959. (Reprinted from *Reshumot* V (1927), 338–348; VI (1930), 398–407; new series I (1945), 197–207; II (1947), 196–208; III (1947), 240–251; IV (1947), 174–187; V (1953), 304–312.)

Hurvits, I., *Mivhar pitgamim*, New York, 1960.

Landau, A., "Sprichwörter und Redensarten," *Jahrbuch für jüdische Volkskunde*, 1923, 335–361; continued by S.M. [?], 362–370.

———, "Bamerkungen tsum yidishn folklor: vegn Sh. Bastomskis zamlungen," *Filologishe shriftn fun YIVO*, I, Vilna, 1926, pp. 13–22.

Lehman, Sh., "Ganovim un ganeyve," *Bay undz yidn*, Warsaw, 1923, pp. 45–55.

[L]itvin, A., "Mayn mames vertlekh," *Lebn un visnshaft*, Vilna, 1912, No. 8–9.

[M]ark, Y., "Shprikhverter vos es iz kiday zey tsu nitsn," *Yidishe shprakh*, II (1942), 28–29, 59–61, 91–93, 152–54, 184–186; III (1943), 58–60, 90–93, 151–153; IV (1944), 58–60, 137–140; V (1945), 87–90; X (1950), 59–62; XI (1951), 55–58; XII (1952), 62–63, 92, 125–126; XIII (1953), 26–28; XIV (1954), 61–62.

Pirozhnikov, I., *Yidishe shprikhverter*, Vilna, 1908.

Rubinshteyn, Sh., "Shprikhverter," *Filologishe shriftn fun YIVO*, I, Vilna, 1926, pp. 411–426.

Tendlau, A., *Sprichwörter und Redensarten deutsch-jüdischer Vorzeit*, Frankfurt a.M., 1860.

Notes

1. This article is a close adaptation of a paper read at the Second World Congress of Jewish Studies, Jerusalem, July 29, 1961. The English translation was made by David L. Gold, from the published Yiddish original entitled "Formale problemen

baym forshn dos yidishe shprikhvort," in *For Max Weinreich on his Seventieth Birthday: Studies in Jewish Languages, Literature and Society*, The Hague, Mouton & Co., 1964, pp. 383–394. The present English translation first appeared in *YIVO Annual for Jewish Social Science* 17 (1978), 1–20. Reprinted with permission of Mouton and Company and YIVO Institute for Jewish Research.

2. Abbreviations in square brackets refer to the bibliography at the end of the article.

3. N. Vaynig, "Geshikhte un problemen fun der yidisher paremyologye," *YIVO bleter*, VIII (1935), 356–370.

4. I. Klimenko, *Das russiche Sprichwort* (Bern, 1946), p. 17.

5. A. Taylor, *The Proverb, and an Index to the Proverb* (Cambridge, Mass., 1931; reprinted, Hatboro, Penna., and Copenhagen, 1962), p. 42.

6. On the *Language and Culture Atlas of Ashkenazic Jewry* see Uriel Weinreich, "Culture Geography at a Distance: Some Problems in the Study of East European Jewry," *Proceedings of the Annual Spring Meeting of the American Ethnological Society*, ed., W.L. Chafe, 1962, pp. 27–39; and "Mapping a Culture," *Columbia University Forum* 6.3, 1963, pp. 17–21.

7. L. Taubes, *Talmudishe elementn inem yidishn shprikhvort* (Vienna, 1928); H. Samet, *Hashpa'at sifrutenu ha'atika al pitgamei ha'am* (Warsaw, 1935).

8. Cf. Sh. Rudyansky, "Di filosofye fun di yidishe shprikhverter," *Lebn un visnshaft* (Vilna), 1912, No. 8–9.

9. Taylor, p. 4.

10. F. Seiler, *Deutsche Sprichwörterkunde* (Munich, 1922).

11. For a brief survey of the regional variants of Yiddish, see U. Weinreich, "Yiddish, Language," *Encyclopedia Judaica*, XVI, 794 ff.

12. B. Hrushovski, "On Free Rhythms in Modern Yiddish Poetry," *The Field of Yiddish*, I (New York, 1954), 223.

13. H.P. Althaus, Introduction to reprint of Ignats Bernshteyn's *Yidishe shprikhverter un rednsartn* (Hildesheim, Germany, 1969), pp. ix–xxvii.

14. H. Schwartzbaum, *Studies in World and Jewish Folklore* (Berlin, 1968), pp. 417–424.

15. I.M. Furman, *Yidishe shprikhverter un rednsartn gezamlt in Rumenye, Besarabye, Bukovine, Moldeve, un Transilvanye* (Tel Aviv, 1968).

16. A. Zivy, *Jüdisch-deutsche Sprichwörter u. Redensarten* (Basel, 1966).

17. D.L. Gold, "Jewish Intralinguistics," prepared for the Eighth World Congress of Sociology, Toronto, August 18–24, 1974.

18. D. Sadan, *Di khokhme fun khokhmes (tsu der biografye fun vort un vertl)* (Tel Aviv, 1967).

19. R. Rothstein, "The Poetics of Proverbs," *Studies Presented to Professor Roman Jakobson by His Students* (Cambridge, Mass., 1968), pp. 265–274.

20. R. Abrahams, "Proverbs and Proverbial Expressions," in Richard M. Dorson, ed., *Folklore and Folklife: An Introduction* (Chicago, 1972), pp. 117–127.

21. V. Voigt, "Les Niveaux des variantes de proverbes (Un ancien problème du folklore sous un éclairage nouveau)," *Acta Linguistica Academiae Scientarum Hungaricae*, 20 (1970), 357–364.

22. E. Ojo Arewa and A. Dundes, "Proverbs and the Ethnography of Speaking," *American Anthropologist*, 66 (1964), No. 6, part 2, 70–85; P. Seitel, "Proverbs: A Social Use of Metaphor," *Genre*, 2 (1969), 143–161.

The Invading Guest: Some Aspects of Oral Transmission

*Pierre Crépeau**

One of the principal defining characteristics of folklore is variation. The comparative study of any single folktale, folksong, or traditional game demonstrates the range of variation. The proverb because it is a fixed-phrase folklore genre (as opposed to a free-phrase genre) tends to vary somewhat less. The proverb "Time flies" for example occurs in precisely that form in English virtually any time it is cited. Variation in a single proverb does occur through time and across cultures. Within a single culture, however, it is generally believed that proverb texts are remarkably stable.

The following essay should serve to dispel the idea that proverb texts do not manifest intracultural variation. Pierre Crépeau's stunning in-depth study of a single proverb from Rwanda presents incontrovertible evidence that variation is not only possible but likely—at least in certain cultures. It may well be that the propensity for improvisation generally in African societies is partly responsible for what appears to be a stylistic difference between African and European proverbs.

This paper has three purposes. First, it aims at introducing the reader to a specific example of Rwandan lore, namely a Rwandan proverb which has been heard in 70 different variants or versions. Second, an analysis of this particular item is proposed from which some conclusions can be drawn as to the principles which seem to regulate its oral

*Reprinted from the *Yearbook of Symbolic Anthropology*, 1 (1978), 11–29.

transmission. And third, it makes some very tentative suggestions as to how oral transmission operates in general. But, before coming to the point itself, I feel it necessary to set forth some of the theoretical assumptions underlying this essay.

Theoretical Assumptions

As the item under study is a proverb, one might expect some clarifications about the problem of the definition of the proverb. Unfortunately, I have none to propose for the moment. Whether a proverb is essentially a metaphoric saying (Forster 1963) or a statement in which the symmetry of content is reproduced in the symmetry of form (Milner 1969:54) is not a crucial issue for the present study. Suffice to say that the Rwandan people can easily distinguish their proverbs from other genres of their verbal arts although they cannot provide clear criteria for the distinction. Sometimes one will hesitate when another is sure that the item is or is not a proverb. But those cases are rare. Most of the time, a proverb is introduced with the stereotyped formula *Abanyarwanda baca umugani bati*: "The Rwandan people chisel a proverb saying," or in elliptical form *Bacu umugani bati*: "One chisels a proverb saying." This way of identifying a Rwandan proverb is for the folklorist of another culture the only sound criterion for deciding which product of Rwandan verbal art is a proverb and which is not. Holding to this one criterion is the only way of avoiding ethnocentrism and of deciding within the Rwandan cultural matrix.

This being said, I would however agree with Greimas (1970:310) that a proverb necessarily implies connotation. It functions at two levels of signification: one referential or denotative, and the other connotative. The two levels of signification are bound together in such a way that the first level is the very expression of the second. This can be figured as:

second level		F		R	C
first level	F	R	C		

In this figure F stands for form, C stands for content and R for relation between form and content (cf. Barthes 1964:130). At the first level of signification, content is determined through an immediate

Level of change	*Object of change*	*Kind of change*	*Result of change*
Linguistic	Terms	Variation	Variant
	Grammatical structure		
Semantic	Terms	Permutation	Version
	Functions	Transformation	New items of folklore

Fig. 1

though arbitrary relation between *designantia* and *designata.* At the second level, content is determined through a mediate relation between *connotantia* and *connotata.* This relation is mediate, that is to say, it is established by the aid of the socio-cultural context and of the enunciative process. The enunciative process includes the situational context and the intentional or functional aspect of the proverb. This brings us to the second assumption.

A new trend is spreading among the folklorists which tends to conceptualize folklore as event rather than as item (Bauman 1971). According to this conception, studies of folklore should consider the happening rather than the objects of folklore. That folklore is a communicative process rather than an aggregate of the traditional materials and that it should consequently be dealt with as such, is a point no one will argue. But one should also bear in mind that if analysis of folklore items cannot pretend to explain the whole of folklore, it nevertheless constitutes a necessary step towards a full comprehension of this cultural phenomenon. Psycholinguistics, sociolinguistics and ethnolinguistics are all necessary complements to descriptive and structural linguistics, but the study of language cannot be reduced to these fields. So it is with folklore. Of course folklore is performance and as such it cannot be fully explained without any attention being paid to its process.

However, in folklore as in language, there is no performance without underlying competence. Folklore is a communicative process of its own, with its own structuring rules. There is the folkloristic *parole*; there is also the folkloristic *langue*. No one would question the legitimacy of descriptive or structural linguistics which are the study of items of language. Why then should one question the legitimacy of analysis of items of folklore from which can be drawn at least some of the rules of its process? The present essay is based on this legitimacy.

The words "variant" and "version" will often be used here. If there is any distinction between the two terms, it is a subtle one. One might venture to say that a variant is nothing but a different way of saying exactly the same thing, whereas a version is saying something related to but different from another version. A variant is a change in form at the pure linguistic level; a version on the contrary implies a switch in semantics. Referring to the above mentioned distinction, one might say that a variant is a change in form at the first level of signification only, whereas a version is a change in content at the first level of signification and consequently in form at the second level. It must be kept in mind however that not all changes in content at the first level of signification are versions. Indeed some of these changes may go as far as to generate a new item of folklore.

Lévi-Strauss, in his *Mythologiques,* has made a constant use of such words as variant, version, permutation, and transformation. As far as I know, he never gave a formal definition of these terms. One is left to figure out the meaning through the uses of the words. If I understand properly, variant and version in the *Mythologiques* are interchangeable although version tends to bc used more naturally when changes in the myths seem to have more analytical value. "Permutation" is a change of terms which leads to a switch in semantics and to a version. As for "transformation," it means a change from one item to another, from one myth to another. It comes at the end of a long series of permutations. Myth A permuting from version to version finally becomes Myth B. The Bororo, for example, transform their myth of the genesis of the cooking fire into the myth of the genesis of water through a long series of permutations of the terms (Lévi-Strauss 1966:18). In fact, transformation occurs when a new function is assigned to opposed terms. As long as the functions remain unchanged there is no transformation. Referring to Lévi-Strauss' canonical formula, changes of a and b are permutations as long as x and y remain untouched; "transformation" is a change in x or y and it generates a new item of folklore. This interpretation seems to be shared by Elli Köngäs Maranda for riddles (1971:54–55). It seems applicable also to many other genres of verbal art, if not all. One can briefly say: a variant is the result of variation at the linguistic level only; a version is the result of semantic variation in terms only; a new item of verbal art is the result of variation in functions. Figure 1 summarizes all these.

"Oral tradition" is often used either for the traditional materials of verbal art or for the process of transmitting from mouth to ear. For the sake of clarity in the present essay, oral tradition will be used exclusively for the products of verbal art, the process itself being termed "oral transmission."

A Rwandan Proverb

First, here are the different variants and versions in which the proverb was heard. All 70 of them were actually heard. I feel it necessary to stress this point as the reader might be inclined to think that some of them are nothing but my logical deductions. There are logical possibilities that a lot more versions or variants might be acceptable to Rwandan culture. We will see later what the restrictions are. Of course, the variants and versions were not heard in the order they are presented here. I arranged them in such a way as to make it possible for the reader, even without knowing the language, to discover at least some of the features of the variational matrix.

The Rwandan text is written according to the rules established by André Coupez (1961 and 1962). The phonetic units, consonants, vowels and semi-vowels, follow current orthography and generally correspond to the *Africa* system of the International African Institute except in some details as, for example, the voiceless front fricative which is written sh instead of ʃ. Consonants and semi-vowels also admit many allophones which are not written. Quantity and tone follow the rules of Africa to which are added particular rules required by specific Rwandan tonal system. Quantity is usually indicated with a double vowel except when found in determined positions. Tone is indicated by the aid of diacritical signs. The Rwandan language has four tones: one low tone which is indicated by the absence of diacritical sign and three high tones which are distinguished by the position and the form of the diacritical signs [´] and [ˇ].

1 *Umutuutsi umusembereza ikwéru akaguca muu mbere*
The Tuutsi you lodge him in the ingle-nook and he throws you out of the front-room.[1]

2 *Umutuutsi umusembereza ikwéru akaguca ruguru*
The Tuutsi you lodge him in the ingle-nook and he throws you out of the upper-room.
3 *Umutuutsi umusembereza ikwéru akaguca ku buriri*
The Tuutsi you lodge him in the ingle-nook and he throws you out of the bed.
4 *Umutuutsi umusembereza haakwéru akaguca muu mbere*
The Tuutsi you lodge him in the ingle-nook[2] and he throws you out of the front-room.
5 *Umutuutsi umusembereza haakwéru akaguca ruguru*
The Tuutsi you lodge him in the ingle-nook and he throws you out of the upper-room.
6 *Umutuutsi umusembereza haakwéru akaguca ku buriri*
The Tuutsi you lodge him in the ingle-nook and he throws you out of the bed.
7 *Umutuutsi umusembereza mu muryángo akaguca muu mbere*
The Tuutsi you lodge him in the lobby and he throws you out of the front-room.
8 *Umutuutsi umusembereza mu muryángo akaguca ruguru*
The Tuutsi you lodge him in the lobby and he throws you out of the upper-room.
9 *Umutuutsi umusembereza mu muryángo akaguca ku buriri*
The Tuutsi you lodge him in the lobby and he throws you out of the bed.
10 *Umutuutsi umusembereza ikwéru akagukuura muu mbere*
The Tuutsi you lodge him in the ingle-nook and he forces you out of the front-room.
11 *Umutuutsi umusembereza ikwéru akagukuura ruguru*
The Tuutsi you lodge him in the ingle-nook and he forces you out of the upper-room.
12 *Umutuutsi umusembereza ikwéru akagukuura ku buriri*
The Tuutsi you lodge him in the ingle-nook and he forces you out of the bed.
13 *Umutuutsi umusembereza haakwéru akagukuura muu mbere*
The Tuutsi you lodge him in the ingle-nook and he forces you out of the front-room.
14 *Umutuutsi umusembereza haakwéru akagukuura ruguru*
The Tuutsi you lodge him in the ingle-nook and he forces you out of the upper-room.
15 *Umutuutsi umusembereza haakwéru akagukuura ku buriri*

The Tuutsi you lodge him in the ingle-nook and he forces you out of the bed.

16 *Umutuutsi umusembereza mu muryángo akagukurra muu mbere*
The Tuutsi you lodge him in the lobby and he forces you out of the front-room.

17 *Umutuutsi umusembereza mu muryángo akagukuura ruguru*
The Tuutsi you lodge him in the lobby and he forces you out of the upper-room.

18 *Umutuutsi umusembereza mu muryángo akagukuura ku buriri*
The Tuutsi you lodge him in the lobby and he forces you out of the bed.

19 *Umutuutsi umusembereza ikwéru akaguteera muu mbere*
The Tuutsi you lodge him in the ingle-nook and he intrudes on you in the front-room.

20 *Umutuutsi umusembereza ikwéru akaguteera ruguru*
The Tuutsi you lodge him in the ingle-nook and he intrudes on you in the upper-room.

21 *Umutuutsi umusembereza ikwéru akaguteera ku buriri*
The Tuutsi you lodge him in the ingle-nook and he intrudes on you in the bed.

22 *Umutuutsi umusembereza haakwéru akaguteera muu mbere*
The Tuutsi you lodge him in the ingle-nook and he intrudes on you in the front-room.

23 *Umutuutsi umusembereza haakwéru akaguteera ruguru*
The Tuutsi you lodge him in the ingle-nook and he intrudes on you in the upper-room.

24 *Umutuutsi umusembereza haakwéru akaguteera ku buriri*
The Tuutsi you lodge him in the ingle-nook and he intrudes on you in the bed.

25 *Umutuutsi umusembereza mu muryángo akaguteera muu mbere*
The Tuutsi you lodge him in the lobby and he intrudes on you in the front-room.

26 *Umutuutsi umusembereza mu muryángo akaguteera ruguru*
The Tuutsi you lodge him in the lobby and he intrudes on you in the upper-room.

27 *Umutuutsi umusembereza mu muryángo akaguteera ku buriri*
The Tuutsi you lodge him in the lobby and he intrudes on you in the bed.
28 *Usembereza umutuutsi ikwéru akaguca muu mbere*
You lodge the Tuutsi in the ingle-nook and he throws you out of the front-room.
29 *Usembereza umutuutsi ikwéru akaguca reguru*
You lodge the Tuutsi in the ingle-nook and he throws you out of the upper-room.
30 *Usembereza umutuutsi ikwéru akaguca ku buriri*
You lodge the Tuutsi in the ingle-nook and he throws you out of the bed.
31 *Usembereza umutuutsi haakwéru akaguca muu mbere*
You lodge the Tuutsi in the ingle-nook and he throws you out of the front-room.
32 *Usembereza umutuutsi haakwéru akaguca ruguru*
You lodge the Tuutsi in the ingle-nook and he throws you out of the upper-room
33 *Usembereza umutuutsi haakwéru akaguca ku buriri*
You lodge the Tuutsi in the ingle-nook and he throws you out of the bed.
34 *Usembereza umutuutsi mu muryángo akaguca muu mbere*
You lodge the Tuutsi in the lobby and he throws you out of the front-room.
35 *Usembereza umutuutsi mu muryángo akaguca ruguru*
You lodge the Tuutsi in the lobby and he throws you out of the upper-room.
36 *Usembereza umutuutsi mu muryángo akaguca ku buriri*
You lodge the Tuutsi in the lobby and he throws you out of the bed.
37 *Usembereza umutuutsi ikwéru akagukuura muu mbere*
You lodge the Tuutsi in the ingle-nook and he forces you out of the front-room.
38 *Usembereza umutuutsi ikwéru akagukuura ruguru*
You lodge the Tuutsi in the ingle-nook and he forces you out of the upper-room.
39 *Usembereza umutuutsi ikwéru akagakuura ku buriri*
You lodge the Tuutsi in the ingle-nook and he forces you out of the bed.

40 *Usembereza umutuutsi haakwéru akagukuura muu mbere*
You lodge the Tuutsi in the ingle-nook and he forces you out of the front-room.
41 *Usembereza umutuutsi haakwéru akagukuura ruguru*
You lodge the Tuutsi in the ingle-nook and he forces you out of the upper-room.
42 *Usembereza umutuutsi haakwéru akagukuura ku buriri*
You lodge the Tuutsi in the ingle-nook and he forces you out of the bed.
43 *Usembereza umutuutsi mu muryángo akagukuura muu mbere*
You lodge the Tuutsi in the lobby and he forces you out of the front room.
44 *Usembereza umutuutsi mu muryángo akagukuura ruguru*
You lodge the Tuutsi in the lobby and he forces you out of the upper-room.
45 *Usembereza umutuutsi mu muryángo akagukuura ku buriri*
You lodge the Tuutsi in the lobby and he forces you out of the bed.
46 *Usembereza umutuutsi ikwéru akaguteera muu mbere*
You lodge the Tuutsi in the ingle-nook and he intrudes on you in the front-room.
47 *Usembereza umutuutsi ikwéru akaguteera ruguru*
You lodge the Tuutsi in the ingle-nook and he intrudes on you in the upper-room.
48 *Usembereza umutuutsi ikwéru akaguteera ku buriri*
You lodge the Tuutsi in the ingle-nook and he intrudes on you in the bed.
49 *Usembereza umutuutsi haakwéru akaguteera muu mbere*
You lodge the Tuutsi in the ingle-nook and he intrudes on you in the front-room.
50 *Usembereza umutuutsi haakwéru akaguteera ruguru*
You lodge the Tuutsi in the ingle-nook and he intrudes on you in the upper-room.
51 *Usembereza umutuutsi haakwéru akaguteera ku buriri*
You lodge the Tuutsi in the ingle-nook and he intrudes on you in the bed.
52 *Usembereza umutuutsi mu muryángo akaguteera muu mbere*
You lodge the Tuutsi in the lobby and he intrudes on you in the front-room.

53 *Usembereza umutuutsi mu muryángo akaguteera ruguru*
You lodge the Tuutsi in the lobby and he intrudes on you in the upper-room.
54 *Usembereza umutuutsi mu muryángo akaguteera ku buriri*
You lodge the Tuutsi in the lobby and he intrudes on you in the bed.
55 *Umutuutsi umusembereza muu mfúruká akaguca muu nzu*
The Tuutsi you lodge him in the corner and he throws you out of the house.
56 *Umutuutsi umusembereza mu kirămbi akaguca muu nzu*
The Tuutsi you lodge him in the living-room and he throws you out of the house.
57 *Umutuutsi umusembereza muu mfúruká akagukuura muu nzu*
The Tuutsi you lodge him in the corner and he forces you out of the house.
58 *Umutuutsi umusembereza mu kirămbi akagukuura muu nzu*
The Tuutsi you lodge him in the living-room and he forces you out of the house.
59 *Umutuutsi umusembereza muu mfúruká akaguteera muu nzu*
The Tuutsi you lodge him in the corner and he intrudes on you in the house.
60 *Umutuutsi umusembereza mu kirămbi akaguteera muu nzu*
The Tuutsi you lodge him in the living-room and he intrudes on you in the house.
61 *Umutuutsi umusembereza mu muryángo akaguteera mu kirămbi*
The Tuutsi you lodge him in the lobby and he intrudes on you in the living-room.
62 *Umutuutsi umusembereza ihéeru akaguca ikámberé*
The Tuutsi you lodge him in the second house and he throws you out of the main house.
63 *Umutuutsi umusembereza ihéeru akagukuura ikámberé*
The Tuutsi you lodge him in the second house and he forces you out of the main house.
64 *Umutuutsi umusembereza ihéeru akaguteera ikámberé*
The Tuutsi you lodge him in the second house and he intrudes on you in the main house.

65 *Umutuutsi umusembereza ikwéru akaguca ikàmberė*
The Tuutsi you lodge him in the second house and he throws you out of the main house.

66 *Umutuutsi umusembereza ikwéru akagukuura ikàmberė*
The Tuutsi you lodge him in the second house and he forces you out of the main house.

67 *Umutuutsi umusembereza ikwéru akaguteera ikàmberė*
The Tuutsi you lodge him in the second house and he intrudes on you in the main house.

68 *Umutuutsi umusembereza mu isămbu akagukuura muu ngo*
The Tuutsi you receive him on the estate and he forces you out of the dwellings.

69 *Umutuutsi umusembereza mu muryángo agakwimura muu mbere*
The Tuutsi you lodge him in the lobby and he chucks you out of the front-room.

70 *Umutuutsi umucumbikira mu kirămbi akaguteera nó muu mbere*
The Tuutsi you put him up for the night in the living-room and he intrudes on you even in the front-room.

Contextual Analysis

Let us take No. 1 as the basic text. This choice is of course arbitrary as I have no means of nor interest in finding which is the *textus princeps*. The particularity of text No. 1 is that it is found in the oldest important corpus of Rwandan proverbs (Kagame 1953: No. 1409) and that its form seems rather archaic. Recourse to socio-cultural context in this case implies the knowledge of house-building as well as of socio-political structure of traditional Rwanda. First, here is a ground-sketch of an average Rwandan compound (fig. 2) and of an average

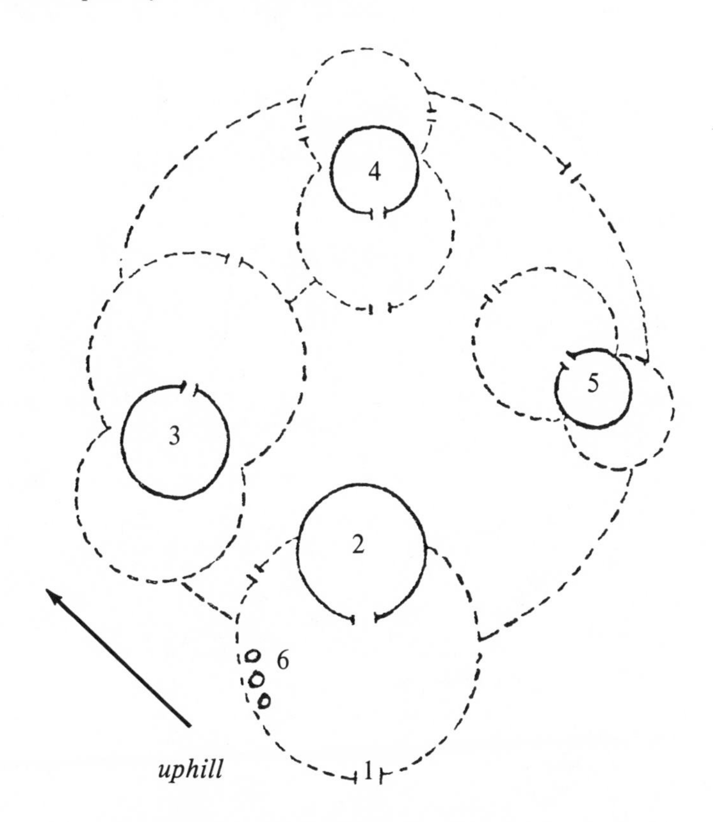

Fig. 2 Ground sketch of a traditional compound (adaptation from Sandrart 1939:38–9)

--- limits of the fences
— limits of the houses

1. *ku irémbo:*	at the gate
2. *ikámberé:*	at the main house
3. *ihéeru:*	up there
Kagŏndo:	Proper name (first secondary house)
4. *igihisí:*	Proper name. Name of the hill on which the house is built (second secondary house)
5. *urutéekero:*	the kitchen
6. *ibiráaro:*	the byres

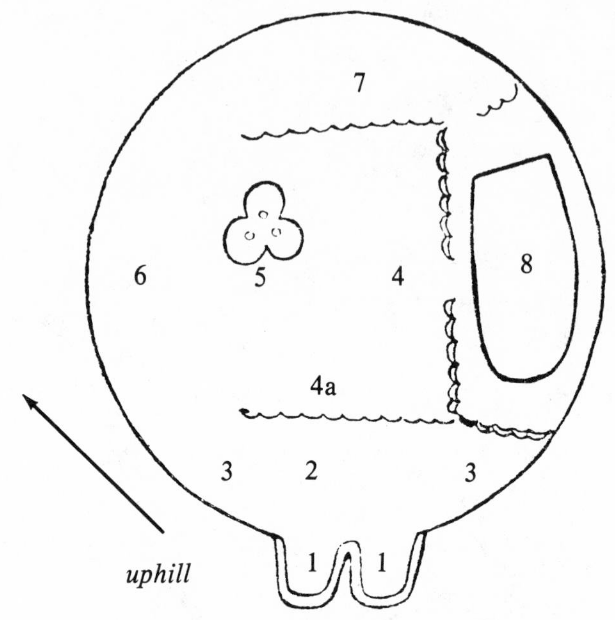

Fig. 3 Ground sketch of a traditional house (adaptation from Sandrart 1939:40)

﹏: plain partitions
﹏: adorned partitions

1.	*ibitabo:*	door-steps
2.	*mu muryángo:*	in the lobby
3.	*muu mfŭruká:*	in the corner
4.	*mu kirămbi:*	in the living-room
	muu nzuugi:	inside the partitions
4a.	*mu ruugi:*	inside the partition
5.	*ku ziiko:*	by the fire-place
6.	*mu mugendo:*	in the passageway
	mu rubúmbiro:	by the fire-place or in the goat-fold
	mu ruhŏngore:	in the calf-fold
	mu mukúbo:	in the fold
	mu ndugú:	in the goat-fold
7.	*muu mbere:*	in the front-room
	haruguru or *ruguru:*	in the upper-room
8.	*ku buriri:*	on the bed

Rwandan house (fig. 3).

Rwanda is a country of hills and mountains. Flat surfaces are almost unknown so that compounds and houses are mostly built on hill-sides, the gates and doors usually perpendicular to the hill-side at some angle, the hill being on either side of the compound indifferently. The area of the compound is flattened sometimes as a result of laborious terracing. To a certain extent this geographical situation is reflected in the naming of the different sections of the compound. The back is called *haruguru* or *ruguru:* "up there" and the front part is called *epfó*: "down." The same applies to the different sections of the house, the remotest part being called *ruguru* which I translate as "upper-room." The more people reside in the compound or the house, the more they go up. This also has some bearing in seating the guests inside the house, the more important being given the "upper" places.

The compound includes the main house in which lives the "master of the compound" and, if he is polygynous, his preferred wife with her offspring. His other wives live in secondary houses with their offspring. Intimate guests are usually put up in the most important secondary house (No. 3 in fig. 2) where they can enjoy more privacy, whereas others are put up in certain sections of the main house. In regard to hospitality, the traditional Rwandan house is composed of two sets of sections: one set which guests are allowed into (No. 2, 3, and 4 in fig. 3) and the other set which is strictly reserved to members of the family (No. 7 and 8 in fig. 3). As for No. 6, it is usually used as a shelter for goats or calves at night in compounds which have no byres. Otherwise, it is used as a passageway to the upper-room. Guests may occasionally be seated in this section, as needed.

As one can see from the ground sketches, some sections of the compound and of the house have one fixed name whereas other sections are given different names. This indeterminacy raises some difficulties in the interpretation of the proverb at its first level of signification. For example, the terms *ikwéru* and *haakwéru* although often quoted in the proverb, are rarely known to informants. There are also some discrepancies in naming section No. 6 of the house.

Kagame (1953:155) gives a comprehensive note to explain the proverb at its first level of signification. This shows that the form in which he quotes it must be archaic and that he expects many a Rwandan reader, for whom his collection is intended, not to understand it properly. Had the text been clear to everyone, the author would not have felt the need for such an explanation. Now, according to Kagame, *ikwéru* means a narrow place near the fire-place between *muu ndugú* and *muu mbere*, respectively No. 6 and 7 in fig. 3. Moreover, people of the upper class speak of *mu mukúbo* and *haruguru* whereas people of the lower class speak of *muu ndugú* and *muu mbere, muu ndugú* being the section of the house where people of the lower class fold their goats for the night.

I checked Kagame's interpretation among many informants, Tuutsi as well as Hutu. None of them confirmed what Kagame had written 20 years ago. First, all of them use indifferently both expressions *muu mbere* and *haruguru* (or *ruguru*). Secondly, *muu ndugú* was known only to informants from the northern region of Rwanda, those from the south using *mu mukúbo, mu ruhŏngore* or *mu rubúmbiro. Mu rubúmbiro* is generally used when goats are folded, *mu ruhŏngore* when calves are byred and *mu mukúbo* when no herds are byred, the section being a passageway to the upper-room. Many a southerner would also use indifferently *mu mukúbo* and *mu rubúmbiro*. One informant separates section No. 6 of the house in two parts: *mu rubúmbiro* is the "lower" part, next to *muu mfúruká* and *mu mukúbo* is the "upper" part next to *muu mbere.* Important guests are seated in front of the upper part, the others in front of the lower part. Thirdly, very few of my informants ever heard of *ikwéru*. One could say no more than: "it is a nice place which is good for people," probably deriving the term from the verbal radical *-éer-* which means to be white, to be good. In Rwanda as in many other African countries, white is a symbol of auspiciousness and black of woe. A lady indentified ikwé*ru* with the corner, another informant with the upper-room. Another placed it in the upper right corner of the living room, close to the upper-room and the bed, in fact opposite to Kagame's identification. This probably occurs when the entrance to the upper-room is on the right side. Finally another identified it with the main house, feeling at the same time that the term must be of foreign origin, probably from Burundi. All these informants were 55 years of age or more. Other informants, who were all under 55, corrected me when quoting the proverb in Kagame's form saying that I should rather say *ihéeru* instead of *ikwéru*. And not only for all of them but also for all my informants, *ihéeru* means at the second house of the compound (No. 3 in fig. 2), in opposition to *ikámberé* at the main house. A wife will also name the compound of her parents-in-law *ihéeru*. Whether this is related to the rule forbidding a wife to pronounce the names of her parents-in-law or any other word phonetically related, I could not establish with certainty, the information I gathered being contradictory. It is quite puzzling that although informants do not understand the term *ikwéru* and some even tend to discard it, it has been heard over and over again during collecting time. All that can be said for the moment is that Kagame's version is still nowadays very often quoted without being understood and is even sometimes questioned. People quote the proverb in its archaic form contenting themselves with its general meaning. But when asked the exact meaning of each term, they fail to provide a suitable explanation and tend to replace the term by another one which is better known to them. We will later see the significance of this fact in regard to oral transmission. Let us note meanwhile that the socio-cultural context of house-building and of rules as to places where guests are put up allows us to grasp the meaning of the proverb at its first level of signification. It means: if you let the Tuutsi in as a guest, he soon considers himself as master of the compound. All the different forms in which this general idea is expressed are variations or permutations of terms, the function of the terms remaining the same throughout. Their signification in regard to oral transmission will be studied in the next section of this paper.

At its second level of signification, the proverb provides a rule of behaviour in one's relations with the Tuutsi. This rule of behaviour is not clearly expressed: it is a conclusion anyone can draw from the description of the Tuutsi's attitude. It is suggested behaviour in anticipation of an expected behaviour. Better be cautious with the Tuutsi, because if you give him a foot he takes a mile. This connotative meaning can be understood only in the light of the socio-political structure of traditional Rwanda. The limits of this paper do not bear but a few remarks on the subject. For further details, the reader is referred to Maquet (1954) and d'Hertefelt (1962). I restrict my comments to what I feel necessary for the understanding of the proverb.

The Tuutsi were the rulers of traditional Rwanda. Although forming but a small minority, they succeeded in establishing a socio-political organization which gave them control over the Hutu peasants and the Twa. This socio-political organization was based on three structures: an administrative framework, a military force and serf bondage. The king was the supreme ruler whose authority was officially unchallengeable, although he was in fact submitted to some restrictions, especially from the queen-mother, the high chiefs and his two councils. Authority was delegated through the three structures so that political responsibility was often shared by two or more persons in one and the same field of action. This peculiar organization created a complicated network of relations which criss-crossed all along the social scale. It also enabled the subjects to play one master off against the other whenever they felt it was in their own interest. To keep his subjects from resorting to trickery, the ruler had to keep himself very well informed of all matters. This gave rise to a specific political attitude to which the proverb alludes, and which Maquet has called the "diffuse authority." That is to say that the ruler did not confine his control to political matters but extended it to all activities of the subject. There existed no field of competence nor time restrictions in the relation ruler/subject. It pervaded the whole life of the subject, down to the most intimate matters.

The Tuutsi was educated to rule. The tendency to pervade others' lives was consequently incrusted in the child's soul very early during the educational process. Thus it soon became a Tuutsi characteristic to interfere with others' lives no matter how private the issue may be. Although shared, to a certain extent, by members of the other two ethnic groups, this attitude is perceived by all as specifically Tuutsi. Of course, this political attitude met with resistance. Anyone would tend to protect his privacy. Therefore the Tuutsi needed to develop specific qualities in relation to their political attitude. Sheer force would have been useless in this case, whereas astuteness, shrewdness and doggedness were very effective. That is why the educational process of the Tuutsi child insisted upon those "qualities" which soon become characteristics of the group.

This partly explains the political success of the Tuutsi. It also partly explains the recent events in Rwanda. As late as last February, the Tuutsi were ejected from secondary schools and from higher educational institutions as well as from most civil servant and clerk jobs. The reason given by the young Hutu generation who were responsible for the deed is that after 13 years of Hutu power, the authorities have not reached what had been proclaimed as a revolutionary goal, namely that the number of Tuutsi in schools and in good jobs should be in proportion to their demographic importance. In fact, close to 100% of the clerk jobs in the private sector were held by Tuutsi. They also numbered near 50% of the civil servants and of the students at the secondary and higher level. Such an achievement is due to the fact that they resorted to all kinds of devices such as falsification of their ethnic origin, exploiting the corruptibility of some Hutu officials, and blackmail. But the most fruitful means they used was marrying their daughters to Hutu officials, thus weaving a powerful network of reciprocal obligations and forcing the new masters to subvert one of the main goals of the revolutionary manifesto. What they could no longer obtain with their long-horn cows, they secured with their "nice-legged" women. As for the foreigner becoming acquainted with Tuutsi, he is soon forced to fight for his last bit of privacy sometimes at the cost of friendly relationships. The proverb alludes to all this and that is why it is so real even nowadays. This might also be one of the reasons why it is so often used and its form subject to so many changes.

Structural Analysis

The proverb under study may be divided into two segments *A* and *B*. The two segments are ordered in a consequential unit: assuming *A*, *B* follows, which can be written $A \longrightarrow B$. Each segment includes two terms *a* and *b*, *a* expressing an action *v* exerted by an agent *s* on some other, *o*, and *b* expressing a local determination *p*. These terms are ordered in such a way that *Aa* is in opposition to *Ba* and *Ab* to *Bb*. The action in segment *A* is one of receiving a guest whereas in segment *B* it is one of forcing someone out of his own place. Moreover, the agent in segment *A* is object in segment *B* and the object in segment *A* is agent in segment B. This structure can be represented as in fig. 4.

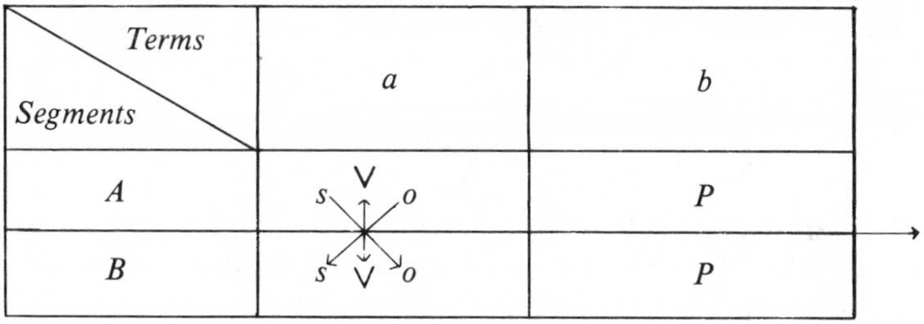

Terms / *Segments*	*a*	*b*
A	*s* V *o*	*P*
B	*s* V *o*	*P*

Fig. 4

Applying the basic text to the structure, one would read as in fig. 5.

You – lodge – Tuutsi	*in ingle-nook*	*and*
He – throws out – you	*of front room*	

Fig. 5

Change may affect any of the four terms. Let us list all the changes:

Aa1. *Umutuutsi umusembereza:* The Tuutsi you lodge him
Aa2. *Usembereza umutuutsi:* You lodge the Tuutsi
Aa3. *Umutuutsi umucumbikira:* The Tuutsi you put him up

Ab1. *ikwéru:* in the ingle-nook
Ab2. *haakwéru:* in the ingle-nook
Ab3. *mu muryángo:* in the lobby
Ab4. *mu kirămbi:* in the living-room
Ab5. *muu mfúruká:* in the corner
Ab6. *ihéeru:* in the second house
Ab7. *mu isămbu:* on the estate

Ba1. *akaguca:* and he throws you out
Ba2. *akagukuura:* and he forces you out
Ba3. *akaguteera:* and he intrudes on you
Ba4. *agakwimura:* and he chucks you out

Bb1. *muu mbere:* in the front-room
Bb2. *ruguru:* in the upper-room
Bb3. *ku buriri:* on the bed
Bb4. *mu kirămbi:* in the living-room
Bb5. *muu nzu:* in the house
Bb6. *ikámberé:* at the main house
Bb7. *muu ngo:* in the dwellings

We can also add in term *Aa* the inversion: *ucumbikira umutuutsi* "you put up the Tuutsi" (*Aa4*). Informants did not volunteer this form but upon enquiry they did accept it as correct. So that altogether we have 4 forms in term *Aa*, 7 in term *Ab*, 4 in term *Ba*, and 7 in term *Bb*. Then the logical possibilities for change in the proposed forms are 4 x 7 x 4 x 7 = 784. There exist hundreds of other possibilities if we include all the different sections of the house and of the compound but their detailed analysis would not add anything to our purpose. I tested all the possibilities arising out of the phrases cited above, also a few of the others. Among all the forms which had not been volunteered, some were accepted as correct, others were firmly discarded as no good and a third group, though structurally correct, were put aside in favor of more usual forms. We will look at all this later on. For the moment, let us keep on clearing the ground.

Referring to the distinction between variant and version, one might ask which of the forms are variants and which are versions or, in other words, which among all culturally acceptable forms imply a semantic change. *Aa2* is an inversion of *Aa1* without semantic impact, except maybe a little stress on the *Tuutsi* in form *Aa1*. The same applies to *Aa4* in regard to *Aa3*. Therefore there are only two versions of the first term: the verbal radical *-semberez-* means "to receive someone as a guest" without indicating any time limits whereas the radical *-cumbikir-* means "to receive someone for the night or for a short period of time." *Ab2* is a variant of *Ab1*: both words vary only in one formal element, namely in the locative class. They meant exactly the same thing. As for *Ab6*, grammatically speaking, it is a variant of *Ab1* for the same reason as *Ab2*: it is another locative form. But, as we have seen earlier, it implies a real semantic switch, at least for most of the informants. *Ab3, Ab4* and *Ab5* are versions since they indicate different sections of the house. So it is with *Ab7* which indicates the whole of the estate. Therefore 6 versions must be retained in term *Ab*. The four forms of term *Ba* are versions. Indeed, as one can see from the proposed translation, the four verbal radicals differ at least in some nuances: *-ci-* means "to throw out," *-kuur-* "to force out," *-teer-* "to intrude on" and *-iomur-* "to chuck out." Some of these nuances are subtle of course, but they do exist. The seven forms of term *Bb* are also all versions as they indicate different sections of the house or of the compound, or the whole of the compound. A difficulty may arise as to form *Bb2* which indicates the same section of the house as *Bb1*. Nevertheless, the cultural meaning of these forms is different, *Bb1* being in relation to the entering guest and *Bb2* being in relation to the geographical set up of the house.

It is time to turn to the reasons for the cultural acceptability of the different logical forms. I said earlier that some sections of the house are strictly reserved to members of the family. Consequently, any of those sections would be culturally unacceptable in term *Ab*. To say for example: "The Tuutsi you lodge him in the upper-room" would be cultural nonsense. I tried it and was rewarded with a big laugh.

If some sections of the house are culturally unacceptable in term *Ab,* there is no such restriction in term *Bb.* Any section of the house or of the compound would suit. But there exists another cultural restriction. For the sake of brevity, let us call the sections reserved to members of the family *F* and sections opened to guests *G.* The opposition *Ab/Bb* can be of two types only: *G/F* or *G/G, F/G* or *F/F* being culturally unacceptable as we have just seen. There is no restriction as to *G/F:* any *G* in *Ab* can be in opposition to any *F* in *Bb.* But there exists a cultural restriction as to *G/G.* This opposition is correct on condition that *G* in term *Ab* indicates a section of the house closer to the entrance than *G* in term *Bb*, or that *G* in term *Bb* be more general than *G* in term *Ab*. When the opposition *G/G* is related to the compound, *G* in term *Ab* must be a secondary house and *G* in term *Bb* must be the main house. When related to the whole estate, *G* in term *Ab* must be more general than *G* in term *Bb*. Thus any of phrases *Ab1, Ab2* or *Ab4* can be opposed to *Bb1, Bb2* or *Bb3, Ab3* or *Ab5* to any *Bb* forms except *Bb6* or *Bb7, Ab6* to *Bb6* only and any *Ab* forms to *Bb7*. For example, one cannot say: "The Tuutsi you lodge him in the living-room and he throws you out of the lobby or of the corner." When quoting the proverb in this form, I drew pitiful comments. As much as my informants were amazed at my knowledge of house-building and so many forms of the proverb, so were they astonished at my ignorance of the structuring rules. One even volunteered the structuring rule saying: "Hey man! that is going backwards!"

It should be noted also that some forms are more common than others. *Ab7, Ba4* and *Bb7* for example appear only once among all proposed forms. I tried all forms 1–68 with the variant *umucumbikira.* My informants agreed as to the correctness of those forms but always immediately volunteered a more common form. Which means that although they were ready to accept these new forms as correct, they preferred forms more commonly used. In this case, we are faced with the weight of tradition. Some forms can be culturally acceptable but the proverb is generally transmitted in other forms. It is a matter of preference, not of acceptability. Tradition is so strong as to transmit forms which are no longer understood in their details. Such is the case, as we have seen earlier, of forms *ikwéru* and *haakwéru.* Of course, the connotative meaning of the proverb is still fully understood. But some references are lost: the *significatum* is still alive in the tradition whereas the *significans* has been partly lost.

Conclusions

There are two sets of conclusions one can draw from the above analysis: rules for the oral transmission of the proverb itself and suggestions in regard to oral transmission in general.

1 The structure of the proverb can generate a great number of logical forms.

2 Not all logical forms are culturally correct. There exist some contextual and structural restrictions as to how the logical forms can be applied. All house sections which are reserved to members of the family are unacceptable in term *Ab.* House sections which guests are allowed into must be in such a position that the more intimate is in term *Bb.* Compound sections must be opposed in such a way that the main house is found in term *Bb.* In reference to the estate, the more general section must be in term *Ab.*

3 Among all culturally acceptable forms, traditional ones are preferred. New forms are accepted as correct but forms which have been heard before are preferred. The preference is strong enough to favour traditional forms in which some of the terms are no longer in common use or even intelligible, rather than new forms in which all of the terms are fully understood.

Our case study is very limited. It concerns one single item among thousands of one genre of verbal art of one population. Its significance in regard to oral tradition in general cannot be but suggestive. A great many more small scale analyses of this kind are needed before case materials will allow some conclusions of cross-cultural significance. The following are hypotheses for further research.

1 The materials of folklore are usually conceptualized as traditional. They constitute a body of knowledge inherited from the past which accordingly is transmitted with a certain fixity. But the

materials of folklore are also mobile and manipulative. Our case study is a clear example of this truism within the same cultural group. When it comes to transcultural transmission, we may expect greater mobility and manipulativeness and less fixity.

2 Change can affect oral tradition in many ways. A new situational context may completely change the connotative signification of an item whereas the denotative signification remains untouched. Materials of folklore may change in form without changing in content. They may also change in form and content. Change may lead to a variant or a version but may also generate a new item of folklore. The variational matrix proposed in fig. 1 is of course very general. It needs to be qualified in the light of other case studies. But it can be useful as a starting point in classifying the different modes of change in oral transmission.

3 Many factors are at play either in orienting or limiting variation in oral transmission. One is tempted to distinguish external factors and internal factors. External factors would be the different kinds of pressures exerted on oral transmission from outside the communicative process itself such as for example social change, political turnover, economic development, cross-cultural contacts, religious missions and so on. Internal factors would be all the possibilities for change inside the communicative process such as the structure of the language, logical appositeness, structural inventiveness and limitation, the weight of tradition and so on. In regard to internal factors, our case study allows us to suggest four rules of change: *(a)* the tendency of oral transmission is to explore as many linguistic and logical forms as possible within each of its genres; *(b)* the structures of the materials of folklore which are determined by the aid of socio-cultural context maintain this tendency within certain limits: *(c)* the weight of tradition operates a choice among all structural possibilities; *(d)* the more an item of folklore is "alive," the more it is subject to change.

Needless to repeat that these are not conclusions but hypotheses which need to be tested by other case materials. Their significance might extend not only to folkloristic research but also to all fields of anthropology related to systems of representations such as cognitive anthropology, educational anthropology, anthropology of religion and so on. Such studies can also be of some importance in applied anthropology and in all cross-cultural contacts be they diplomatic, economic or religious in nature. Foreign aid bodies and international boards as well as missionary groups would also profit by a better knowledge of educative processes which can be gained from studies of this type.

Notes

1. This is a very literal translation meant to keep the original image. What the Rwandan call the front-room (or the front of anything) is always in regard to the person concerned. Here it means the section of the house which is in front of the entering person. As it is the farthest away from the entrance, the section should have been called the back-room. But the original image would have been lost.

2. *ikwéru* and *haakwéru* vary only in the locative classification (*i vs haa*), the meaning of which is the same. Both words are consequently translated into the same English word.

Bibliography

Barthes, R. 1964: "Eléments de sémiologie." *Communications* 4:91–135.

Bauman, R. (ed.) 1971: "Toward New Perspectives in Folklore." *Journal of American Folklore* 84, special issue.

Coupez, A. and Meeussen, A.E. 1961: "Notation pratique de la quantité vocalique et de la tonalité en rundi et rwanda." *Orbis* 10:429–33.

Coupez, A. and Kamanzi, Th. 1962: *Récits historiques rwanda.* Tervuren, Musée royal de l'Afrique centrale.

d'Hertefelt, M. 1962: "Le Rwanda," M. d'Hertefelt, A.A. Trouwborst and J.H. Scherer, *Les anciens royaumes de la zone interlacustre méridionale: Rwanda, Burundi, Buha,* Tervuren, Musée royal de l'Afrique centrale, 9–112.

Forster, E.A. 1963: "The Proverb and Superstition Defined," unpublished Ph.D. thesis, University of Pennsylvania.

Greimas, A.J. 1970: *Du sens: essais sémiotiques.* Paris, Seuil.

Kagame, A. 1953: *Imigani y'imigenûrano.* Kabgayi, Editions royales 7.

Köngäs Maranda, E. 1971: "Theory and Practice of Riddle Analysis," *Journal of American Folklore* 84:51–61.

Lévi-Strauss, C. 1966: *Du miel aux cendres.* Paris, Plon.

Maquet, J.J. 1954: *Le système des relations sociales dans le Rwanda ancien.* Tervuren, Annales de Musée royal du Congo belge.

Milner, G.B. 1969: "De l'armature des locutions proverbiales: essai de taxonomie semantique." *L'Homme*, 9:349–70.

Sandrart, G. 1939: "Cours de droit coutumier," unpublished m.s., Astrida.

Toward a Theory of Proverb Meaning

*Barbara Kirshenblatt-Gimblett**

The consideration of variation in folklore must include both variation in text and variation in meaning. In this short essay, Professor Kirshenblatt-Gimblett explores the multiple meanings of several familiar proverbs. It may seem obvious enough that proverbs may be understood differently by different individuals in different contexts, but one must keep in mind that most proverb collections consist of nothing but long lists of proverbs presented without any discussion whatsoever of their meanings. For readers especially interested in proverb meaning, the work of Arvo Krikmann is recommended. See, for example, On Denotative Indefiniteness of Proverbs *(Tallinn, 1974) and* Some Additional Aspects of Semantic Indefiniteness of Proverbs *(Tallinn, 1974).*

Proverbs sound authoritative. The truths they proclaim feel absolute. This impression is created by the proverb's traditionality and the weight of impersonal community consensus it invokes. The proverb's form reinforces this effect by sounding so "right." Neat symmetries and witty convergences of sound and meaning, tight formulations of logical relations, highly patterned repetitions, structural balance, and familiar metaphors encapsulate general principles and contribute to the feeling that anything that sounds so right must be true (see Malof 1966). This is an instrumental part of the proverb's strategy. But this does *not* mean that proverbs do state absolute truths. Proverbs are just

*Reprinted from *Proverbium*, 22 (1973), 821–827.

supposed to sound like they do. When examined in terms of their actual use in specific situations, we see that a proverb can be made to express more than one meaning, that sometimes these meanings are contradictory, and that a proverb's meaning, rather than being autonomous of the proverb's use as we are led to believe by proverb collections, is indeed contextually specified.

My purpose here will be to explore some of the sources of a proverb's multiple meanings and usages as a way of demonstrating that it expresses relative rather than absolute truths and is therefore responsive to the fact that situations, in turn, can be evaluated in more than one way. Alternative proverbs and alternative ways of using one proverb provide options for evaluating and responding to a situation. The choice of which alternative to use is based on a combination of (1) the participants' perception of the situation; (2) the repertoire of proverbs available to the participants and their perception of the meaning and usage possibilities of them; and (3) what it is they want to accomplish in the situation. Not all proverbs which could be made to fit the situation semantically will fit socially.

Sources of Multiple Meaning and Usage

Although proverbs have the potential to mean more than one thing, not all of these meanings will necessarily be realized in the proverb performances of a given community or individual. But this does not mean that the investigator can assume that all users of the proverb mean the same thing by it. Just as we must take care when studying the proverbs of another culture not to assume that their proverbs mean the same thing as English ones that seem similar, so too must we be sensitive to intracultural differences in the understanding of a given proverb as well as variation from individual to individual.

"A rolling stone gathers no moss." According to Milner, the exact meaning of this proverb was "the topic of a minor leader in *The Times* late in October 1966, which was followed by a number of letters in the correspondence columns. One writer claimed that in Scotland the allusion is to a stone roller, which must not be permitted to remain idle for long, or it will gather unwanted moss. The Scottish interpretation of this saying is therefore said to be: 'Keep abreast of modern ideas, keep your brain active.' In England, on the other hand, the allusion is to the desirable qualities of the moss found draped over stones in a peaceful brook." (Milner 1969: 201) Seen positively, this proverb affirms stability and the gains made thereby. In addition to these two options, University of Texas students, especially those who identify with counterculture values, suggested that the proverb meant that it is good to keep moving because then one does not become weighed down with a family and material possessions. They evaluated the moss on the stones in the peaceful English brook negatively. When asked about the meaning of this proverb, the class of about 80 Texas students actually presented all three possibilities: (1) a rolling stone gathering no moss is like a machine that keeps running and never gets rusty and broken; (2) a rolling stone is like a person who keeps on moving, never settles down, and therefore never gets anywhere; (3) a rolling stone is like a person who keeps moving and is therefore free, not burdened with a family and material possessions and not likely to fall into a rut. But the students were surprised at each other, because in most cases, each student was only familiar with one, or at most, two of the possible readings.

Sources of multiple meaning in "Rolling stones gather no moss" include (1) what is understood by the image presented in the metaphor (stone roller, stone in brook); (2) what is understood as the general principle expressed by the metaphor (movement promotes efficiency, stability promotes tangible gains); (3) how the general principle is evaluated (tangible gains are worthwhile, tangible gains are not worthwhile); (4) the requirements of the situation in which the proverb is used regardless of what one actually believes in principle (does one want to console or criticize the stable person; does one want to console or criticize the wanderer).

"A friend in need is a friend indeed (in deed)." When asked the meaning of this proverb, the Texas students again surprised each other with the following readings: (1) Someone who feels close enough to you to be able to ask you for help when he is in need is really your friend; (2) Someone who helps you when you are in need is really your friend; (3) Someone who helps you by means of his actions (deeds) when you need him is a real friend as opposed to someone who just makes promises; (4) Someone who is only your friend when he needs you is not a true friend. These alternate readings provide the basis for such parodies of this proverb as: "A friend in need is no friend of mine"; "A friend in weed (marijuana) is a friend indeed."

Sources of multiple meaning in "A friend in need is a friend indeed (in deed)" include (1) syntactic ambiguity (is your friend in need or are you in need); (2) lexical ambiguity (indeed or in deed); (3) key (Is proverb being stated "straight" or "sarcastically"? Does "a friend indeed" mean "a true friend" or "not a true friend"?). The readings provided here and the ambiguities they are based on do not exhaust the possibilities but merely pinpoint the most common ones. As noted above for "Rolling stones gather no moss," further possibilities are provided by the requirements of the situation in which the proverb is used.

Given all these possibilities, how do the participants know what the proverb means? Can they be counted on to share the same basic understanding of the potential meanings of the proverb? Since an important aspect of proverb use is the indirectness it affords and the tacit understanding it assumes, the proverb user who provides an explanation in order to disambiguate the proverb would be doing so as a last resort. Furthermore, if both parties are familiar with the proverb but the listener does not understand its application, the proverb user's explanation can be construed as an admission that his performance is unsuccessful even though he is able to demonstrate its logic, if pressed. Such an explanation would be easier to accept if the proverb itself was new to the listener and the need for such an explanation was anticipated and the gloss skillfully incorporated into the performance. Ideally, however, such explanations should not be necessary in ordinary conversation, there being other cues which help the listener to understand the statement the proverb is intended to make. For example, stress, juncture, tone of voice, and semantic fit are important in at least distinguishing:

a friend in need is a friend in deed
a friend in need is a friend indeed.

Paralinguistic features can serve to signal that the proverb is intended sarcastically. And assuming the performance is successful, the immediate context will support the reading intended by the proverb user.

In addition to optional and sometimes contradictory readings for a single proverb, there are within both community and personal repertoires proverbs which contradict each other or which provide conflicting options for evaluating similar situations: "You are never too old to learn" or "You cannot teach an old dog new tricks"; "Out of sight out of mind" or "Absence makes the heart grow fonder"; "Look before you leap" or "He who hesitates is lost"; "The more the merrier" or "Too many cooks spoil the broth"; "Nothing ventured nothing gained" or "Better safe than sorry"; "Haste makes waste" or "Strike while the iron is hot." These pairs and many others that could be brought forth, dramatize the notions that (1) proverbs express relative rather than absolute truth; (2) a proverb's meaning and "truth" are conditioned by the context; (3) a proverb that fits semantically may not be socially appropriate in terms of what the participants in the situation wish to accomplish; (4) a person tends to select a proverb on the basis of what the situation requires rather than simply or solely because of either a given proverb's semantic fit or its "truth" in some abstract sense; (5) situations can be evaluated in more than one way.

Does haste *always* and under *any* circumstances make waste? Does absence *always* make the heart grow fonder? Are you *never* too old to learn? Does money *always* talk? The question is not only *when* does haste make waste or *when* does money talk. The question is equally *when is it appropriate to say that it does*. Sometimes it may be important to use a given proverb even though it may not really be "true" whereas at other times it may be politic *not* to use a proverb that really does seem to be "true." Let us explore these possibilities in terms of an example.

"Money Talks"

1. John is bemoaning his failure to land a job with a new firm. He explains to his friend, Harry, that even his father's offer of a large contract could not convince them to hire him. *Money does not talk and there is no point in pretending that it does.*

2. After hearing John describe how even the promise of a large contract did not get John hired, Harry says, "Money talks?" *Money does not talk and by using the proverb ironically to mean the opposite of what it normally states, Harry is able to state that this situation is an exception to what is supposed to be a general rule.*

3. John and Harry are competing for the same job in a new firm. Harry thinks he is better qualified and believes that John got the job

because of the contract John's father gave the firm. Not willing to admit that John was actually hired on his own merits, Harry is bitter and says to his wife, "Money talks," *Money does not talk. Thinking and saying so help Harry to rationalize the situation to himself and to his wife.*

4. John earned the job on his own merits even though his father did provide the firm with a large contract. Harry, however, cannot accept that John is better skilled and believes the contract was really what got John the job. However, since John is now in an excellent position to help Harry to enter the same firm, Harry refrains from saying what he thinks in order not to antagonize John. *Money does not talk and even if one party believes that it does, it is not in his best interests to say so.*

5. John recognizes that he got the job because of his father's contract. Despite the fact that John's abilities are superior and that he deserved to get the job on his own merits, company politics were such that his hiring was made contingent on his father's contract. In discussing the matter with Harry, who has also been trying to enter this firm but without success, John says bitterly, "Money talks." *Money talks. The participants recognize this. It pays for John to say so, partly because in so doing he acknowledges the injustice of the situation and offers Harry some consolation.*

6. John brags to Harry about how he won his new job by virtue of his superlative abilities and naively overlooks the fact that his new boss was probably bribed into hiring him by the promise of his father's large contract. Harry, who is well qualified and who has struggled for a long time for the same position, is resentful and is tempted to say "Money talks" but refrains because, knowing that John is now in a position to help Harry enter the firm, he does not want to antagonize him. *Money talks and at least one participant knows that it does but it is not in his best interests to say so.*

7. John is celebrating his success in landing a job with Harry. John has made every effort to train himself for the position but to no avail until his father promised the firm a large contract. However, John does not associate his success with his father's contract. He thinks his own efforts finally paid off. *Money does talk. Harry accepts John's view that money did not get John the job and knows it would be in poor taste at this moment to even try to support the view that "money talks."*

8. John gets the job because of his father's contract. However, he thinks he landed the job on the strength of his own abilities. His good friend Harry, who is as well qualified and who has struggled for the same position for a long time, is very discouraged. In John's efforts to console Harry by making him believe that his failure to get the job is not a reflection on Harry's abilities but is contingent on factors beyond Harry's control, John tries to make his own success look smaller by saying, "Money talks." *Money does talk. John does not think that it does but says so in order to console Harry.*

In these examples, the base meaning of the proverb, "Money talks," is relatively constant: "If you give money to someone, he will be favorably predisposed to granting your wishes." What varies is therefore (a) whether *in fact* the money given did indeed have a positive effect; (b) whether at least one of the participants thinks it did; and (c) whether it was appropriate or consistent with what the participants wanted to accomplish in the interaction to say that money influenced the course of affairs. These three variables, which appear to be independent of each other, may be combined in eight different ways, all of which are represented in the situations described above and summarized in the following diagram:

	In fact money had positive effect	Potential user of proverb thinks money had positive effect	It pays for potential user of proverb to say money had positive effect
Example 1	−	−	−
Example 2	−	−	+
Example 3	−	+	+
Example 4	−	+	−
Example 5	+	+	+
Example 6	+	+	−
Example 7	+	−	−
Example 8	+	−	+

As we can see from the above chart, this proverb may or may not be used regardless of whether or not money did indeed talk and regardless of whether or not the participants think that it did. The multiple usages and socially situated meanings of the proverb, "Money talks," as found in the examples presented here, are *not* a result either of an ambiguity in the proverb metaphor or of the proverb's yielding multiple base meanings but rather of the *various convergences of social situation, participant evaluation, and interactional strategy.*

Conclusions

In recent years, more scholars have addressed themselves to the analysis of proverbs in their immediate social contexts, both actual and hypothetical, as well as in their larger cultural setting (see the pioneering work of Firth 1926; Herskovits 1930; Herzog and Blooah 1936; see also the more recent contributions of Parker 1958; Messenger 1959; Dundes and Arewa 1964; Seitel 1969; Jason 1971). It is generally recognized that proverbs are a rhetorical strategy serving the intentions of the speaker (see Burke 1961; Abrahams 1968, 1969) and that proverbs must be studied in their immediate contexts of use.

Important contributions to the study of proverb meaning have been made by Jason (1971) who explores the capacity of a proverb metaphor to yield more than one abstraction or base meaning (see p. 620)[1] and by Messenger (1959) who analyses the capacity of a situation to be evaluated in more than one way. He explores how, in a Nigerian judicial system, various proverbs, even contradictory ones, may be invoked by opposing parties to uphold their respective evaluations of a given situation.

Worthy of more attention in future studies of proverb use are (a) the multiplicity of base meanings which any one proverb can yield; (b) the variety of ways any one of these base meanings can be integrated into various social situations; and (c) the availability of alternative proverbs for evaluating any given situation. When these possibilities have been pinned down for a particular individual and/or speech community, we might explore which possibilities are realized more frequently; how many of them figure in the repertoire of any one individual; and how one speaker chooses from among the options available to him when he must interpret or use a proverb.

One of the aims of this paper has been to explore some of the sources of a proverb's multiple meanings and possible usages in order to facilitate a reconceptualization of the locus and nature of proverb meaning. We have attempted to go beyond Burke's illustration of how one proverb can be applied to four different situations which "are all distinct in their particularities; each occurs in a totally different texture of history yet all are classified together under the generalized heading of the same proverb" (Burke 1957: 4).

Firstly, we considered the proverb's capacity to yield more than one abstraction. Not all proverbs are metaphoric and by examining a proverb such as "A friend in need is a friend in deed (indeed)" we found that there are other sources of multiple base meanings besides alternate readings of the proverb metaphor, as was the case in "Rolling stones gather no moss." From our analysis we found that some sources of multiple base meanings for any one proverb may include, in addition to (1) what is understood by the concrete image presented in the proverb metaphor and (2) what is understood as the general principle expressed by this image, such factors as (3) how this general principle is evaluated (positive/negative), (4) syntactic ambiguity, (5) lexical ambiguity, and (6) key (serious, sarcastic, etc.). Alternate base meanings and the availability of contradictory proverbs in the individual's repertoire enable the proverb user to accommodate the many fine distinctions and qualifications to which each particular life situation is subject. But these multiple base meanings are only one source of different types of usage for a given proverb and only one component of "proverb performance meaning." Our analysis of "money talks," where the base meaning was held constant and the other components of proverb performance were varied, was intended to delineate a range of usage possibilities which did *not* hinge on alternate readings of the proverb. These different usages in turn were shown to condition "proverb meaning."

We may conclude from the foregoing analysis that "proverb meaning" ultimately emerges from a proverb's use in a specific context and that it is not the meaning of the proverb per se that need be our central concern but the meaning of proverb performances:

Proverb (Performance) Meaning	=	Participants' Evaluation of Situation	+	Participants' Understanding of Proverb's Base Meaning	+	Interactional Strategy of Proverb User

The determining of a proverb's base meanings (we will have already made an advance if we begin with the assumption that a proverb has more than one base meaning) is but the first step. It provides the investigator with a foundation for examining the understandings that emerge when these base meanings are socially situated. But the base meanings of a proverb must not be confused with "proverb meaning" or more accurately, "proverb performance meaning," which may be defined as that which emerges from the integration of proverbial (base meaning) and situational meaning (participant evaluation of situation plus interactional strategy). In everyday life proverbs *only* exist as socially situated meanings in contrast with proverb compilations in which proverbs are "unsituated" and appear to express absolute truths.

Note

1. It is interesting to note here the reverse pattern. There are instances where the concrete *image* in the proverb metaphor is either understood in as many as three different ways or perhaps not understood at all while the base meaning of the proverb, no matter how the image is understood, remains substantially the same. For example, when asked what was referred to by the concrete image in "Little pitchers have big ears," some University of Texas students said, "Little boys playing pitcher for baseball games have big ears"; a very few said, "A small jug (pitcher) has big handles (ears) on each side"; others said, "Little pictures (paintings or illustrations) have big ears" and expressed bewilderment because they could not see the sense in such an image. When asked, "What does it mean when someone says, "Little pitchers have big ears," the eighty students were unanimous: "It means that a child is around who is hearing adults discuss things he should not hear." They varied, however, as to the most familiar use of the proverb. Some said that this proverb was typically addressed to the child as a way of telling him to leave the room so that adults could finish their conversation. Others said that the proverb was typically addressed by one adult to another to signal, without the child knowing, that they should change the subject and cease discussing the topic which the child is not allowed to hear.

Bibliography

Abrahams, Roger. "Introductory Remarks to a Rhetorical Theory of Folklore," *Journal of American Folklore* 81 (1968): 143–158.

——— "A Rhetoric of Everyday Life: Traditional Conversational Genres," *Southern Folklore Quarterly* 32 (1968): 44–59.

"The Complex Relations of Simple Forms," *Genre* 2 (1969): 104–128.

Arewa, E. Ojo and Alan Dundes. "Proverbs and the Ethnography of Speaking Folklore," *American Anthropologist* 66, no. 6, pt. 2 (1964): 70–85.

Burke, Kenneth. *The Philosophy of Literary Form* (New York, 1957).

Firth, Raymond. "Proverbs in Native Life with Special Reference to those of the Maori," *Folk-lore* 37 (1926): 134–153, 254–270.

Herskovits, Melville J. "Kru Proverbs," *Journal of American Folklore* 43 (1930): 225–293.

Herzog, George and C.G. Blooah. *Jabo Proverbs from Liberia* (London, 1936).

Jason, Heda. "Proverbs in Society: The Problem of Meaning and Function," *Proverbium* 17 (1971): 617–623.

Malof, Joseph. "Meter as Organic Form," *Modern Language Quarterly* 27 (1966): 3–17.

Messenger, John. "The Role of Proverbs in a Nigerian Judicial System," *Southwestern Journal of Anthropology* 15 (1959): 64–73.

Milner, G.B. "What is a Proverb?" *New Society* 6, no. 332 (1969): 199–202.

Parker, Richard B. "Lebanese Proverbs," *Journal of American Folklore* 71 (1958): 104–114.

Seitel, Peter. "Proverbs: A Social Use of Metaphor," *Genre* 2 (1969): 143–161.

Proverbs: A Social Use of Metaphor

*Peter Seitel**

The meaning of proverbs is best revealed by actual usage in social situations. Folklorist Peter Seitel tries to develop a model to show how there must be a semantic fit between the meaningful parts of a proverb and the cultural context in which it is actually cited. For a classic study of proverbs studied in context on the basis of extended field observation in a German village, see Mathilde Hain, Sprichwort und Volkssprache. Eine volkskundlich-soziologische Dorfuntersuchung *(Giessen, 1951). For Seitel's field experience with his model, see "Saying Haya Sayings: Two Categories of Proverb Use," in J. David Sapir and J. Christopher Crocker, eds.,* The Social Use of Metaphor *(Philadelphia, 1977), pp. 75–99.*

This article will present a system for viewing proverbs as the strategic social use of metaphor; that is to say, the manifestation in traditional, artistic, and relatively short form of metaphorical reasoning, used in an interactional context to serve certain purposes. It will be the task of this paper to show why it is reasonable and interesting to view proverbs in this way, to suggest areas of investigation which present themselves in this light, and to offer some preliminary conclusions drawn from my own researches. The proposed method is a development from the ethnographic approach used by other investigators, who have taken as their goal the explication of meaning in proverbs through a description of the cultural context in which they appear.

*Reprinted from *Genre*, 2 (1969), 143–161.

George Herzog and C.G. Blooah, *Jabo Proverbs from Liberia* (London, 1936) give ethnographic details concerning the content of most proverbs presented and often the social situations to which they may be applied. In an article on Maori proverbs, Raymond Firth has stated the general principles of this type of approach.

> The essential thing about a proverb is its meaning—and by this is to be understood not merely a bald and literal translation into the accustomed tongue, nor even a free version of what the words are intended to convey. The meaning of a proverb is made clear only when side by side with the translation is given a full account of the accompanying social situation—the reason for its use, its effect, and its significance in speech.[1]

In an article entitled "Proverbs and the Ethnography of Speaking Folklore,"[2] E. Ojo Arewa and Alan Dundes expand on this basic idea. They not only delineate the various aspects of the "social situation" of proverb use but also see proverbs as part of the total communication system operative in a given society. As a mode of social communication, proverbs may then be handled within the framework outlined by Dell Hymes in an article entitled, "The Ethnography of Speaking."[3] When applied to proverbs, this general method for describing the cultural patterns that languages use yields the following questions:

> One needs to ask not only for proverbs and what counts as a proverb, but also for information as to the other components of the situations in which proverbs are used. What are the rules governing who can use proverbs, or particular proverbs, and to whom? upon what occasions? in what places? with what other person present or absent? using what channels (e.g. speech, drumming, etc.)? Do restrictions or prescriptions as to the use of proverbs or a proverb have to do with particular topics? with the specific relationship between speaker and addressee? What exactly are the contributing contextual factors which make the use of proverbs or a particular proverb, possible or not possible, appropriate or inappropriate?[4]

The core of interest in the Arewa and Dundes article is essentially the same as that of the earlier work by Firth; that is, to reach an understanding of proverbs by thoroughly describing the ethnographic context. Arewa and Dundes have extended and delineated more precisely the questions to be asked concerning the relevant aspects of social context.

The system for studying proverbs presented here owes much to Hymes' "ethnography of speaking" approach. Rather than viewing proverbs as an instance of patterned speech to be fit into a system designed to handle a much broader range of data, however, I shall take an alternate approach by setting a goal of proverb study and then adducing whatever methods seem appropriate to the attainment of this goal. This does not in any way question the validity of the "ethnography of speaking" method; the system presented here merely takes as its first step the consideration of proverb usage itself, to determine whether certain problems arise which are characteristic of it alone or whether in proverb usage certain general problems are most readily accessible to investigation.

This article takes as its central question: Given that a person has memorized a certain number of proverb texts, by application of what set of rules does he speak them in a culturally appropriate manner and by what criteria does he judge the correctness of another's usage? Alternately stated, the goal of the method presented is to delineate the culturally shared system which enables a person to use proverbs in a socially acceptable manner.

With this central concern, a certain line of investigation may be followed. First, what is a proverb? That is, how does one recognize that which he is going to study? Second, what is the data available for the study? Third, what are the tools available for the analysis of the data? Fourth, what conclusions may be drawn on the basis of the data?

It will become evident that the first two questions in practice cannot be separated. Definition of a phenomenon for study depends, of course, on the type of data available. An investigator who observes proverb usage in a natural conversational setting and in his own language will define "proverb" differently from an investigator whose data are collections of texts. Proverbs in English may be provisionally defined as short, traditional, "out-of-context" statements used to further some social end. That proverbs are short and traditional is a generally accepted feature of definition. That they are used for a social end or a "strategy" has been noted by Kenneth Burke.[5] What is meant by "out-of-context" is simply that a proverb in some way violates the "usual" rules of conversation. That is a proverb may be acceptable at a given time within the order of a conversation, but the proverb's syntax, subject matter, or other features violate in some (acceptable) way the "usual" context. "A stitch in time saves nine" applied to the need for minor automobile repairs before a long trip introduces the subject of sewing into a context where it appears to have no place. "Seeing is believing" in judgment of a purported statement of fact stands out from the normal conversational flow because of its unusual syntax. "Business is business," applied to the morality of New York Chemical Bank's role in the economy of South Africa violates usual English rules which specify the permissible combination of words. Leaving the definition at present to the criteria mentioned above, let us consider how the data available for the study limited the application of this definition.

Proverb use among the Ibo people of Eastern Nigeria (Biafra) was studied through library materials. Three types of data were used: ethnographic, textual, and literary. The ethnographic materials were the monographs of Uchendu[6] and Basden,[7] as well as other books and articles on Ibo society. Also employed was a collection of 1022 proverb texts made by Northcote Thomas as part of his report on the Ibo-speaking peoples of Nigeria.[8] Three novels of Chinua Achebe[9] provided examples of proverb uses in traditional contexts. While the ethnographic and textual works are generally accepted as "hard" scientific data, an explanation must be given of how and why one may use novels as repositories of factual information.

The rationale which allowed the use of novels as sources for the realistic portrayal of proverb use was essentially this: if it could be shown that the novelistic depictions of cultural features (exclusive of proverb use) were substantially accurate, then it would not be unreasonable to assume that accounts of proverb usages were similarly true to life. To this end, novelistic description of such things as social organization, residence rules, burial customs, cosmology, and performances of items of verbal art other than proverbs were compared with accounts from the ethnographic sources on the same cultural features. The novels were shown to be accurate in every instance, allowing for the fact that variations exist within what was then Ibo territory.

Using novels as ethnographic data on proverb use has certain inherent limitations. Aside from the fact that the rational foundation rests on the inductive leap outlined above, only certain proverbs and aspects of proverb use are available for study. If, for example, there are Ibo proverbs set off from usual context by unusual syntax or violation of permissible combinations of words, one could not detect this because all the proverbs appear in English translation. One manner of departing from the normal context, however, does remain recognizable even in translation—the abrupt shift in subject matter when a proverb such as "a stitch in time . . ." is used. This kind of "out-of-contextness" is recognizable in a novelistic setting because the contexts in which proverbs appear are described. Many proverbs deal with animals, but few if any of the novelistic contexts of proverb use have animals in them. With respect to the definition first proposed, then, the proverbs will be limited to those set off by subject matter. This type of proverb has been termed the "metaphorical proverb" because the relationship between it and the social situation to which it is applied may be termed metaphorical.[10] The novels yielded 150 instances of proverb use in social contexts (uses of proverbs in the authorial voice for descriptive purposes were eliminated).

The features of social context of proverb use were then recorded, selecting out as many social features mentioned by Arewa and Dundes as the smallness of the sample allowed. For example, the relative age of the speaker and intended hearer, their relative social status and sex could be employed because of the few discriminations needed on each dimension. But a category such as kin relationship could not yield significant results because of the relatively large number of possibilities in relation to the small size of the sampie. Also recorded was the intention of the speaker in using the proverb—knowable in most cases because it is the craft of the novelist to make internal motivations evident. The type of occasion was noted—ceremonial, formal reception of a visitor, village meeting, informal discussion, etc.—as was the presence or absence of introductory phrases such as, "the elders have a saying that . . ."

It should be noted that all of these categories refer to the context in which a proverb is spoken. An equally important aspect of proverb use to be described is the metaphorical relationship between the imaginary situation presented in the proverb and the social situation to which it refers. To understand proverb use one must understand the mechanism of this metaphor and how it is manipulated to serve social ends. As an aid to developing a conceptual terminology with which to analyze this relationship, consider the following heuristic model:

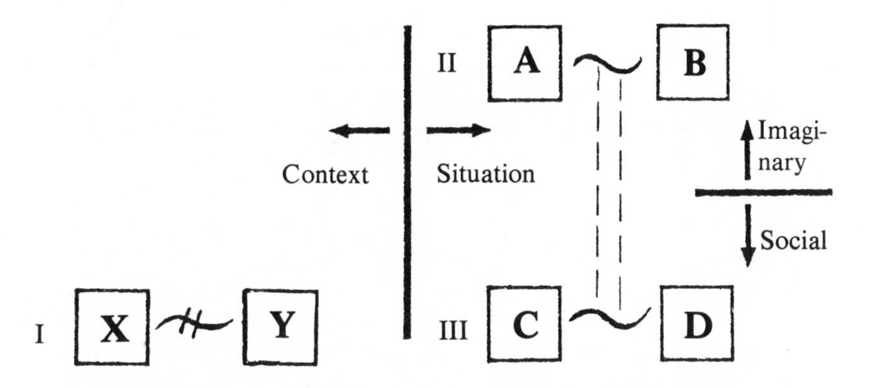

X and Y are, respectively, the speaker and the intended hearer of a proverb and ≁ represents the relationship which obtains between them—features of which are age, sex, status, etc. Part I of the diagram thus represents the social context of proverb use. Parts II and III represent, respectively, the proverb situation and the social situation to which the proverb is applied.

The symbol ~ refers to a relationship which is seen by the speaker as obtaining both between the objects (or people) in the social world (C and D) and between the concepts in the imaginary proverb situation (A and B). Because the diagram represents a *logical* structure, the symbol ~ represents a relationship of a logical nature which obtains between the substantive terms of the proverb situation (A ~ B) and also between the substantive terms of the social situation (C ~ D). This relationship may therefore be named by relational words such as "implies"—to characterize the relationship between the substantive terms "smoke" and "fire" in a usage of "where there's smoke there's fire." Another example is the relational word "equals"—to relate substantive terms in "a penny saved is a penny earned." The relational word may also name an action which is occurring or has occurred between the substantive terms such as "recognition"—a usage of "it is a wise parent who knows his own child." The symbol ~ can never stand for a substantive term.

The parallel dotted lines drawn between the relationship symbols (~) in II and III represent the drawing of an analogy between the two relationships. Thus, we may visualize that X says to Y that A is to B as C is to D (or A:B :: C:D). The terms "context" versus "situation" and "imaginary" versus "social" are added to aid both in visualizing the parts of the diagram to which these refer and in keeping them distinct from one another in subsequent usages.

To give an example of how the model represents the areas of investigation of proverb use: A father is discussing with his adolescent son the advisability of the son's associating himself with a certain group of boys, one of whom has earned a very bad reputation. To his son's argument that all of the rest of the members are reputable individuals, the father may answer, "If one finger brought oil it soiled the others." Here X and Y are the father and his son. The relationship between them (≁) has dimensions of age, status, kin relationship. The context (I) may or may not be relevant—formal teaching session, informal discussion over a meal, etc. The proverb situation (II) is made up of the term "finger which brought oil" (A) and the term "other fingers" (B). The relationship between them (∼) is "soiling." The social situation described (III) is a boy of bad reputation (term C) bringing disrepute (the relationship ∼) to the other members of his group (term D). The fact that the relationship in the social situation is seen by the father as somehow the "same" (that is, "spoiling" in both cases) is shown by the parallel dotted lines.

If the son objects by saying that this doesn't apply to him personally, the father might say "If you lie with the puppy you'll get fleas." In this example, the social context (I), remains the same as in the first case, but here the proverb situation is made up of the term "you, lying with the puppy" (A) and the term "fleas" (B), the relationship (∼) being "getting." The social situation (III) here consists of the son's associating with the aforementioned group (term C), and a bad reputation (term D), the relationship (∼) here, also one of "getting." The parallel dotted lines represent the drawing of the analogy: you lying with the puppy is to fleas as you associating with that group is to a bad reputation. This example may be seen as being of the same rational structure as the first, but with one significant difference. In the second instance the son appears in two places—as the hearer (X) and as a subject in the social situation (C).[11] The dual role of the son in this instance points up another aspect of proverb use—one which I have termed "correlation."

By correlation I mean the manner in which the speaker "matches up" the terms in the proverb with the people in the social situation and possibly in the social context. This may be described with a set of terms borrowed from language grammars: first, second, and third persons, singular and plural. To see how these apply to proverb use, it is easiest to give examples of a single proverb used in several of the six types of possible correlation. If I journey to a friend's house on an urgent matter, during the course of preliminary exchanges of courtesy (as an Ibo) I might say, "A toad does not run in the daytime unless something is after its life." The meaning would be clear—I have come because I have a matter to discuss (the toad running in the daytime is to something which is after its life as I, visiting, am to matter to be discussed). The correlation would here be first person singular because the person to whom the "toad" refers is "I." However, if you come to see me, and I say this proverb to you, the correlation is second person singular, because the person to whom the "toad" refers is then the person to whom the proverb is spoken (you). Further, if I speak to you about the frequent visits a third person makes to a certain house, alluding to the fact that I feel suspicious activities are going on, I may use the same proverb. Here the correlation is third person singular, because the person referred to is neither the speaker nor the person to whom the proverb is addressed. I leave it to the reader's imagination to construct hypothetical situations for using this proverb in the plural correlations of first, second, and third person; that is, the "toad" as we, you (pl.), and they.

Although the above six types of correlations were most often found in Achebe's novels, other types, made up of a combination of the six, are also possible. If there are two terms within a proverb which one wants to correlate with two people in a certain social situation, this usage is possible and may be handled within the "correlation" scheme. Consider, for example, a situation in which a man of high status visits a man of lower status, and the latter treats the former with generous hospitality. When the man of high status expresses his gratitude, the man of lower status may reply with modesty (don't thank me because) "a woman can place only so much of her leg over her husband." That is, beings of lower status can only do so much—very modest indeed. The correlation here is both first and second person singular, for terms referring to both the speaker and hearer are present in the proverb usage. The importance of correlation to understanding proverb usage may be noted by imagining a reversal in the correlation of the above proverb.[12] That is, in reference to the same situation, the man of high status speaks the proverb to the man of lower status. The usage would then be, rather than a modest statement, a blatant insult. Note that in a first and second person correlation, the social context is the same as the social situation. It appears that proverb use of this kind is one of great delicacy.

Another concept important to the description of proverb use is "strategy." By strategy I mean essentially what Kenneth Burke proposed the term to mean—a plan for dealing with the situation which the proverb names. As an answer to an implied (or perhaps stated) question, "what to do?" the proverb is an attempt to resolve the personally felt conflicts which arise from perceived contradictions in a social situation. That is, a conversational proverb use is an attempt to solve a situational problem which the speaker perceives in a manner which the speaker believes is most suitable. This is most evident in proverb usages where advice is being given: "look before you leap" is usually used as an attempt to resolve the perceived contradiction between quick decisive action and thorough weighing of alternatives; "he who hesitates is lost" (although perhaps not used metaphorically in all cases) is often an attempt to resolve the same contradiction. Proverb usages such as the one described above for "if one finger brought oil it soiled the others" give advice regarding the proper choice of alternatives—here an admonition to break off what is perceived to be a damaging relationship. Proverbs may also be used to resolve the contradictions between what a person feels a social context should be and what he perceives it to be at present. The usual use of "the toad does not run in the daytime unless something is after its life" is an attempt to bridge the gap or to mediate between a simple social visit and a context in which an important matter may be discussed. The speaker perceives the initial context as mere greeting behavior; he has a desire for a different kind of context. The proverb is spoken to resolve this felt conflict—in favor of the speaker's desire. Proverb usages in which the social situation described is the same as the social context of use are manifestations of this kind of conflict resolution.

For Ibo proverb usages, and perhaps for proverb usages in general, a speaker may attempt the resolution in what may be seen as two mutually exclusive ways. First, he may propose to defeat one side of the contradiction, giving victory to the other; this is the intent for the usages described in the preceding paragraph. Second, he may propose that the contradiction which he perceives in a situation and which the intended hearer also perceives is in fact the natural state of the world and must be endured. This type of strategy, which might be called "restraint" or "consolation," is evident in the instance of one elder seeking to comfort another, described by Achebe in *Arrow of God* (p. 213). When the speaker hears of the disappointment his friend has experienced because of an abnormal domestic relationship between his daughter and son-in-law, he consoles him by saying (don't let this bother you because) "there are more ways than one of killing a dog." That is, there are more ways than one of ordering a domestic relationship. This proverb usage also indicates the difficulty one would have in ascribing strategies to proverbs on the evidence of the text alone.

The major areas of the proposed method for studying proverb usage are the social context, the proverb situation, the social situation, and the concepts of correlation and strategy. These will be used in the next section, first in a brief report of the library research on the Ibo materials, and then in a discussion of ways of implementing the approach in a field research context.

It must be repeated that the results of the library research rest on the inductive leap discussed before, and hence must be taken as provisional; however, several interesting patterns do emerge from the materials. As one might suspect from the examples given above for the case of double correlation, there is a significant connection between the speaker's intent and the type of correlation employed. For example, for proverb usages in which animals are correlated with people, the rule appears to operate that for first person correlation the intent is a justification of one's own actions or position on a given social issue. The proverb quoted above, "the toad does not run in the daytime unless something is after his life," is usually used in first person correlation to state one's intention of and justification for bringing up a matter for discussion.[13] "The lizard that jumped from the high *iroko* tree to the ground said he would praise himself if no one else would" is spoken by a man who has come to request the sponsorship of an elder in beginning his yam garden. With this proverb usage he states that he must mention his own personal attributes and feels justified in doing so.[14]

A second person correlation for proverb usages in which animals occur may be found only a few times in Achebe's novels. In each case, however, the proverb is used in a negative appraisal of the intended hearer's actions and with intent which may be characterized as insult. One of these instances is especially interesting because the proverb cited here for a second person occurs in other usages in a first person correlation. "A toad does not run in the daytime unless something is after its life" is spoken by an elder who has received a visit from a younger relative of his.[15] The elder is quite displeased with the youth's discourteous manner, which violates not only norms for respectful treatment of elders but also the cordial relationship which is supposed to obtain between people who stand to one another as kin of the mother's brother/sister's son type. To add to the elder's expression of displeasure he introduces the proverb with "we have a saying that . . ." implying that either the youth does not know the proverb—the most frequently used one in the novels—or that the elder is paying ironic over-courtesy.[16]

Third person correlations for animal subjects, as one might expect, are used in the novels for negative judgments. "Unless the wind blows we do not see the fowl's rump" is used of friends who desert when adversity arises.[17] "Did you expect the leopard sired to be different from the leopard?" remarks negatively on the resemblance between father and daughter.[18] "When the mother-cow is chewing grass its young ones watch its mouth," remarks upon bad habits passed from parent to child.[19]

These examples should not be construed as evidence for a general rule that proverbs are used in support of oneself and against others. These examples are drawn only from those proverb usages which include animal subjects—30 out of 150.[20] The results are given here merely to suggest the aspects of proverb use which are part of the proposed method of investigation. Among the remaining 120 are usages which support the actions and opinions of others and some which are self-deprecatory for the purposes of courtesy and humor.

A somewhat similar pattern emerges for those proverbs in which a word such as "child" or "boy" occurs. First person correlation of "child" is common and has no negative connotations.[21] Second and third person correlations are deprecatory[22] with one basic exception—when the proverb is addressed to a child. In such a usage, the elder may be reprimanding the child, but in no sense may his remarks be taken as insult. "A boy who tries to wrestle with his father gets blinded by the old man's loin cloth" is spoken to a son to warn against disobeying his father.[23] Were this said by one grown man to another, it would clearly be aggressive and derisive in tone. Unfortunately, no such pairs of social contexts and situations exist in the novels for the same proverb. But an indication of the shift in the speaker's intention and in the application of the metaphor may be found in two instances of the same proverb—one in the Northcote Thomas collection and one in *Things Fall Apart*. "A baby on its mother's back does not know the way is long" is said by a priestess to a young child whom she wishes to comfort just before she will carry the young girl the long distance to an oracle cave.[24] This proverb also occurs in the Thomas collection in the section "Wealth and Poverty," where it is translated as "the child which is carried on the back does not know that travelling is a labor."[25] The proverb is to be applied "to a spendthrift son" or, it would appear, to any person who lives on the wealth of his parents rather then by his own labor. This is another clear instance of a change in application signalling a change in the speaker's intent and in the very meaning of the metaphor. The more specific problem of proverb use to children will be taken up below.

The extension of this type of study to field research requires that the lines of investigation suggested in the heuristic model of proverb use be followed in two ways. First, in interviews with proverb speakers, hypothetical situations should be constructed for a single proverb. Each situation should differ from another by a single value on one of the dimensions cited—type of correlation, socially defined characteristics of the person to whom the proverb applies (age, sex, social standing, etc.), aspects of the social context in which the proverb is spoken, etc. The informant should be asked whether the proverb may be used in this way: if it can, he should give an exegetical statement (if possible) which approximates the meaning of the usage. Questions should be asked such as, if the usual use of the proverb is a first person correlation, is it possible to use it in a second person correlation, and what does it mean so used? If a proverb is usually used by a senior in age to a junior, can it be used in any other way? Does a proverb have the same meaning whether it is applied to a man or a woman? Can this proverb be spoken if people who stand in certain kin relationships to the speaker are present? For any single proverb, the distinctions to be made for proper use, and the consequent questions to be asked are great in number. The aim is to construct usages of the same proverb in which a minimal difference in application signals a difference in meaning. When this information is available for a representative number of proverbs, patterns of use will emerge as they have to a limited extent for the Ibo materials.

The second way of applying the proposed method to field studies is to record instances of proverb use in their natural social contexts. The participants might be questioned at a later time as to the relevant factors which caused the choice of one proverb as opposed to another. This would provide the frame for questions regarding the substitutability of proverbs under certain circumstances. In both types of study, the aim should be to isolate the minimal differences in the features of social context and social situation which signal a change in proverb meaning and proverb selection.

Recalling the short discussion of the proverb, "a child on its mother's back does not know the way is long," we may ask whether the proposed method can offer a framework for dealing with special use of proverbs to children. That children occupy a special status in a system of proverb usage is suggested by a few reports on African societies. Otto Raum states that proverbs are not to be used at all to children below a certain age among the Chaga. Stories are thought to be the proper mode of moral instruction.[26] From a personal account I have the fact that among certain Swahili-speaking cultures on the coast of Tanzania a proverb use to a child is usually accompanied by a story said to "explain" the meaning of the application of the proverb. What these seem to suggest is that the metaphorical reasoning employed to understand proverbs is thought to be acquired by a process of developmental learning, and, also, that cultural concepts in the system of metaphorical proverb use (the proverb terms) must be invested in the child's mind with proper cultural meanings.

The process of metaphorical reasoning has been discussed as the application of an imaginary (proverb) situation to a real (social) situation through a process of correlation. If one wanted to simplify this process so that it could be learned by a child, he would try to make the desired correlation as unambiguous as possible. One of the ways to do this is to "literalize" one of the proverb terms; that is, to make part of the proverb nonmetaphorical. This is what is evident in the usage of the proverb, "a child on its mother's back does not know the way is long," directly to a child. In the Arewa and Dundes article, 12 proverbs are given which are said to relate to child-rearing. Although no definite indication is given as to which proverbs are regularly addressed to children, it is interesting to note that 10 out of the 12 have the words for "child" or "mother" in them. The problem of a "literal" correlation in usage to children may offer evidence on indigenous ideas of developmental growth of reasoning capacity.

To discuss the educational process of investing proverb terms with proper cultural meanings, it is necessary to refer again to the heuristic model of proverb usage. It will be recalled that the process of metaphorical reasoning requires drawing a parallel or an analogy between the relationships which obtain between A and B, and between C and D. But how are these relationships known? Of what are they made? And how does one communicate this to a child?

I believe that the direction in which these answers may be sought is indicated by drawing an analogy. It will be recalled that in the social context (sector I of the diagram) the symbol ≁ represents the relationship between the speaker and the hearer (X and Y respectively). It is, as we have seen, a shorthand representation for the sum of the culturally defined features of the relationship which obtains between them. That is, for example, if both are male, features of the relationship are: relative sex of speaker and hearer—same; sex of speaker (or hearer)—male: Their relative and/or absolute ages also comprise features of the relationship, as do the political, ritual, and social statuses of the participants. It is to be emphasized, first, that these features are culturally defined and, second, that the sum of these features comprises the relationship between speaker and hearer. The composition and definition of the relationship (∼) which obtains between the proverb terms, A and B (sector II), may be understood in an analogous way.

A proverb term, for example "child," is characterized by a number of cultural features which together comprise the metaphorical concept "child"—dependence, innocence, irresponsibility, ignorance, etc. These are ascribed differentially from society to society; children in one society may be thought to be completely irresponsible while they may not be thought so in another. Terms are invested with culturally defined features by virtue of appearing or of having once appeared in a certain culturally recognized environment. For "child," the feature of dependence may come as a result of the environments connected with suckling and later feeding by the mother. Irresponsibility as a feature may result from cultural practices and beliefs regarding the entrusting of certain tasks to children. In a similar manner other features come to define the metaphorical concept "child." But cultural environments are not exclusively social or natural settings. We have, for example, the expression, "the child who cried 'wolf,' " a possible feature of the concept "child" which comes not from any social environment but from a story to warn children. That the tortoise is slow but steady is a feature of our concept of "tortoise" which also derives from a story. The environments which invest proverb terms with features (alternately stated, symbols with associations or "valences") may be social, imaginary, or naturalistic. Thus we may state that terms in a proverb, just like the participants in a proverb-speaking social context, are invested with culturally defined features which are relevant for proverb usage.

When two terms appear in juxtaposition within the proverb situation, the sets of features characteristic of each combine so that features which correspond between the terms make up the relationship ($\sim$) while others, for which there is no correspondence between the terms, drop out. That is, each term may have a very large number of features associated with it, but when both are part of the same stated situation, only certain of the features apply. Following the example of "child": if one says of an incompetent employee "you shouldn't send a child to do a man's work," certain features of "child" are implied because of the juxtaposition with "man,"[27] that is, indecision, incompetence, etc. But in the previously discussed proverb, "a child on its mother's back does not know the way is long," child is here invested with slightly different features by virtue of juxtaposition with mother (or mother's back): ignorance of the ways of the world in comparison with an adult and dependence on an adult. A proverb such as "a child cannot pay for its mother's milk," sets up a relationship between child and mother (mother's milk) which has the features of exclusivity, nurturance, inappropriateness of certain social forms which imply distance between individuals (paying), and the relationship among certain groups of kin in Ibo usage.[28] These examples are adduced to suggest that the relationship between proverb terms consists, then, of the sum of the logical correspondences in the culturally defined features characteristic of the terms, just as the relationship between the participants in the social context of proverb use consists of the sum of the culturally defined features characteristic of the participants.

This provides a hypothesis to explain the problem of proverb usage to children. Because it is necessary for the hearer of a proverb to know the features of the terms (so that he can understand the relationship and, hence, the metaphor), a child is told stories either along with or instead of proverbs so that he can see the terms, later to be used in proverbs alone, in the environments which define their features. Alternately, proverb use in general or the use of specific proverbs is delayed until a child is thought to have had sufficient social experience, i.e. to have observed the social environments which invest proverbs with their proper features.

In this short paper I have attempted to present a method for dealing with the phenomenon of proverb use. It has been my purpose to extend proverb study beyond the perusal of texts, and beyond a check-list of questions to be answered, to the construction of a heuristic model of proverb use, focussing on the central problem of the social application of metaphor. The system's aim is understanding, here taken to mean the ability to produce and to interpret proverb usages in culturally acceptable ways. The purpose of presenting this method is to show the boundaries of the area for investigation and to suggest a few of the problems therein.

As a necessary by-product of the presentation, a vocabulary for talking about proverb usages was developed. I have tried to make it as simple as possible, introducing only the widely used concepts of person and number from an "outside" discipline. The other words used—context, situation, relationship, feature, term, correlation, and strategy—have been given their usual meanings or a restricted part of their usual meanings. The discussion of the use of literature for ethnography, the short examples of results from a study of Achebe's novels, and the concept of the nature of metaphor (as part of the discussion on child proverb usage), may be taken as useful spin-off and/or as Shandyesque digressions.

And yet it appears that the most important question which might be raised about proverbs has been neither asked nor answered: why study them at all? Again let me answer with an analogy: as white rats are to experimental psychologists and as kinship terms are to cultural anthropologists, proverbs can be to folklorists. That is, by pushing around these small and apparently simply constructed items, one can discover principles which give order to a wider range of phenomena. Proverbs are the simplest of the metaphorical genres of folklore—song, folktale, myth, folk play, etc.—and the genre which clearly and directly is used to serve a social purpose. By investigating the relatively simple use of metaphorical reasoning for social ends in proverbs, one can gain insight into the social uses of other, more complex metaphorical genres.

Although relatively simple in their application of metaphor, proverbs are one of the most complex genres in that they are most sensitive to social context. That is to say, the social rules which one must master in order to use and interpret proverbs correctly are probably the most numerous and complex of those for any genre. Given a logical and workable method, it is possible to ascertain them; and if it is possible for the most complex—proverbs—it will also be possible to write rules for the use and interpretation of less context-sensitive genres.

The simple, yet subtle and complex, nature of proverb use makes its study an important step in understanding the general problem of the social uses of metaphor. To a person interested in the social purposes which literature of all kinds may serve, the investigation of proverbs can offer significant insight.[29]

Notes

1. "Proverbs in Native Life with Special Reference to the Maori," *Folk-Lore*, XXVII (1926), 134.
2. "Proverbs and the Ethnography of Speaking Folklore," *American Anthropologist*, LXVI, No. 6, Pt. 2 (1964), 70–85.
3. *Anthropology and Human Behavior,* ed. Thomas Gladwin and William C. Sturtevant (Washington, D.C., 1962), pp. 15-53.
4. Arewa and Dundes, op. cit., p. 71.
5. *The Philosophy of Literary Form* (New York, 1957), pp. 3–4.
6. Victor Ch. Uchendu, *The Ibo of Southeast Nigeria* (New York, 1965).
7. G.T. Basden, *Among the Ibos of Southern Nigeria* (London, 1921) and *Niger Ibos* (London, 1938).
8. *Anthropological Report on the Ibo-Speaking Peoples of Nigeria*, 6 vols. (London, 1914).
9. *Things Fall Apart* (London, 1958) and *No Longer at Ease* (London, 1960) and *Arrow of God* (London, 1964).
10. W.R. Bascom, "Stylistic Features of Proverbs, a Comment," *Journal of American Folklore*, LXXVIII (1965), 69.

11. Although the proverb has the syntactic form "If you lie with the puppy . . ." it should not be thought that the son in the usage described appears in three places: as hearer (X), as a term in the social situation (C), and also as term "you" in the proverb situation. To the contrary, the "you" of the proverb term (A) "you, lying with the puppy" is the X "you" of impersonal statement, not the "you" of second person address. The proverb usage would have exactly the same logical structure were the proverb to read "lying with the puppy brings fleas."

Two points must be emphasized. First, that the model and the entire system proposed does not describe or explain syntactic or surface structure; it is designed to investigate the logical structure and the rational process that underlies proverb use. Second, that a term in the social situation (C or D) can never also be a term in the proverb situation. The proverb derives its essence, and the metaphor its meaning, from the fact that the terms A and B are related to each other in one system (imaginary), and this very relationship is said to characterize the relationship between two terms, C and D, in another separate system (social).

12. In the first usage the metaphorical analogy is man: wife::man of high status: man of low status; the speaker is the man of low status and thus the correlation is second person-first person. In the reversed usage, the analogy remains the same; but the speaker is the man of high status and thus the correlation is first person-second person.

13. Achebe, *Things Fall Apart*, pp. 19, 282; *Arrow of God*, pp. 171, 254.

14. Achebe, *Things Fall Apart*, p. 20.

15. Achebe, *Arrow of God*, p. 25.

16. This pattern is also reported by Arewa and Dundes for Yoruba proverb usage, op. cit., p. 79.

17. Achebe, *Arrow of God*, p. 72.

18. Ibid., p. 91.

19. Achebe, *Things Fall Apart*, p. 65; Achebe, *Arrow of God*, p. 213.

20. It should be noted that the results given here are for single-type correlations. A double correlation for animal subjects, "A fowl does not eat into the belly of a goat" (Achebe, *Arrow of God*, p. 93), does not follow the rule for single correlations of animal subjects. It resembles the example of double correlation given above in the text in that social context equals social situation and the metaphorical analogy refers to the differential statuses of the speaker and hearer.

21. See, for example, Achebe, *Things Fall Apart*, pp. 61, 151.

22. See, for example, Achebe, *No Longer at Ease*, p. 75.

23. Achebe, *Things Fall Apart*, p. 123.

24. Ibid., p. 92.

25. Thomas, *Anthropological Report*, Proverb Number 28.

26. *Chagga Childhood* (London, 1940).

27. Similarly for the term "man," which not only has associations of competence when juxtaposed with "child" but is also used in a juxtaposition like "are you a man or a mouse?"

28. Achebe, *Things Fall Apart*, p. 151.

29. I would like to thank David Sapir for his comments on this paper and for his helpful suggestions.

Proverbs and Practical Reasoning: A Study in Socio-Logic

*Paul D. Goodwin and Joseph W. Wenzel**

Proverbs are part of traditional communication, often serving to persuade, exhort, or criticize. For this reason, it is perfectly appropriate to examine proverbs in terms of rhetorical strategy and technique. In addition to the use of analogy discussed in the previous essay, one can find other patterns of logical argument expressed in proverbs. In this paper by Goodwin and Wenzel, we see how proverbs are viewed from the perspective of specialists in speech communication.

The study reported here originated in some perennial questions about the nature of human rationality. Modern conceptions of reason have ranged from the belief that "the laws of logic are the laws of thought"[1] to the supposition that the term "rational" should be applied to any sort of consistency within the cognitive field of an individual.[2] In contrast to those views is an emerging account of human reason that recognizes the shared social character of the rules and standards by which an argument is evaluated.[3] Human rationality, on this view, is grounded neither in a purely formal logic, nor in mere psycho-logic, but rather in a kind of *socio-logic*—a socially developed sense of practical reasoning. The motive power of reasoning may be an individual's striving for cognitive consistency, and the techniques employed may include some formal rules, but their ultimate source

* Reprinted by permission of the Speech Communication Association from the *Quarterly Journal of Speech*, 65 (1979), 289–302.

and sanction is the experience of a community of persons thinking and acting together over time. Rules of correct reasoning as a form of social knowledge, thus, are "confirmed through recurrent action."[4] If the principles of such a socio-logic do not exhibit the rigor of scientific method or the systematic elegance of formal logic, they nevertheless serve to guide ordinary persons in reasoning and arguing about their mundane affairs. Indeed, they may be more useful than a formal logic, for they are expressed in terms that are immediately intelligible. They are, many of them, proverbial.

Proverbs readily come to mind with this conception of socio-logic because of certain familiar examples: "One swallow doesn't make a summer" cautions against hasty generalizations; "Don't judge a book by its cover" warns against faulty reasoning from signs; and so forth. On the basis of such simple examples, we began to speculate: Is it possible that the proverbs of some cultures might reflect a fairly elaborate logical system? Might one find amid the multitude of proverbs the common folk's equivalent of a logic textbook? If anything like such a folk logic exists, we hypothesized, it would reflect, at least, (1) an implicit typology of patterns of legitimate reasoning, (2) rules to guide correct inference, and (3) cautions against specific fallacies. We determined to test that hypothesis by searching for such rules of reasoning in the proverbs of what may be called Anglo-American culture. Our purpose was not to conduct an ethnographic study of that amorphous culture, but rather to address more general conceptual questions: Do Anglo-American proverbs suggest an elaborate system of logical principles? Would the study of proverbs help to illuminate the nature of rationality as a culturally based socio-logic? The remainder of the study presents our findings. We will briefly discuss the nature of proverbs and their utility for conveying folk wisdom, present a collection of examples that can be arrayed in parallel with the logical principles of typical texts on argumentation, and finally discuss the significance of the findings.

The Uses of Proverbs

A proverb may be defined as a "short pithy saying . . . popularly known and repeated, usually expressing simply and concretely, though often metaphorically, a truth based on common sense or the practical experience of mankind."[5] Doubtless, the qualities included in the definition contribute to a proverb's "catching on," and enduring. But a proverb, to endure, must also be useful. It must have strategic value in coping with some relatively common human problem or situation. Burke describes that function:

> [S]ituations are real; the strategies for handling them have public content; and in so far as situations overlap . . . the strategies possess universal relevance. . . .
>
> Consider a proverb, for instance. Think of the endless variety of situations, distinct in their particularities, which this proverb may "size up" and attitudinally name.[6]

A person who can invoke a proverb in a given situation, therefore, is not dealing with an unknown. The proverb defines the situation and prescribes a response. As Taylor puts it, "As a guide to life's problems, the proverb summarizes a situation, passes a judgment, or offers a course of action."[7] Characteristically, proverbs deal with the eternal and universal human concerns—love and money, family and friends, work and play—concrete problems that confront everyone. What this study uncovered was a vast array of proverbs that teach also how to think straight in reasoning about those concerns.

The essential function of proverbs is a rhetorical one, for they are used primarily in deliberation about questions of practical conduct. Whether people are deliberating internally or sharing counsel with another, proverbs serve to establish norms for actions. They endure not only because of their rhetorically effective form, but also because of their substantive capacity to shape attitudes and action. Abrahams has remarked on the rhetorical nature of folklore generally:

> Folklore, being traditional activity, argues traditionally; it uses arguments and persuasive techniques developed in the past to cope with recurrences of social problem situations. In fact, the very traditional nature of the expression is one of the important techniques of persuasion in a tradition-oriented group. . . . Folklore functions normatively, as a cohesive force.[8]

Proverbs are thus a part of the folk wisdom that makes communal life possible. People can reason together only to the extent that they share rules for reasoning.

The utility of proverbs as vehicles of conventional wisdom depends on the rhetorical effectiveness of both their form and function. Two somewhat paradoxical observations illustrate that point. The first concerns the contextual flexibility of proverbs: On the surface, in their form of expression, many proverbs appear to be entirely context-bound (and, indeed, some do apply to quite limited cases); yet most function in a nearly limitless range of application, well beyond the concrete terms in which they are (metaphorically) expressed. Thus, "A stitch in time saves nine" and "An ounce of prevention is worth a pound of cure" no doubt originated in the contemplation of specific experiences, and each calls to mind specific images; but either can function in countless circumstances. Each proverb is successful, not only because it gives good general advice, but also because it does so in a way that affords intellectual pleasure. The proverb moves the mind from the concrete image evoked by its familiar terms, through apprehension of the implicit metaphor, to a novel application to the problematic situation.

A second paradoxical observation concerns the existence of contradictory proverbs. Although at first glance such contradictions suggest inconsistency, on reflection they may be found to achieve consistency at a higher level. Indeed, they constitute a unique kind of solution to conflicting human tendencies, for the contemplation of contrary proverbs leads to a moderation of impulses. Knowing both "Look before you leap" and "He who hesitates is lost," one is inclined to hesitate just long enough to look! And no doubt many young lovers have found a middle way between "Absence makes the heart grow fonder" and "Out of sight, out of mind." Farb reports a West African proverb exchange in which a Yoruba father cites a proverb to justify disciplining his child and is countered by the mother's citation of another proverb on tempering discipline with love.[9] He reports also that "proverbs and other wise sayings are central to the African judicial process, and litigants quote them to support their cases in much the same way that lawyers in European cultures cite legal precedents to bolster their arguments."[10] Reviewing uses of proverbs in Western culture, Taylor reports that "In the Renaissance men made collections entitled 'The Crossing of Proverbs,' that is to say, collections setting one proverb against another,"[11] Out of the clash of such contradictories, one supposes, emerged a sensible middle course, All these observations show how proverbs constitute a rich resource in situations of private or public deliberation. Their formal properties arrest attention, and thereby fulfill their function of inviting their users to weigh wisdom based on experience.

One has the impression that proverbs are not so widely used nowadays as once they were.[12] Perhaps this is because proverbs are more likely to appear in the utterance of older members of a community or family and the decline of the extended family has diminished their movement from generation to generation. Perhaps the youthful, hip, urban orientations of contemporary culture militate against the popular use of proverbs. As Aristotle observed, "The use of maxims is appropriate only to elderly men . . . For a young man to use them is—like telling stories—unbecoming; to use them in handling things in which one has no experience is silly and ill-bred: a fact sufficiently proved by the special fondness of country fellows for striking out maxims, and their readiness to air them."[13] Perhaps the decline in proverb use is simply due to changing fashions in expression. One compiler has suggested that the use of proverbs is a habit "of which, if we become alive to it, we should probably try to break ourselves, either from a striving after originality, or because sententiousness is one of the bugbears of the modern mind."[14]

Despite their apparent decline, however, proverbs are not entirely absent from current speech. The late President Lyndon Johnson was reported to be a great user of proverbs, often earthy, but effective.[15] Senator Sam Ervin delighted his colleagues and the public audience with folksy observations during the Watergate hearings. A recent press release from Senator William Proxmire's office concerning the Bicentennial Youth Debates made wry use of the proverb "Hope, which makes a good breakfast, is a sorry supper."[16] Another public official whose effectiveness owes much to proverbial expression is Jim Kemp, a director of the Chicago area Regional Transportation Authority, whose "Kempisms" were cited by his colleagues as effective means of persuasion. Examples include "Hard times will make a monkey eat red pepper" and "That which goes around the devil's back must buckle under his belly."[17]

Reflection on everyday experience will no doubt recall many instances in which the key words of a proverb are cited in everyday conversation: "The grass is always greener . . . ," "Don't count your chickens . . . ," "A bird in the hand . . . " The truncated form suggests how completely these proverbs have been integrated into thought patterns. Finally, we should observe that proverbs, or candidates for proverb status, are constantly being created. Of today's pithy sayings (e.g., "When you're hot, you're hot"; "What you sees is what you gets"; "Different strokes for different folks"), though most may soon be forgotten, a few may find places in the proverb collections of the future.

Though their popularity may wax and wane, proverbs are always available. So long as persons seek effective expression of the fruits of their experience, they will produce short, pithy sayings that other persons will remember and repeat. For, to cite one of Abraham Lincoln's favorites, "A word fitly spoken is like apples of gold in pictures of silver."[18]

Proverbs and Patterns of Argument

The method of this study was to search for proverbs in the English language that reflect or illustrate logical principles, and to match them to a conventional classification of patterns of reasoning or argument. Because it offered one convenient, clear, and comprehensive system, we followed the categories employed in the first edition of Ehninger and Brockriede's widely used textbook.[19] Like other forms of social knowledge, the use of a classificatory system is a matter of interpretation; the categories themselves may be construed in different ways, and many arguments (and proverbs) may be assigned to more than one category.[20] Therefore, we claim merely the sanction of well-established custom for our categories, and an intuitive reasonableness for the assignment of proverbs to categories. Our chief source of proverbs is *The Home Book of Proverbs, Maxims and Familiar Phrases*, which has been described as the largest collection in the English language.[21]

Substantive Argument

Sign. Aristotle believed that all rhetorical argument is based on probabilities and signs.[22] Undoubtedly, most reasoning and argument begins with some perception of the outward appearances of phenomena. When arguers take such perceptions as signs of something else and draw conclusions accordingly, they reason from sign.[23] Perhaps because such mental processes are so fundamentally necessary, a large number of proverbs deal with them. Although we found few proverbs that discuss the mode of reasoning explicitly, dozens embody the principle of reasoning from signs. A few examples are,

> A man is known by the company he keeps. (387–0)
> The bird is known by its note. (177–8)
> The empty vessel makes the greatest sound (677–0)
> Fraud and Deceit are always in Haste. (886–6)

The largest number of those proverbs we have assigned to the topic of reasoning from sign have to do with potential fallacies. Examining them before considering proverbs that suggest reliable ways of inferring from signs may be instructive. Many proverbs warn that appearances are deceiving (83–2); therefore: "In appearances place no trust" (82–4). Variations on this theme abound: "You can't judge a horse by its harness (82–3); "All that glistreth is not gold" (991–0); "The handsomest flower is not the sweetest" (835–5); "Men's characters are not always written on their foreheads" (82–4); and "None can guess the jewel by the casket" (82–2).

Many proverbs caution against hasty sign reasoning about human character. The familiar observation that "Clothes make the man" (367–5) may be interpreted as a reflection on the way things are rather than the way they should be. For the wise know, "It's not the gay coat makes the gentlemen" (373–7). Even sacred cloth may mislead: "The hood makes not the monk" (1620–6) and "Many wear God's cloth that know not their Master" (363–9). Not only character, but other human capacities may be misjudged from outward signs. Thus, "Many can pack [shuffle] the cards that cannot play" (285–5); "Not every man is a huntsman who can blow the horn" (81–3); and "They that are booted are not always ready" (221–4).

Finally, we note proverbs that caution against careless sign reasoning about phenomena other than human character and capacity. Examples include, "There is not always good Cheer where the Chimney smoaks" (330–1) and "Brag's a good Dog, but dares not bite" (229–6).

Through all of the examples cited so far run certain underlying contrasts: appearance vs. essence, outward show vs. inner reality, and the like. Perhaps this lies behind the common person's version of the "philosophical pairs" that Perelman and Olbrechts-Tyteca invoke to explain dissociative reasoning and arguments.[24] Certain proverbs teach by example that a shrewd attention to contrasting concepts (e.g., general-particular, symbol-thing, appearance-reality) may save the reasoner from faulty inferences based on merely accidental connections. The same contrasting pairs have a role in those proverbs which suggest how one may go about reasoning from signs more reliably. The appearance-reality pair predominates. One proverb teaches that "A common jar often holds noble nectar" (82–3); therefore, "Do not look upon the vessel, but upon that which it contains" (78–7). One may sometimes discover that "A Saint in the Face may be a Fiend at Heart" (80–0).

In the field of human character, a familiar contrast is invoked between word and deed: "Actions speak louder than words" (11–7); "I have always thought the actions of men the best interpreters of their thoughts" (11–11); "The fole is knowen by his wordis and the wiseman by his werkis" (858–6). Here, then, is clear instruction to base sign reasoning on firm grounds: look beneath the surface; seek the essence of things; and, in judging human character, place more reliance on what persons do than on what they say.

Sign reasoning may also be legitimate when based on some understanding of the nature of things or the necessary connections among species. Examples that convey those notions include: "The best carpenters make the fewest chips" (289–9); "By the Husk you may guess at the Nut" (82–2); "In seeing the stubble one may judge what the grain was" (305–7).

As the number of examples may suggest, sign reasoning is the subject of many proverbs. As we hypothesized, proverbs were found which illustrate the pattern in themselves, others point to legitimate grounds for sign reasoning, and still others warn of potential fallacies.

Cause. A consideration of sign reasoning inevitably leads to relations of cause and effect, for on deeper analysis many things taken as "signs" turn out to be effects of that which they signify. The usual distinction drawn in textbooks is based on the notion that sign reasoning draws an inference from the regularly recurring connection between two phenomena without analyzing the nature of the connection. Cause-to-effect and effect-to-cause reasoning go a step further to posit a definite causal link between the phenomena.[25]

Among the most familiar proverbs are several that exhibit cause-effect reasoning. So familiar are some that they are frequently expressed in condensed form: "Spare the rod . . ." (344–8) and "As the twig is bent . . ." (2371–7). Other examples range from

"Chaunge of pasture makth fat calves" (314–4) to "He who lies down with dogs, will rise with fleas" (610–7).

Reasoning from effects to causes is also well illustrated by proverbs, e.g., "Where there is smoke, there must be fire" (812–1) and "Where bees are there is honey" (144–8).

A few proverbs comment on causal relations in a more abstract way. That every effect has a cause is expressed in the saying "A bell never rings by accident" (164–2). Another abstract observation occurs in a proverbial statement that may be of learned origin: "The cause having ceased, the effect ceases also" (305–4). Regardless of the origin of this particular form of expression, however, the idea is a common one, a part of the ordinary person's understanding of rational connections.

Comparatively few, also, are the proverbs warning against fallacious causal reasoning—perhaps because most of the errors in causal reasoning stem from substantive ignorance or misunderstanding rather than from formal characteristics of such inferences. There is thus little scope for general cautions. The fallacy most commonly discussed in textbooks is the *post hoc, ergo propter hoc* argument: "after this, therefore because of this." It is represented in proverb lore by "It does not follow that the archer aimed, because the arrow hit" (90–2).

Parallel Case. Reasoning or argument based on parallels may be abstractly characterized as follows: Case A is known to have feature *x*; case B is similar to case A in essential respects; therefore, case B will be found to have *x* also.[26] This is the sort of argument that Aristotle meant by "example" (i.e., *paradigma*), the direct comparison of two cases, situations, events, or entities.[27] In respect to this pattern, we find again proverbs which embody and illustrate the type, others that suggest legitimate grounds for such comparisons, and still others that caution against the pitfalls of such arguments.

The most familiar example of a proverb that embodies the principle of parallel cases occurs in several variant forms, e.g., "Sauce for the goose is sauce for the gander" (1011–6) and "As is the Gander, so is the Goose" (1011–3). "As like as two peas in a pod" (1427–8) and "Like father, like sonne; like mother, like daughter" (771–0) also invoke family affiliation as a basis for comparison. What makes parallel case arguments legitimate, it appears, is the ability to assign the items compared to the same class at an appropriate level of judgment. Thus, king and commoner may be compared as men, for both "put their pants on one leg at a time" (uncollected). On the other hand, for some purposes, the proverb holds, "Purple must be compared with purple [i.e., royalty with royalty]" (390–7). The notion has its philosophical correlate in a rule of formal justice, as explicated by Perelman: *"those who are essentially similar should be treated alike."*[28] This is one of several instances in which proverb makers and users appear to have found by experience conclusions that the learned have reached through a philosophic analysis of concepts.

The caveats that apply to parallel cases are of two kinds. One includes the general objection to ill-founded parallels: "Comparisons are odious" (390–9) and "Comparisonis do ofttime greate grieuance" (391–1). The other harks back to sign reasoning, cautioning a close attention to essential characteristics rather than appearances as the proper basis for comparison. Thus, "The fox changes his fur, but not his nature" (882–9) and a wolf in sheep's clothing should not be treated as one would a lamb (2555–2).

Finally, a few proverbs provide neat expressions with which to expose faulty comparisons: "No more lyke than an apple to an oyster" (87–2); "I know chese from chalke" (310–8); and "As analogous as Chalk and Cheese, or a Cat and a Cartwheel" (310–9).

Analogy. Argument from analogy and parallel cases are often confounded in texts on practical reasoning and logic. We will not argue the issue here, but merely follow Ehninger and Brockriede's categories.[29] Unlike the direct comparison which underlies parallel cases, analogies are based on a four-part resemblance of relationships: A is to B as C is to D. This is what Aristotle meant by *analogia*, a term first used to denote geometric proportions.[30] A small but significant set of proverbs embody, and thus teach, the principle of analogy. Examples include: "Grace is to the body what judgment is to the mind" (1018–13); "A great Man and a great River are often ill Neighbours" (1029–17); "Fish see the bait, but not the hook; men see the profit but not the peril" (1892–13); and "A garden must be looked unto and dressed as the body" (935–15). Aside from the general cautions about comparisons, we found no proverbs dealing pointedly with fallacious analogical reasoning.

This may be the place to comment on the important connection between analogical reasoning and proverbs in general. By their very nature, proverbs entail analogical reasoning. Because of the implicit inferential pattern underlying the utterance of most proverbs in a given situation, one can neither apply a proverb nor understand its application without at least an intuitive grasp of the logic of analogy. For example, a sage who reminds a parent, "As the twig is bent, so grows the tree," implies an argument based on an analogical warrant: The relationship between discipline of one's child and the way the child turns out in maturity is essentially similar to the relation between nurture of a seedling and the shape of the mature tree. In quasi-mathematical form, discipline : adult : : nurture : tree. Although some proverbs may be used in a strictly literal sense (e.g., "a stitch in time" may apply to sewing), they are more often metaphorical and the logical structure underlying metaphor is analogy. Hence, proverbs have the effect of reaching that particular pattern of reasoning in a unique and general way.

Generalization. An argument by generalization moves from observations about a number of specific instances to a conclusion about the larger class to which the instances belong.[31] Much of the learning that takes place in early life is the result of the generalization process, as when a child learns that "hot" means the same unpleasant thing whether applied to a dish or a radiator. Proverbs deal explicitly with this experience in "The burnt child dreads the fire" (727–2), and more generally in "Once bitten [burnt], twice shy" (725–8). In both proverbs the mental habit of generalizing is explicitly recognized. The rule in generalization is that "Experience is the teacher of all things" (724–5), but there are several caveats against hasty generalization. These cautions are found in "Once does not make a custom" (477–3), "One flower makes no garland" (835–12), and, finally, "One swallow does not make summer" (2253–5).

Despite the caveat against hasty generalization, however, in dealing with people, proverb lore seems to counsel a strict standard. "False in one thing, false in all" (751–6) is the rule. There are many other examples, both from the "guard your own name" point of view, and from the point of view of the critical social actor, "He that deceives me once, shame fall him; if he deceives me twice, shame fall me" (533–3).

Finally, two additional interesting observations are available in proverbs on generalization. The first is a comment on a sort of stimulus generalizaton. Sometimes it is difficut to determine the cause of a bad experience, and so "He that hath been bitten by a serpent is afraid of a rope" (727–5), and, similarly, "A dog once scalded fears cold water" (727–3). The second observation is that, although experience may be the best teacher, the errors which are most instructive are also often injurious. And so, "Wise men learn by other men's mistakes; fools by their own" (855–2).

Classification. The argument from classification holds that what is true of a class will also be true of the individual members of that class.[32] People expect, for instance, that one politician or rock star will share the characteristics of politicians or rock stars in general. Thus, when the argument from classification is used in proverbs, an expressed or implied identification is posited between the subject of the proverb and the referent in real life. In order to make use of "You can't teach an old dog new tricks" (615–6), someone must be identified as the old dog. Or, in Plautus' "Lover, lunatic. (Amans, amens)" (1486–12), there must be a commonly understood subject—a lover.

Proverbs which deal with classifications should be easily categorized by the label or type with which they deal. Thus many proverbs deal with "thieves," such as "When false thieves fall out true men come to their own" (2298–2) and "Save a thief from the gallows and he'll cut your throat" (2299–9). Similarly, the body of proverbs about "wolves" includes "Wolves may lose their Teeth, but not their Nature" (2553–1), "The sheep are happier of themselves, than under care of the wolves" (2088–6), and, one of the most famous of the proverbial phrases, "wolf in sheep's clothing" (2555–2 in variant forms). The "thief" proverbs may have literal or metaphoric referents, but the "wolf" in the second group is almost certainly metaphorical.

Classification is especially important since the name that people make for themselves (i.e., how they are classified) will determine the attitudes of others toward them. Pliny the Younger observed, "I have said everything when I have named the man" (1653–11). Many other proverbs attest to the power of names, some seriously—"Give a dog an ill name and hang him" (605–8), and some wryly—"He that hath the name to be an early riser may sleep till noon" (1656–3). The combination of importance and permanence makes naming or classifying a serious business, one to be treated with care. Names can change people: "Call one a thief and he will steal" (2296–11); and they can bring dire consequences: "A man at whom everybody points dies without being ill" (1658–2).

Proverbial lore thus recognizes arguments from classification as an important type, and provides some general advice for dealing with them. On the one hand, one is admonished to look to essential nature, as in these examples: "Of an eufll father commeth neuer a good childe" (1134–8); "What is hatcht by a hen, will scrape like a hen" (1131–6); and "Plant the Crab-Tree where you will, it will never bear Pippins" (2368–8). On the other hand, one is urged to beware of hasty classifying, for "Many a good coowe hath an euille caulfe" (1135–2) and "All that breed in the Mud are not Eels" (239–3).

Statistics. Ehninger and Brockriede's final type of substantive arguments are those based on statistics.[33] Not surprisingly, few proverbs deal with statistical arguments. Until modern times, statistics have not been commonly employed in everyday discussions. The few proverbs on the subject are all of recent origin, and all are negative. The warnings include "You may prove anything by figures" (802–1); "Figures won't lie, but liars will figure" (802–1); "Figures are like alienists [psychiatrists]; they will testify for either side" (uncollected); and, finally, "There are three kinds of lies: lies, damned lies, and statistics" (802–1). These biting comments seem to exhaust the commentary of our source on the subject.

Authoritative Argument

The argument from authority[34] receives more attention, direct and indirect, in proverb lore than any other argument type, perhaps because everyday argument frequently hinges more on the reputation of the speaker than on the soundness of the argument. In many instances, sign and generalization arguments may be intermediate steps in a reasoning chain which will arrive at a conclusion concerning a putatively authoritative source. When a proverb states that "'Tis character persuades, not empty words" (318–7), the point is that the credibility of the source is the primary component of authority, regardless of what type of argument is being made. People will believe what is unlikely from one they trust before they will believe what is likely from one they do not. Proverbs argue that good authority should be heeded, but that much authority is not as good as it seems.

Proverbs themselves, of course, are arguments from authority, and illustrate some of the difficulties with such arguments. A proverb may, for example, be prefaced with some phrase such as "They say . . . " or "You know what they say." These phrases invoke the common acceptance which buttresses the acceptability of proverbs and without which they lose their authority. When the preface "They say . . . " is challenged by "*Who* says?," the answer is necessarily insufficient. Either one accepts the "they say" convention and gives ear to the wisdom in the proverb, or one does not. The person who will not accept a proverb as authoritative must be convinced of the soundness of the advice by means of some other argument.

Proverbs that promote acceptance of authority fall into two categories. First is a group that admonishes one to take and heed counsel. The most familiar of these is "Two heads are better than one" (1096–1). But there are many others: "Do not anything without taking counsel" (429–9); "He that will not be counselled, cannot be helped" (430–5); "Good counsel never comes amiss" (431–7); and "He that refuseth to buy counsel cheap, shall buy repentance dear" (433–1). A second group of proverbs points out that the experience of others is valuable, and often less painful than that acquired first-hand. Examples of the "value experience" type include " 'Tis good to follow the old fox" (880–8); "A new broom sweeps clean, but the old one finds the corners" (247–5); "The bark of an old dog should be heeded" (612–11); "One Nestor is worth two Ajaxes" (430–9); and "Wise men learn by others harms, fools by their own" (725–0).

The proverbs which repudiate authority do so in many ways, for many factors affect credibility. The skeptical group includes "The devil can cite Scripture for his purpose" (566-2); "Believe none of what you hear, and only half of what you see" (uncollected, but attributed to Mark Twain); "Children are to be deceived with comfits, and men with oaths" (532–5); "Every cook praises his own broth" (420–3); "False folk should have many witnesses" (751–7); "Approve not of him who commands all you say" (827–12); "It is easy when we are well to give good advice to the sick" (23–10); and "He who accuses himself cannot be accused by another" (8–7). Proverbs also comment upon many special cases. Authorities may be impeached for several shortcomings, such as lack of impartiality—"It depends upon whose ox is gored" (291–3); perceptual difficulty—"In the kingdom of the blind the one-eyed man is king" (197–8); failure in managing one's own affairs—"Physician, heal thyself" (599–4); and base motive—"He gives advice such as the cat gives to the mouse" (22–12). This list could be extended, as could the list of proverbs that comment on authority by means of sign arguments, generalizations, and others.

Motivational Argument

The final argument type in Ehninger and Brockriede's scheme is motivational proof,[35] consisting of appeals based on the audience's values, motives, and desires. Such arguments are sound when the underlying values are rationally justified, unsound when they are warranted by no more than blind prejudice or passion. As Perelman and Olbrechts-Tyteca observe, "values enter, at some stage or other, into every argument," for "One appeals to values in order to induce the hearer to make certain choices rather than others and, most of all, to justify those choices."[36] Conventional wisdom, too, recognizes that "We may convince others by our arguments; but we can only persuade them by their own" (91–9).

Proverbs give evidence that emotions and desire are potent influences by including so many cautions against giving the passions free rein, and by pointing out the dangers of being carried away by the emotional appeals of others. "Rule your desires lest your desires rule you" (553–13) and "His own desire leads every man" (553–9) are general warnings about the power of unreason, and there are many others, e.g., "You will conquer more wisely by reason than by passion" (1941–9) and "When the judgment's weak the prejudice is strong" (1872–11). These injunctions warn against hasty or ill-considered actions, and against allowing emotions to rule over reason. The majority of proverbs which deal with this subject are admonitions of this sort, perhaps because it is hardly necessary to encourage people to do what they normally do anyway. People's opinions (of which values are a substantial part) have much to do with their actions, for "Opinion governs all mankind" (1721-0).

Proverbs do not offer much about the formal properties of motivational arguments, but some yield incisive comments on specific cases. It is said, for instance, of the use of flattery (a sycophantic use of a motivational appeal) that "There is no remedy for the flatterer's bite" (826-11). If a person finds "support" for some action already decided on, the proverb points out that motivations can be rationalized in many ways: "He who wishes to kill his dog can always find symptoms of rabies" (604-9). Finally, one should note that motives and values are addressed in a more specific and substantive fashion by the thousands of proverbs that comment on the good and bad objects of human striving. The proverbs that endorse health, thrift, sobriety, and so forth, all legitimize specific motivational proofs.

General Rational Principles

In addition to proverbs that illustrate or comment on specific patterns of reasoning, many others articulate more general principles about intelligent or reasonable behavior. They occur in such numbers and variety that we are able to give only a small sampling here.

In the first place, we note numerous proverbs that comment on features of human psychology that may adversely affect reasoning. The most general of these observe that folly is a universal danger: "If folly were grief, every house would weep" (839-10); "Folly is the product of all countries and ages" (840-5); and "We have all been fools once in our lives" (847-3). More specifically, proverbs warn of the danger of wishful thinking: "What ardently we wish, we soon believe" (161-6); and "A fool believes the thing he would have so" (851-8). Or, they caution against unseemly haste: "Folly rushes in through the door, for fools are always bold" (850–4); "He speeds to repentance who judges hastily" (1280–14); and "He that looks not before, finds himself behind" (865–14). Even the pitfall of mistaking the symbol for the thing finds its proverbial expression in "He who cannot beat the ass, beats the saddle" (105-4).

The conditions of belief and doubt, credulity and skepticism, are discussed in a number of proverbs. They present another interesting illustration of contraries that, taken together, suggest the wisdom of the middle way. Perhaps because "It is easier to believe than to doubt" (162-13), humanity is reminded that "naught is of more service to mankind than a prudent distrust" (592-9) and "He will never do well who easily believes" (452-15). Lest one err by an excess of doubt, however, the contrary proverb holds: "Better be too credulous than too skeptical" (452-12).

Reason and good judgment are the subjects of several proverbs, as in the following examples in which they are contrasted with such unreflective sources of belief as faith, passion, and custom:

> Conscience without judgment is superstition. (405-6)
> The Way to see by Faith is to shut the Eye of Reason. (744-9)
> Contradiction should awaken Attention, not Passion. (416-5)
> Custom without Reason is but an ancient Error. (476-2)

The conditions for the exercise of judgment are touched on in a number of proverbs. One of these is calmness in the face of provocation: "When angry count 10 before you speak. If very angry 100" (67-2). And in argument one should remember that "A soft answer turneth away wrath" (72-13). Reason is also served by a realistic outlook. Because "Facts are stubborn things" (742-3), one must face them squarely. For, "What can't be cured, must be endured" (683-12); "You can't make an omelette without breaking eggs" (671-7); and "In al gardeins, some flowers, some weedes" (936-3).

A necessary part of sound deliberation is to seek appropriate counsel, for "Two eyes can see more than one" (730–3). Hence, the following proverbs: "The first degree of folly is to hold one's self wise, the second to profess it, the third to despise counsel" (839–11) and "Verily, he hazardeth too much, who reposeth himselfe in his own judgement" (1279-9). The need for counsel leads to a consideration of means of deliberation, and one of these, debate, presents another interesting example of contradictory sayings: "Debate destroys despatch" (528-1) and "There is danger in delay" (546-7); but "Swift decisions are not sure" (535-3) and, therefore, "Decide no suit until you have heard both sides" (1281-14).

Finally, a few proverbs recognize the pragmatic character of human reasonings and the field dependence of the standards that apply to them. In the first place, proverbs recognize that human experience is not constrained by absolute laws, that "Circumstances alter cases" (356-8). Though proverbs embody general rules to live by, they acknowledge exceptions or reservations that apply to those rules. We have already noted the "crossing of proverbs," the contrary sayings that serve as a check on one another. There exist, also, proverbs meant as specific exceptions to general rules. Thus, fools are generally to be avoided, but "A fool's bolt may sometimes hit the mark" (824-7). And, although good counsel is a valuable commodity, "Too much Consulting confounds" (429-10). The variability of custom, and hence of appropriate behavior, is recognized in "Every land has its own laws, customs, and usages" (433-5). In short, proverbs of this kind call one's attention to specific situations as the pragmatic grounding of reasoning, and thereby insist on attention to the material context in which an inference is made. One consequence is the need to qualify one's conclusions, for "The only certainty is that nothing is certain" (309-7) and "All wholesale judgments are loose and imperfect" (1280-6). The fault of overstated claims is explicitly noted: "Blame-all and praise-all are two blockheads" (457-7). "Positive men err most of any men" (308-18), and "Positiveness is an Evidence of poor Judgment" (308-18). The obvious solution is a sensible caution in drawing conclusions: "Almost and well nigh saves many a lie" (53-3). The foregoing proverbs provide striking confirmation, in the wisdom of the common folk, of Toulmin's analysis of the substantive character of ordinary arguments.[37] Apparently, ordinary people have intuitively grasped what Toulmin demonstrated philosophically, namely, that the historical, situational, pragmatic character of ordinary arguments requires attention to all of their substantive features if they are to be adequately understood and criticized. The proverbs in this paragraph speak directly to the need to recognize reservations and qualifications as critical parts of an inference process.

Conclusion

In answer to the main question posed in this investigation, we conclude that the proverbs of Anglo-American culture do indeed illustrate a significant number of logical principles. Moreover, our specific hypotheses were broadly confirmed. Although the claim cannot be made with the same force for each specific argument type, it is generally true that proverbs (1) reflect an implicit typology of patterns of reasoning or argument, (2) illustrate and comment upon legitimate patterns of inference, and (3) caution against general and specific fallacies. Taken as a body of conventional wisdom, proverbs serve the common run of humanity in the same way that a textbook on logic or argumentation serves the formally educated. Proverbs offer a general set of rational strategies for deliberating about life's problems. We found a fairly close match with Ehninger and Brockriede's categories of inferential patterns, but it is likely that the material might have been organized differently so as to correlate with almost any other textbook on argumentation or practical logic.

Clearly, of course, the logical principles illustrated by proverbs lack the systematic elegance of a textbook or theoretical treatise. Some types of inference come in for a much greater share of attention than others; some important logical principles are neglected (e.g., formal validity); and inconsistencies between contrary proverbs are left unexplained. The probable cause of this difference is that proverbs have developed empirically, each one coined more or less independently in response to specific situations. It is rather remarkable, therefore, that a collection can be made that so closely approximates the abstract and theoretical analysis of a learned treatise or a textbook. If this collection of proverbs can be regarded as representing the logic of the common folk, scholars should be heartened by the degree of rational competence suggested.

Even more important than the discovery of proverbs that reflect specific logical principles, perhaps, is the discovery that proverbial wisdom may help to illuminate the ordinary person's understanding of the nature of popular argument. We have not attempted to explicate the categories and details of that understanding here, although the subject deserves discussion. To indicate the sort of question that might be pursued, however, we suggest reflection upon all the proverbial statements that bear on authority, credibility, and character. That body of traditional wisdom seems to support Aristotle's observation that the speaker's "character may almost be called the most effective means of persuasion he possesses."[38]

Likewise, we have noted in passing some correlations between proverbial principles and notions grounded in philosophical analyses of argument, e.g., Perelman's "rule of justice" and "philosophical pairs." These incidental observations suggest that it might be fruitful to come at the study of proverbs from a different angle in order to discover the assumptions that inform general bodies of proverbial wisdom, for example, on the nature and value of advice or of deliberation or of testimony. Furthermore, such an investigation could potentially yield categories to facilitate cross-cultural study of proverbs bearing on attitudes toward rational processes in general. (E.g., would a culture that sets great store by *machismo* also value counsel highly?)

Others have recognized the value of the study of proverbs as an entree to cultural studies generally. We submit here that proverbs may also illuminate the uses of argument, and the character of socio-logic.

Notes

1. For a review of this position see Mary Henle, "On the Relation Between Logic and Thinking," *Psychological Review*, 69 (1962), 366–78.

2. Jesse G. Delia reviewed the evidence for that view of psycho-logic in an early essay: "The Logic Fallacy, Cognitive Theory, and the Enthymeme: A Search for the Foundations of Reasoned Discourse," *Quarterly Journal of Speech*, 56 (1970), 140–48.

3. Delia, for example, no longer equates rationality with natural cognitive processes as he did in the work previously cited. See his more recent article: Jesse G. Delia, "Constructivism and the Study of Human Communication," *Quarterly Journal of Speech*, 63 (1977), 66–83; see esp. p. 82.

4. Thomas B. Farrell, "Knowledge, Consensus, and Rhetorical Theory," *Quarterly Journal of Speech*, 62 (1976), 9.

5. *The American College Dictionary*, ed. Clarence L. Barnhart (New York: Harper and Brothers, 1957).

6. Kenneth Burke, *The Philosophy of Literary Form*, 2nd ed. (Baton Rouge: Louisiana State Univ. Press, 1967), pp. 1–2.

7. Archer Taylor, "The Study of Proverbs," *Proverbium*, 1 (1965), 7.

8. Roger D. Abrahams, "Introductory Remarks to a Rhetorical Theory of Folklore," *Journal of American Folklore*, 81 (1968), 146.

9. Peter Farb, *Word Play* (New York: Bantam, 1975), p. 119.

10. Ibid., p. 118.

11. Taylor, p. 7.

12. The only relevant study we have found supports that conclusion, but it is rather dated: William Albig, "Proverbs and Social Control," *Sociology and Social Research*, 15 (July-Aug. 1931), 527–35.

13. Aristotle, *Rhetoric*, trans. W. Rhys Roberts, in *The Basic Works of Aristotle*, ed. Richard McKeon (New York: Random House, 1941), 1395a 2–7.

14. Janet E. Heseltine, "Introduction," *The Oxford Dictionary of English Proverbs* (Oxford: Clarendon, 1935), p. vii.

15. David Halberstam, *The Best and the Brightest* (Greenwich, Ct.: Fawcett, 1969), pp. 528–29.

16. Senator William Proxmire, press release, 22 March 1976.

17. Larry Ingrassia, "Kempisms: Lively Listening," *Chicago Sun Times*, 25 Apr. 1976, p. 2.

18. On Lincoln's use of this proverb, see Harry V. Jaffa, "Expediency and Morality in the Lincoln-Douglas Debates," *The Anchor Review*, No. 2 (Garden City, N.Y.: Doubleday, 1957), p. 199.

19. Douglas Ehninger and Wayne Brockriede, *Decision by Debate* (New York: Dodd, Mead, 1963): see chapters 10–12.

20. Douglas Ehninger and Wayne Brockriede, *Decision by Debate,* 2nd ed. (New York: Harper & Row, 1978), pp. 43–44, 89–91. The changes in classification in the second edition are mainly simplifications by combination; we believe they do no violence to the findings we based on the more differentiated categories of the first edition.

21. *The Home Book of Proverbs, Maxims and Familiar Phrases,* sel. and arr. Burton Stevenson (New York: Macmillan, 1948). Citations are by page and entry number, e.g., (203-8) refers to the eighth numbered entry on page 203.

22. *Rhetoric,* 1357a 30–35.

23. Ehninger and Brockriede. p. 131. This and subsequent references are to the first edition.

24. Ch. Perelman and L. Olbrechts-Tyteca, *The New Rhetoric: A Treatise on Argumentation,* trans. John Wilkinson and Purcell Weaver (Notre Dame: Univ. of Notre Dame Press, 1969). Part Three, Chapter 4.

25. Ehninger and Brockriede, pp. 131–32.

26. Ibid., pp. 139–42.

27. James S. Measell, "Classical Bases of the Concept of Analogy," *Journal of the American Forensic Association*, 10 (Summer 1973), 3–5.

28. Ch. Perelman, *The Idea of Justice and the Problem of Argument,* trans. John Petrie (London: Routledge & Kegan Paul, 1963), pp. 81–82.

29. Ehninger and Brockriede, pp. 139–44.

30. Measell, pp. 5 ff.

31. Ehninger and Brockriede, pp. 134–38.

32. Ibid., pp. 145–47.

33. Ibid., pp. 148–54.

34. For a discussion of this type of argument, see ibid., pp. 158–62.

35. Ibid., pp. 162–66.

36. Perelman and Olbrechts-Tyteca, p. 75.

37. Stephen Edelston Toulmin, *The Uses of Argument* (Cambridge: Cambridge Univ. Press, 1958). See especially chapter III.

38. *Rhetoric,* 1356a 13.

Uses of the Proverb in the Synoptic Gospels

*William A. Beardslee**

Because of the power of the proverb as a persuasive device, it should not be surprising to find proverbs in traditional political and religious rhetoric. Proverbs are an integral part of the so-called Wisdom Literature of the ancient Near East. There is a whole book of proverbs in the Old Testament *and, as the following essay by a professor of religion shows, proverbs are also a factor in the* New Testament. *For a sampling of the oldest recorded proverbs, see Edmund Gordon,* Sumerian Proverbs. Glimpses of Everyday Life in Ancient Mesopotamia *(Philadelphia, 1959).*

Today Christian theology is grappling again with the question of how to relate its perspective of faith, which is concrete and historical, to other perspectives from which men find meaning and express their deepest convictions. For a long time theology, and especially biblical theology, believed that it did not have to confront this problem. Men held that a directly kerygmatic or confessional approach was sufficient, and that the concrete historical standpoint of faith could simply speak for itself, without taking any account of other positions. Now we see the one-sidedness of a simply confessional approach, partly because such an approach has great difficulty in dealing seriously with the problem of hermeneutic: If the standpoint is simply given, it is hard

*Reprinted from *Interpretation. A Journal of Bible and Theology,* 24 (1970), 61–73.

to deal with the fact that with the passage of time standpoints change. Today we really cannot stand in the same "biblical" perspective as Jeremiah or Paul. Equally important in showing the one-sidedness of the confessional approach was its frequent failure to take its dialogue partners seriously. To the outsider, such a theological stance has often seemed to be one which could talk but could not listen.

In biblical theology the new interest in communication between the particular stance of the faith which is believed and other perspectives is shown in several important ways. One of the most important of these is the renewed interest in the wisdom tradition. Confessional theology and the theology of sacred history often found the Wisdom Literature to be almost an embarrassment. But wisdom has left extensive marks on the Law, the Prophets and even the cult; and in the New Testament its influence is particularly prominent in the Synoptic Gospels. Such a tradition has to be taken seriously. Its presence and influence can in large part be understood through the fact that in the Hebraic and Jewish world wisdom served precisely the function referred to above, that of building a bridge between the perspective of faith and the experience of men outside the circle of faith.

The interpretation of existence, through which a connection could be seen between a particular faith and the meanings found by other men, took place in two rather different ways in the Wisdom books, through practical wisdom and through speculative wisdom. Speculative wisdom, the Near Eastern precursor and background of philosophical speculation, attempted to grasp the meaning of increasingly wider circles of existence, and ultimately to grasp a vision of the whole. This side of the wisdom tradition was immensely important for Christian theology, particularly in providing christological categories. The early Christian faith in the universal significance of Christ was often expressed in terms taken from wisdom speculation: Logos, the wisdom of God. Speculative wisdom is not absent from the Synoptic Gospels. The interpretation of Christ in wisdom categories began very early, as early as the thinking presented in Q, where Christ is already seen as Wisdom or at least in wisdom terms.[1]

Despite the growing interest in speculative wisdom's contribution to early Christian theology and to Gnosticism, the present paper will be entirely directed to the proverb, an element from the other style of wisdom, practical wisdom. This is the style which is by far the more important in influencing the Synoptic Gospels. Matthew, Mark, and Luke, quite unlike later Christian theology, draw far more heavily on practical wisdom than on the speculative tradition. Practical wisdom, the older and less technical side of the tradition, simply looked at the events of a man's life for recurring patterns. This interest in the daily, human existence is characteristically shown in the Synoptics by the presence of the two wisdom forms, the proverb and the parable.

Recent study of the Synoptic Gospels has fixed a great deal of attention on the parables, and in particular on an analysis of how they "work,"how they make their point. Fuchs, Wilder, Jüngel, Linnemann, Robinson, Funk, and Via are among the names which suggest the concentration of attention on the parables in the attempt to move beyond positions established principally by Jülicher, Dodd, and Jeremias in clarifying the function of the parable.

In the meantime, the proverbs in the Synoptic Gospels have received comparatively little attention, though Bultmann studied them in detail; and the discovery of many Synoptic proverbs in the Gospel of Thomas has recently turned some attention to them.[2] It is easy to understand why this form has not attracted much attention. Parables are not unique in the Synoptics, but they are distinctive. It is not so easy, on the other hand, to point out any distinctive marks of the Synoptic proverbs or to move backward through the layers of Synoptic tradition and make a judgment about what was characteristic of the use of the proverb by Jesus himself. Furthermore, we are still in reaction against the "moralization" of the Synoptic kerygma, and any interpretation of the Gospels which tends to reduce their meaning to mere general moral truths—as Jülicher's interpretation of the parables tended to do, for instance—is anathema to contemporary interpreters.

The present paper takes the limited task of reflecting primarily on the form and function of proverbs in the Synoptic tradition. It will also glance at the historical problem of the relation of this proverbial tradition to Jesus, without undertaking the detailed form-critical analysis which this latter problem necessarily involves when carried through thoroughly.

It is clear that the proverb is a less definite form than the parable—less specific in its function and therefore more easily capable of being transferred from one setting to another, so that the proverb, for instance, appears frequently in apocalyptic and gnostic settings as well as in wisdom settings. Nonetheless it is a striking fact that proverbs are abundant in the Synoptics, not only in the sayings tradition common to Matthew and Luke, but also in Mark. Furthermore, despite the facts that (1) these proverbs have often been combined with prophetic-apocalyptic sayings and with legal sayings, and that (2) proverbial forms like the macarism or beatitude have been shifted from a wisdom framework to an eschatological one, it is worth noting how much of the old practical wisdom setting of the proverb remains in the Synoptic Gospels. There were strong factors leading toward a utilization of speculative wisdom traditions in early Christianity, in contrast to practical wisdom traditions. In spite of this trend, the Synoptic Gospels, and especially Q as the main deposit of wisdom traditions in the Gospels, are characterized by the strong predominance of practical wisdom, insofar as they are characterized by the presence of wisdom traditions. Although it is also true that the wisdom sayings have to some extent been given a specifically "religious" interpretation, even this tendency is sharply limited. Only a few of the sayings classified by Bultmann as wisdom sayings make any explicit reference to God or the Kingdom.[3] By contrast, such a common-sense document as *The Sentences of Sextus* is far more explicitly "religious."[4] This is not to suggest that the Synoptic proverbs are secular either in the sense of the secular strand in ancient Near Eastern wisdom or in the modern sense. Practical wisdom of the proverbial type was deeply fused with faith in the Jewish tradition, and this fusion continues in the Synoptics. But the dimension of faith does not cause God and religion to appear as a separate realm. The power of the orientation of practical wisdom in the Synoptic tradition is shown by the way in which a wisdom form such as the macarism or beatitude, though transferred to a prophetic or eschatological function, still retains its practical reference to the concrete behavior of a man among his fellow men.[5]

We may enter our discussion of how the proverb works with Bultmann's discussion of the subject.[6] He says that proverbs express general truths which can become the possession of the hearer, but that this is not the whole story; for in a particular concrete situation such a statement can lose its character of general truth and become an address to a particular person or group, qualifying the "now" of the person addressed. He points both to the coming of the Kingdom and to the encounter with opponents as elements in the situation of Jesus which could give concreteness and address-character to proverbial statements. We may take this as our starting point and work toward a further clarification.

In the first place, it is somewhat misleading to speak of the proverb as a statement of a general truth. It is a statement about a particular kind of occurrence or situation, an orderly tract of experience which can be repeated. In this sense, though it is not a narrative, the proverb implies a story, something that happens, the moves through a sequence in a way which can be known. The relation of the proverb to narrative can be illustrated by noting how motifs from the Old Testament proverbs are paralleled in some of the parables of Jesus:

Parable of the chief seats: (Luke 14: 7–11, itself provided with a typical proverbial summing up at the close)

Do not put yourself forward in the king's presence
. . . .
for it is better to be told, "Come up here,"
than to be put lower in the presence of the prince.
—Proverbs 25:6f.

Parable of the friend at midnight: (Luke 11:5–8)

Do not say to your neighbor, "Go and come again,
tomorrow I will give it"— when you have it with you.
—Proverbs 3:28

Parable of the two foundations: (Matt. 7:24–27 // Luke 6:47–49)

When the tempest passes, the wicked is no more.
but the righteous is established for ever.
—Proverbs 10:25; cf. 12:7

These thematic parallels, which could easily be extended to many other Synoptic parables, show the close connection between the proverb and the story—not, of course, the story of the group, but stories of a man's existence. But the main point to note is that while the proverb is a kind of generalization, it really is a prediscursive form of thought, and not a truly general statement. That is, what a collection of proverbs confronts one with is not a systematic general analysis of existence, but a cluster of insights. Part of the skill of the wise man is to know when it is time to use which insight. Cautious and middle-of-the-road as much proverbial wisdom is, it does all have what may be called this existential element, the necessity of confrontation in choosing what little story or little history applies to this particular case. Hans Heinrich Schmid has emphasized this aspect of wisdom in his recent book, which provides a useful corrective to an interpretation of wisdom as "nonhistorical."[7]

The result of the above section has been to relativize the contrast between generalization and confrontation. Even the most "cracker-barrel" type of wisdom has in it an element of confrontation, and correspondingly, the confrontation cannot meaningfully take place without some kind of field or background against which it sharpens a particular demand. The fact that the imperative and the question are basic proverbial forms, along with the most widely used form, the statement, indicates this confrontational challenge to insight and action in the proverb.

Though there are in Mark and Q (and in material peculiar to Luke and Matthew) examples of proverbs which express a rather general folk wisdom, with its rather relaxed and sometimes even resigned attitude toward the making of choices, it is evident that in the most characteristic Synoptic sayings this wisdom is immensely concentrated and intensified. The primary means of intensification are paradox and hyperbole.

Paradox is related to the antithetical formulations which are so widespread in proverbial literature. We can bypass the antithesis between two different types of man or existence, as in Proverbs 10:1: "A wise son makes a glad father, but a foolish son is a sorrow to his mother." The kind of antithesis which provides the background for the Synoptic paradox is the antithesis which expresses a reversal of situation. The story which lies behind the proverb is a story of reversal of fortune. This is also a very ancient proverbial form. Probably its original form, and certainly a very ancient widespread usage, was the function of expressing the disastrous consequence of exceeding one's role. "He that exalts himself shall be humbled," in common sense wisdom is a warning against what the Greeks called *hybris*. Don't step out of place. Similar formulations appear, for instance, in a Babylonian source from about 1440 B.C. (in form these particular sayings are derived from the "omen"): "If (he thinks), 'I am heroic,' he will be shamed; if (he thinks), 'I am weak,' he will become mighty."[8] These proverbs presuppose an order, and warn against transgressing it. Of this type we may cite such Synoptic proverbs as:

> Everyone who exalts himself will be humbled, and he who humbles himself will be exalted (Luke 14:11; cf. Luke 18:14; Matt. 23:12).
>
> Many that are first will be last (Mark 10:31; cf. Matt. 20:16; Luke 13:30).
>
> What does it profit a man, to gain the whole world and forfeit his life? (Mark 8:36 par.).
>
> Whoever would be great among you must be your servant, and whoever would be first among you must be slave of all (Mark 10:43–44 par.).

Now we come to a saying which I classify as a paradox rather than an antithesis:

> Whoever loses his life will preserve it (Luke 17:33; cf. Mark 8:35 par.; John 12:25).

Here the antithesis is so sharp that it can be rightly called paradox. But note that these sayings have been arranged in a kind of ascending scale of sharpness of contrast, so that one can say that gaining the whole world and losing one's life, or becoming servant of all, is paradox as well. But, at any rate, with the final saying we have reached the distinctive intensification of proverbial wisdom in the Synoptic tradition. Here the reversal situation is so sharp that the imagination is jolted out of its vision of a continuous connection between one situation and the other.

The paradox of intensified antithesis is putting pressure on the very presupposition on which the clusters of wisdom-insights had been gathered together. This presupposition is the project of making a continuous whole out of one's existence. All the antithetical sayings about reversal of status involve some shaking up of this project, but the final one in the series involves such a paradox that the visible or, better, the conscious continuity of the project is done away. You may humble yourself with an eye to being exalted later on, but so far as the conscious field of decision is concerned, it is difficult to hold in view the possibility of later gaining one's life while casting it away.

Nonetheless, the saying is a paradox and not just a negation of the project of making a whole out of one's existence, since it affirms that in spite of all, life is conferred through this paradoxical route.

For the purpose of classifying proverbial sayings, we have defined paradox in a very specific way, as an intensification of the "reversal of status" type of antithesis which is widely known in proverbial literature. We could define paradox more broadly, but instead choose for our broader term, "hyperbole." Here we can include a wide range of intensified or exaggerated language. Once again, the phenomenon is a widespread one in proverbial literature, as one can easily discover by looking at the many parallels to Synoptic proverbial sayings. Though these sayings fall into a variety of types, it is easy to rank them again in some kind of rough scale of intensity or exaggeration:

> Foxes have holes, and birds of the air have nests; but the Son of man has nowhere to lay his head (Matt. 8:20 par. Luke 9:58).
>
> Leave the dead to bury their own dead (Matt. 8:22 par. Luke 9:60).
>
> If you have faith as a grain of mustard seed, you will say to this mountain, "Move hence to yonder place," and it will move (Matt. 17:20; cf. Luke 17:6; Mark 11:23; Matt. 21:21).
>
> It is easier for a camel to go through the eye of a needle than for a rich man to enter the kingdom of God (Mark 10:25 par.).

These hyperbolic passages reach their distinctive intensification in some of the longer wisdom poems of the Sermon on the Mount from which we can cite only one sample:

> Love your enemies, do good to those who hate you (Luke 6:27; cf. Matt. 5:44).

In terms of its role in proverbial wisdom generally, it is often the case that hyperbole is associated with a kind of sardonic humor at the fate of the other fellow. Though I think that the question of humor in the Gospels has not been well treated, I am not going to try to enter into that subject here. In the Synoptic Gospels there is little of this sardonic humor which distances itself from the other whose fate is depicted in the proverb—though it can be seen in such a saying (not strictly proverbial) as: "You blind guides, straining out a gnat and swallowing a camel!" (Matt. 23:24). On the whole, however, it is clear that the role of humor to provide distance, so characteristic of much wisdom, is not characteristic of the Synoptic proverbs; and this is not surprising, since distance is usually associated with moderation and with retaining a self-image rather than with the coming of a new self-image. In the Synoptics, hyperbole is used, like paradox, to jolt the hearer out of the project of making a continuity of his life. "Love your enemies" illustrates this, and the form in which this saying appears in the Didache (1:3) illustrates the tendency of wisdom to draw even such an hyperbolic saying back into the continuity of the project of life: Love your enemies and you will have no enemy.

From the above sketch we conclude that while many of the proverbial sayings in the Synoptics are general enough that they do not offer any distinctive clues to the specific style of life being advocated in them, the proverb does have a distinctive usage in the Synoptics in which paradox and hyperbole challenge the typical proverbial stance of making a continuous project out of one's life, but a usage which paradoxically views this challenge as itself the way of life. For the reflective interpreter, this use of paradox raises the question To what extent can the disjunctive "jolt" or reorientation demanded by the paradox be retrospectively seen in a larger coherent framework, and to what extent must it remain as an abrupt break in perception?

As is not unexpected, the kind of confrontation sketched here for the proverb is strikingly similar to what some of the writers named at the beginning of this paper have worked out for the parable. Both are forms of faith-speech which direct the hearer to his present existence. Wilder speaks of the secularity of the parables.[9] Funk notes that the new logic of the parables turns out not to be an isolated entity over against the world in its everydayness, but the mundane world transmuted.[10] The proverb is not so indirect as the parable; it is too compressed for that, but it does share the parable's use of the familiar experience of every day to jolt the reader into a new insight.

If this is a correct judgment about the intensification of the proverb by paradox and hyperbole, can anything be said about the fact that there are many proverbs which do not, so far as we can tell, share in this intensification, that simply represent the widespread tradition of practical wisdom? Briefly, yes. For one thing, the Synoptic message does not always proceed by way of reversal. "Seek, and you will find" (Matt. 7:7) is a typical proverb of continuity; and continuity also has its place in this proclamation, even though continuity does not so clearly disclose the characteristic features of the message. The presence of these more general proverbs in the Synoptic tradition is immensely significant precisely as indicating what one may call the field of intensification. For these proverbs arise from the life of man in his everyday existence, in his relation to his actual world, his neighbor and enemy, his family and work, and not least to himself. There was a tendency in the tradition for the nonparadoxical common sense to prevail over its paradoxical intensification; and for that reason students of the Gospels, searching for something distinctive, have been unfriendly toward the proverbial elements. But this situation can be viewed the other way around. The intensified proverb and even the parable find their field or setting in the context of everyday life, and the fact that this is their setting is emphasized by the presence of these more general proverbial sayings. The strongly practical orientation of the bulk of the proverbs in the Synoptics is the context from which the paradox and hyperbole arise and from which their meaning is oriented. We may contrast the situation in the Gospel of Thomas where many Synoptic proverbs occur, but for whatever reason, virtually all of those which have been cited here as most distinctive of the Synoptic orientation are absent. Reversal of situation is not the way faith is understood in Thomas, but rather clarification of situation; and at the same time situation is not understood in the practical and everyday manner of wisdom, but is interiorized.[11]

A language event is not just a verbal structure; and no doubt our interpretation has been influenced by our picture of the Synoptic message as a whole, including the presentation of Jesus' actions as well as his words—as, indeed, the interpretations of the parables are as well. But even though this paper has grouped together proverbial materials from various Synoptic strata,[12] the coherence of the picture drawn arises in good measure from its point of historical origin. If we could undertake a more detailed form-critical analysis we should show, despite all the judgments of probability involved, that the proverb, like the parable, comes into the tradition from its use by Jesus himself, and that the same is true of its intensification by paradox and hyperbole, which is the distinctive mark of the use of the proverb in the Synoptics.

For the modern interpreter, the prominent place of the proverb in the Synoptic Gospels, and presumably in the speech of Jesus himself, is important from several points of view. As noted above, even the somewhat everyday and conventional proverbs are important, as reminding the reader of the everyday field of concern to which faith and action must relate. The characteristic thrust of the Synoptic proverbs, however, is not the cautious and balanced judgment so typical of much proverbial literature. Such middle-of-the-road style has as its presupposition the project of making a continuous whole out of one's existence. The intensification of the proverb in paradox and hyperbole functions precisely to call this project into question, to jolt the hearer out of this effort, and into a new judgment about his own existence.

It is evident that the gnomic, proverbial form cannot express the whole framework or perspective from which the challenge to insight and action issues. The perennial efforts to bring the perspective to expression lead, so far as the present subject is concerned, rather in the direction of speculative wisdom. This effort is an inevitable task, but the direct speech of the proverb, like that of the parable, simply bypasses it. Both proverb and parable presuppose that the hearer's own perspective already gives him a basis from which to respond to the challenge being given.

Since the proverb assumes that there is a common human body of experience on which to comment, the use of this form tends to point in the direction of a hermeneutic based on a common human nature. This direction has often been followed in Christian theology, and despite the view of some modern thinkers that there is no constant human nature (within limits this is certainly correct), this line of interpretation is still an important one. Such a hermeneutic would not necessarily have to flatten the distinctively Christian perceptions. But it would recognize that the same reality which is described in explicitly Christian or christological terms can also be spoken of in other ways, and that a significant response to the substance of the message of faith can be made without the expression or response to any explicitly christological affirmations.

If we can recognize the authentic speech of the gospel in a paradoxical or hyperbolic proverb, we should be prepared to recognize that there is no one standard form of Christian speech, but that the point of the message may be made in a great variety of ways in various circumstances.

The "intensification" of the proverb, as has been pointed out, has to do with the shifting of its function from that of identifying some repeatable tract of experience, useful to know about when engaged in the project of striving to make a coherent whole out of one's existence, to that of jolting the hearer out of this hoped-for continuity into a new judgment about his existence. The term intensification suggests that impossible standard which is set so often in the Synoptics. Here we cannot examine the question of the "practicality" of the Synoptic message, but can only comment on one facet of this question. The intensification of the proverb is, of course, related to the use of proverbs in an eschatological framework. Eschatology often has a large speculative component, partly derived, in fact, from speculative wisdom. That the Synoptics have little of this speculative expression of eschatology, and instead set it forth through the intensified proverb (as well as in other ways) is an important clue to the kind of eschatological faith that they present. In particular it is worth noting that speculative eschatological dualism often leads to detachment from present existence, a detachment that is heightened in Gnosticism. The Synoptic proverbs, for all their intensity, do not fall into this pattern of detachment, but instead keep the hearer very much in this world. It is sometimes said that a radical eschatology is radically world-denying, or that it anticipates a total reversal of existence. The presence of these intensified wisdom sayings, however, shows that such an analysis is far too oversimplified. Though eschatological urgency may easily take the direction of abandonment of the present, this kind of eschatological hope produces a faith sharply focused on the present, and ready to make demands on the present which are (as we can say without carrying the subject further) beyond common sense possibility.

Finally, the proverbial form itself cannot answer the question raised above, whether the jolt or challenge to make an abrupt break in one's relation to himself and his neighbor can retrospectively be brought into some unified vision, or whether it has to remain an outright "leap." It has been suggested above that in the Wisdom Literature there is no absolute break between the generalized statement and the existential challenge. The sayings themselves fix attention on another point, and the shift of vision which they demand is one which leaves the self open to the claim of the other. Since the other's existence is not just momentary, but itself needs continuing coherence, the quest for coherent vision is not excluded by the paradox and hyperbole of these central Synoptic sayings. They do insist that one's vision of a coherent world of faith not close him off from the demand of the world outside.

Notes

1. Thomas Arvedson, *Das mysterium Christi* (Uppsala: Lundquist, 1937), pp. 209 ff.; Ulrich Wilckens, *Weisheit und Torheit* (Tübingen: J.C.B. Mohr [Paul Siebeck], 1959), pp. 197 ff.

2. Rudolf Bultmann, *History of the Synoptic Tradition*, trans. by John Marsh (New York: Harper & Row, Publishers, 1963), pp. 69–108; Helmut Koester, "One Jesus and Four Primitive Gospels," Harv ThR, XLI (1968), 203–27.

3. Bultmann, op. cit., pp. 73–81.

4. See Henry Chadwick, *The Sentences of Sextus* (Cambridge: Cambridge University Press, 1959).

5. For a discussion relating the beatitude or macarism to the present theme, see William A. Beardslee, *Literary Criticism of the New Testament* (Philadelphia: Fortress Press, 1970), Chap. 4.

6. "General Truths and Christian Proclamation," in *History and Hermeneutic* (JThC, IV; New York: Harper & Row, Publishers, 1967), pp. 153–62.

7. *Wesen und Geschichte der Weisheit* (Berlin: A. Töpelmann, 1969).

8. Ibid., p. 127.

9. Amos N. Wilder, *The Language of the Gospel* (New York: Harper & Row, Publishers, 1964), p. 81.

10. Robert W. Funk, *Language, Hermeneutic, and the Word of God* (New York: Harper & Row, Publishers, 1966), p. 195.

11. A study of the function of the proverb in the Gospel of Thomas would be a separate project, but it is nonetheless indicative of a different stance from that of the proverbs chosen above to illustrate paradox and hyperbole. Only Logion 4 (many first shall be last) and Logion 86 (foxes have holes) appear in Thomas. Reversal sayings do occur, such as Logia 5, 6 (what is hidden will be manifest) and hyperbolic ones as well: e.g., Logion 26 (mote and beam) and Logion 45 (grapes from thorns).

12. A sketch of wisdom elements in several Synoptic strata is offered by Beardslee in "The Wisdom Tradition and the Synoptic Gospels," JAAR, XXXV (1967), 231–40.

The Proverbial Wisdom of Shakespeare

*F.P. Wilson**

Literary folklorists have paid much attention to the use and function of proverbs by numerous authors from antiquity to modern times. They have also sought to discover the possible sources of specific proverbs cited by a particular author. One obvious but nonetheless indispensable aid for source study in proverbs consists of dictionaries of proverbs. Proverb dictionaries to be sure are not always well compiled. Some dictionaries include purely literary "proverbs" which were never orally circulated; others indicate the "earliest" recorded version of a proverb when in fact much earlier recorded versions could have been cited.

The questions of literary use of proverbs and of reliable dictionaries of proverbs are addressed in the following paper by F.P. Wilson who edited the third edition of the Oxford Dictionary of English Proverbs *which appeared in 1970, seven years after his death. The paper was Wilson's presidential address to the Modern Humanities Research Association in 1961.*

For other representative samples of Shakespearean proverb scholarship, see Richard Jente, "The Proverbs of Shakespeare with Early and Contemporary Parallels." Washington University Studies *(Humanistic Series), 13 (1926), 391–444; Charles George Smith,* Shakespeare's Proverb Lore *(Cambridge, 1963), and Horst Weinstock,* Die Funktion elisabethanischer Sprichwörter und Pseu-

*Reprinted by permission of the Modern Humanities Research Association from F.P. Wilson, *The Proverbial Wisdom of Shakespeare* (London, 1961), pp. 1–14.

dosprichwörter bei Shakespeare *(Heidelberg, 1966). For additional studies, see Wolfgang Mieder,* Proverbs in Literature: An International Bibliography *(Berne, 1978).*

I

A Proverb, so wrote James Howell in 1659, is "a very slippery thing, and soon slides out of the Memory," and he recommends a reader "to have his Leger-Book about him. . . .to Register therein such that Quadrat with his Conceit and Genius." For some twenty-five years I have kept a ledger-book of proverbs whether they quadrated with my conceit or not. I cannot say that I have kept one very systematically, but at least I have kept one. At the moment one of my tasks is to prepare for press a revised and enlarged edition—it will be a third edition—of the *Oxford Dictionary of English Proverbs*. This is an historical dictionary of proverbs; that is, it aims at citing for each proverb the earliest literary reference, whether in manuscript or printed book, with a few examples from later centuries. It is not a period dictionary. It records proverbs from Anglo-Saxon times to our own. Therefore it has to be highly selective and to omit many hundreds of sayings which never had much circulation and are now obsolete. One Dictionary there is which attempts to give every English proverb within a certain period, the period from 1500 to 1700, and it does so with rich documentation. The editor was the late Morris Palmer Tilley, and his dictionary was published in 1950 by the University of Michigan. I shall often have occasion to refer to it. The University of Michigan Press has granted the Clarendon Press unrestricted use of Tilley's Dictionary, a sign that the generous brotherhood contracted among men of learning in all parts of the world, to which this Association is a living witness, extends also to learned presses.

A man with a hobby is apt to resent any aspersions cast upon the usefulness of his occupation. For him it suffices that the occupation is innocent and keeps him busy and interested when he is too tired to do anything else. Let this be one excuse for my hobby of collecting proverbs; but I have others. Men have been attracted to the study of proverbs for a variety of reasons: for their value for philology, for psychology, for folk-lore, for the history of manners, or because they are said to illuminate the national character. My own interest is mainly literary. A knowledge of proverbs may help us to establish a text: it may help us to interpret its meaning; it may help us to discover with what tone a passage is to be read or spoken. The reader of eighteenth-century and nineteenth-century English literature is seldom at a loss to recognize a proverb and its meaning. Proverbs have remained a constant ingredient of popular literature, especially the novel; but by the late seventeenth century they had begun to disappear from poetry and polite literature and many became obsolete and are now unrecognizable without study. In the time of Shakespeare, however, the proverb was an important figure in rhetorical training, and the many collections of proverbs published in the sixteenth and seventeenth centuries provided material for dramatists and pamphleteers, politicians, orators, and preachers. No writer is richer in proverbs than Shakespeare. "The nature of his work" wrote Johnson,

> required the use of the common colloquial language, and consequently admitted many phrases allusive, elliptical, and proverbial, such as we speak and hear every hour without observing that they can ever grow uncouth, or that, being now obvious, they can ever seem remote.

The problem of definition I have discussed in a paper on "English Proverbs and Dictionaries of Proverbs" contributed to *The Library* in June 1945, and more learned hands than mine, such as Professor Archer Taylor's, have written books about it. To the various early attempts at a definition objections may be raised. John Ward, who died vicar of Stratford-upon-Avon in 1681, required six things of a proverb: it had to be short, plain, common, figurative, ancient, true. But many proverbs are not figurative—"forget and forgive," for example, which Shakespeare puts to the noblest use near the end of *King Lear:* and while most proverbs are short, plain, common, ancient, true, so are the ten commandments. Indeed the commandments are much truer than the proverbs, which often contradict each other. Nicholas Breton could not have written a pamphlet called *The Crossing of Commandments*. Some have required that a proverb shall have the power of variant reference, and the best proverbs have that power; but some of the weather proverbs like "September blow soft Till the fruit is in the loft" are restricted in their application. Some writers point to the fact that almost all proverbs are anonymous. In different countries and at different times they may seem to spring up by the process of polygenesis of which Professor Dámaso Alonso spoke to us so persuasively a year ago; yet the most striking, we may plausibly conjecture, descend from one inventor, who must for ever remain nameless, as surely as the man who first sang in his head the original verses of *Sir Patrick Spens*. Popularity is another test which some apply. "It is the Common-people alone" says Howell, "that have the priviledge of making Proverbs." A sixteenth-century writer, Thomas Bowes, said that the English make foreign words native by passing them to and fro upon the file of their teeth; and in this way the people "make" proverbs as they "make" ballads.

The Oxford Dictionary's definition insists that a proverb must be popular: "a short pithy saying in common and recognized use." This applies well to the proverbs we assimilated in childhood, and it applies also to some newcomers of which the latest to come to my notice is "Your head will never save your heels." But the editor of an historical dictionary is forced to ask, "In common use when, and in what circles, and how common?," questions it is not always easy to answer. The most famous reference to a proverb in the whole of Shakespeare is no doubt Lady Macbeth's

> Letting "I dare not" wait upon "I would,"
> Like the poor cat i' th' adage;

and in his day the saying that "the cat would eat fish yet dare not wet its feet" was in such common use that he could refer to it thus obliquely. But today perhaps only one in a thousand recognizes the adage and how apt it is to the occasion. Here is the power of variant reference at its highest.

In the paper printed in *The Library* to which I have referred, I urged the lexicographer to include not only sentences but proverbial phrases and similes and to err on the side of inclusiveness, not exclusiveness. I was thinking of the generous nature of an Elizabethan's conception of a proverb, including as it did not only established similes, bywords or popular phrases which we might call catchphrases, and mere tags and clichés, but also apophthegms and moral precepts of a sententious nature. Tilley was well aware that much that he included was not strictly proverbial in the modern sense, and a year before his death in 1947 he wrote to me to say how much he relied on what the sixteenth and seventeenth centuries understood as proverbial. "Where no evidence from the collections turned up," he went on, "I have depended partly on the repetition of a thought and partly on 'hunch.' At times I have even admitted idiomatic phrases that seemed proverbial. I have erred decidedly on the side of inclusiveness." If Tilley had excluded everything except gnomic sentences now or formerly in popular use, his dictionary would have been half as big and half as useful.

II

Shakespeare lived in the two great proverb-making centuries of the English tongue—the sixteenth and the seventeenth. They were the centuries in which England exported almost nothing yet imported great riches without seeming to injure the balance of the language. I once attempted to draw up a list of the collections of English proverbs published between 1640 and 1670, that is, between the collection of 1640 known as George Herbert's and John Ray's of 1670. I found twenty-one and have since found two more. Consider how much has survived from the sixteenth century. Apart from the rich collections of proverbs mainly of native growth published by John Heywood in his *Dialogue of Proverbs* of 1546, enlarged c. 1549, consider the dictionaries and grammars and dialogues which give foreign proverbs and their English counterparts: the Latin-English ones done by Thomas Cooper, John Baret and John Withals and such revisers of Withals as Abraham Fleming and William Clerk; or the Spanish by William Stepney and John Minsheu; or the Italian by James Sanford and John Florio—Florio in his dialogues but not in his dictionary; or the French by Palsgrave, Holyband, Delamothe, and (richest of all) Cotgrave. Or consider the number of translations from that great disseminator of proverbs Erasmus: the *Dicta Sapientum* of c. 1526, Taverner in 1539, Nicholas Udall in 1542, William Baldwin in 1547, Robert Burrant's *Precepts of Cato* with the annotations of Erasmus, in 1545, and so on. One purpose these and other scholars had was to increase the "copy" (*copia*, copiousness) of their native language, and they and their like put before the English public a vast quantity of proverbs, proverbial phrases and similes, wise saws, apophthegms, anecdotes, for the English people to file their teeth on, if they chose to. Often of course they did not choose to, but sometimes they did. The proverbial phrase "To call a spade a spade" strikes one as being very English. And if a man wished to argue that a nation's proverbs throw light on a nation's character and wished at the same time to be patriotic, he might take the phrase as indicative of the honesty and forthrightness of the English character. In fact it came into English very early in the sixteenth century—my earliest example is from Rastell's *Four Elements*, printed c. 1526–7—and from the Latin *ligonem ligonem vocare*, a phrase included of course in Erasmus's great thesaurus of proverbs.

What appears to be another importation is the proverb "An empty sack can't stand upright." The earliest English example that I can give is from Giovanni Torriano's *Select Italian Proverbs* of 1642 (p. 90): "*Sacco vuoto non può star in piedi* An emptie sack cannot stand upright." It is still in popular use in England. In Cambridge in 1942 I heard it used with great effect by a sergeant in the Home Guard.

The translators were as bent on enriching the vernacular as the lexicographers. In some ways they are more interesting than the lexicographers, because when they translate a proverb they show the proverb in lively action not (as it were) as a stuffed specimen in a showcase. Sometimes I imagine—no doubt I fondly imagine, for the evidence can never be complete—I can observe the actual moment at which a proverb or proverbial phrase came into the language. Take as an example one of the earliest secular plays in English, *Calisto and Melibea*, printed by John Rastell about the year 1529. Most of the play is adapted from *La Celestina*, and in the adaptation several Spanish proverbs are borrowed and make their first known appearance in English dress: "Tomorrow is a new day" (*Manaña es otro dĩa*) "As soon goes the lambskin to market as the sheep's," "The half knows what the whole means." And to these we may add an expression without which it is difficult to see how a romantic lover could get on: *adoro la tierra que huellas*, "I worship the ground you tread on." In this way a language is enriched.

An interesting case is the weather proverb which has a seasonable airing every year in the English popular press: "Cast ne'er a clout till May be out." If there is one thing clear it is that May is the month, not the blossom of the hawthorn-tree. The evidence at present available to me suggests that it was imported in the early eighteenth century from the Spanish proverb "Hasta Mayo (pasado Mayo) no te quites el sayo," a proverb which appears in the early seventeenth-century

Vocabulario de Refranes of Gonzalo Correas Iñigo. Captain John Stevens (s.v. Mayo) in his very useful *New Spanish and English Dictionary* of 1706 gives this translation: "Do not leave off your Coat till *May* be past, that is Leave off no Cloaths." His dictionary is rich in proverbs, as indeed is the Spanish tongue, and it is his practice to give the idiomatic English equivalent whenever possible. The fact that he is here so literal suggests that the proverb was not yet familiar to him in an English dress. Not until 1732 do we find the rhyme: "Leave not off a Clout, Till *May* be out," and then it is No. 6193 in that "vast confus'd heap of unsorted Things, old and new," the collection of 6496 numbered proverbs collected by Thomas Fuller, M.D., under the name *Gnomologia*.

It is no part of my duty today to question the truth of this popular proverb, but I would point out that one Spanish version is more flexible: "Hasta el cuaranta de mayo [June 10], no te quites el sayo; y si el tiempo es importuno, hasta el cuaranta y uno." The English form makes no such concession to climatic conditions and is the same in Scotland as in England. If my history of the proverb is right—and any day a lucky discovery may prove it wrong—then the inhabitants of Great Britain should ask themselves whether the Spanish saying was adjusted to the meridian of Madrid or of Seville, and at the same time should bear in mind that we borrowed it before we adopted the Gregorian calendar.

The borrowing has been most successful. Perhaps it is mainly responsible for such currency as the archaic or dialectal word "clout" possesses in England today. Contrast the failure to take root of another proverb from the same language. Many a preacher, orator, or dramatist has valued the homely proverb for its power of putting him on a friendly and familiar footing with his audience, and so has many a traveller into foreign parts. Perhaps the traveller also values it because it persuades him if not his audience that his command of the language is greater than it is. I have found one of the many proverbs in *Don Quixote* of some service in these respects: "Paciencia y barajar," "patience and shuffle the cards" as the unlucky but persistent cardplayer may cry out to the dealer. Tilley gives the proverb under "Patience and shuffle" and can quote only one example; and that is from Shelton's translation of *Don Quixote!*

Whether they came into the language early or late the proverbs used by Shakespeare were for the most part thoroughly English. Very occasionally he used what appears to be a foreign proverb or maxim, and I should like for a few minutes to examine two of these, for it is a puzzle how he came across them. The discovery of a pre-Shakespearian instance might give a clue to his reading, unless we suppose that he picked up these trifles, as undoubtedly he picked up more important matters, from hearsay.

One of these sayings is a proverb or maxim which Pistol repeats in slightly different form in 2 *Henry IV*, II iv 171 and V v 97, both forms garbled by him or by Shakespeare or by the printer. Professor E.M. Wilson tells me that the original was probably Spanish, not Italian, and in choice Castilian would take the form "Si Fortuna me atormenta, la esperanza me contenta"; if Fortune torments me, Hope contents me. Tilley treats it as proverbial but gives no example after Shakespeare before 1640. There is, by the way, a French saying very like it: "Le désir nous tormente, et l'espoir nous contente, Desire torments us and hope contents us." (The Folio reading at II iv 171 is, perhaps by accident, half French: "Si fortune me tormente, sperato me contente.") It is found with English translation in 1592 in "The Treasure of the French Tongue" added to *The French Alphabeth* by G. Delamothe, a Protestant refugee, one of the many foreign teachers resident in sixteenth-century and seventeenth-century London who tell us so much about the English language in the time of Shakespeare. Delamothe could have supplied the proverb which Shakespeare quotes in French at 2 *Henry VI*, V ii 28—"La fin couronne l'oeuvre," but obviously he cannot be the source of Shakespeare's Spanish saying.

Richard Farmer thought he had found the source, and in his classic *Essay on the Learning of Shakespeare* (1767), in which he sought to show that Shakespeare had little or no learning but took his knowledge of the classics and modern languages from English books, he pointed to two examples of this saying, one of them in a book called *Wits, Fits and Fancies* by Anthony Copley. In the enlarged second edition of the same year Farmer says that the book "seems to have had many Editions," but only three are known, one in 1595 and two in 1614. (The copy in the Folger Library with the date 1596 is a mere variant of the edition of 1595.) Here is the passage:

> Hannibal Gonsago being in the low Countries ouerthrowne from his hors by an English Captaine, and commanded to yeeld himselfe prisoner: kist his sword and gaue it the English man saying: Si Fortuna me tormenta, Il speranza me contenta.

Some editors of Shakespeare refer the reader to the 1595 edition of Copley's work. Professor M.A. Shaaber in his New Variorum edition of 2 *Henry IV* is an honourable exception: "I have not succeeded in locating this passage in Copley's book." It is, however, in the augmented editions of 1614: but as 2 *Henry IV* was written about 1597 and printed in 1600, Copley's book cannot be the source of Shakespeare's knowledge, unless indeed we assume (as we have no right to) that an augmented edition with this passage was published in time for Shakespeare to make use of it by 1597. Where Copley found the story I do not know. Many of his jests and anecdotes he translates from the *Floresta Española* of Melchior de Santa Cruz de Dueñas, but not this.

The other example of the saying which Farmer refers to is in Sir Richard Hawkins's *Voyage into the South Sea. Anno Domini 1593*, p. 13. Hawkins had lost his pinnace in a storm off Plymouth Harbour, and writes:

> These losses and mischances troubled and grieved, but nothing daunted me; for common experience taught me, that all honourable Enterprises, are accompanied with difficulties and daungers; *Si fortuna me tormenta; Esperança me contenta*: Of hard beginnings, many times come prosperous and happie events.

But what Farmer does not say is that while Hawkins wrote an account of his voyage of 1593 he wrote it late in life and died while it was passing through the press in 1622. So we still do not know how the saying came to Shakespeare's hand.

The other foreign proverb I have in mind, again a proverb which never became English, Shakespeare puts to much more powerful use because he brings it into a much greater context. We are introduced to Iago in the first scene of *Othello* where he and Roderigo awaken Desdemona's father and Iago shouts at the old man the foul images of sex which spring to his mind. And one of these images is in the sentence: "I am one, sir, that comes to tell you your daughter and the Moor are now making the beast with two backs." Tilley gives "the beast with two backs" as proverbial and cites *Othello* but no other example before 1650. One of his examples is from an English translation of Rabelais; in France the expression is much older than Rabelais. But in an English book it is found in 1611—in the French-English Dictionary made by Randle Cotgrave. Both under the word "beste" and under "dos" he gives the French form "Faire la beste à deux dos ensemble," adding the gloss "To leacher." Still, Cotgrave belongs to the year 1611 and *Othello* to 1604, so Shakespeare could not have learnt it from Cotgrave. We noticed that "Si Fortuna me tormenta" had a close parallel in French, and this is characteristic of the traffic of proverbs in the romance languages. "The beast with two backs" is Italian as well as French, and Shakespeare could have found it in a book printed in London in 1591, "Far la bestia a due dossi," one of the 6150 proverbs John Florio printed in the *Giardino di Ricreatione* (p. 105), a companion volume to his *Second Fruits*. However the saying came to Shakespeare, it can hardly have been familiar to his audience; yet the meaning of these words on the lips of Iago no more needed a gloss than they do today.

III

In what I have said and in what I am about to say I would not be thought to be decrying Tilley's *Dictionary*. If he had lived to see its publication he would at once have set about providing a supplement. It is to his praise that he has produced a firm foundation upon which a supplement may be based. But there are signs that demands are being made upon his work which it was not expected to meet. So too with the *Oxford English Dictionary*. We know it is so good that we are tempted to use it as a kind of lazy-tongs which will save us from the labour of making our own enquiries, a practice to which the editors of that Dictionary would have been the first to object. Tilley is now in danger of being maltreated in this way. In reviewing his dictionary (*The Review of English Studies*, 1952, iii, 195) I said that in future it would seldom be necessary for an editor of Shakespeare or of any sixteenth-century or seventeenth-century author laboriously to collect his own set of proverbial parallels: a reference to Tilley would usually suffice. And this is true. But no dictionary of proverbs can ever be definitive, and the shortcomings of Tilley may be illustrated from his treatment of Shakespeare's proverbs, an excellent treatment immensely better than any we had before. He told me that his initial interest in proverbs began with Shakespeare's, especially in connexion with the so-called borrowings by and from Shakespeare, which are not borrowings at all: and at the end of his dictionary he gave references to more than 2000 proverbial or semi-proverbial quotations given in the dictionary from Shakespeare. This valuable work needs to be supplemented in three ways. First, earlier examples can be found of many of the proverbs for which Tilley's earliest is from Shakespeare. Secondly, Tilley failed to add Shakespearian examples to many of the proverbs which he cites. And thirdly, while he is remarkably inclusive, proverbs may be found in Shakespeare and other writers which do not appear in his dictionary. I will say a few words about each of these three ways.

I have been especially interested in discovering earlier examples of the proverbs for which Tilley's earliest is from Shakespeare. In my review of Tilley I gave forty-four instances of these proverbs.* The only way of proving that a saying or phrase was absorbed by Shakespeare from the diction of common life and was not invented by him is to find an example in an earlier writer. That Shakespeare invented many a saying or phrase and gave it such currency that many a user forgets the original and assumes it to be proverbial, I do not doubt. Like some of the sayings of Sancho Panza they have become proverbs *since* he used them. But just as certainly many a saying and many a phrase which we take to be his invention came to his audience with the surprise not of discovery but of recognition. Doubtless he could have invented "My dancing days are done" or "Wit, whither wilt thou?" but as certainly he did not. Among other sayings for which earlier examples may be added to Tilley's Shakespearian ones are:

> A coward dies many deaths, a brave man but once. You set an old man's head on a young man's shoulders. Sleep is the image of death. Youth and age will never agree. To be flesh and blood as others are. God stays long but strikes at last. Injuries are written in brass. Man's extremity is God's opportunity. There is nothing but is good for something. He may go hang himself in his own garters. Confess and be hanged. First thrive and then wive. It is better to wear out than rust out. Let well alone.

*In the original publication of this paper, Wilson included an appendix containing some one hundred and twenty-five additional instances of proverbs with recorded versions earlier than their appearance in Shakespeare's works. We elected not to reprint the appendix inasmuch as a number of these proverbs are mentioned in the paper. Ed. Note.

These and others will be found in my reviews of Tilley as also such proverbial phrases as "To come in with the conqueror, To live within compass, To lick into shape" and such proverbial similes as "As dry as a biscuit, As flattering as a spaniel, As honest a man as ever broke bread."

A straightforward example is the line in 3 *Henry VI* (V iii 13) "For every cloud engenders not a storm." Tilley's only quotation apart from Shakespeare is from Giovanni Torriano's great dictionary of Italian-English proverbs and proverbial phrases of 1666. If Shakespeare required a literary source for this not very profound reflection, he could have found one in Abraham Fleming's revision in 1584 of the highly popular English-Latin dictionary for children and beginners originally compiled by John Withals. Here it appears (on sig. A4) as the translation of a hexameter which I have not been able to trace: *"Non stillant omnes quas cernis in aëre nubes*, All the clowdes which thou seest in the ayre do not yeeld rayne."

Not so straightforward is the repetition of a thought which either did not settle into a fixed form at all or settled late after Shakespeare's death. Tilley is usually alert for independent instances of the same thought in works of his period. The one I choose got into the dictionaries from 1616 and appears in Tilley in the form: "Go forward and fall: go backward and mar all." He quotes from *Macbeth*:

> I am in blood
> Stepp'd in so far that, should I wade no more,
> Returning were as tedious as go o'er.

But he might also have quoted from Anthony Munday's *Zelauto* of 1580: "I am not so farre ouer shooes: but I may returne yet drie, nor I am not so far in, but I may easily escape out"; and from Minsheu in 1599: "I had waded so farre in it, as without helpe I could not get ouer, nor without danger and shame returne backe." I do not know why he does not cite *Richard III*, IV ii 65: "I am in So far in blood that sin will pluck on sin."

Under the same heading of examples of which Tilley's earliest is from Shakespeare I give a simile and a phrase. I cannot attach any significance to the fact that my earlier instances both come from the same dictionary, Richard Huloet's *Abcedarium* of 1552, another English-Latin dictionary. Tilley gives under one entry (F 328) "To swim like a fish (duck)" For "swim like a fish," which is not

Shakespearian, he gives one example and that from Fletcher and Massinger's *Sea Voyage* of c. 1622; an earlier one is in Harington's *Orlando Furioso* of 1591: "*Orlando* nakt and light, swam like a fish." Of "swim like a duck" his only example is Trinculo's words in *The Tempest* (II ii 120). Huloet gives "Swymme lyke a ducke. *Tetrinno. as.*" Huloet gets the meaning wrong, for I am assured that *Tetrinno* ought to mean "I quack like a duck." Nevertheless he gives the simile which Shakespeare was to use. In the same dictionary I find (under "Trowell") "*thrullisco. as. ang.* to laye on wyth a trowell." Here is a phrase which, as I have always thought, Shakespeare himself made proverbial. I still think so; for whereas Huloet is strictly literal, Shakespeare's Rosalind applies the expression ironically and metaphorically to Touchstone's fine language, so making it possible for us to apply it to any excess whether of style or manners.

The second way in which Tilley's dictionary needs to be supplemented is by adding to the proverbs which he gives the Shakespearian references which he neglects. In a recent reading of Shakespeare's early history plays I have noted five omissions in *Henry VI*, Part I, in Part 2 eight, in Part 3 ten, and in *Richard III* eighteen. And while I am not anxious—now or at any time—to get involved in the problem of the authorship of *Henry VI*, Part I, I venture to point out that the disparity between the use of proverbial or semi-proverbial language in that play as against the other three plays, a disparity already marked in the lists which Tilley supplies, becomes the more striking if we add the proverbs which he missed. One example of these omissions may be noted—from 3 *Henry VI*, III iii 152: "Having nothing, nothing can he lose." This is Tilley's N331: "They that have nothing need fear to lose nothing." An example earlier than Shakespeare is in Roper's *Life of More* (1557, ed. Hitchcock, p. 7): "He nothinge havinge, nothing could loose." This command of the diction of common life is apparent in Shakespeare's earliest work as in his latest. No other English poet, not even Chaucer, held in his memory so many proverbial sayings.

Under this heading as under the first I take an example of a thought which did not crystallize into a set form in the time of Shakespeare. Tilley gives as proverbial "You are a right Englishman, you cannot tell when a thing is well." It appears more or less in this form in many seventeenth-century dictionaries of proverbs—in the 1616 edition of Withals, in Clarke (1639), in Howell (1659), in Ray (1670), and so on. Tilley's earliest is from Withals, but I think he would have added, if he had thought of it, Falstaff's "It was alway yet the trick of our English nation, if they have a good thing, to make it too common." Years earlier we find a pre-Shakespearian example. In 1545 Stephen Gardiner wrote to Sir William Paget: "They saye that an Englishe man in al feates excellith if he could leaue whenne it is wel, which they cal *tollere manum de tabula*." Gardiner, it will be noticed, puts up the proverbial signpost, "They say."

The third way in which Tilley may be supplemented is by the addition of proverbs which do not appear in his dictionary at all yet were used by Shakespeare. There must still remain sayings in Shakespeare which his audience recognized as proverbial and we do not. Among those omitted by Tilley are "as good be an addled egg as an idle bird"; "as like as a crab is like an apple," a variant of A291; "between asleep and awake"; "when angry count a hundred." This last is an example of a proverb which became fixed in shape and word very late. Other ways of allaying anger than counting a hundred were suggested. The popular Jacobean preacher Thomas Adams recommended the reciting of the Greek alphabet "as a pause to coole the heate of choler" (1616, *Diseases of the Soul*, p. 16). The moral of 2 *Henry VI*, I iii 150–1 appears to be: when angry, walk once round the quadrangle. In *Richard III* (I iv 118) the second murderer about to murder the sleeping Clarence suffers some dregs of conscience and with grim irony observes: "I hope this passionate humour of mine will change: it was wont to hold me but while one tells twenty."

Another saying of a proverbial nature which Tilley missed altogether is "Fair dovecots have most doves." (His P588, "Priests and pigeons (doves) make foul houses" is a different proverb.) In this form it appears in H. Peters's *Dying Father's Last Legacy* of 1660, while F. Hawkins in *Youth's Behaviour* of 1663 gives "Doves flock to fair houses." From these I move backwards (like the crab) to Greene's *Menaphon* of 1589 (Grosart vi 47: "Doves delight not in foule cottages"), and to one of the *Three Proper and Witty Familiar Letters* which passed between Gabriel Harvey and Edmund Spenser and were printed in 1580. Harvey quotes three of his brother John's variations in pseudo-quantitative verse on a theme in Ovid's *Tristia* (I. ix 7, *Adspicis ut veniant ad candida tecta columbae*), the simplest and shortest of which is

> See ye the Dooues? they breede, and feede in gorgeous Houses:
> Scarce one Dooue doth loue to remaine in ruinous Houses.

Earlier still is this passage in Robert Burrant's *Precepts of Cato* of 1545 ("Seven Wise Men," C2): it is translated from a comment by Erasmus on the proverb "In time of prosperity friends will be plenty, in time of adversity not one among twenty."

> Ouid compareth suche flatterynge frendes vnto Piggions who as longe as the doufehouse is freshe and newe, they abyde and haunt there, but yf it begynne ones to wexe olde and rotten, they wyll flee [a]way from it to another.

Finally we come to Shakespeare or at least to *Henry VI*, Part I (I v 21). The great Talbot comments on the defeat of the English soldiers by the witchcraft of Joan of Arc:

> A witch by fear, not force, like Hannibal,
> Drives back our troops and conquers as she lists:
> So bees with smoke and doves with noisome stench
> Are from their hives and houses driv'n away.

These homiletic similes drawn from nature—like "Every cloud engenders not a storm" or "Constant dropping will wear the stone" which Shakespeare used no less than eleven times—were stock ornaments when he began to write. As he reached maturity he tended to drop them or to transform them into metaphor, no longer hooking them on with an "as" or a "so," no longer making them serve as mere amplification. But in his early work, as in the early work of such a sententious poet as Drayton, proverbial and semi-proverbial expressions tend to come in clusters; as for example, in *Richard III*, II iii 32:

> When clouds are seen, wise men put on their cloaks;
> When great leaves fall, then winter is at hand;
> When the sun sets, who doth not look for night?
> Untimely storms make men expect a dearth.

Moreover, what is semi-proverbial assumes by association proverbial authority. By 1590 "Doves are driven from dovecotes by stench" might be considered proverbial but not "Bees are driven from their hives by smoke." So in 2 *Henry VI*, III i 53, Suffolk poisons the mind of Henry against Gloucester with "Smooth runs the water where the brook is deep," a proverb known to medieval England, and continues: "The fox barks not when he would steal the lamb," which then assumes all the authority of a proverb. So in 3 *Henry VI*, II ii 17, "The smallest worm will turn, being trodden on" is followed by "And doves will peck in safeguard of their brood."

IV

To conclude. Shakespeare's mind received its stores from books, more still from speech. What he borrowed from books he so transmuted that only rarely can we trace with certainty where he had been reading. How much he took from speech we may surmise from his proverbs. He was an observer of men and manners in court and city, town and country, church and tavern. Whether he often cried "My tables—meet it is I set it down," as Shaw represents him doing in *The Dark Lady of the Sonnets*, may be doubted. What he heard was stored away in his retentive memory. He could count on his proverbs being known to his audience, just as were his images, images as familiar as the chamberlain putting his master's shirt on warm, or that image of heaven peeping "through the blanket of the dark" which excited Johnson's risibility but does not excite ours. While the learned word and the learned allusion are by no means absent from his work, yet basic to his style are these images drawn from the goings-on of ordinary life and these proverbs assimilated from the diction of common life. When the occasion demanded they were called from the "vasty deep" of his memory, and they came at his call to receive their appropriate language and rhythm.

The Bird That Fouls Its Nest

*John G. Kunstmann**

While some scholars are interested in literary uses of individual proverbs, other scholars prefer to observe an individual proverb in as many contexts as possible. Such scholars often seek to find the earliest recorded version of a proverb and to track it through space and time wherever and whenever it has appeared. Such ambitious historical/comparative investigations normally require familiarity with dozens of languages as can be seen in Professor Kunstmann's rich compilation of an impressive number of versions of one proverb. For a global, book-length study of a single proverbial expression (describing or referring to the natural phenomenon of rain falling while the sun is shining), see Matti Kuusi, Regen bei Sonnenschein. Zur Weltgeschichte einer Redensart, *FFC 171 (Helsinki, 1957). For references to many other studies of individual proverbs, see Wolfgang Mieder,* International Bibliography of Explanatory Essays on Individual Proverbs and Proverbial Expressions *(Bern, 1977) and Lutz Röhrich,* Lexikon der sprichwörtlichen Redensarten. *2 vols. (Freiburg, 1976).*

As far as is known, the proverb, "It is an ill bird that fouls its own nest," was first recorded in complete form in Latin by Egbert von Lüttich in verse 148 of his *Fecunda Ratis*. There it reads: *nidos commaculans immundus habebitur ales*. The *Fecunda Ratis* is a

*Reprinted from *Southern Folklore Quarterly*, 3 (1939), 75–91.

collection of fables, proverbs, maxims, and similar material and was finished *ca.* 1023 A.D.[1] From this year on, the proverb concerning the nest-befouling bird appears frequently in the literature (the term is used in the broadest sense of the word) of Western and Northern Europe, down to our days. Scholars have made known from time to time the places where they have met this adage, notably Hoffmann von Fallersleben,[2] K.F.W. Wander,[3] W.H.D. Suringar,[4] Ida von Düringsfeld and Otto von Reinsberg-Düringsfeld,[5] Joseph Haller,[6] Müllenhoff-Scherer-Steinmeyer,[7] Vincent Stuckey Lean,[8] G. Walz,[9] Max Förster,[10] Friedrich Seiler,[11] and Richard Jente.[12] Through their industry, they have made available the material for research into the origin, the dissemination, the formal changes, the meaning, and the application of this proverb.

On the following pages I propose to build on this foundation.

Under *I* I shall give a chronologically arranged list of occurrences of the Medieval Latin versions of the proverb anent the nest-befouling bird. These Medieval Latin versions are commonly conceded to be the root whence stem the various vernacular versions.[13] To furnish a "union list" of all available vernacular forms of the proverb, from the Straits of Gibralter to the North Cape and from the German-Slavic line to Iceland, would serve no useful purpose at this time. For I am mainly concerned with the origin of the proverb. Once the provenience of the Medieval Latin, or mother proverb is discovered, the parentage of the descendant vernacular versions is also established. In listing the Medieval Latin versions, I shall not confine myself to an indication of the places where the proverb may be found, nor shall I limit myself to listing such places as contain the proverb in its complete form. I shall cite the proverb in full, and in its context, wherever it so occurs. This is necessary for a study of the formal changes, of the meaning, and of the changes in application of the proverb during the last nine hundred years. I shall include in the list allusions to and adaptations and extensions of the proverb. To the list I shall append samples, one for every important West and North European language, of the (modern) vernacular versions of the proverb.

In no sense of the word do I consider this list, or the unpublished list containing the occurrences of the proverb in the various vernaculars *my* list. I may have contributed a few citations to the great number gathered by the scholars whom I have mentioned and by others whom to mention in every case limitations of space forbid. I hereby acknowledge gratefully my indebtedness to them.

Under *II* I shall, using the material presented in *I*, discuss very briefly some aspects of dissemination of the Medieval Latin versions. Because of the omission of the vernacular versions, I shall not consider at this time the geographical distribution of the proverb over Western and Northern Europe.

Under *III* I shall attempt to answer the question: Who or what is this bird that fouls its own nest? The answer to this question, if it be correct, should, at the same time, answer the question of the proverb's provenience.

I. Medieval Latin Versions

(1)*Ca.* 1000 A.D. *At Henricus Trevirensis, cui summa rerum commissa erat, circumspecto claustro: Enimvero, ait, talis nidus bonas aves decet! Et Kebo, Lorisham abbas, vir nominis reverendi prae multis et eo die pro nobis plus caeteris sentiens, sed et crebro nos postea donans et consiliis invans: Si placet, ait, ipsarum avium hunc nidum qualis per omnia sit, primitus ab abbate audiamus, ut de caeteris, quid agamus, integrius scire valeamus. [Commissarii imperatoris S. Galli coenobium visitant,* 966*].* "Ekkehardi IV. Casus S. Galli. c. X," *Monumenta Germaniae Historica,* SS. II. 128, 33 ff. Cf. *Proverbia Communia*, ed. Hoffmann von Fallersleben, *Horae Belgicae, Pars Nona,* p. 42, no. 676: *Tis goet sien aen den nest, wat voghel daer i woont. Nidus testatur, ibi qualis avis dominatur;* Dr. Jellinghaus, *Die Proverbia communia mittelniederdeutsch, aus einer Bordesholmer Handschrift vom Jahre 1486.* Programm (Kiel, 1880), p. 20, no. 641: *Tys ghud to seende an dem neste wat vaghels dar inne wand;* Suringar, *Bebel,* p. 133, no. 498; *Ex nido avem indicamus;* p. 536; p. 208, where he quotes from *Klosterspiegel*, X, 21: *Es ist ein böser Vogel, der in sein Nest hofiert, und doch tragen's die Mönche nicht aus dem Kloster:* Grimm, *Deutsches Wörterbuch*, XII, 2, 397, where Eyering I, 89 is quoted: *am nest wird man leichtlichen innen was für ein vogel wont darinnen.*

(2)*Ca.* 1023 A.D.

Nidos commaculans immundas habebitur ales:
Pelex nec factis claret nec nomine digna.

Egbert von Lüttich, *Fecunda Ratis.* vv. 148–9, Cf. Fischart, *Das philosophische Ehzuchtbüchlein* (Scheible, *Das Kloster*, X, p. 545): *Vettel . . . nistet gern inn fremde Näster.*

(3)*Ca.* 1046 A.D.

Sed dicit nova lex: in dextram mandibulam te
Si quis cedat, ei paciens prebeto aliam tu.
Composite mala vestra satis defenditis acta!
Turpe est quod proprium violas, onocrotale, nidum.
Ad defendendum sapientes estis iniquum.
Ad rectum stulti. . . .

Sexti Amarcii Galli Piosistrati *Sermonum Libri IV*, ed. M. Manitius (Leipzig, 1888). These lines are taken from Book III, vv. 759 ff.

(4)*Ca.* 1151–52.

Nec petit hic standi veniam, nec stare quod ipsum
Hic patior, grates, quas mihi debet, agit,
Restituit pretium nutrita monedula merdam,
Gracculus et cuculo, quem fovet, hoste perit.

Magister Nivardus (?), *Isengrimus*, ed. E. Voigt (Halle, 1884), Book IV, vv. 525 ff.

(5)12th cent.

Progenies avium mala foedat stercore nidum.

Cod. 2521, Vienna (formerly Hs. philol. 413), in Haupt-Hoffmann, *Altdeutsche Blätter*, 1 (Leipzig 1836), 10; also Hs. 1966, Germanic Museum (Nuremburg), and (?) cod. lat. 7977 (Kaisheim 77), Munich (13th cent.). See Müllenhoff-Scherer, *Denkmäler*,[3] II, p. 147: Jacob Werner, *Lateinische Sprichwörter und Sinnsprüche des Mittelalters* [=*Sammlung mittellateinischer Texte*, ed. A. Hilka, no. 3] (Heidelberg, 1912), p. 72.

(6) 12th cent.

Est mala que proprium demerdat avicula nidum.

Cod. Lat. 17142, Munich, formerly Scheftlarn. See Seiler, *Z. f. d. Ph.*, XXXXV (1913), pp. 238, 286, 289.

(7) After 1172.

Non est illa valens que nidum stercorat ales.

C 58/275, Zurich (Wasserkirche). See Müllenhoff-Scherer, *l.c.;* Wander, *o.c.*, IV, *s.v.* "Vogel," section on Latin versions.

(8) End of 12th cent.

Ericus se ad astandum fratri natura pertrahi dixit, probrosum referens alitem qui proprium polluat nidum.

Saxo Grammaticus, *Gesta Danorum*, Book V., ed. P.E. Müeller, I (Copenhagen, 1839), 195.

(9) *Ca.* 1250.

Qui spuit in propriam, probra spargit propria, barbam:
Nidum, quo residet, sordida foedat avis.

Albert von Stade (Albertus Stadensis), *Troilus*, ed. Merzdorf, Lib. V, v. 939. I quote this from Suringar, *Bebel*, pp. XLIX, 207. Cf. "sein eigenes Ponim verschänden" = "ein Glied seiner eigenen Familie herabsetzen." Abraham Tendlau, *Sprichwörter und Redensarten deutsch-jüdischer Vorzeit* (Frankfurt a. M., n.d. [1860?]), pp. 228 f., no. 721. See also no. (14), below.

(10) 13th cent.

Turpis avis, proprium que fedat stercore nidum.

Cod. 1365 (formerly 3356), Vienna. Also in a Basle Ms.; see Werner, *o.c.*, p. 98, and Wander, *o.c.*, IV, *s.v.* "Vogel," section on Latin versions.

(11) 14th cent.

Es ist ein ungenemer vogel, der do befleckt sein eigen nest: Est avis ingrata, que defedat sua strata.

"Schwabacher Sprüche des XIV. Jahrhunderts," *Sitzungsberichte der Münchner Akademie,* II, 25–38, no. 73; cf. *Z. f. d. Ph.,* XLVII (1916), pp. 243 ff., 250. See also Werner, *o.c.,* p. 26 (Basle Ms.), and nos. (16) and (24), below.

(12) End of 14th cent.

Turpiter errat avis, proprium que stercore nidum,
Cuius erit custos, contaminare studet.

Gower, *Vox Clamantis,* V, 835; cf. Walz, *o.c.,* pp. 80 f.

(13) First quarter of 15th cent.

Est avibus proprium fedis corrumpere nidum.

(14) First quarter of 15th cent.

Expuis in barbam, si membra domestica ledis;
Est avibus proprium nidos corrumpere fedis.

(13) and (14): Cod. A XI, 67, University Library, Basle; cf. Werner, *o.c.,* pp. 26 and 31.

(15) 15th cent.

Degenerans olidum facit ales stercore nidum.

Peder Lolles samling af danske og latinske ordsprog, optrykt efter den aeldste udgave af 1506 af R. Nycrup (Copenhagen, 1828) [bruchstücke einer hs. des XV. jh. in universitets-jubilaeets danske samfund nr. 57, blandinger II, 1, 39 ff.], no. 231; cf. H. Reuterdahl, *gamle ordspråk på latin och swenska efter en Upsalahs.* (XV jh.) utg. (Lund, 1840), 204; Axel Kock och Carl af Petersens, *Östnordiska och Latinska Medeltidsordspråk. Peder Låles Ordspråk och en motsvarande Svensk Samling,* I (Copenhagen, 1889–1894), p. 160, no. 205: II (Copenhagen, 1891–92), p. 119.

(16) *Ca.* 1450.

Est avis ingrata, que defedat sua strata.
Es ist ein vngenemer vogel, der do wefleckt sein eygen nest.

Breslau-Lüben Ms., 1459 A.D. See Joseph Klapper, *Die Sprichwörter der Freidankpredigten* ("Wort und Brauch," XVI) (Breslau, 1927), p. 79, no. 425, and no. (11), above. Klapper lists on p. 24 as nos. 176 and 177 from Breslau Ms. I. Q. 50: Est avis ingrata, que defedat sua strata, and Est avis ingrata, que stercorat in sua strata.

(17) Third quarter of 15th cent.

Turpis avis nidum defedat stercore suum.

Camenz-Frankenberg Ms. I. Q. 363. Klapper's signature of the ms. (I. Q. 353, Bl. 108), *o.c.,* p. 79, is evidently a misprint. Klapper lists on p. 36, as no. 617, from Breslau Ms. I. Q. 617: Turpis avis proprium defedat stercore nidum.

(18) End of 15th cent.

Tis een vuul voghel, die sijn nest ontreint.
Vilis et ingrata volucris fedans sua strata.

Proverbia Communia, no. 677. See Hoffmann von Fallersleben, *Altniederländische Sprichwörter*. . . . p. 42, and no. (25), below.

(19) *Ca.* 1495.

Nemo suae patriae confingat scandale, nidum
Defoedans proprium, pessima fertur avis.
Nymand schendt seyn vaterlandt
Das er nicht werde genant
Eyn vogel der do vnreyn ist
Vnd schmeyst ym selber in seyn genist.

Fabri de Werdea, *Proverbia metrica*, n. 166 v. 393. See Suringar, *Bebel*, p. 207; *Erasmus*, pp. XXX f.

(20) 1508

Pessima est avis, quae proprium nidum defoedat: hoc est: Malus est, qui vel uxorem vel propriam patriam et familiam vel suos parentes aut sorores infamat.

Henricus Bebelius, *Proverbia Germanica collecta atque in Latinum traducta,* quoted from Suringar, *Heinrich Bebels Proverbia Germanica* (Leiden, 1879), p. 21, no. 44.

(21) 1514–15.

It is ein vûl vogel, de syn eigen nest beschit.
Foeda suum volucris defoedans stercore nidum.

Hoffmann von Fallersleben (ed.), *Tunnicius* (Berlin, 1870), p. 80, no. 952; p. 176.

(22) 1539 and 1552. Richard Taverner, *Proverbs or Adages of Erasmus* (London, 1539 and 1552), in referring "It is an evyl byrde that defyleth her owne neste" to Erasmus, evidently has in mind Erasmus' "Qui domi compluitur." See V. Stuckey Lean's *Collectanea*, IV (1904), 9: Tav., f. 59, 1552. The reference to Erasmus I owe to Professor Richard Jente (Erasmus 4338, p. 659 of the 1518 edition of the *Adagia*). Cf. Suringar, *Erasmus*, p. 345, nos. CLXXXVII, 3 and 4: "Qui domi compluitur, huius ne deum quidem miseret," with references to Franck and to Egenolff (1541 and 1548).

(23) 1566–1598.

Turpis avis spurcum proprium facit upupa lectum.

Gartner, *Proverbialia Dicteria* (1566–1598), p. 113. Cf. Suringar, *Bebel*, p. 207. See no. (26), below.

(24) *Ca.* 1570.

Est avis ingrata, quae defoedat sua strata.
Welcher sein eigen nest bescheist,
Billich ein boeser vogel heist.

Bruno Seidel, *Loci Communes proverbiales de moribus, carminibus antiquis conscripti, cum interpretatione Germanica nunc primum selecti et editi* (Basle, 1572), p. 174. See Seiler, *Deutsche Sprichwörterkunde*, p. 125; *Z. f. d. Ph.*, XLV (1913), p. 279.

(25) 1521 to 1634 (?).

It is a foul bird that bewrays his own nest.
Vilis et ingrata volucris foedans sua strata.

Lean, *Collectanea,* IV, p. 9, quotes "Bewrays. W. 1586," and on p. 10, he quotes "Vilis et ingrata volucris foedans sua strata. W., 1586." Does Lean have in mind John Withals, *Dict. in English and Latin* (London, 1521, and later editions, up to 1634) and does he quote from the edition of 1586?

(26) Undated.

Turpis avis foedum proprium facit upupa nidum.

J. Eiselein, *Die Sprichwörter und Sinnreden des deutschen Volkes in alter und neuer Zeit* (Freiburg, 1840), 621.

EXAMPLES OF MODERN VERNACULAR FORMS OF THE PROVERB

They are cited from the well-known collections of Wander, Düringsfeld, and Haller.

Portuguese: Aquella ave he má, que em seu ninho suja.
Spanish: Aquella aue es mala: que su nido estraga (o :cága).
Italian: Cattivo uccello che sporca il suo nido.
French: Cet oiseau est méchant, qui chie en son nid.
Dutch: Het is een vuile vogel, die zijn eigen nest ontreinigt.
English: It is an ill bird that fouls its own nest.
German: Es ist ein böser Vogel, der in sein eigen Nest hofiert.
Danish: Det er en slem Fugl, som besmitter sin egen Rede.
Swedish: Elak fogel, som sölar sitt egit näste.
Norwegian: D'er ein klen Fugl, som skjemmer sitt eiget Reid.
Icelandic: Sá es foglinn verstr es i sjálfs sins hreiþr dritr.

II. Some Aspects of Dissemination of the Medieval Latin Versions

The list in *I* seems to make it fairly clear that there was current before the year 1000 A.D. a proverb or a proverbial expression that had to do with the behavior of birds in their nests: A clean nest does honor to its feathered inhabitants; they are good birds. An unclean nest does not do honor to its occupants; these birds are bad birds. A good bird keeps his nest clean. A bad bird does not keep his nest clean; he soils it, befouls it. That such a proverb or proverbial expression must have been fairly well known at the time when the Imperial Committee visited the monastery of St. Gall in 966, is apparent from Ekkehard's account (I, 1). Ekkehard's spokesmen do not have to quote the postulated maxim; they can *allude* to it.

An expression of this sort lends itself well to moralizing. Most likely, therefore, teachers and preachers and such as prepared sermon-helps seized this "proverb" and standardized and disseminated it. They, members of the Church, are responsible for the monastic, ecclesiastic, Latin, moralizing tradition of this proverb, and they are the authors of its metrical form; *hexameter*, e.g. I, 2–7, 10, 14, 21; *distich*, e.g. I, 9, 19; *leonine verse*, e.g. I, 11, 13, 15, 18, 25. A verse, they knew, is more easily memorized and retained. It becomes a "quotation." There is, to be sure, a certain amount of variation in the Latin versions that are handed down to us. The bird that soils its nest is *ales immundus, degenerans, probrosus* or *avis (volucris) mala, non valens, sordida, pessima, foeda,* or, most frequently, *turpis, ingrata,* or *vilis et ingrata.* And the soiling is called *commaculare, violare, (stercore) foedare* (or *defoedare*), *demerdare, stercorare, polluere, contaminare, fedis corrumpere,* or *olidum facere nidum.* Again, in some instances, a specific bird is named as the evildoer (*onocrotalus, monedula, upupa*). In most citations, however, the bird remains an anonymous fowl. On the other hand, the metrical form places a certain restraint on the choice of vocabulary, and the result is "standardization." This is noticeable, from the 12th century on, especially with those versions of the proverb which occur in collections, i.e., as isolated sayings, without a (story) context. A context would naturally make for variation of expression, to suit a special situation or occasion. By the year 1400, approximately, two versions, both leonine, seem to be on the way to becoming the favored versions: *Turpis avis, proprium que fedat stercore nidum,* and *Est avis ingrata, que defedat sua strata.*[14] A glance at the modern standard forms of the vernacular versions of our proverb at the end of *I* makes it very probable that they are the lineal descendants of the one or the other of these two Latin versions.

III. Who or What is the Bird That Fouls Its Own Nest?

This much, then, seems to be plausible, viz., that there was in the beginning a widely distributed, Medieval Latin saying concerning the bird, or a bird, that fouls its own nest, and that all the modern vernacular versions derive from it. This view explains satisfactorily the *dissemination* of the proverb over western and northern Europe after *ca.* 1000 A.D. It would be wrong, however, to assume blithely that such an assumption explains the *origin* of our proverb. Any attempt to explain the *origin* of the proverb must take into consideration the possibility that there existed somewhere in western Europe in early medieval times a *vernacular* saying about a filthy, nest-befouling bird and that this *vernacular* saying was used by a monastic teacher, who transformed it into a Latin verse and thus originated the Latin tradition. This (later) Latin stream may very well have existed side by side with one or several vernacular streams which flowed subterraneously, i.e., which merely did not happen to come into evidence in medieval literature. In this connection, it is interesting to look at the passage in Egbert von Lüttich's *Fecunda Ratis*, the first complete form of our proverb in European literature. To be sure, it is recorded in Latin, and thus seems to lend weight to the opinion that subscribes to the theory of the Medieval Latin origin of our adage. It must not be forgotten, however, that it was Egbert's intention to collect proverbs, etc., *that were current among the folk and that had never before been written down "in communi sermone, nusquam scripta"* (so in his dedication to Bishop Adalbold of Utrecht). Hence it is possible that our proverb—as proverb—did exist in the vernacular of the Dutch Lowlands at Egbert's time. On the other hand, Egbert made use of the ecclesiastical literature and of the classical heritage in the compilation of his anthology, and since he does not distinguish in the arrangement of his "*rustici sermonis opusculum*" between indigenous and non-indigenous proverbs, one is unable to tell whether his proverb concerning the nest-befouling bird is one deriving from classical antiquity or one that sprang from the soil of Egbert's native country or some other (west) European land some time during the early Middle Ages. Similarly one might argue for a Latin or for a vernacular origin of the expression on which the banter in the *Casus S. Galli* rests.

The inquiry, whether the Latin form from which descend the vernacular versions was "original" or whether it, in turn, was derived from a vernacular source or tradition, or whether it derives ultimately from older, classical or ecclesiastical, etc., traditions, can be answered, in my opinion, by answering another question, viz., Who or what is the bird that fouls its own nest?

About 15 years ago, the thought occurred to me that the bird in the proverb, "It is an ill bird that fouls its own nest," might well be a specific bird. I was pleased when Professor Richard Jente wrote me, in answer to a different matter, on October 24, 1931: "This (It is an ill bird, etc.) is a good example of a medieval proverb based on an old Latin one, but made more definite. I even suspect that in the new form it alluded originally to some definite bird of which a story was told such as the proverb sums up." I am satisfied that I have identified the nest-befouling bird and that the culprit is the hoopoe (*upupa epops L.*). Elsewhere I have presented what to me constitutes the proof for my assumption.[15] I need, therefore, at this time only summarize the reasons for my belief in the hoopoe as the ill bird that fouls its own nest, and cite by way of proof and illustration such material as is not included in the previous publication.

The *upupa epops L.* is one of the world's most infamous sterquilinous birds. As a matter of fact, it is among the fowls of the air what the skunk is among the beasts of the field. Most names of the hoopoe which are not onomatopoeic, particularly in France, in the Netherlands, the Scandinavian countries, and in Germany, connect it with dirt, dung, excrements, and stench, and make it out to be an unclean bird. Even when the hoopoe is called by its various "standard" names, it is often described as an unclean, unsavory bird. Sometimes the reference to the hoopoe contains only a brief statement, an epithet, to the effect that it is a filthy bird; sometimes a more or less detailed etiological account is given, explaining the genesis of its coprolitic and scatophagous manners; again, a knowledge of the cause of its offensive odor is presupposed and hence there are only allusions to an etiological account. Popular belief in the hoopoe's habits and traits of uncleanliness is practically coexistent with the geographical occurrence of the bird. This bad reputation of the hoopoe is recorded as early as the Pentateuch. It is a part of the ornithological lore of today. It is true, of course, that speaking of the Old World in general and of Germany in particular, the rise of industrialization and the growing importance of urban centers has caused the hoopoe to be forgotten. For most people it has ceased to be a living reality and has become, at best, a name only.[16] The oldest reference to the filthiness of the hoopoe seems to be in the list of birds of abomination, found in Leviticus XI and in Deuteronomy XIV.[17] The Arabs share this view (but see below). The oldest allusion in Greek literature to the putrid emanations of the hoopoe seems to be the passage in Aristophanes' *Birds*, 641 ff.[18] From this time on, there is a cloud of witnesses, testifying to the belief of classical antiquity, the Middle Ages, and of modern times in the "ill"ness of the hoopoe. The witnesses include such authors as Aristotle, Aelian, Pliny, St. Jerome,[19] St. Cyril,[20] Isidore of Seville, Rhabanus Maurus, St. Hildegard, Odo de Ciringtonia, Vincent of Beauvais,[21] Albert the Great, Johannes de Janna.[22] Many vernacular passages furnish additional proof that the hoopoe = filthy bird tradition was firmly established in medieval Europe. Here belong among others, Guillaume le Clerk, Heinrich von dem Türlin, Der Stricker, Konrad von Megenberg. In addition, there are a good many medieval and modern folk tales, etc., from France, Italy, Rumania, Bukovina and Transylvania, Carniola, Lusatia, England and, especially, Germany.[23]

It is scientific observation and pseudo-scientific lore, the latter based chiefly on biblical and classical tradition, which makes the hoopoe out to be a filthy bird. The passages, quoted in *The Hoopoe*, pp. 40–60, may be roughly divided into two groups: first, such as characterize the hoopoe as a filthy bird because it eats filth or chooses filthy dwelling and feeding places; and, second, such passages as describe it as a filthy bird because it befouls its nest. It is this latter trait of the hoopoe, that of befouling its own nest, which, I think, lives on in our proverb.

It must be admitted that the hoopoe's *name* occurs but rarely in connection with the proverb. Usually the proverb mentions no bird by name. Only in the following instances have I found the hoopoe mentioned specifically as the bird that fouls its nest:

Est avis ingrata, que defedat sua strata. Talis est upupa, per quam significantur fornicarii et adulteri. [Breslau-Lüben Ms., 1459 A.D.: see above *I*, (16)].

Der Vogel kan nit sein der best. // der scheisset in sein eigen nest. [Thomas Murner, *Die Schelmen Zunfft*, 1512; the hoopoe is not named, but there is an illustration featuring the hoopoe].

In sein eigen nest hofieren wie ein widhopf (=hoopoe). [Sebastian Franck, 1541: see above *I*, (22)].

Turpis avis spurcum proprium facit upupa nidum. [Gartner, *Proverbialia Dicteria*, publ. 1566–1598: see above *I*, (23)].

Turpis avis foedum proprium facit upupa nidum. [See above *I*, (26)].

It must also be admitted that the hoopoe is not the only bird that is said to befoul its nest. In the list in *I*, two more such birds are mentioned, *onocrotalus* and *monedula.* And in *The Hoopoe*, pp. 62, 65–72, I have enumerated others of this ilk. There I also give my reasons for assuming that, if not originally, then certainly ultimately, the hoopoe is the ill bird that fouls its own nest. In my opinion, the *onocrotalus* and the *monedula* and the other birds mentioned as rivals of the hoopoe eventually dropped from the ken of the people who were using our proverb. They eventually understood the bird in question to be the hoopoe, even though they did not mention it specifically. They did not have to mention the hoopoe by name, because the hoopoe, as the names and passages cited in *The Hoopoe* indicate, had become in the mind of the folk the one representative filthy bird that befouls its own nest.

The final step in the development of our proverb is that not even the hoopoe is thought of any longer when the proverb is quoted, except perhaps in certain rural districts. As has been pointed out before, knowledge of or rather familiarity with birds in general and with the hoopoe in particular is dying out, even in countries where the hoopoe was fairly well known up to the beginning of the nineteenth century. Because the hoopoe was never really at home in England (see note 16) we are not surprised at the non-appearance of its name in the English form of the proverb. But even in Germany, where it seems to have been well known up into recent times, the hoopoe is mentioned less and less frequently. It is my impression that it occurs only in such nineteenth and twentieth century writers as are "close to the soil."

In the modern vernacular proverb, "It is an ill bird that fouls its own nest," we have, then, a paroemiological formulation of a belief or beliefs which derive from classical, Graeco-Roman sources by way of medieval ecclesiastical and "scientific" writers. Ultimately, however, the belief in the malodorous characteristics of the hoopoe, which finds expression in our modern European proverb, seems to rest on oriental, Egyptio-Semitic lore. For there is strong likelihood that the allusion to the fetor in the nest of the hoopoe in Aristophanes' *Birds* is an allusion to something not commonly known in Greece at that time. E. Oder suggests rather convincingly that the Athenians were not very well acquainted with this bird, else they would have made more of its stench.[24] He claims that nowhere in their literature do they mention the noisome odor of the hoopoe.[25] In this, I think, Oder errs. To me, the passage in the *Birds* loses all significance if one rules out the allusion to the offensive smell of the nest. But the fact remains that the Athenians do not make much of this trait which elsewhere is one of the first traits to be noted. And for this reason, the statement in Aelian, *Hist. Anim.* XVI, 5, becomes significant: this story (about the hoopoe; it has nothing to do directly with the stench emanating from the bird and its nest) has come to the Greeks from the Orient, and one must not think of the European hoopoe as mentioned in this oriental story, but of the Indian hoopoe, previously described by Aelian.[26] This remark of Aelian's indicates, rather late, it must be admitted—Aelian belongs in the latter part of the second century A.D.—that there was knowledge of the introduction of hoopoe lore from the Orient into Greece. There is, however, this difficulty that the story to which Aelian refers, while it is a hoopoe-story, has nothing to do with the hoopoe as the, or an, ill bird that fouls its own nest. It has to do with that other very important bit of hoopoe lore, the filial piety of the hoopoe, a trait which seems diametrically opposed to that of the uncleanness of the bird. The one characteristic is a vice and surrounds the bird with mephitic stench, while the other characteristic is a virtue and envelops it with the odor of sanctity, in the tradition of the Egyptians, the Arabs, and the peoples of medieval Christian Europe and Byzantium.[27] *And it is this story of the filial piety of the hoopoe which,* according to Aelian, *was introduced into Greece from the*

Orient. Does not the one story preclude the other, or one belief cancel what is apparently a denial of the belief?

I had for a long time assumed that filial piety was one trait of the hoopoe and that its dirty habits were another, that both existed side by side, as happens not infrequently in popular belief. For this reason, I did not connect these two bits of hoopoe lore one with the other. I permitted them to have being separately. I was inclined to demand oriental origin for both, but, as it were, two separate oriental origins—two oriental sources whence flowed two parallel streams into the Graeco-Roman world and on into medieval Europe.

I am now convinced that there is only one oriental source for the two traditions. And for this reason, I am even more certain than before that the modern European proverb, "It is an ill bird that fouls its own nest," has its roots in the Egyptio-Semitic Orient. *This one oriental source I find in the story of the burial of the hoopoe's mother in the head of the young hoopoe.* This story is told in order to praise the filial piety of the young bird, to explain the origin of the fetor of the hoopoe, and, incidentally, also that of the hoopoe's crest.[28] It is really the filial piety of the hoopoe which causes the infamous stench to cling to it.

This assertion rests on the story told *ca.* 870 A.D. by Ibn Koteiba, while writing the biography of the Arabic poet Umajja ibn Abi s Salt, who died nine years after the Hegira. There the following verses, a part of a *Kamil* by Umajja ibn Abi s Salt, are recorded:

> Nubila erant et caligo densaeque tenebrae:
> Prodiit en matris corpore onustus epops.
> Lecticam cristae praebebant, donec haberet
> Credi cui posset sarcina cara locum.
> At frustra petiit finem requiemve laboris:
> Gestat gestabitque hoc pietatis onus.[29]

Nebelgewölk und Finsternis und ein Wolkenergusz, zu den Zeiten, wo der Wiedehopf seine Mutter ins Leichentuch hüllte und auf die Suche ging [var, sich verproviantierte],

um ihr eine Ruhestätte zu bereiten und sie da zu bestatten: da richtete er ihr auf seinem Hinterkopf das Grab auf, indem er ein weiches Lager

> bereitete. Dann erhob er sich mit seiner Last zu den Vögeln [oder: mit den Vögeln], seine Mutter tragend, ohne sich zu krümmen
>
> Unter ihrer Last, und so lief er, sich als Sohn mit seiner Last aussöhnend, und man vermiszt nicht die braune Farbe seines Rückens.
>
> Und man sieht ihn schwerbelastet schreiten unter ihrem Totenbett, solange er geht und solange die Zeitläufe sich ablösen.[30]

Schulthesz, the author of the German translation of the Arabic verses, adds: "Die Legende erklärt den Gestank, der dem Wiedehopf vom Nest anhaftet," and J. van Leeuwen, from whom the Latin paraphrase is quoted, cites Ibn Koteiba as observing, "ferunt enim upupam matris morte functae corpus in capite collocasse, donec locum sepulcro idoneum inveniret; ibi autem mansisse corpus crista abditum, causamque hanc esse tetri odoris quem upupa solet spargere."

Here, then, we have the "explanation" of the stench of the hoopoe. This stench was something new in the nostrils of the Athenians. It came to them from the Orient. They passed it on, in their (pseudo) scientific writings, just as they preserved in their poetry the story of the burial of the bird parent in the head of the young bird. The only changes which Aristophanes—it is he who alludes to the stench of the hoopoe in his *Birds*, and it is he who tells the story of the filial piety of a bird in the same play—makes, are in the name of the bird: he changes the hoopoe into a crested lark (the hoopoe is a crested bird!), and in the sex of the parent: it is the father bird who dies and is buried.[31]

It is a long flight from Yemen to England and Iceland. On the way, the filial piety and the stench of the hoopoe which used to be united as cause and effect in one oriental story, became separated into two unrelated parts. One of them, the tradition concerning the filial piety of the hoopoe, came to an untimely end in the sixteenth century. The other lives on in the proverb, "It is an ill bird that fouls its own nest."[32]

Notes

1. *Egberts von Lüttich Fecunda Ratis, zum ersten Mal herausgegeben, auf ihre Quellen zurückgeführt und erklärt von Ernst Voigt* (Halle, 1889), p. 36. See also F. Seiler, *Deutsche Sprichwörterkunde* (Munich, 1922), pp. 91, 71–73, 79; id., "Deutsche Sprichwörter in mittelalterlicher lateinischer Fassung," *Z. f. a. Ph.*, XXXXV (1913), p. 279; A. Taylor, *The Proverb* (Cambridge, Mass., 1931), p. 51.

2. Hoffmann von Fallersleben, "Altniederländische Sprichwörter nach der ältesten Sammlung," *Horae Belgicae, Pars Nona* (Hanover, 1854); *id.* (ed.), *Tunnicius, Dic älteste niederdeutsche Sprichwortsammlung von Antonius Tunnicius gesammelt und in lateinische Verse übersetzt* (Berlin, 1870).

3. K.F.W. Wander, *Deutsches Sprichwörten-Lexikon*, vol. III (Leipzig, 1873), *s.v.* "Nest"; vol. IV (Leipzig, 1876), *s.v.* "Vogel."

4. W.H.D. Suringar, *Erasmus over nederlandsche spreekwoorden* (Utrecht, 1873): *Heinrich Bebels Proverbia Germanica* (Leiden, 1879).

5. Ida von Düringsfeld—Otto von Reinsberg-Düringsfeld, *Sprichwörter der Germanischen und Romanischen Sprachen*, vol. II (Leipzig, 1875), no. 561.

6. Joseph Haller, *Altspanische Sprichwörter und sprichwörtliche Redensarten aus den Zeiten vor Cervantes*, I (Ratisbon, 1883), pp. 317–319, no. 266.

7. Müllenhoff-Scherer, *Denkmäler deutscher Poesie und Prosa aus dem VIII–XII. Jahrhundert*, third edition, ed. by E. Steinmeyer (Berlin, 1892), I. pp. 63 ff.

8. Vincent Stuckey Lean's *Collectanea*, vol. IV (Bristol, 1904), pp. 9–10.

9. G. Walz, *Das Sprichwort bei Gower mit besonderem Hinweis auf Quellen und Parallelen*, Munich Diss. (Nördlingen, 1907), pp. 80–81.

10. Max Förster, "Das elisabethanische Sprichwort nach Th. Draxe's Treasurie of Ancient Adagies (1616)," *Anglia* XLII = N. F. XXX (1918), pp. 361 ff.

11. Friedrich Seiler, see note 1.

12. Richard Jente, "The Proverbs of Shakespeare with Early and Contemporary Parallels," *Washington University Studies*, vol. XIII, *Humanistic Series*, No. 2 (April, 1926) = Whole No. LII, pp. 402–3.

13. *Zeitschrift für deutsche Philologie*, XLVII (1916), p. 250.

14. *ingrata*, i.e., *non grata*, as in *persona non grata*. There is also an *ungrateful bird*. This is the bird that lays eggs in strange nests. I have collected a considerable amount of the lore of this bird and intend to publish it in the near future.

15. *The Hoopoe. A Study in European Folklore*. Dissertation, The University of Chicago, 1938. Cited henceforth as *The Hoopoe*. Cf. Hoffmann-Krayer, "Wiedehopf," *Handwörterbuch des deutschen Aberglaubens*, IX, coll. 565–570.

16. The hoopoe is not known in America. It is an old-world bird. It hails from Africa. It seems to be fairly common on the continent of Europe. In England, it is something of a rare bird. See *The Hoopoe*, p. 1.

17. The "Second Moses," Maimonides (1135–1204), furnishes a list of 24 unclean birds. The hoopoe is no. 23. "Signa mundarum avium non explicantur ex Lege, quae solum immundarum censum instituit, et reliquae species concessae sunt. Species porro prohibitae sunt viginti quatuor." *De cibis vetitis,* chapter I, section 14, cited in Samuel Borchart, *Hierozoicon sive de animalibus S. Scripturae*, ed. Ern. Frid. Car. Rosenmüller (Leipzig, 1796), III, p. 119.

18. Cf. J. van Leeuwen, *Aristophanis Aves. Cum Prolegomenis et Commentariis* (Leyden, 1902), p. 103, note 642; also his excellent *Excursus de epope avium rege, o.c.,* pp. 261–270. I owe the reference to the *Excursus* to the kindness of Professor Archer Taylor. See also M. Ludwig Keimer, *"Quelques remarques sur la huppe (upupa epops) dans l'Égypte ancienne," Bulletin de l'Institut Français d'Archéologie Orientale,* XXX (1930), pp. 305–331, esp. 324 f. Hippolyte Boussac, "La huppe dans l'ancienne Égypte," *Le Naturaliste*, 29e année, 2e série, no. 496, ler novembre 1907, pp. 251–3, I have not seen.

19. *in Zachariam*, cp. 5: "Épopa appellant ab eo, quod stercora humana consideret. Avem dicunt esse spurcissimam, semper in sepulchris, semper in humano stercore commorantem. Denique et nidum ex eo facere dicitur, et pullos suos de vermiculis stercoris alere putrescentis." Quoted from Bochart, *o.c.,* III, p. 114.

20. *Libro III, de adoratione:* "(upupa) aviculae genus est, quae paludum foedissimas perpetuo circumvolat, atque ex coeno et sordibus pastum petit."

in Zachariam, t. III: "(upupa) avis est coeno gaudens, stercore vescens, et in vermium greges ferocius insaniens, et immundissima quaeque pro alimento usurpare solita."

Homilia decima de festis Paschalibus: "Upupa, inquam, impura est avicula, quae vermibus et ventris excrementis vesci gaudet imprimis." All three passages are quoted, in the original and in translation, in Bochart, *o.c.,* III, p. 114. See also pp. 123 f.

21. *Bibliotheca Mundi Vincentii Burgundi ex ordine Praedicatorum Venerabiiis Episcopi Bellovacensis Speculum Quadruplex* (Duacr, 1624), *Spec. nat.,* lib. XVI, c. 148, coll. 1235–6, with many references.

22. *Summa que Catholicon appellatur fratris Johannis Ianuensis sacri ordinis fratrum predicatorum . . . emendata per prestantem virum magistrum Petrum Egidium* (1520), *s.v.* "Vpupa"; "Upupam greci appellant quia stercora humana comedat et fetenti pascatur fimo. Auis est quedam spurcissima christis extensis galeata: semper in sepulchris et humano stercore commorans." The *Summa* was originally published in 1286. Works such as the *Summa* and the *Bibliotheca Mundi* are good examples of medieval encyclopedias which copied together existing information and, in turn, were copied and excerpted.

23. I should like to add here a medieval hoopoe-passage which heretofore had escaped me. It is found in *Monumenta Germaniae Historica, Legum Sectio V. Formulae,* ed. by K. Zeumer (1886), in the "Additamentum e codice formularum Senonensium," p. 226:

16 Volat upua, et non arundo,
Isterco commedit in so frundo,
Humile facit capta dura,
Sicut dilatus in falsatura
Falsator. Vadit
21 Tamquam latro ad aura psallit . . .

The text is evidently not good. This much seems to be clear: the "upua" is the "upupa"; the "arundo" is most likely the "hirundo"; "Isterco commedit in so frundo" is perhaps "Stercus commedat in sua fronde" = the hoopoe eats dung in its leafy nest.

24. E. Oder, "Der Wiedehopf in der griechischen Sage," *Rheinisches Museum*, N. F. XLIII (1888), 541–56, esp. p. 550.

25. J. van Leeuwen, *o.c.*, pp. 267 f. with note 1 on p. 268.

26. J. van Leeuwen, *o.c.*, pp. 268 f.

27. See *The Hoopoe*, chap. III, "The Hoopoe, an Exponent of Filial Piety," pp. 22–29; M. Ludwig Keimer, *o.c.*, pp. 325 f.

28. See *The Hoopoe*, chap. I, "The Crested Bird," pp. 1–10.

29. J. van Leeuwen, *o.c.*, p. 267.

30. Friedrich Schulthesz, "Umajja ibn Abi ṣ Ṣalt. Die unter seinem Namen überlieferten Gedichtfragmente gesammelt und übersetzt," *Beiträge zur Assyriologie und semitischen Sprachwissenschaft*, ed. Friedrich Delitzch-Paul Haupt, VIII, Heft 3 (Leipzig, 1911), p. 26, verses 5 ff. [the passage in Arabic, poem no. XXV], p. 85, lines 9 ff. [translation]; p. 84 has an introduction to the legend of the hoopoe and additional references. Cf. E. Power, S.J., "Umayya Ibn Abi-S Salt," *Mélanges de la Faculté Orientale*, I (Beyreuth, 1906), no. 5, pp. 197–222; esp. pp. 200, 220–222; de Goeje, *Ibn Qotaiba, Liber Poesis et Poetarum* (Leyden, 1904), pp. 279 f. (Arabic only). I hereby wish to acknowledge gratefully the kind assistance rendered me in connection with the Arabic material by Professor Martin Sprengling of the Oriental Institute of the University of Chicago.

31. *Birds*, vv. 471 ff. J. van Leeuwen, *o.c.*, p. 268, note 3, cites "another" head burial, Theocritus VII, 23. He denies that this is a head burial and claims that the scholium on the passage is wrong. To me the interpretation of the ancient commentator is an additional proof for the acquaintance with this legend. On the Aesopian fable concerning the burial of the parent bird in the head of the crested lark, which Aristophanes retells, and on the Theocritus-scholium see also C.E.C. Schneider (ed.), *Fabulae Aesopicae a Francisco de Furia Florentino . . . collectae* (Leipzig, 1810), no. 415, p. 168; Claudius Galenus, *de simplicium medicamentorum temperamentis ac facultatibus*, ed. by C.G. Kühn (Medicorum Graecorum opera quae exstant, XII [Leipzig, 1826]), Lib. XI, cap. 37, pp. 360 f.; A. Gronovius (ed.), *Aeliani de natura animalium* (Heilbronn, 1765), p. 1110 [his reference to Cruquius' commentary on Horace's ode 12 of Book IV is somewhat misleading; Cruquius explains there the "fine feathers" of the pheasant into whom the young prince Itys has been transformed: see *Q. Horatius Flaccus cum commentariis etc.*, ed. by Cruquius (Leyden, 1597), p. 242]; Pauly-Wissowa, *Real-Encyclopädie der Classischen Altertumswissenschaft* XXIX, col. 312 (O. Stein, "Indien bei Megasthenes") and I.A.' coll. 101 f. (W. Schultz, "Rätsel" von "Ungeboren," der seinen Vater oder seine Mutter auf dem Kopfe trägt). On the migration of the (Arabic) story concerning the head burial to the African tribe of the Soroko see Albert Wesselski, "Alters-Sinnbilder und Alters-Wettstreit," *Journal of the Czechoslovak Oriental Institute* IV (Prague, 1932), no. 1, pp. 6–8. The reference to Wesselski I owe to the kindness of Professor Archer Taylor. As a *curiosum* I cite Bochart, *o.c.*, III, p. 115: lam vide, lector, praeclaram metamorphosim upupae in alaudam, cuius auctor Pandectarius: Alauda (inquit) Arabice est upupa avis. Imo Arabice alauda vox est nihili. Sed is ex alhudhud (the Arabic article *al* plus the Arabic name of the hoopoe *hudhud*) fecit alaudam. Sic Athenienses de alauda fabulari, quod de upupa Brachmanes observat Aelianus Historiae libri decimi sexti capite quinto.

32. It is possible that the story of the filial love and of the head-burial of the hoopoe was originally told, not of the hoopoe, but of the fabled phoenix, and was then transferred to the hoopoe whose description is not unlike that of the phoenix in some

texts. On some of the phoenix lore bits of traditions concerning the sacred scarabaeus may have become superimposed, and thus may have been brought about the change from the original sweet odor of the phoenix to the odor of dung which is associated with the *sacer scarabaeus* and which now clings to the hoopoe in popular tradition. See J. van Leeuwen, *o.c.,* pp. 269 f.

Stuff a Cold and Starve a Fever

*Stuart A. Gallacher**

The study of individual proverbs may lead into many fields, for example, law and medicine. In the case of so-called medical proverbs, some may question whether such traditional dicta as "An apple a day keeps the doctor away" should be considered as belonging to the proverb genre at all. Such sayings are almost always understood literally whereas most proverbs can be interpreted metaphorically. Because of the literal nature of medical adages, they can appropriately be cited only in a very limited number of contexts. "Stuff a cold and starve a fever" might well be considered as a folk belief or superstition rather than a proverb. On the other hand, it is included in proverb collections—one can find it in The Oxford Dictionary of English Proverbs, *for example. Proverb and/or superstition, this folk remedy for colds and fevers remains current in American oral tradition. Professor Stuart A. Gallacher's brief consideration of it ends with an illuminating discussion of the possible folk principles of thought which underlie it. For other examples, see Russell A. Elmquist, "English Medical Proverbs,"* Modern Philology, *32 (1934–35), 75–84. For further consideration of the folk theory mentioned by Gallacher, see M.H. Logan, "Selected References on the Hot-Cold Theory of Disease,"* Medical Anthropology Newsletter, *6:2 (February, 1975), 8–14.*

The origin or real meaning of this rather common expression is still cause for conjecture.[1] Some scholars believe the expression to be

* Reprinted from the *Bulletin of the History of Medicine*, 11 (1942), 576–581, by permission of the Johns Hopkins University Press.

elliptical with the meaning: if you stuff a cold, you will have a fever to starve.[2] Others believe it should be interpreted literally. After investigating the possible medical theories upon which it might be founded, I believe it was meant to be taken literally. It is rather a product of lay thinking of comparatively recent times than a traditional medical maxim or popular superstition. Only one element, starve a fever, is, according to medical knowledge, justifiable to a certain degree. The elliptical meaning seems at first glance to be in harmony with medical thought, but it, too, is not fully in agreement with medical knowledge, since all colds are not without more or less fever.[3]

I have been unable to find an equivalent expression in any other modern tongue which might have influenced our expression. Since the present meaning of starve (to deprive of food) and the meaning of cold (the disease) first occur in the sixteenth century,[4] the English form of our expression cannot be older than that century. The earliest examples, however, are from around the middle of the nineteenth century,[5] and, singularly, at a time when both fevers and common colds were epidemical in England.[6] These epidemics certainly afforded ample opportunity for someone to coin an expression indicative of a popular treatment for two of our most common ailments. In addition, such a simple statement is rather to be looked for when sufficient, capable medical attention is not available. Household remedies circulate rapidly in the absence of competent medical advice.

What is the historical evidence of the treatment of fevers and colds? It has been the practice since the early stages of medicine to make the patient fast or carefully feed him if suffering from a fever.[7] In the medicine of India one fasted to rid oneself of a fever.[8] Part of a compound Indian proverb attests this ancient and modern practice.[9] In western medicine the diet has always been an important factor. Robert Bently Todd (1809–1860) deviated from the strict dietary treatment and began to feed the fever-stricken patient, and, to be sure, he and his colleagues sometimes went to excess. Since his time, however, fevers have been scientifically fed.[10]

The common cold—*gravedo* in ancient Roman and *coryza* in ancient Greek medicine—likewise was treated by careful observation of the stricken person's diet.[11] There are no instances of stuffing, or feeding in the sense of stuffing. *Gravedo* did not imply the meaning of a person having been chilled or exposed to cold as the word cold suggests to laymen today. To be sure, the old principle *contraria contrariis curantur*[12] might imply the stuffing of colds, but, as far as I can determine, there are no medical cases recorded of its application in the treatment of colds. The reversed principle *similia similibus curantur*[13] of Paracelsus likewise is not found in the treatment of colds. Both types of thinking were property of the so-called informed physicians and were practiced by them and not the laity. Physicians are not (and were not) wont knowingly to state false doctrines as maxims, since their reputations depend upon their ability to effect a cure. It is perhaps singular, too, that nowhere is our expression commented upon by physicians in their treatment of fevers, since the element dealing with fever does not run obnoxiously counter to medical knowledge. On the other hand, when physicians speak of the treatment of colds our expression comes in for a sharp denouncement, since the element dealing with a cold is unsound.[14]

A likely theory, I believe, underlying the origin of the expression, dates from ancient times, from Hippocrates who says, "As the soil is to trees, so is the stomach to animals. It nourishes, it warms, it cools; as it empties it cools, as it fills it warms."[15] In harmony with this, Hippocrates also presented regimen for winter and summer eating in which he expressed the principle of eating as much as possible in the winter to keep warm, and lightly and of limited foods in the summer to keep cool.[16] This type of logic, however, was found only among the learned of that time, and did not have common currency among the laity until more recent times. Of course, people at all times and to a certain extent have been aware of the phenomenon observed by Hippocrates, but not until the advent of scientific medicine and competent physicians who have constantly enlightened the common folk in the matter of eating has the laymen been conscious of it to any marked degree.[17] Nowadays this has become common knowledge. The layman recognizes no obstacle if one says, summer and fever signify heat, and winter and "to catch cold" imply cold. The layman knows the respective reliefs from heat and cold, namely, little or no food and sufficient food or plenty of it.

The layman's acquisition of early medical principles has not been accompanied by a vivid realization of all their implications. He has always been notorious for his ability to think along the lines of least resistance. The layman's application of these principles then to our expression is, to reduce heat, one must remove that which produces it (starve a fever), to produce heat, fuel must be supplied (stuff or feed a cold). This is a logical solution with respect to common-folk thinking. Thus, one can say, that the principles underlying our expression are founded upon principles of medicine in its early period of development. Our expression, however, was not coined by physicians. The elements of contrast, *starve: stuff* and *fever: cold* with the element of alliteration *st* (or *f* in the variants with *feed*) speak rather for a lay origin than for a learned medical one. Contrast and alliteration are elements frequently found in proverbs,[18] and are more the mark of the common folk than the learned man, notwithstanding the intricate forms of alliteration found in ancient and modern poetry.

Therefore, in the light of the above, and since our expression first occurs at about the same time that the common folk was becoming aware to a greater extent than ever before of what it thought to be good medicine, I agree with George Redway, one of the first to comment upon the expression, when he says, "a cold is to be fed, and a fever is to be starved."[19] This is the light in which the common folk understands it today and understood it years ago. The elliptical meaning is the viewpoint of those people somewhat better informed than the common folk, and it is they who read such a meaning into the proverb.

Notes

1. Cf. Archer Taylor, "The Study of Proverbs," *Modern Language Forum*, XXIV (1939), No. 2, 75–6, "What does *Stuff a cold and starve a fever* mean? Probably, the two injunctions are taken literally, but they are understood by some to signify *If you feed a cold, you will have a fever to starve*. As a matter of fact, indeed, the saying is sometimes reversed and quoted as *Starve a cold and stuff a fever*, but this perhaps is the version of a fever-smitten glutton."

2. Cf. Edward H. Marshall, *Notes and Queries,* 6th Series, III, 429, in which he suggests Socrates', πσλλάκις γὰρ τό γε λιμοῦ αγαθὸν πυρετοῦ κακόν ἐστιν, καὶ τὸ πυρετοῦ ἀγαθόν λιμοῦ κακόν ἐστιν (Memorabilia, III, viii. 7) [for oftentimes what is good for hunger is bad for a fever, and what is good for a fever is bad for hunger] to have something in common with the elliptical meaning of which he is in favor. See also ibid.,

IV, 54, the assertion of E. Leaton Blenkinsopp, "I have heard it 'stuff a cold, etc.,' the expression is elliptical, for '(if you) stuff a cold, (you will have to) starve a fever.' "

3. Cf. W.A. Wells, *The Common Head Cold and Its Implications* (New York, 1929), pp. 154–5, "A cold is a fever, the inflammation being localised in the respiratory mucous membranes." See also W.G. Smillie, *The Common Cold* (New York and London, 1937), p. 13, "Sometimes there occurs an increase to 100 degrees F. or even higher." In particular see the early opinion expressed by John W. Hayward, *Taking Cold* (London, 1873), p. 21, "The diseased states produced by taking cold are—local congestion and inflammation, and general fever."

4. Cf. James A. H. Murray, *A New English Dictionary* (Oxford, 1893), II, 609, "Cold," 4 b; IX, Pt. 1, 847, "Starve," 7.

5. Examples in writing are not numerous. Cf. W.G. Smith and J.C. Heseltine, *The Oxford Dictionary of English Proverbs*, p. 405, "Stuff a cold and starve a fever," 1852, E. Fitzgerald, *Polonius 9*; R.F. Burton, *Vikram and the Vampire* (New York, 1870), p. 61, "a fever starve, but feed a cold"; and Vincent S. Lean, *Collecteana, English and Other Proverbs, Folklore, etc.* (Bristol, 1902), I, 507, "Feed a cough and starve a fever; Feed a cold and starve a fever." Lean gives no sources for his references. Cough and cold are likely variants, since one is so closely associated with the other. R.F. Burton, above, attributed the saying to the learned physician *Charndatta*. Others, as well as myself, have been wholly unable to find Burton's *Charndatta*. This physician is not to be found in copies of the manuscript Burton is supposed to have used. There are, however, two famous Indian physicians, Candrata and Cakradatta, who practiced ca. A.D. 1000 and 1060. Burton might have had knowledge of either of them and added this information as pure embellishment.

6. Cf. J.G. Townsend, *A Review of the Literature on Influenza and the Common Cold* (Washington, D.C., 1924), Supplement #48, Public Health Reports, p. 61, "Stallybrass also calls attention to the epidemic years of England, which are, 1789–90, 1802–3, 1830–32, 1840–41, 1848–49, 1854, 1869–70, etc."

7. Cf. Theodor Hirsch, *Die Entwickelung der Fieberlehre und der Fieberbehandlung* (Berlin, 1870), p. 96, "In den älteren Schulen galt als Axiom, dass jeder Fiebernde auf knappe Diät gesetzt werden müsse. . . ." Cf. also W.G. Spencer, *Celsus, de medicina* (Loeb Classical Library, Cambridge, Mass., 1935), I, 233, "Hence for the first days there is to be abstinence from food; . . . . But his best medicine is food opportunely given; the question is when it should first be given." Cf. also p. 237, "The fourth day, however, is generally the most suitable date for beginning to give food."

8. Cf. Julius Jolly, "Medicin" (*Grundriss der Indo-Arischen Philologie und Altertumskunde* [Strassburg, 1901]), III, Heft 10, 73, "Im allgemeinen gilt die Regel zu Anfang Fasten, späterhin Beförderung der Verdauung durch entsprechende Diät, zuletzt Arzneien, etc."

9. Cf. Otto Böhtlingk, *Indische Sprüche* (St. Petersburg, 1873), 512, "Das Studium giebt uns Macht über die Vedas, das Fasten Macht über das Fieber, etc."

10. Cf. Hirsch, ibid., "die allgemeine Regel aber, während des ganzen Verlaufs keines acuten Fiebers jemals wirklich nährende Kost zu verabreichen, beruht sicher zum Theil auf der falschen Präsumption, dass unter allen Umständen die Oxydation der aufgenommenen Nährstoffe die Verbrennung im Körper, also auch die Stärke des Feibers, d. h. die Temperaturerhöhung vermehren müsse. Und bei diesem Punkte ist

allerdings vorzugsweise das Verdienst einiger englischen Aerzte, vor allen Todds, die alte Lehre gestürzt zu haben, wenn sie auch freilich nun oft genug in den entgegengesetzten Fehler verfallen sind." See also note 1, "Bekannt ist Todds Aeusserung, dass er als rühmendste Inschrift für sein Grab die drei Worte wünsche 'he fed fevers.' "

11. Cf. W.G. Spencer, ibid., p. 375, "In the case of gravedo, he should lie in bed on the first day, neither eat not drink, cover the head, and wrap wool around the throat; on the next day he should get up, and still abstain from drink, or, if he must have some, take not more than one tumbler-full of water: on the third day he may eat the crumb of bread, but not much, with some small fish, or light meat, and water for drink." Cf. also pp. 371–2 for Celsus' description of gravedo, "This closes up the nostrils, renders the voice hoarse, excites a dry cough; in it the saliva is salt, there is ringing in the ears, the blood-vessels in the head throb, the urine is turbid. Hippocrates names all the above coryza; I note that now the Greeks reserve this term for gravedo, the dripping they call catastagmus. These affections are commonly of short duration, but if neglected may last a long while. None is fatal, except that which causes ulcers in the lung."

12. Cf. S.W. Lambert and G.M. Goodwin, *Medical Leaders* (Indianapolis, 1929), p. 42, "Themison (Themison of Laodicea, 123–43 B.C.) formulated this method of therapeutics by the exhibition of drugs and hygienic procedures producing conditions the opposite of the pathology theoretically inferred as existent with the phrase *contraria contrariis curantur.*"

13. Cf. Ibid., p. 96, "He (Paracelsus, 1493–1541) substituted for the *contraria contrariis curantur* his own *similia similibus curantur* which later became the bone of contention in the great medical schism in American medicine of the early nineteenth century."

14. Cf. T.B. Rice, *The Conquest of Disease* (New York, 1927), p. 155, "For instance, we have the old advice, 'Stuff a cold and starve a fever.' This should be written 'Stuff a cold and you will need to starve the fever which follows,' if we would have it stated correctly." See also Russell L. Cecil, *Colds, Cause, Treatment and Prevention* (New York and London, 1927), p. 88, "In mild colds diet does not play a very important part in the treatment. The patient may eat moderately of any wholesome food and feel none the worse for it. In severe colds accompanied by fever the diet should consist of liquids and soft, easily digested foods. The old proverb, 'stuff a cold and starve a fever' is unsound in that a cold should not be fed any more than is necessary. Whatever food is taken should be simple and nutritious." See also W.A. Wells, ibid., "The diet should be light and free from nitrogenous foods. Nothing could be farther from the right than the injunction 'Feed a cold and starve a fever.' A cold is a fever. . . . Overloading the stomach is directly harmful. . . ."

15. Cf. W.H.S. Jones, *Hippocrates* (London and New York, 1931), IV, 83.

16. Cf. Ibid., p. 45.

17. The matter of proper diet has gone a step further. There are those who believe disease may be prevented by use of a "balanced diet," the elimination of malnutrition. There are others who discount the part malnutrition plays as a preventive measure. See W.G. Smillie, ibid., p. 63, wherein, in commenting upon diet and vitamins A and D as preventive measures for colds, he says, "But there is no evidence whatever that any of these various factors prevent a cold. The well-fed, healthy youngster will, as a rule, throw off the ill effects of a cold more rapidly than the ill-nourished child that does not follow the few simple rules of good personal hygiene. However, one should not delude

himself into thinking that he can prevent a cold by any known dietary regimen, not even by the highly recommended method of large doses of codliver oil."

18. Cf. Archer Taylor, *The Proverb* (Cambridge, Mass., 1931), pp. 143 and 137.
19. Cf. *Notes and Queries*, 6th Series, IV, 54.

Reliability and Validity of Proverb Interpretation to Assess Mental Status

*Nancy C. Andreasen**

Whereas literary scholars may seek to interpret proverbs or study how authors interpret proverbs, psychologists and psychiatrists ask subjects or patients to interpret proverbs for diagnostic reasons. Various proverb tests have been devised to measure intelligence or identify schizophrenics. This applied use of proverbs is in marked contrast with conventional social scientific proverb research. Anthropologists and folklorists try wherever possible to record proverb usage in natural contexts. Psychologists, on the other hand, construct artificial contexts in which proverbs are introduced.

There is a considerable literature in which psychological reports of proverb testing is featured. The following essay by Nancy C. Andreasen reviews some of the apparent strengths and weaknesses of psychological proverb tests. For an earlier essay in which proverb tests are considered, see Paul Satz and L. T. Carroll, "Utilization of the Proverbs Test as a Projective Instrument: An Objective Approach through Language Behavior," Journal of General Psychology *67 (1962), 205–213. For a folkloristic appraisal of some of this literature, see Wolfgang Mieder, "The Use of Proverbs in Psychological Testing,"* Journal of the Folklore Institute, *15 (1978), 45–55.*

Proverb interpretation has been a standard part of the mental status examination for many years. Like most forms of epigrammatic wit,

*Reprinted by permission of Grune & Stratton, Inc., and the author from *Comprehensive Psychiatry*, 18 (1977), 465–472.

proverbs can be quite profound, pithy, and entertaining, and perhaps consequently many psychiatrists find themselves particularly fascinated with this portion of the mental status examination. So ingrained is the tradition of asking about proverbs, in fact, that this area may be explored even when other aspects of mental status such as memory or orientation are left unexamined.

What can an interviewer learn about a patient's mental status by asking him to interpret a series of proverbs? Traditionally, proverbs have been used in order to help determine whether a patient has a thought disorder of some type. According to Goldstein, the fundamental impairment producing a thought disorder is inability to think abstractly.[1,2] Benjamin was one of the earliest investigators to use proverbs to assess deficits in thinking, and he emphasized their usefulness in diagnosing impaired ability to abstract in schizophrenia and organic disorders, stating that highly literal or concrete interpretations were characteristic and almost pathognomonic.[3] Gorham attempted to develop a standardized test which could be used clinically.[4] He described a three-point scoring system for rating abstractness and concreteness which he found to have an inter-rater reliability of 0.95. Applying the test to schizophrenics, he found it to be highly successful in differentiating them from normals.[5] Meadow et al. also applied the test to schizophrenics and were able to replicate Gorham's findings in terms of both interrater reliability and impairment in abstract thinking among schizophrenics.[6] Shimkunas et al., on the other hand, found the correlation between ability to abstract and intelligence to be so high that the proverb test seemed to do little more than to duplicate the function of an intelligence test.[7,8] In their studies autistic interpretation of proverbs appears to be a more significant indicator of schizophrenia than concreteness.

Most previous investigations of proverb interpretation have been limited to one clinical diagnosis, schizophrenia, and this group is usually compared to normals. Consequently, prior investigations have not closely resembled the actual clinical situation in which proverb interpretation is usually used, where proverbs are seen as an indicator of thought disorder and therefore an aid to differential diagnosis. In a clinical situation the interviewer is blind concerning the patient's diagnosis: the patient's proverb interpretations are supposed to help him discover it. Further, in most clinical situations, interviewers do not have precise guidelines for rating proverbs in terms of abstractness or concreteness. Instead they usually describe a patient's interpretations as concrete or bizarre based on their own prior experience.

This investigation was undertaken in order to assess the value of proverb interpretation in actual situations. It had several goals: 1) to evaluate interrater reliability in scoring proverb interpretations when psychiatrists follow their usual clinical practice and are kept blind as to diagnosis; 2) to examine the value of proverb interpretation as an indicator of thought disorder; and 3) to assess the usefulness of proverb interpretation as an aid in differential diagnosis. It examines these aspects of proverb interpretation in terms of three common illnesses which are a challenge to differential diagnosis: schizophrenia, mania, and depression.

Methods

Proverb interpretation was used as a standard portion of interview and evaluation in a consecutive series of 14 schizophrenics, 15 manics, and 15 depressives admitted to the inpatient psychiatric service at the University of Iowa Hospitals. Diagnoses were made using the Research Diagnostic Criteria developed by Spitzer, Endicott, and Robins, and only patients meeting these criteria were included in the study.[9] The patient groups did not differ significantly in age or education, although the depressed group contained more women.

Each patient was given ten proverbs to interpret, using a standard list obtained from the Mental Examiner's Handbook.[10] The ten proverbs are as follows:

1. All that glitters is not gold.
2. Don't cross the bridge before you come to it.
3. Too many cooks spoil the broth.
4. Straws show which way the wind blows.
5. A stitch in time saves nine.
6. Still waters run deep.
7. It's an ill wind that blows nobody good.
8. Wild colts make good horses.
9. The hot coal burns, the cold one blackens.
10. Make yourself honey and the flies will eat you.

Each patient was asked to indicate what the proverbs meant and was given an illustrative example before he was asked to make his first interpretation. ("For example, you might interpret 'The grass always looks greener on the other side of the fence' as meaning that people often find things they don't have to be more attractive or important than the things they actually do have.") All interpretations were tape-recorded and later transcribed.

The transcribed proverb interpretations were then distributed to the faculty and residents within the University of Iowa Department of Psychiatry. A total of 31 staff members were asked to participate, and 24 completed the ratings for the study, including seven faculty members and 17 residents. Prior to distribution the 44 sets of proverb interpretations were randomly mixed so that raters would have no clues as to diagnosis. In the instructions they were told that the proverb interpretations had been collected from a group of patients seen on the inpatient service and that they were being asked to rate them for "a study to determine the value of using proverb interpretation to assess mental status" with a particular interest in whether psychiatrists can agree with one another in rating proverb interpretations. They were asked to rate each patient on five different aspects of proverb interpretation, using the customary clinical standards which they would ordinarily use during a mental status examination. They were asked to code their ratings on a one to three scale as follows:

Correctness:	3 = correct	2 = partially correct	1 = not correct
Abstractness:	3 = abstract	2 = partially abstract	1 = not abstract
Concreteness:	3 = concrete	2 = partially concrete	1 = not concrete
Bizarreness:	3 = bizarre	2 = partially bizarre	1 = not bizarre
Personalization:	3 = personal	2 = partially personal	1 = not personal

One major purpose of this investigation was to evaluate interrater reliability in a clinical situation. Data analysis to assess interrater reliability was of two types, the kappa statistic and two-way analysis of variance to develop an intraclass correlation coefficient. The kappa, developed by Fleiss, measures the reliability between two raters when chance agreement is taken into account.[11] The intraclass correlation coefficient, developed by Ebel, generates a number "*r*" which reflects interrater reliability after two-way analysis of variance has been used to determine the variance due to rater differences, the variance due to subject differences, and the experimental error.[12] Both the kappa and the "*r*" have roughly the same numerical significance as other measures of correlation; that is, the correlation must be greater than approximately 0.6 in order to be statistically significant. It was hypothesized that interrater reliability would be relatively low when measured by these two statistics.

A second major purpose of the investigation was to determine whether blind raters would be able to make ratings which would differentiate the various groups on the basis of their proverb interpretations. That is, would manics differ significantly from schizophrenics in their degree of bizarreness, abstractness, concreteness, personalization, and correctness? It was hypothesized that manics and schizophrenics would resemble one another more than manics and depressives, and that schizophrenics and depressives would fall somewhere in the middle.

Results

Table 1 contains the intraclass correlation coefficients of the 24 raters. Although the raters were blind as to diagnosis, the data are portrayed in terms of diagnostic categories. As the table indicates, interrater reliability is generally quite low. None of the coefficients would be considered large enough to be significant, if a level of 0.6 is considered to represent reasonably good agreement. Agreement is somewhat better when the patients are schizophrenic than when they are depressed or manic, but the differences are not marked. The data were also broken down so that ratings by faculty and residents could be compared in order to determine whether more experienced clinicians would be able to achieve better agreement than less experienced clinicians. Residents and faculty did not differ significantly, however, and consequently ratings were pooled thereafter for purposes of data analysis.

Table 2 approaches the issue of interrater reliability through use of the kappa statistic. For this portion of the study a small subset of the data was used. Two faculty members and four residents were randomly selected from the total pool of raters by choosing every fourth rater from a list ranked by the order in which the ratings were turned in. Each of these raters was then compared with each of the others to assess interrater reliability with the kappa. Data were

Table 1. Interrater Reliability of 24 Raters in Proverb Assessment*

	Schizophrenics (N = 14)	Depressives (N=15)	Manics (N = 15)
Personalization	0.3402	0.0495	0.5195
Bizarreness	0.5000	0.1434	0.3518
Concreteness	0.3327	0.5531	0.3216
Abstractness	0.4239	0.5361	0.3423
Correctness	0.5781	0.5176	0.3911

*Based on "r" an intraclass correlation coefficient derived from 2-way analysis of variance: ratings > .6 could be considered significant.

Table 2. Per Cent of Agreement Between Paired Raters *On Specific Proverb Ratings*

	No. of Categories	No. of Rater Pairs	No. of Possible Agreements	No. of Observed Agreements	Per Cent of Agreements
Rating					
Correct	3	15	45	20	44
Abstract	3	15	45	15	33
Concrete	3	15	45	18	40
Bizarreness	3	15	45	12	27
Personalization	3	15	45	6	13
Diagnosis					
Manics	5	15	75	20	27
Depressives	5	15	75	25	33
Schizophrenics	5	15	75	26	35
Faculty-Resident Status					
Faculty-Faculty	15	1	15	4	26
Faculty-Resident	15	8	120	39	32.5
Resident-Resident	15	6	90	28	31

*Based on number of Kappas indicating statistically significant agreement between rater-pairs.

analyzed in order to measure agreement in three different situations: when the ratings were examined in terms of 1) describing the quality of thinking disorder (correctness, abstractness, etc.), 2) diagnostic categories, and 3) resident faculty status. The kappa score was determined for each pair of raters on each set of variables, and the score was then tested for statistical significance. Table 2 summarizes the percent of statistically significant agreements occurring between paired raters when the data are analyzed in terms of these three different variables.

As Table 2 indicates, a high percentage of agreement is never reached when the data are examined using the kappa statistic, just as was the case with the intraclass correlation coefficient. The best agreement was reached when raters assessed concreteness and abstractness, but the highest percentage of agreement on any category was only 44%. Agreement is even poorer when the data are analyzed in terms of diagnostic categories. Blind raters were able to agree with one another best when rating schizophrenics, but they only agreed 35% of the time, and agreement was somewhat worse for mania and depression. When residents and faculty members were compared with one another in terms of their ability to achieve agreement, the percentage of significant kappas tended to remain relatively low,

Table 3. Quality of Proverb Interpretation by Depressives and Schizophrenics as Assessed by Single Raters and All Raters

	Rater # 1			Rater # 2			All Raters		
	Mean Rating of Depressives ($N = 15$)	Mean Rating of Schizophrenics ($N = 14$)	Z Statistic	Mean Rating of Depressives ($N = 15$)	Mean Rating of Schizophrenics ($N = 14$)	Z Statistic	Mean Rating of Depressives ($N = 15$)	Mean Rating of Schizophrenics ($N = 14$)	Z Statistic
Correctness	1.80	1.27	3.78*	1.93	1.43	3.40†	1.83	1.34	15.28*
Abstractness	1.93	1.21	4.55*	2.07	1.64	2.61‡	1.95	1.60	9.52*
Concreteness	1.60	1.86	−1.62	1.60	1.71	.66	1.71	1.92	−4.90*
Bizarreness	1.07	1.79	−4.89*	1.27	2.00	4.47*	1.10	1.73	−10.06*
Personalization	1.20	1.71	−3.40†	1.07	1.43	2.79†	1.13	1.45	−9.20*

Ratings are based on a 1-2-3 rating scale with 1 = absent, 2 = partial, and 3 = present. The Z statistic indicates whether the 2 groups differ significantly.
* $p < 0.001$. † $p < 0.01$. ‡ $p < 0.05$.

Table 4. Quality of Proverb Interpretation by Manics and Depressives as Assessed by Single Raters and All Raters

	Rater # 1			Rater # 2			All Raters		
	Mean Rating of Manics ($N = 15$)	Mean Rating of Depressives ($N = 15$)	Z Statistic	Mean Rating of Mainics ($N = 15$)	Mean Rating of Depressives ($N = 15$)	Z Statistic	Mean Rating of Manics ($N = 15$)	Mean Rating of Depressives ($N = 15$)	Z Statistic
Correctness	1.33	1.80	3.29†	1.67	1.93	1.69	1.43	1.83	11.62*
Abstractness	1.33	1.93	3.85*	1.73	2.07	2.14‡	1.57	1.95	10.72*
Concreteness	2.07	1.60	−2.88†	2.00	1.60	−2.50‡	2.15	1.71	−11.10*
Bizarreness	2.20	1.07	−8.52*	1.93	1.27	−4.19*	1.71	1.10	−18.00*
Personalization	2.33	1.20	−7.76*	1.80	1.07	−5.57*	1.81	1.33	−21.28*

Ratings are based on a 1-2-3 rating scale with 1 = absent, 2 = partial, and 3 = present. The Z statistic indicates whether the 2 groups differ significantly.
* $p < 0.001$. † $p < 0.01$. ‡ $p < 0.05$.

suggesting that the poor agreement is not due to a lack of clinical experience among the residents. The pair of faculty raters, who would presumably have the most clinical experience, had the poorest agreement of all.

Although agreement between raters tended to be quite poor, suggesting that proverb interpretation does not yield reliable data, it seemed relevant to raise the question of validity as well, recognizing that answers would be based on unreliable data. That is, the data were also analyzed to determine whether the three diagnostic groups differed significantly in their style and quality of proverb interpretation. In terms of validity, this data analysis would indicate whether it is useful to ask a patient to interpret proverbs in order to help establish a diagnosis. These data are summarized in Tables 3, 4, and 5. They tend to suggest that although proverb interpretation is unreliable, it may be valid or useful.

These three tables portray the mean ratings of proverb interpretation on the five variables as assessed both by two different single raters and by all 24 raters. Rater 1 is the author. Rater 2 is another experienced faculty clinician. Data concerning single raters are shown here because they more nearly approximate an actual clinical situation. That is, proverb interpretation is ordinarily used as a part of the mental status examination by a single psychiatrist who is trying to use the patient's ability to interpret proverbs as a clue to diagnosis.

Whether the mean differences are significantly different on each of the five variables is assessed by using a "Z statistic":

$$Z = \frac{\bar{x}_1 \quad \bar{x}_2}{\sqrt{\frac{SE_1}{n_1} + \frac{SE_2}{n_2}}}$$

Because the number of measurements appears in the denominator, and because the number of measurements is considerably larger for all 24 raters (360) than it is for single raters (29), the Z statistic for all raters tends to be much higher (and therefore more significant statistically) than it is for single raters. In a sense, the highly significant differences achieved by all 24 raters are misleading, since proverb interpretation is not typically scored by having 24 different clinicians rate patients.

As Table 3 reveals, highly significant differences in all five aspects of proverb interpretation are observed when the data by all raters are pooled. These differences are much less significant in the case of the two single raters, but they too found significant differences in all aspects except concreteness. Both single raters and all raters agreed in the direction of the differences between the groups. When compared to schizophrenics, depressives interpreted proverbs more correctly, more abstractly, less concretely, less bizarrely, and with less personalization. These differences tend to concur with the clinical

Table 5. Quality of Proverb Interpretation by Manics and Schizophrenics as Assessed by Single Raters and All Raters

	Rater # 1			Rater # 2			All Raters		
	Mean Rating of Manics (*N* = 15)	Mean Rating of Schizophrenics (*N* = 14)	Z Statistic	Mean Rating of Manics (*N* = 15)	Mean Rating of Schizophrenics (*N* = 14)	Z Statistic	Mean Rating of Manics (*N* = 15)	Mean Rating of Schizophrenics (*N* = 15)	Z Statistic
Correctness	1.33	1.29	3.36	1.67	1.43	1.58	1.43	1.34	3.13†
Abstractness	1.33	1.21	8.04	1.73	1.64	5.55	1.57	1.60	–0.944
Concreteness	2.07	1.86	1.38	2.00	1.71	1.73	2.15	1.92	5.41*
Bizarreness	2.20	1.79	2.82†	1.93	2.00	.37	1.71	1.73	–0.405
Personalization	2.33	1.71	3.58†	1.80	1.43	2.39†	1.81	1.46	10.26*

Ratings are based on a 1-2-3 rating scale with 1 = absent, 2 = partial, and 3 = present. The Z statistic indicates whether the 2 groups differ significantly.
* $p < 0.001$. † $p < 0.01$. ‡ $p < 0.05$.

experience of most psychiatrists and are in expected directions. Rater 1, who has a more extensive interest in observing and measuring thought disorder than Rater 2, tended to make more discriminating ratings of higher statistical significance, a difference reflected in her more divergent mean scores.

Table 4 displays the differences in the scores of manics and depressives. These two diagnostic categories are the most divergent, as one would expect on the basis of clinical experience. Again, single raters and all raters agree on trends, with Rater 1 achieving more statistical significance than Rater 2. Manics differ from depressives in their proverb interpretations by being less correct, less abstract, more concrete, more bizarre, and more personalized.

Table 5 compares the mean ratings of the manics and schizophrenics. As might be expected, these two groups were the most difficult to differentiate. Indeed, the pooled ratings only discriminated these two diagnostic categories in three aspects of proverb interpretation, and at less significant levels than in the case of the two previous comparisons between diagnostic groups. Manics tended to be rated as somewhat more correct, more concrete, and more personalized, with no differences in bizarreness or abstractness. Rater 2 rated the two groups differently only in the area of personalization, and only at the 0.05 level. Rater 1 considered manics to be more bizarre and more personalized, with no differences noted in correctness, abstractness, and concreteness. Thus there is less agreement between single raters and all raters when confronted with a distinction between the disturbed cognition of the manic and the disturbed cognition of the schizophrenic, although there is some indication that manics are more disturbed.

Discussion

The use of proverb interpretation is firmly entrenched in psychiatric tradition. Yet its value in a clinical setting has never been carefully explored in a systematic or quantitative way. Most studies only examine proverb interpretation in schizophrenics, and yet proverbs are asked of nearly all patients seen, even if the diagnosis of schizophrenia is not entertained. Like any other test of psychopathology, the value of using proverb interpretations to assess mental status should be evaluated with the dual criteria of reliability and validity.

Applying the first criterion this investigation indicates that in a clinical setting blind raters are unable to achieve adequate reliability. Two different statistical techniques, the kappa statistic and the intraclass correlation coefficient, both lead to this conclusion. Although both Gorham and Meadow et al. found rather good reliability in their studies of proverb interpretation, they achieved this reliability at the expense of blindness: only schizophrenics were evaluated, and the high reliabilities obtained on ratings for abstractness and concreteness may have been due to lack of variance among subjects and preconceived expectations about the type of thinking disturbance to be found in a schizophrenic sample. The present investigation provides a more realistic estimate of reliability in an actual clinical setting, in that clinicians evaluated patients on the quality of their thinking without any knowledge of their diagnosis. When the clinician is blind concerning diagnosis, reliability drops markedly.

The data concerning validity are more difficult to interpret. At first glance, one might conclude that proverb interpretation is quite valid, even if it is not reliable. For highly significant differences are found in the mean ratings of thinking disturbance among schizophrenics, manics, and depressives when scores from all raters are averaged. Yet this is probably a situation in which statistical data analysis could lead to a somewhat misleading conclusion. Although extremely high levels of significance are reached by comparing mean scores for all raters across diagnostic groups, this method does not approximate accurately the actual clinical situation in which proverb interpretation is assessed. In most clinical situations, a single rater examines a series of patients. Therefore, mean scores for single raters were also compared across diagnostic groups, based on the recognition that this would probably provide a more realistic test of validity. This test of validity indicates that a single rater can use thinking disturbances to discriminate diagnostic subtypes quite well in the case of manics and depressives, less well but still impressively in the case of depressives and schizophrenics, and much less well in the case of manics and schizophrenics. As differential diagnosis becomes more difficult, ability to discriminate tends to decrease. In the case of manics and schizophrenics, the differences are only slightly greater than one might obtain by chance alone.

Thus at best proverb interpretation may have relatively good validity but poor reliability, and the greatest validity is obtained in those cases when differential diagnosis is not a problem. At worst, therefore, the validity of using proverbs in a clinical situation is somewhat questionable.

But even if validity were not somewhat questionable, would it be of any value if good reliability cannot be achieved? The answer is probably negative: a clinical symptom or sign on which two raters cannot agree is usually of little practical use, even though it may be a matter of great importance. Medicine in general and psychiatry in particular are replete with examples: the loudness of cardiac murmurs, blunting or flatness of affect, the amount of pain a person is experiencing, etc. The problem with such significant symptoms is that they lead to significant decisions about diagnosis and treatment. And yet if two different observers cannot agree that affect is flat or pain severe, at least one of them will be led to make a bad decision about a matter of considerable significance. Patients will be called schizophrenic when they are depressed or depressed when schizophrenic, and pain will be overmedicated or undermedicated. Consequently, when dealing with signs or symptoms for which reliability is poor, physicians should be very wary about basing major decisions on them.

What implications does this have for the use of proverb interpretations as part of the mental status examination? It implies that they are of little value as an indicator of thought disorder and as an aid to differential diagnosis and that they are therefore of little practical use. They carry a heavy weight of tradition, and no doubt many clinicians will be reluctant to give them up. Yet they are probably likely to be misleading in the hands of most clinicians because of their poor reliability, and their widespread use should probably be discontinued.

References

1. Goldstein K: The significance of special mental tests for diagnosis and prognosis in schizophrenia. Am J Psychiatr 96:575–588, 1939.

2. Goldstein K: Abstract and concrete behavior: An experimental study with special tests. Psychol Monographs, 53:1–151, 1941.

3. Benjamin JD: A method for distinguishing and evaluating formal thinking disorders in schizophrenia, in Kasanin JS (ed): Language and Thought in Schizophrenia, Berkeley, University of California, 1944.

4. Gorham DR: A proverbs test for clinical and experimental use. Psychol Rep 2:1–12, 1956.

5. Gorham DR: Use of the proverbs test for differentiating schizophrenics from normals. J Consult Psychol 20:435–440, 1956.

6. Meadow A, Greenblatt M, Solomon HC: "Looseness of association" and impairment in abstraction in schizophrenia. J Nerv Ment Dis 118:27–35, 1953.

7. Shimkunas AM, Gynther MD, Smith K: Abstracting ability of schizophrenics before and during phenothiazine therapy. Arch Gen Psychiatry 14:79–83, 1966.

8. Shimkunas AM, Gynther MD, Smith K: Schizophrenic responses to the proverbs test: abstract, concrete or autistic? J Abn Psychol 72:128–133, 1967.

9. Spitzer RL, Endicott J, Robins E: Research Diagnostic Criteria (RDC) for a Selected Group of Functional Disorders, ed. 2, 1975. Available from Drs. Spitzer and Endicott at Biometrics Research, New York State Psychiatric Institute, 722 West 168th St., New York, NY, 10032.

10. Wells FL, Ruesch J: Mental Examiners Handbook. New York, Psychological Corp., 1945.

11. Fleiss JL: Statistical Methods for Rates and Proportions. New York, John Wiley & Sons, 1973, pp. 143–147.

12. Ebel RL: Estimation of the reliability of ratings. Psychometrika 15:407–424. 1951.

A Proverb Test for Attitude Measurement

*Franziska Baumgarten**

Another psychological use of proverbs involves attitude measurement. Such tests, however, are not concerned with mental illness or intelligence. Rather, proverbs are employed as a means of eliciting normally difficult-to-obtain statements about personal values and philosophy. In the following pioneering study, Franziska Baumgarten asked Swiss subjects to select a small number of proverbs from a corpus of more than two hundred and to indicate verbally whether they agreed or disagreed with the thought or sentiment expressed. By this means, she hoped to ascertain workers' views towards work and life. One of the few later studies along similar lines is a doctoral dissertation (University of Southern California, 1960) by Robert Reveal entitled "The Development and Validation of a Proverbs Test for the Selection of Supervisors."

I

The economic as well as the socio-political developments of the recent decades have awakened a wide interest in the mentality of employees, in psychologists and sociologists as well as personnel supervisors. For the former this is primarily a purely scientific question: What is the psychical structure of a given employee? What

* Reprinted by permission of Personnel Psychology, Inc. from *Personnel Psychology*, 5 (1952), 249–261. Translated into English by Lee and Morton Silberstein.

is his level of psychical development? Does working in a particular occupation cause him psychological damage and which?

For the supervisor the one and only question of importance is: Has the employee a real interest in his work or does he solely consider it a means to earn a living? Will he fit in with his co-workers or will he isolate himself from them? In other words can he adjust to the group or will he be a source of malcontent?

The answers to these questions will determine the approach to a given worker: The degree of trust that is put into his loyalty and faithfulness, into his actions and words. For these reasons it has been attempted for decades by means of psychological tests to determine the vocational aptitude as well as the character of each worker. The emphasis was placed on the individual job applicant.

Previously applied psychological test methods made it possible to recognize the necessary qualifications for specific occupations. However, the testing of character traits in spite of wide and varied efforts has shown no satisfactory results.[1]

The last war has made these difficult problems even more complex. Greater attention became focused on the masses as a political factor and mass psychological aspects have also been extended to workers as a group; hence, to the entire personnel body. In modern economy factories, stores, etc. are constantly enlarging. Undertakings with more than 5000 employees are no longer rarities. It is therefore obvious, that even knowing all the "individuals" cannot yield a satisfactory picture of the group spirit. The new pressing questions can be formulated as: What is the nature of the personnel working under an owner or manager? Is it possible to obtain a total picture of this group? In this manner the problems of mass psychology have also become important to management.

Therefore a new, very responsible and difficult task is arising in the field of industrial psychology.

II

Before testing the mentality of a group, mentality as a concept will have to be clarified.

Many erroneously identify character with mentality. The latter involves character traits, but only those that exhibit a pronounced moral tendency. Furthermore, mentality involves the way of thinking, reasoning and the ability to judge. These play an active part and determine the social and economic attitudes; which means, to take cognizance of what the personnel considers right or wrong, approves or disapproves, appreciates or criticizes.

At present for this purpose (especially in America) questionnaires with hundreds of questions are used. Many arguments have been propounded against this method, which continued in use, because it was the best available. The Rorschach and Szondi tests have also been proven unsuitable for this purpose. In order to examine the problem of mentality, it has been necessary to develop a new method.

This has been found in the "Sprüchetest" (Proverb Test), which consists of a collection of 240 proverbs concerning human labor and social relationships. Many individual problems in these fields have been included; e.g.: the effect of work, social status of the vocations, work techniques, remuneration, fairness, suitable conduct, existing social conditions etc.[2]

The examinee is to select from this collection eight proverbs he considers correct and eight others, which he thinks are incorrect. He will then indicate either orally or in writing why he agrees, or disagrees with each chosen proverb. This method is one of indirect questioning. An attitude is provoked in respect to the problems contained in a given proverb through activation of emotions and experiences. In this manner the test makes possible free expression on a self-chosen topic. It has been used in conjunction with other evocative tests to examine the mentality of 98 workers of a large Swiss industrial firm. Some of the results are set forth in the following.

III

Most frequent were the proverbs in the field of *labor*. 37% used: "Work makes life sweet." Such a choice alone indicates a positive adjustment to work. The latter assumption has been fully confirmed by the reasons given for this selection; namely: that work gives meaning and purpose to life. It diverts people from their troubles and wards off boredom; deters them from foolish acts and makes them content. A summary of these opinions shows that work has a psycho-hygienic value. Several examinees thought that work also strengthens the body and is a means toward advancement in life. In one case it was mentioned that work provided a chance to prove one's capabilities and gave the satisfaction of being useful.

From these assertions it is evident that work is not considered a means within itself, but a means to an end. It is interesting to note that the *spiritual effects* of labor are far more dominant than the physical ones. In only two cases it was stated that work has a favorable influence on the body, while in 19 instances its good effects on the mind were mentioned. This clearly non-materialistic position taken by the examinees, as shown by their popular choice of the axiom: "Work makes life sweet" and their spiritual explanations thereof, is directly contrary to what would customarily be expected.

Other proverbs from the field of labor also indicate on the whole a positive approach toward work; i.e.: "Work shames no one." "Those who work, eat." "No reward without diligence."

One might especially stress some of the criticisms of these maxims in this category; such as: "Work does shame when munitions are produced." An attitude, with which one must agree. Also in reference to the last mentioned proverb above, one examinee said: "And yet, there are people who profit by the labor of others." To the saying, "In the sweat of thy brow thou shalt eat thine bread," one protested: "Why should bread only be eaten in the sweat of one's brow?" This is a justified comment, if modern vocational theory intends to create and promote the satisfaction of work.

Three proverbs from the field of labor caused an especially strong opposition from some of the examinees. The first one was: "As the labor, so the pay." An exceptional reaction to this axiom was: "Good pay for good labor." But others said: "Unfortunately this is not true;" or "Rarely is the pay commensurate with the work;" and "Many deserve more wages." Some quoted from their own experience. "This proverb is not correct, because I think the pay I get for my work is too low." "Our wage raises are not always equal to our work performance." The testees refer to several facts known to them: "This is not true. There are workers, who work beyond their energies; yet, when they ask for corresponding pay, they are told that their performance is unsatisfactory. Naturally the boss pockets the lion's share." "This for example does not hold for our Army, because the military insurance settles every case in its favor." "The coal shoveler and the construction worker do much more strenuous work than a travelling salesman, teacher or secretary." "Some people have harder and heavier work than others and earn much less than those who do nothing at all." It is evident that the examinees read the newspapers and are informed about current events.

A second proverb that found disapproval reads: "Bitter work, sweet slumber." It was not only pointed out that easy labor may also bring sweet slumber, but it was specifically stressed that after "bitter work one usually does not sleep well." One said: "I do not think that somebody who dislikes his work will sleep well."

Much animosity was also caused by the saying, "One's position is indicative of one's capability." Some emphasized: "By far not all are equal to the position they hold." Others said: "Many a man would be suited for something better, but he hasn't had the luck." For this "too little" or "too much" fitness or aptitude for a position reasons like favoritism, contacts, relatives, seniority, automatic promotions, etc. were given. The unfavorable reaction to this proverb clearly indicates that many employees are dissatisfied with the jobs they hold.

From this short discussion it is evident, the manner in which the negative and positive sides of the problems of human labor were appraised by the examinees.

IV

A large number of the chosen proverbs dealt with practical and proper conduct. For example: "In all that you do think of the end result." "Ability brings advancement." "One learns by trying." "A wise man takes advice." "Many know much, but one never stops learning." "Foresight is better than hindsight." "To the courageous belongs the world." "Every weapon is good in a strong hand." "Only that is lost, which is given up as lost." It seems therefore that the examinees attach great importance to the problems of suitable and inappropriate behavior and conduct. They have definitely recognized that success or failure may depend on a certain type of behavior; consequently they have stressed those proverbs that set up rules of conduct. It is interesting that in the maxim, "Only that is lost, which is given up as lost," it is expressly emphasized that every difficult situation has a solution. One testee said: "Success depends solely on an iron will." Three examinees express their opinions in the "should-form": "One should never give up . . . , but hold out and don't lose your nerve." To be further noted is that some of the quoted proverbs were criticized in the form of a rejection. For example to the proverb: "Where one can't walk through, one has to slip through," one answered: "Adjustment is not every man's talent." Two replies which were fully in the spirit of the saying, "He who wants, must take," were given. These are: "Otherwise somebody else will take it." "One who doesn't defend his rights only gets left-overs." Yet 5% of those tested voiced their disagreement, e.g.: "This proverb was especially applicable during the War." "This axiom might instigate one to steal." "An unhealthy attitude, that in small and large matters must lead to conflicts with one's neighbors."

Since the rules of conduct are of a rational nature (developed through common sense) their acknowledgment simultaneously means the recognition of that which is sensible. Therefore, it can be concluded, that the examinees were surely not "dulled" by their work. Their common sense had been retained to a high degree and they were intent on its further cultivation. Furthermore, the preference of proverbs containing rules of conduct indicates a tendency towards self-improvement; i.e. the possibility to reach a higher intellectual plane, which seems a condition for such behavior. These results are even more noteworthy, since the maxims were predominantly selected from two fields: human labor and social relationships. Only rarely were proverbs chosen which dealt with practical behavior. However, they were occasionally selected, which must be taken as evidence for the special interest in this topic. In connection with the inclination towards logical reasoning stands the discrimination of the examinees, which, as indicated by the examples given, is determined by their ethical attitude.

V

Of the moral problems that of *justice* proved to be most interesting to the examinees. They chose proverbs relating to this topic most frequently and at every occasion expressed their opinions to questions concerning it. It runs like a red thread through all answers given. Without a doubt it constitutes a sore spot with a large number of the testees. This emphasis was especially noticeable. The saying, "A judge must have two equal ears," which in poetic form describes his impartiality, was picked by a considerable number of employees; an indication of how actual and alive they consider this problem of justice. The sensitivity toward this problem may be the cause for two affirmative and 16 negative answers to the saying: "Might makes right." Some of the comments were: "The weak are also entitled to justice." "This is valid for an undemocratic state, but justice should always come *before* might." A third said: "Might is not the sole factor; wisdom also plays a role."

From this attitude it is understandable that those proverbs offending the principle of justice were chosen to be criticized; e.g. two sayings with the same meaning: "One works; the other gets the gravy." "One carries the wood, the other warms himself with it." These facts were confirmed by those tested on the basis of their experience or knowledge. They said: "One works and others take the profit." "There are always people who eat by the sweat of others." "Quite true, that's just what's happening today in the politics of those in power." "The working people carry the load of wood, and the capitalists warm themselves on the profits." "There were always great inventors. Yet, I know of none whose work was ever properly repaid." One examinee even set up the rule: "He who carries the wood should also warm himself with it."

It would be incorrect to consider these opinions of the employees, solely, as expressions of personal resentment. Their criticism does not purely refer to personally experienced injustices, but unfortunately, our social order offers too many occasions for objections of the existing code of justice. The testees exhibited the proper sensitivity for same. Furthermore, they resigned themselves to the facts, as expressed by a chosen saying: "Not merit but luck brings success." "Also merit brings success." The others realized, that besides achievement a lucky incident decides one's progress in life. As one bitterly expressed: "You have to have luck in life—like a man who's born a millionaire."

VI

The examinees focused their attention specifically on the field of *social relationships* by choosing numerable proverbs relating to this topic.

It is not surprising that the well known and here in Switzerland much quoted saying, "One for all and all for one," was frequently selected (14%). Those who chose it must feel particularly strongly about its validity, as one wrote: "This fundamental concept of the Swiss state is the general basis of any community endeavor." However, the consequences that would result from adherence to this maxim were pointed out: "If this were so, there would be no wars and fewer poor people." And again, although the employees were asked to substantiate the accuracy of the axiom, they resorted to the "should-form:" "One should not only think of oneself, but also of one's fellow man." "A good man should not only think of himself." "A friend should be there for all, not only for himself." These opinions sound like an obligation to oneself. The idea of social peace found its expression (among others) in the choice of proverb: "Surrender stops all wars." Some agreed with it. Others argued: "Wrong, think of Munich 1938." "Today's events prove the contrary. We have learned from Hitler." One defined the type of surrender: "Not giving in, as such, silences further wars, but only yielding justifiably." Some indicated the negative results. One of the latter is the increase in greed; "Give them a finger and they'll take the whole hand." "If you yield, they will take all." Another is the loss of independence, "Give in and become a slave?" One testee limited the validity of this saying with the remark: "To give in one also needs understanding." Another notes that peace does not depend on one partner alone, "If evil does not will it, then good cannot live in peace."

In a number of instances (13%) the following axiom was selected: "He, who does not meddle, always has peace." One half of the examinees agreed with this, the other opinions pointed out the necessity for interference. "When one sees that things are going wrong, one has to interfere; even though the peace may be disturbed." This indicates a strong feeling of social responsibility, simply expressed here: "I also have a feeling of responsibility." Or, "That is correct, but who lives according to this proverb is a weakling without character or an opinion of his own." This evidence of responsibility is one of the most heart-warming testimonials of the mental maturity of the group, who prefers to disturb the peace rather than passively accept an injustice. It is an expression of the proper comprehension of the social obligations of the individual and a noble concept of human dignity.

It is interesting to note the viewpoint taken by 11% to the saying, "Other fields are always greener." A number realized that envy is involved: "If one judges the fields without jealousy, one sees that both will yield a good crop." Some limited the general validity of this concept: "Some people only think that their crop is the best." They criticized the envious: "This maxim is only valid for people of low mental level."

Two proverbs, asserting pessimism about social relationships, were also chosen. The first reads: "He who waits for help will be left waiting." 8% of the employees affirmed the accuracy of this saying, e.g.: "That everybody ought to know." The second proverb stated: "Learn to stand on your own two feet. Then you'll know what you are standing on."

Two opinions were voiced against this pessimism: "I am sure, that in spite of everything bad, there are still people one can depend on," and "If this were true, it would mean the end of every friendship. One can always rely on real friends." These answers demonstrate that there exists more distrust than trust towards others. Yet, the universality of this pessimistic saying is denied.

In this connection the following proverb must be emphasized: "The dog, who finds a bone, leaves his master." The protest against this saying is quite interesting. No single candidate accepted this proverb as correct. It was remarked that a good dog will never leave his master for the sake of a bone. One examinee characteristically wrote: "If you are a good teacher then you will have so trained your dog, so that he can abandon the bone." This shifts the emphasis from the "dog" to the "master" and denies the onesidedness of the blame.

"One who pays well has good servants." 6% of the testees answered in the affirmative to the proverb. Perhaps, for the reason that they feel deeply about their insufficient pay. However, 9% sided against it. One pointed out: "Good treatment also makes for good servants." (According to this a "good word" is as well appreciated as "good wages.") Another thought: "Those are not the best servants, who are well paid." A third said: "Also well paid servants may steal." "We may also fall victim to a swindler." Strangely to say, in this manner the employees protect the employer and comment (that with good wages): "Kindness may be misused." "Sometimes good-naturedness may be abused."

Such opinions evidence strong social feelings and a fair sense of justice. The payer as well as the "payee" must be decent human beings to deserve consideration.

VII

In consideration of this sober interpretation of the existing "world order," the examinees deserve double credit for defining their *ethical values* in a precise manner. 25% of those questioned accepted honesty as the correct philosophy of life: "Honesty lasts longest." They firmly believe that honesty is the best policy. Their reasons are mostly of a practical nature; e.g.: "One trusts the honest." "Through honesty one can live and think freely." Contrarily, the consequences of dishonesty are very unpleasant: "Eventually, all things come to light." "All crime will be avenged on earth." This type of reasoning is pure utilitarianism. A moralist would say that this does not constitute proof of an ethical position. On the other hand, a sociologist would consider it quite gratifying that the personal experiences of the employees were of such a positive nature.

Yet, that the examinees do not only recognize ethical values from a materialistic point of view, but also possess an ethical sensitivity, is evidenced by the considerable negation (21%) of the following proverb: "Deceiving is more honest than stealing." One testee thought contemptuously that this was a stupid folk-saying; but with three exceptions the others stressed that these actions were equally bad. "Neither of the two is honest." "The difference has only legal significance." From the denial of this maxim one can see, that the examinees have no desire to differentiate the nuances of moral conduct. Deceit is something shameful, stealing also is reprehensible. It does not depend on the degree of dishonesty.

Toward the ethical assessment of part of the testees also speaks the fact that on several occasions proverbs were put into the "should-form." This means for example, in reference to those just discussed: "You should not deceive or steal." In relation to the proverb, "Honesty lasts longest": "That's the way it should be;" In, "Small thieves are hanged, the big ones run free." "One should hang the big thieves and let the small ones run free."

VIII

Further selected proverbs cannot be discussed here. They only confirm what has already been shown, that the personnel group tested on the whole manifested an ethical attitude, moral maturity, social sense, democratic convictions, a tendency toward constructive conduct, toward an esteem of work, a sharp reasoning faculty and critical sense. As a group the employees demonstrated many positive characteristics.

It was particularly pleasant to note the objectivity of the answers. None of the examinees expressed himself in a form of speech often heard in conversation: "I am not that kind, I don't do things that way." Instead they specifically pointed out the positive exceptions to objectionable proverbs. One might have expected that in their opinions the employees would have shown a partiality to their own needs. Actually, hardly any examinees complained about injustices that they themselves experienced. Though they occasionally passed severe judgment on the "bosses" and the "rich," they also defended their partner in the employment situation, namely the employer. Many seem to be free from a "supervisor complex." Therefore, they can judge without restraint the social conditions, have a proper understanding of the individual's social responsibilities and an insight into the motives of human conduct. The critical handling of many sayings permits the conclusion that the examinees have by no means been "dulled" by their work, but have retained common sense and freedom of expression. This, without doubt, is not a lethargic, insensitive, homogeneous mass (as one frequently pictures the personnel group), but a group of sensible, capable observers and socially sensitive individuals. These conclusions naturally do not exclude the possibility that there are individual employees who do not possess the discussed characteristics; but here the group as a whole is of prime interest.

The distribution of the chosen proverbs has been graphically, grosso modo, presented in Fig. 1. This method of the Sprüchetest (Proverb Test) with which these results were achieved, has been found to be more practical than others used in Psychology until the present.

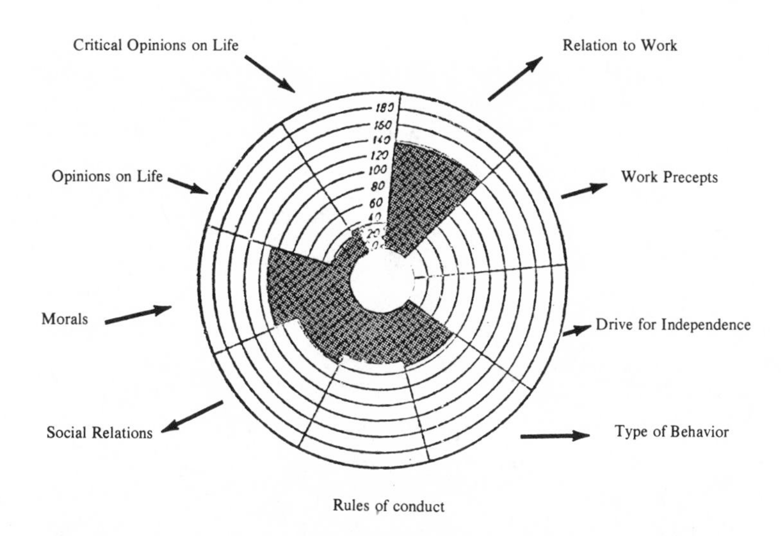

FIGURE 1. DISTRIBUTION OF THE SELECTED PROVERBS INTO THE VARIOUS FIELDS DISCUSSED

The above test of the mentality of a personnel body by means of a psychological method is probably the first one of its kind. It will be necessary to test other groups. This will show whether the results found, taken from a group working under very favorable conditions, constitute an exception or the rule.

Notes

1. F. Baumgarten, *Die Charakterprüfung der Berufsanwärter,* Zürich, 2nd ed. 1947.
2. Details in op. cit., p. 64 ff.

Chinese Proverbs and Their Lessons

*Alfred Lister**

The attempt to extrapolate attitudes and values from proverbs constitutes an important part of earlier proverb scholarship. Unlike the previous essay, authors rarely consulted informants about the philosophical implications of their proverbs. Rather, the authors drew their own conclusions concerning the moral and didactic content of proverbs from a given culture. From contextless collections, writers were only too quick to generalize about the alleged wisdom or character of a people as determined from sampling a selected proverb corpus.

In the following paper by Alfred Lister, we find a representative example of nineteenth century proverb research in which Chinese proverbs are examined with a view to delineating patterns of Chinese thought. The very title of the paper indicates the author's debt to Bishop Richard Trench's 1853 treatise On the Lessons in Proverbs. *In considerations of proverbs from a culture foreign to the author, one invariably finds the author unable to resist the temptation to cite a purportedly parallel proverb from his own culture. Occasionally these parallels are in fact cognate, but more often than not, the proverbs are genetically and historically unrelated.*

We have elected to include this older paper because we feel it does represent a longstanding approach to proverb content. For other typical examples of the approach, see William Elliot Griffis, Proverbs of Japan: A Little Picture of the Japanese Philosophy of Life

*Reprinted from *The China Review*, 3 (1874–75), 129–138.

as Mirrored in Proverbs *(New York, 1924) and Clifford Henry Plopper,* Chinese Religion Seen Through the Proverb *(Shanghai, 1926).*

When the far-reaching researches which are now daily carried on into the history of language shall have been pushed a little further than at present, it is not improbable that, instead of tracking the descent of mere words, philologists may begin to devote themselves to whole sentences; and, naturally, these sentences will be nothing but proverbs, "the fragments of an elder wisdom, which, on account of their brevity and aptness, have been preserved amid a general wreck and ruin." If a list could be made out of all the proverbs which are common to all known languages—a larger number, I suspect, than most persons would imagine—how much would be done towards a more intimate acquaintance with that ideal home of the Aryan race which nestled in the light that never was on sea or land, somewhere on the northern slope (was it not?) of the Himalayas! What should we not know of the inmates of that shadowy house, their experiences of life, their hopes, their fears, their disappointments, and whether they had learned to distrust the mouth of a gift horse! For although the occurrence of the same idea to various nations might be fortuitous, the words in which it is clothed remain for a prey to the comparative philologist, and it will go hard but he will press them into the service. A list of primeval proverbs will, I am persuaded, do much to restore to us the language of the primeval home. Nay even, we may hope ere long to be in possession of the conversation that was exchanged across the coffee and hot rolls on that eventful morning when the elder brother strolled out after breakfast and lost himself in an Aryan constitutional, whilst his younger companion was sauntering in an irrevocably opposite direction!

Badinage, however, apart, there can be no doubt that the proverbs of a people are most pregnant with instruction if rightly considered. "The genius, wit, and spirit of a nation are discovered in its proverbs." "In them is to be found an inexhaustible source of precious documents in regard of the interior history, the manners, the opinions, the beliefs, the customs of the people among whom they have had their source." These observations are true of the proverbs of any one nation, treated separately, but how much more true if we take the whole world for our province, and study those terse sayings which are so valuable as guides in the conduct of life as to have occurred or to have been transmitted to the people of every country, whose wisdom is so indispensable that no society is without them?

Nothing more forcibly awakens the attention of the collector of Chinese Proverbs than the numerous and extraordinary coincidences between them and the sayings of other nations; resemblances so literal sometimes, as to suggest that a European or Indian proverb has been transplanted bodily, rather than that it has grown up independently in two or more soils. These coincidences if found, say, between English and German proverbs, would be nowise remarkable, but China is supposed to lie so much outside of all the rest of the world, not to say outside of all human interest, that it is almost one of the first canons of Sinology that the student shall forget there is such a thing as European literature, for he will never want it anymore. Never, never let him venture to illustrate anything Chinese by anything from the western world!

It is nevertheless a fact that in Chinese proverbs, as in Chinese everything else, the most instructive coincidences between Western and Eastern thought are to be found. Archbishop Trench remarks that the proverb, *Man proposes, God disposes* is possessed, he is inclined to believe, by every nation in Europe. But the same proverb exists, *totidem verbis*, in Chinese, and exists in the form of a sort of jingle, just as it does in several Western countries.[1] I shall have more to say by and by of the recognition of God which it involves. The excellent Latin adage, *Maxima reverentia debetur pueris*, is exactly reproduced in a Chinese form, as is also that one used by our Lord against the obstructive Pharisees, *If the blind lead the blind both shall fall into the ditch*. Sometimes the same thing is said in a different way. At home we remember that, "Necessity is the mother of invention"; the Chinese more tersely put it that *Need breeds device.*[2] We say "Like master, like man"; but they, *Like mistress, like maid*; to which they also add this excellent warning, *Master easy, servant slack*. Their comparison of a welcome service to *A present of coals in a time of snow*, recalls Solomon's "Cold of snow in the time of harvest," and like many other proverbs points to a birth-place in the North of China. But very often the Seric version does more than just repeat or vary its western counterpart; it expands, or even explains it. Such an expanded proverb will be found in this: *Happiness never comes double—misfortunes never single*; or in this: *The pitcher that is always at the well gets broken—your general hardly escapes death in battle.* Nor have I, perhaps, ventured too far in saying that a Chinese proverb may be a welcome aid in explaining one from another country. There is a proverb of Solomon's which I never understood till I found its Chinese reflex. It is this, "As a jewel of gold in a swine's snout, so is a fair woman which is without discretion." The ordinary explanation is that beauty so placed is incongruously placed, or, as some have said, that the fallen woman is still a jewel of gold, though in a degrading position, a sentimentality not to be ascribed to Solomon. But how nervous and vivid does the metaphor become when read in the light of this Chinese aphorism: *Air and graces invite best, as carelessly stored treasure invites a thief.* That is the idea. The jewel of gold in the swine's snout cries out, "Come steal me," to every passer-by, and the airs and graces of the fair woman without discretion proclaim her virtue an easy prey to him who first cares to attempt it.

Such are a very few out of numberless instances in which popular thought in China and in the West has, as it were, interlocked. But if we are to learn any lesson from Chinese proverbs it is perhaps more fitting that we study those which seem (at first sight, for I doubt whether investigation would not discover prototypes elsewhere) peculiar to the country. If it be asked, what is the distinguishing note of Chinese proverbs? I would say—as far as one cares to speak at all of what a life-time may be spent in collecting, and no completeness attained—a certain quiet and keen longheadedness, a somewhat cynical and worldly view of human nature, but a piercing insight into it, reminding one most of those incisive Florentine bywords recovered for us by the unwearied diligence of George Eliot. And thus the proverbs of China are marked more by wisdom than by sweetness, for they have sprung from the hearts of a hard-working not too much rejoicing people. They turn more on the foibles of humanity than its excellences; and though the Chinese possess abundant religious proverbs, they have (if I may coin a new use for an old word) few *Christian* ones, *i.e.* those in which the claims of our common humanity and the duty of love to our neighbour are enforced. We hear much of requiting kindnesses, but very little of doing kindnesses; much of loving your friend, but not one word of loving your enemy. The most Christian proverb I can recollect in a large collection is that *A divided orange tastes just as good*; nor have I met any so tender as

"He's some body's bairn," by which, in Yorkshire, the duty is recalled of helping one who seems to have no friends.

Perhaps however, a spirit of gentle loving-kindness is not a general characteristic of proverbs anywhere, but for a trenchant and caustic wit and terseness many Chinese proverbs might have been the utterances of the immortal Mrs. Poyser herself. Our own excellent adages about the "new broom," and the "beggar on horse-back" are well reproduced in this: *Who came into office but this morning has the more orders to give*, and this: *He lifts his feet high who has put on boots for the first time*, both of which are proverbs turning essentially on Chinese habits and customs. He was a keen observer of human nature who first recorded the ingratitude of men for what cost them nothing in the saying, *Free sitters at a theatre who cry down the play*, or another unreasonable but very human trait in this: *The thrown-in is more thought of than the bought.* That *nobody speaks to Mr. Poor in the street, but very distant relatives of Mr. Rich find him out even amongst the hills*, has been equally noticed by Solomon, who observes that "The poor is hated even of his own neighbour, but the rich hath many friends." A similarly cynical, but I fear very true, Chinese proverb reminds us that *Great folks may set the town in a blaze, common people mustn't even light a lantern*; another declares that *Polite attentions generally mean "I want something,"* whilst another still further warns us that *The riches of one family are the hatred of many.* That man did not take an enthusiastic view of human nature who first declared that *"Coachmen, Sailors, Innkeepers, Horsedealers, and Police-runners all deserve beheading whether they have done anything or not*, but at times one is inclined fervently to agree with him, as well as to endorse the truth of this: *It is easier to visit friends than to live with them*,—a hard saying, but profoundly true.

If however in studying Chinese proverbs we have to accept the Machiavelian rather than the optimist view of life and of ourselves and our fellow creatures, we cannot but perceive "what a body of popular good sense and good feeling is contained in the better, which is also the more numerous portion of them; what a sense of natural equity, what prudent rules for the management of life, what shrewd wisdom, what frugality, what patience, what perseverance, what manly independence are continually inculcated by them. What a fine knowledge of the human heart do many of them display; what useful and not always obvious hints do they offer on many most important points, as on the choice of companions, the bringing up of children, the bearing of prosperity and adversity, the restraint of all immoderate expectations. And they take a yet higher range than this; they have their ethics, their theology, their views of man in his highest relations of all, as man with his fellow man, and man with his Maker. Be these always correct or not, the student of humanity can never, without wilfully foregoing an important document, and one which would have helped him often in his studies, altogether neglect or pass them by." How wise a warning, but alas! how unheeded it is apt to be, to a restless lad anxious to leave his father's roof, that *Simple birds fly first,* and how witty a caricature of "raw haste, half sister to delay" in the portraiture of the man who *will plant a tree in the morning and must needs saw planks from it at night.* There is a grain of wholesome consolation to those who vainly aspire after a higher social status in the reminder that *All ten fingers can't be the same length*; they are encouraged to look for better times by the hopeful saying, *Even a potsherd gets a chance to be turned over,* or as we should say, "every dog has his day"; and they are taught that all things cannot happen alike well to all by this: *Cheap grain is the death of the farmer.* St. Paul most probably merely set before his Corinthian and Galatian churches a proverb with which they were well acquainted when he warned them against one or two troublesome fellows with the words "A little leaven leaveneth the whole lump," but the Chinese put it in the way that comes more personally home to us than either this or Solomon's fly in the pot of ointment, when they say, *No ease for the mouth where one tooth is aching.* An exquisitely apposite reproof to the noise and wrangling of such contentious fellows is contained in the proverb, *A full bottle won't shake, a half-empty one will*; the Scotch have one to the same effect, something about "toom kists" (empty boxes) making most noise. Such a "glib-tongued fellow"[3] might take the warning necessary to restrain his endless loquacity from this: *Diseases enter by the mouth, misfortunes issue from it,* which recalls our Lord's definition of that which defileth a man;[4] or from this: *A coach-and-four cannot bring back a word once uttered,*—a proverb which, in one shape or other, exists in perhaps every language.

Here is a wise reproof for one who will have everything done *his* way and no other. He is told, *Horse and cow face wind differently, i.e.* "there are more ways of killing a cat than choking her with cream." If it be his youthful inexperience that is at fault he is reminded that *Old horses know the road,* whilst he who is hurrying to that most haste which is worst speed is warned, *Better go home and make a net than jump into a pool after fish.* None but a shop-keeping people would have put a very common proverb into this form, *Don't smash your goods to kill a rat.* We say, "You mustn't burn your ship to kill the cockroaches," both proverbs throwing an uncomfortable light on the nature and number of uninvited visitors to ships and Chinese shops respectively. Another excellent piece of shop-keeping wisdom is this; *If you don't run away from your goods, your goods won't run away from you.* A waste of good material is deprecated in the following, uncomplimentary as it is to His Majesty's forces: *Good iron is not used for nails, nor good men for soldiers;* or in this; *Any water will do to wash a boat.* The duty of circumspection and foresight is enforced as follows; *See your guest, then make your feast,* and of economy in this; *Save wine till guests come,* in regard to which two last I may remark that no nation possesses more proverbs breathing a spirit of hospitality and politeness than the Chinese. *Let the host rest when his guests are gone,* not only points out a duty to those who have eaten our bread and salt, but also slyly hints at the relief which even the kindest host experiences when he has his house to himself again. That *Hospitable detention is three parts false, weather detention is wholly true,* is perhaps too analytical to be pleasant, but at least it points to an unfailing practice of politeness. The usefulness of sayings similar to some of those cited above in dealing with a people like the Chinese cannot be exaggerated. It is the peculiar advantage attaching to the citation of a proverb that it is something put beyond dispute, accepted and settled as true, a first principle, like the axioms of science, or the multiplication table. The silencing effect of an apt and telling proverb, let off, as it were, right in the faces of a possibly angry, and certainly gesticulating and blatant Chinese crowd must be seen to be believed. If it happen to be a proverb from the classics, so much the better. It will be asked, however, are not some of these popular proverbs very gross either in their words or their sense? Proverbs gross in sense I have not met with, nor do I think they can be much in common use, though probably a *search* for such, especially in certain company, would discover abundance of them. But all vice is more kept in the background in China than in Europe. Yet it cannot be denied that some, though not many, Chinese proverbs, excellent in their sense, are yet

Shakespearianly "large jests," in their wording, partly from the homeliness attaching to all old sayings, partly from the fact that the Chinese speak without reserve of many subjects which the English of the nineteenth century have relegated to the *tacenda.* As an old collector has it, "The useful notions which many ill-worded proverbs do import, may, I think, compensate for their homely terms; though I could wish the contrivers of them had put their sense into more decent and cleanly language."[5] But such proverbs are almost always quoted apologetically.

It somewhat detracts, however, from the crushing effect referred to above, if your interlocutor be prepared with another proverb of an exactly opposite tendency. For proverbs, like all other documents, are of various interpretations, and it is never hard to find one to serve the turn. You might for instance try to convince an educated Chinaman of the folly of his apathy as to all extra-Chinese subjects by quoting his own proverb *Sitting in a well staring at the sky*, but he would reply with the most pernicious axiom China possesses, *A graduate may know all things without having stirred out of his door*, almost the only proverb I know which does not contain even a grain of truth. There is a whole series of contradictory maxims on the vexed question of the relation of personal appearance to disposition. One, more terse than wise, bids us *Know a man by his looks,* another will have it that *Looks are born in the heart,* which is indeed what Solomon said; "As he thinketh in his heart so is he." But in opposition to these we are told, *A man is not always to be judged by his face any more than the sea measured with a bushel,* and just as the seer of old was cautioned, "Look not on his countenance, or on the height of his stature," *If you judged by appearances Tsze-yu would be now here.* Now Tsze-yu was a statesman of whom Confucius was pleased to approve, and Confucius himself was so ugly that they called his face The Five Mountains. Finally, the controversy may be summed up in this witty saying: *A red-nosed man may be no drunkard, but he will always be called one.*

A set of similarly conflicting proverbs exists on the never-to-be-settled question of appearances and the opinions of others. *A wise man is cautious and avoids the appearance of evil,* says one proverb, the canny carefulness of which is more than followed up by this; *Don't lace your boot in a melon field, nor adjust your hat under a plum-tree,* and this; *If you don't belong to the family don't go into the house, i.e.* lest you be taken for a thief or person on a worse errand. But there is also a proverb which heroically bids you *Never mind what other people think*, and another which avers that *Right heart need not fear evil seeming.* We may also remember that Confucius himself visited the infamous Nan-tsze, and was excessively angry at the suspicions of one of his favourite disciples, so far forgetting himself as to swear! The fact is that a proverb can only represent one phase of a question. There is a time to judge a man by his looks, and a time to forget his looks: there is a time to respect appearances, and a time to scorn appearances. Most proverbs are but half truths at best, but this, which appears appropriately to sum up the controversy of seeming *versus* being, is wholly true: *If you wish no evil known of you there is no way but to do none.*

I will cite one more curiously contradictory set of proverbs on the subject of Government and the Administration of Justice, and I need hardly say that in China, where offical employment is constantly before the mind of the people as the *summum bonum* of existence, the proverbs turning upon it are many. At first sight they seem hopelessly and irreconcilably conflicting, and it is not till we get a clue to their opposing statements that we are enabled to arrange them into two well-marked classes—those that give a faithful picture of public business as it is supposed to be—and those that treat of it as it is. Should any person come upon a collection of the first alone, he would believe that China is such a Utopia of philanthropic government and spotless administration as this world has not seen, except in the dreams of visionary enthusiasts. He would find this written down as the mark of a good man: *To seek out worthy officers and promote them: to perceive his faults and reform them.* He would find this pithy and admirable little maxim: *Public business first, private after,* which in itself is nearly all that is wanted. He would find that *The sword of justice is swift, but will not wound the innocent*, and the typical official described as *The idol of ten thousand hearths*.[6] He would find official rectitude enforced by this saying; *When Princes walk purely the people are happy,* and by this, addressed to such Princes: *Before you are your children—the people; above is all-seeing*[7] *God!*

But if the collector were to leave these somewhat stilted sayings of officials about themselves, and turn to the more homely phrases of the people about them, what a falling off would he discover! The relation between the two is something of that between a school-boy's elegant copy-line, "Good penmanship is commendable," and the scrawled, mis-spelt, and blotted performance which follows. *The upright official cannot be altogether rid of rascally subordinates*, is a little unsettling to the Utopian vision; still more so this: *The Magistrate is not so dreadful as his men;* or this: *You may be arrested by mistake but not released;* or this: *Thirty blows right or wrong;* or this grim joke: *Pull in your head or stick it out, off it must come,* which, amongst other meanings signifies that, once before the Magistrate, whether you are innocent or guilty, submissive or contumacious, the result will be much the same. The wholesale, and, it might seem to those who do not know its causes, unreasoning terror which will seize upon a Chinese neighbourhood on the occurrence of any event which might attract official attention to it is thus expressed: *When you beat the mule the horse is frightened also; i.e.* innocent and guilty shake in their shoes alike. This fear is further implied in the caustic saying; *The people are a flock of sheep delivered over to the the wolf and tiger.*

> Of other care they little reckoning make
> Than how to scramble at the shearers' feast,
> And shove away the worthy bidden guest;
> Blind mouths! that scarce themselves know how to hold
> A sheep-hook, or have learned aught else the least
> That to the faithful herdsman's art belongs!
> What recks it them? What need they? They are sped;
> And when they list, their lean and fleshy songs
> Grate on their scrannel pipes of wretched straw,
> The hungry sheep look up and are not fed,
> But, swoln with wind and the rank mist they draw,
> Rot inwardly, and foul contagion spread;
> Besides what the grim wolf with privy paw
> Daily devours apace, and nothing said.

While we live let us keep out of the Courts, when dead out of Hell, expresses forcibly, but not one whit too forcibly, the people's horror of their rulers, whilst the causes of the evil are hinted at in the saying: *Officials won't flog a bearer of presents,* or in this very quaint proverb (in rhyme in the original): *Even a pig's head is cooked when the fire once gets to it; when money gets to the judge there will hardly be justice;* and finally, in this more pointed warning: *Public officers have their gates facing south, but he who has only cause and no cash had better keep out of them.* Some of these bitter sayings no doubt partly take their rise in that tendency to rail at all existing institutions which is as common to Englishmen as Chinese, but there is also considerable truth in this; *Men who have had justice do not grumble, level water does not flow.*

Perhaps something not altogether alien to these two classes of proverbs may be found in our own country. The compliments often passed from the Bench to the Bar, and from the Bar to the Bench may stand for the Utopian maxims on things as they ought to be; the suppressed growls of the public, and the deep curses of suitors, for comments on things as they are. If lawyers, instead of merely hearing what they say "on their scrannel pipes of wretched straw" of each other, as to how society in general and justice in particular cannot get along without them, were to study (without fee or reward) what society in general and litigants in particular say about them—not about individuals of course, but about the system of shameful delays, and shameless costs, of mere sacrificing of justice to the tithing of legal mint, anise, and cummin—we might (if costs were once and forever abolished) have such a Reform of Law as we are not likely to have whilst Law is so paying an iniquity as it is.

That is one lesson from the Chinese proverbs on the relations of man to man. But I promised, in a quotation which I introduced at the beginning of this article, proverbs on the relations of man to his Maker. Incredible as, I regret to say, it will seem to many readers, it is nevertheless a fact that the Chinese have abundant proverbs implying not only a belief in God, but also a humble trust in Him, which, in the better sort of them, is not, I think, wholly imperceptible in their lives. They have also a startling number about fate, and at first sight it might seem doubtful whether fate or God were greater. But when we find that fate is a creature of God, His will in fact, we perceive that it is only another name for what we call providence. But names have a wonderful influence in confusing *things.* That the Chinese name for God is also, as it has been in almost every nation, the name of the sky, has led persons to deny that they acknowledge Him at all. That they do not acknowledge the profane caricature of the Divine nature set forth in the corrupt theology of almost all our pulpits (I care not of what denomination) I gladly, nay even rejoicingly admit. Long may they continue ignorant of *him*. But in "The Lord, the Lord God, merciful and gracious, long-suffering, and abundant in goodness and truth, keeping mercy for thousands, forgiving iniquity and transgression and sin, and that will by no means clear the guilty," I must maintain that they do cherish a flickering belief. To object that they say *Heaven* (which I deny—we choose to translate it so) where we would have them say *God,* is simply to point out that they give to a very complicated conception a less abstract name than we do. And I never can quite understand what the prattle about "a personal God" means, unless a god with arms and legs.

I have already noticed their proverb, *Man proposes, God disposes;* I have never met with a more beautiful expansion of it than this; *Man has a thousand, a myriad plans for himself; God has only one plan for him.* The same vein of thought runs through this; *Man cries "Now, now!" God says "Not yet, not yet."* We are reminded that *Blessings come from God*; but the most beautiful of this class of proverbs, almost worthy to rank with our own about the wind and the shorn lamb, is that *God never drives a man to desperation,* but will, with the temptation also make a way to escape, that he may be able to bear it. This most religious proverb forcibly recalls that exquisite Spanish one; "God never wounds with both hands;" "not with *both*, for He ever reserves one with which to bind up and heal." The original of that is, "No hiere Dios con dos manos," and I should be glad if those who stumble at what has been said above about a Chinese knowledge of God would recollect what is the ultimate etymology of *Dios*.

But indeed if we come to the region of morality we shall find that God, who is not far from any man, has not left himself without witness among these people, that they should seek Him, if haply they might feel after Him and find Him. One of their truest proverbs declares that *The right path is in each man's mind*, which, hopelessly unorthodox as it sounds, is only what has been said by a higher authority in another place.[8] He who is in the world but not of the world, "persecuted, but not forsaken; cast down, but not destroyed," is said to be *Ground at but not thinned*, in allusion to the grinding of jewels, which metaphor is not in itself the less pleasing that the words were used by Confucius to prove that *he* could touch pitch and not be defiled—a dangerous doctrine. The indirect good consequences of good are thus held up to admiration: *A good man protects three villages, a good dog three houses*; whilst of evil we are warned that

Sin is the root of sorrow. Finally, the evanescent nature of even our best impulses is amusingly commented on in a reference to the man who *Falls to beating the priest the minute he has finished his prayers.*

Very many Chinese proverbs, like those of other nations have been put into the form of rhyme. It is all but impossible, however, to translate these into English rhyme or even jingle (the original is often no more) without losing that exquisite terseness which characterizes them. Here is one attempt, just twice as long as it ought to be

> When your Court talk is not enough
> Eke it out with local stuff;

a hit at the affectation of those who set up to speak Pekingese on the strength of a few sentences, which being exhausted, they are driven to patch up their conversation with village *patois* pronounced with an attempt at metropolitan twang, just as a well-known imposter tried to atone for his ignorance of French by such fustian as "We did gazzer flowers."

I must content myself with citing only a few more of the excellent proverbs which take a not unkindly outlook upon life and manners. On that saddest of subjects, the approach of old age and decay, I know no better one than this, *Men grow old, pearls grow yellow, there is no cure for it;* nor a more effective warning as to the instability of all human plans than this: *Man has a thousand purposes. Death comes one morning and ten thousand may wait.* "In that very day his thoughts perish." He who thinks to fence himself against all possible misfortunes is reminded, *The harder the tree, the harder the weevil.* There is a ridicule of ambitious attempts, but also a grain of consolation for their failure in the adage, *He who failed to draw a tiger made it into a dog.* "It will always make a night cap, said the girl who tried to make a shirt." *A sheep was never known to climb a tree,* is a pungent but not unkindly satire on a man whom nothing can rouse to effort or enterprise, We predict that "He will never set the Thames on fire," but the Chinese version is much the better. *Let your ideas be round, but your conduct square,* is a happy definition of the golden mean between prejudiced conservatism, and unprincipled laxity. That *a clever woman always gets a fool to her husband* has perhaps occurred to others besides the Chinese; and he who would seek domestic peace and ensure it should consider this: *To comply with your brother's wish is to disappoint your sister-in-law.* There are many sly hits at matrimonial infelicity, made and circulated by the wretched men no doubt, and including a version of our own, *The hen that crows*; but they are all compensated in this: *One day of wedded life deserves a hundred days of kindness.* Finally, the head and crown of Chinese proverbs is that *"Do as you would be done by" will serve as a motto for a life-time.*

In selecting the above, my task has been rather the difficulty of leaving out a vast number of excellent and witty proverbs, than of finding the few that I have been enabled to arrange. I trust that even these few will not be deemed too many. "The fact that they please the people and have pleased them for ages—that they possess so vigorous a principle of life as to have maintained their ground, ever new and ever young, through all the centuries of a nation's existence—nay, that many of them have pleased not one nation only, but many, so that they have made themselves a home in the most different lands—and further, that they have, not a few of them, come down to us from remotest antiquity borne safely upon the waters of that great stream of time which has swallowed so much beneath its waves—all this, I think, may well make us pause, should we be tempted to turn away from them with anything of indifference or disdain."

Notes

1. L'homme propose, Dieu dispose; La gente pone y Dios dispone: Der Mensch denkt's, Gott lenkt's: the Chinese form is 謀事在人成事在天.

2. In the original publication of this paper, there was an appendix containing texts of all of the Chinese proverbs in Chinese. Ed. Note.

3. Confucius said, "I hate your glib-tongued fellows!" Analects XI. 24.

4. Matthew XV. 10–20.

5. I may cite one in Premare's collection, 別人屁臭自家香; and another, something corresponding to our "Don't meet trouble half-way," which, even in Chinese, I should not like to put on paper.

6. Originally said of 司馬光.

7. I forestall a criticism on this translation by stating that I am perfectly aware that the character is 靑.

8. Romans II. 14. 15.

The Humour of Spanish Proverbs

*A.A. Parker**

Sometimes the attempt to isolate characteristics or themes in a corpus of proverbs centers on one feature in particular. In the following essay, first presented as the Canning House Ninth Annual Lecture in May, 1962, a professor of Spanish at the University of London seeks to describe the elusive element of humor as he finds it expressed in Spanish proverbial form. However, the more general question raised by this paper is, as in the preceding paper, to what extent, if any, can peculiar or specific features of one cultural group be delineated through the analysis of the proverbs of that group? Can Spanish proverbs or the Spanish versions of international proverbs yield insights into Spanish thought patterns, philosophy, or world-view? In terms of humor, the question might be rephrased as: does what a people laugh at reveal their attitudes toward life? The obvious answer would appear to be yes, but the actual documentation necessary to support such an assertion is not always so easy to provide.

For a further consideration of Spanish proverbs, see Josef Felixberger, Untersuchungen zur Sprache des spanischen Sprichwortes *(München, 1974). For another essay devoted to humor in proverbs, see M.H. Rezvanian, "L'humour dans les proverbes persans,"* Proverbium, *14 (1969), 399–407.*

* Reprinted by permission of the Hispanic and Luso-Brazilian Councils from A.A. Parker, *The Humour of Spanish Proverbs* (London: Hispanic and Luso-Brazilian Councils, 1963), pp. 3–23.

An appropriate phrase with which to begin a talk on proverbs would seem to be an apology for carrying coals to Newcastle. Surely it is not only unnecessary but also impertinent to talk about the humour of Spanish proverbs to an audience interested in Hispanic matters, since *Don Quixote* makes any talk on this subject quite unnecessary. One need only read through any of the chapters in which Sancho Panza is particularly loquacious to see these proverbs as living speech—very much alive and kicking, since they are used as they should be used, to give not only point but a punch to a particular statement. The contrast between what Cervantes does and the best I can hope to do is the contrast between a lively conversation and a dictionary. Dictionaries have their uses, but I must at the start do some justice to my subject not only by paying tribute to Cervantes but by quoting a short passage from him to illustrate what I mean by living speech—that the humour of proverbs depends not only on what they say but on the way they are applied.

One of the practical jokes played upon Don Quixote and Sancho by the Duke and Duchess is the wooden horse Clavileño, on which they are to sit blindfold and be persuaded that they will be carried into the sky. Both of them have already been made to believe that Dulcinea is enchanted and that the spell can only be broken by Sancho giving himself 3,300 lashes on his seat. Shortly before they mount the wooden horse Don Quixote implores Sancho to retire indoors and give himself at least 500 lashes as a first instalment towards the rescue of his lady. "Good Heavens," said Sancho, "Your Honour must be out of his mind! This is like the saying: 'You can see I'm pregnant, yet you ask me whether I'm a virgin.' Now that I've got to go on a journey seated on a hard plank, your Honour wants me to hurt my behind?" *¿En priesa me ves, y doncellez me demandas?*—One might be tempted to think that Cervantes must have made it up himself, but it is to be found in a proverb collection of his day.[1]

Proverbs can exercise a strong fascination and can even lead scholars to dedicate to them a lifetime of specialized study. They have, of course, the fascination of all folklore—the problem of origins, the question of chronological range and geographical distribution: how long has any one of them been alive, how far round the world has it travelled? There is, further, the fascination of seeing the changes they undergo as they pass from mouth to mouth and country to country. The men of the Renaissance, with Erasmus at their head, admired the things that proverbs say: they were awed that wisdom had been reached by common and ignorant people and was not the prerogative of Holy Writ and the authors of classical antiquity. Nowadays it is perhaps not so easy to feel this particular admiration. The proverbs that by now have been collected from all over the world run into hundreds and hundreds of thousands; moreover, the literature we can now turn to for enlightenment and edification is so fantastically vast that we are perhaps too *blasés*: at any rate, proverbs in bulk, purely as regards their content, tend to be rather boring because of their generally platitudinous nature. It is not easy to be patient for long with all these rolling stones, birds of a feather, new brooms, straws and camels. But this does not seem to me to be as true of the proverbs of Spain as it is of those of other countries. It may be that I have a prejudice born of the ignorance that specialization breeds, but it does seem to me that we Hispanists are fortunate in this respect, in that Spanish proverbs have to a marked degree the saving grace of humour, and humour of an agreeably astringent kind. I do not mean that if you wade through all the numerous collections of the innumerable Spanish proverbs[2] you will be splitting your sides for every minute of the months it will take you to read them, but the chances are that you will be tempted to smile at least once on every page, and I rather doubt whether the same thing holds good of the collections of other national proverbs.

Spaniards themselves do not as a rule stress this particular quality. Obsessed as they are with the existence of their national characteristics, they rarely seem able to see beyond them. Thus Aurelio Espinosa, the distinguished scholar in the field of comparative folklore, writes this in his introduction to the Spanish selection in a collection of proverbs from many nations:

> Spanish proverbs and proverbial expressions are, of course, in a great measure, the Spanish forms of similar materials that are common to the folk-lore of Europe, and even to universal folk-lore, but many are fundamentally and typically Spanish in origin, and depict very accurately some of the outstanding traits of the Spanish character. . . . They are a true and direct expression of the psychology of the Spanish people.[3]

Espinosa does not, however, specify what these traits are. Ever since Francis Bacon affirmed that "The genius, wit and spirit of a nation are discovered in its proverbs," many have tried to use proverbs to define national or racial temperament. No side of their study seems to have been prosecuted so vigorously, but the results are insignificant. This is not surprising when we consider, first the elusiveness, indeed the doubtful existence, of such a thing as a national character, and secondly the fact that vast numbers of proverbs in any one language are found also in many other languages. Proverbs, in fact, like all folk-lore, are to a large extent international. An example of the danger of deducing the Spanish character from a proverb comes from the first big collection of proverbs published in England by James Howell in 1659, comprising proverbs in five languages. On the Spanish *Antes moral que almendro* ("Rather a mulberry than an almond tree") Howell comments: "This proverb doth agree with the complexion of the Spaniard, who is more slow and flegmatick in his actions than other nations: as the Mulberry is amongst trees, who buds very late, and not till the asperity of the cold weather be quite past; wherefore that tree is taken for a Symbol of wisdome, as the Almond tree, that buds betimes, is of rashnesse. . . ."[4] I doubt whether anyone nowadays would consider Spaniards a particularly slow and phlegmatic people. It is true that when Howell wrote, gravity was a quality cultivated in Spain; but only a few years previously Lope de Vega had justified the particular form he had given to the national drama by appealing to the "choleric" temperament of his countrymen who, according to him, were so impatient that they could not be made to sit still in a theatre for two hours unless the play had a crowded and swiftly moving action. One would think, then, that this proverb, like so many others, pointed not to a psychological fact but to a moral aspiration.[5]

The attribution of gravity to Spanish proverbs is found also in the following early comparison of the proverbs of the three major Latin countries; in each case it would seem that the qualities already believed to characterize the peoples were read into their proverbs:

> The Spanish and Italian proverbs are counted the most Curious and Significant—the first are remarkable for Gravity and fine Instruction, the Latter for Beauty and Elegance, tho' they are a little tinctured with Levity and have too much of the Amour. This last Variety is the Imperfection of many of the French, tho' otherwise they are very Fine and Bright, and solemnly Moral as well as Facetious and Pleasant.[6]

Another Englishman who published a collection of Spanish proverbs, John Collins in 1823, does not refer to national characteristics, but begins his preface by saying: "Spanish Proverbs have long been celebrated for their pith and humour."[7] However, fashions in humour change and the humour of Collins's volume lies not so much in the proverbs he selects as in the comments he adds. Thus on the proverb *A la mujer barbuda, de lejos la saluda* ("Greet a bearded woman at a distance")[8] he remarks: "Advising persons to avoid women with beards, they being of warm and impetuous dispositions." I should have thought there was a simpler reason for this advice.

One must, I think, be chary in detecting national characteristics. It is interesting to contrast Espinosa's remarks on the Spanish proverbs with the late Professor Saurat's introduction to the French section in the same collection. He seems anxious to exclude any typically French characteristics as being derogatory to the universality of his national culture.

> The point which strikes one in French proverbs is that they are not particularly French. Indeed, I doubt whether any proverbs are truly national. . . . Proverbs are obviously a form of literature which appeals to the widest public of all, and the widest public is only reached by getting down to the lowest and therefore the broadest possible level. This again does not mean that French proverbs are not typical of France. But it means that they are typical of that part of the French which is similarly a part of the psychology of any other people . . . . Perhaps in the case of French proverbs we can see merely that general tendency which is so visible in French literature to reach after universal statements, statements which can be regarded as valid for the whole world.[9]

So true does this appear to be that in France the distinction between proverbs and literary maxims often seems to be deliberately blurred. Dictionaries of French quotations are full of proverb-like sayings such as *Qui borne ses désirs est toujours assez riche* and *Quand on n'a pas ce que l'on aime, il faut aimer ce que l'on a.* But these and countless others like them are quotations from literary authors: in these cases, Voltaire and Thomas Corneille respectively. It is not therefore quite so surprising to find that collections of French proverbs contain famous sayings such as these, with no author's name: *Rien n'est beau que le vrai* and *Le coeur a ses raisons que la raison ne connaît point,* which even a nodding acquaintance with French literature tells us are by Boileau and Pascal. Not only, then, do French proverbs reach after universal statements, but the universal statements of literature seek to become proverbs and to oust those of the people.

There are similar cases, though far fewer, in English. *Knowledge is power* is by Bacon; *To err is human, to forgive divine,* though originally a French proverb, comes to us from Pope; and there is no danger of our forgetting the authorship of *To be or not to be*: these sayings are proverbs now. In Spain the situation is very different: sayings from the national classics are not to be found in collections of proverbs. Literary proverbs do of course exist in Spanish; but though we may well fail to detect them when we meet them in the works of Spanish literature,[10] there is never any likelihood of our failing to detect a popular proverb in a similar setting. For, unlike literary proverbs, the Spanish popular ones (by which, of course, I mean the genuine folk creations) have a distinctive style, with which their humour is closely bound up. This can best be illustrated by showing how the form and wording of a Spanish proverb tend to deviate from the normal or standard international pattern.

The advisability of not running risks is expressed in French by *Il ne faut pas mettre les étoupes trop près du feu*[11] ("One mustn't put the tow too near the fire"). This is a piece of sound advice, couched in the form of a didactic general statement. This first of all becomes in Spanish *Si el fuego está cerca de la estopa, llega el diablo y sopla* ("If the fire is near the tow, the Devil comes along and blows"). The general warning is still there, but it is submerged in the unfortunate result of not heeding it; the general statement gives way to a concrete action; and since you will suffer if your property catches fire, the action of catching fire becomes more significant and vivid if it is personalized as malignant. Further particularity is then given to this by turning it from an unlikely eventuality into a probable one: and so we get a second form of the proverb, *El hombre es fuego, la mujer, estopa; llega el diablo y sopla* ("Man is fire, woman, tow; the Devil comes along and blows"). We have thus moved away from the possibility of careless people leaving tow too near the fire to nature having created women too near to men. The remote possibility of an accident becomes a closer kind of conflagration from which there is no escape.

Some scholars in European proverb lore have distinguished a western and an eastern type of proverb—the former being a general, didactic observation while the latter is concrete and often includes dialogue.[12] In Western Europe, for instance, one says *Lazy people always have holidays,* while in Eastern Europe the proverb runs: *They said to the lazy man, "Today is a holiday." Then he answered, "Tomorrow and the day after, too."* The difference in form is striking. With the eastern form are associated the Arabic proverbs. The fact that the most typical Spanish proverbs belong to the eastern type invalidates a geographical division, unless, of course, it is ultimately a question of Arabic origins. Since it is now fashionable to look to Arab culture for the roots of many things Spanish, it is odd that proverbs have not yet, as far as I know, been brought in to help prove this thesis. If, in fact, the distinction is between eastern and western, the affinity of the Spanish forms with the east is clear enough. Compare these three examples. Arabic: *The kettle reproached the kitchen spoon. "Thou blackee," he said, "thou idle babbler."* Spanish: *Dijo la sartén a la caldera, "Quítate allá, culinegra"* ("Said the frying pan to the kettle, 'Get away there, black bottom' "). *The Oxford Dictionary of Proverbs* gives the modern English form as simply *Pot and kettle,* the implication being that both are equally black; but the real proverb is found in 1639 as *The kettle calls the pot black arse.* If there is a line of descent here, it would clearly seem to be from Arabic to Spanish, to English. But this distinction between eastern and western forms of proverbs has been disputed, since the great majority of Arabic and Greek, and of other proverbs from Eastern Europe, resemble in form those current in Western Europe. Perhaps the distinction should rather be between a primitive and a more advanced form, the primitive form being one much closer to a purely folk culture, the advanced form deriving from a folk environment that is closer to a literary culture. By primitive I do not mean a chronological category, for I think there is plenty of evidence to suggest that the primitive form of many Spanish proverbs can and does develop out of the more literary form. For instance, in the early seventeenth century we find as a Spanish proverb "The bath has sworn not to turn black white"; three centuries later this had become: "Why does the negress have a bath if she can't turn white?" The change is in the direction I have defined.[13] I hope it will also be clear that I am not using the term primitive in any disparaging sense. On the contrary; I consider what I call the primitive type of proverb far superior to the so-called western form. This concrete, particular, more immediate and personal quality is what gives the proverbs that possess it a strength and bite. It also makes them funnier. Compare, for example, the abstractness of the standard European proverb *Charity begins at home,* with the personal particularity with which the Spanish people have expressed the same idea: *Más cerca están mis dientes que mis parientes* ("My teeth are nearer than my relatives"). This concrete, particular and personal form is characteristic of the best Spanish proverbs and I particularly wish it to be noted, especially when I compare one of them with its English or French counterpart.

I have now reached my main theme of humour. The last proverb I have quoted is funny because of the disrespectful way in which family ties, with all the high loyalties involved, are placed lower in the scale of values than the act of chewing. The tow, fire and Devil proverb is funny because of the way in which love is deprived of any idealization by being turned into the Devil's bellows; here too there is an ironical lack of respect, whereby a high established value is made rather ridiculous by a derogatory comparison. This seems to me to be at the heart of the humour of Spanish proverbs and I should like now to illustrate some of its variations.[14]

The first form that may be isolated is that of ambiguity, when respect is ostensibly paid to conventional values in the form of a respectable observation which, however, is susceptible of a slyly destructive twist. For instance: *No le quiere mal quien le hurta al viejo lo que ha de cenar* ("No ill-will is shown to the old man if his supper is stolen from him"). The respectable meaning is that moderation in eating is good for the health of old men; but this is conveyed through the implication that stealing can be justifiable if you can claim that it does the victim a good turn. Another amusing example is a proverb that belies its implied good advice by presenting it in the breach rather than in the observance. *A good example is the best sermon* is a rather prim proverb which English borrowed from Italian. Compare the form in which the same advice is given in Spanish: *Si el prior juega a los naipes, ¿qué harán los frailes?* ("If the prior gambles, what can you expect the friars to do?") Not only is there a pithy example of the maxim where the Italian and English proverb has merely a tame general precept, there is also the sly suggestion that priors might, or even do, gamble at cards.

The last illustration I quote of this ambiguity is *Hartóse el gato de carne, y luego se hizo fraile* ("The cat had its fill of meat and then turned friar"). There is a respectable meaning here if we take it as a warning that the outward show of piety can be hypocritical,[15] but in our hard and cynical age we are more likely to take it as an anti-clerical jibe—the lazy, gluttonous friar, like the cruel, bloated aristocrats in the older Russian films. But it is not really funny if it is only anti-clericalism of this crude kind. The humour of this proverb lies in the fact that it also expresses a spiritual truth: it is easier to praise God—to be a pious and law-abiding citizen—if you are not starving: the cat first had its fill of meat and *then* turned friar. But the anti-clerical insinuation (especially through the fact that *gato* can also mean "thief") is inescapable, and it is the juxtaposition of the two interpretations—one a truth of the spiritual life, the other a mocking reference to the religious life—that gives the proverb a bite.

This last example points to a second type of humour, where the irreverence is direct, without any ambiguity. The most striking examples of these are anti-clerical or even apparently anti-religious proverbs, of which there are quite a number. The great Feijóo, who in common with most representatives of eighteenth-century Enlightenment had little use for folk proverbs, was scandalized at this one: *Ante la puerta del rezador, nunca eches tu trigo al sol* ("In front of the door of the man of prayer never put your corn to dry"). "Temerarious, impious and scandalous," said Feijóo, "for it directly expresses distrust of the fidelity and honesty of devout people."[16] The trouble with Feijóo was that among his many virtues he did not really include a sense of humour. Non-Catholics are sometimes shocked at the familiarity with which jokes are made about religious matters in Catholic countries. No irreverence, much less blasphemy, is intended, and one must bear this in mind when smiling at these apparently irreverent proverbs. There is also, however, another reason for anti-clericalism in Spanish proverbs. In the greater part of Spain the life of the peasant is a hard struggle against poor soil and an unrelenting climate. Spain is, on the whole, a poor country, and the peasantry are conscious of living a life of privation: in past centuries, whence most of my proverbs come, they must, of course, have been very much more conscious of it. This finds expression in several proverbs, of which I instance one, not on this occasion an example of humour: *Escarba la gallina por su mal, y saca el cuchillo que la ha de degollar* ("The hen scratches about on the ground but does herself no good, for she unearths the knife that will cut her throat"). Actually this is one of the oldest of all proverbs. In ancient Greece it was *The goat, the knife*, and referred to a story that when a goat was about to be sacrificed, no knife could be found; but the pawing of the animal revealed a knife in the ground and the sacrifice was carried out.[17] In some versions of the proverb the goat becomes a sheep. In Spain the change to a hen is most significant, for it turns the religious sacrifice of the original proverb into economic exploitation and hardship. Hens, unlike goats or sheep, but like peasants, scratch about on the soil to find their nourishment—in Spain this is *por su mal*, it does them no good.

Awareness of this kind of background seems to me important for understanding large numbers of Spanish proverbs, for they show the folk reacting against these conditions by various forms of self-defence. One form is the assertion of independence, the refusal to cringe: *Debajo de mi manto al rey mando*, or the variant *al rey mato*. ("Underneath my cloak I command the King"—or "I kill the King"). In other words, every man is his own master: in the inviolability of his own personality he can rise above political or economic oppression. Another reaction is the refusal to admit any superiority in those more favoured by fortune—e.g. *Más sabe el necio en su casa, que el sabio en la ajena* ("The ignorant man in his own house knows more than the educated man in somebody else's"). This was a proverb that shocked Don Quixote when he first heard it on Sancho's lips,[18] though in the context in which I am placing it, it is more impressive than our own *An Englishman's house is his castle*.

A third reaction of the Spanish peasant to his economic status is that of inward revolt, or a refusal to submit to what he is told is good for him. *No me den consejos, sino dineros* is its most forthright expression—"Don't give me advice, give me money." Gracián denounced this proverb: "Good advice," he said, "is money, and is worth a treasure; and for him who lacks good advice, a whole India, or even two would not suffice."[19] Which only goes to confirm one's suspicions that Gracián was rather a heartless prig. *Poverty is no disgrace* or *Poverty is no sin*, say the international proverbs, which, while perfectly true, is cold comfort to the desperately poor. So that when the same proverb *Pobreza no es vileza* was preached to the Spanish poor, they added *mas es ramo de picardia* ("Poverty is no sin, but it's a branch of knavery"), i.e. it breeds crime. This rather grim, though true, statement has its humorous counterpart: *El hurtar es cosa linda si colgasen por la pretina* ("Stealing would be a pleasant occupation if only they hanged you round your middle"). In Spanish folk-lore, if nowhere else, hanging *is* a deterrent.

This natural refusal to accept poverty as an unqualified virtue, and this natural preference for the satisfaction of hunger rather than good advice or moral exhortation, are the explanation of what might at first sight appear a cynical attitude to religion. It is not cynicism but common sense; and if it is irreverence, it is irreverence with the saving grace of humour and in no sense malevolent. For instance, this is the way a Spanish proverb expresses our *Enough is as good as a feast*, or *Too much of a good thing: Rogar a Dios por santos, mas no por tantos* ("Pray to God for saints, but not for so many of them"). There is also here the attitude that I referred to earlier: the refusal to be impressed by anything that is much prized, which is at bottom, I think, a way of asserting oneself against the inferiority forced upon one by the more satisfied members of society. This is why even sanctity is not spared.[20] Another amusing example is *Entre santa y santo, pared de cal y canto* ("Between a holy woman and a holy man place a stone wall"): even where both are saints it is better to keep the tow away from the fire. The wittiest of all these comments on sanctity—and I think it is extremely witty—is this: *El estiércol no es santo, mas do cae hace milagro* ("Dung is not holy, but wherever it falls it works a miracle"). I think this startling juxtaposition of two such disparate things, of something so revered as sanctity and something so coarse as dung, is worth examining. If the statement were in the affirmative ("dung is holy because it works a miracle") it would be funny enough, but it would be merely expressing an unexceptionable statement—there are other things besides sanctity that are holy. By putting it into the negative the proverb gives this statement an ironical and irreverent undertone which makes it much more funny: the insinuation is that of course we cannot say dung is holy, but none the less the miracles it works (as against miracles worked in other ways) are at least practical and useful, for they do help us to grow food.

One last example of the humour of irreverence. The old and widespread proverb *Fortune favours fools* has a highly original Spanish equivalent: *A los bobos se les aparece la Madre de Dios* ("It is to fools that the Mother of God appears"). The Dictionary of the

Spanish Academy takes pains to give it a respectable meaning: "This denotes that some people are favoured by fortune without our knowing how."[21] But the irreverence of saying that only half-wits see apparitions of Our Lady needs no stressing. The seventeenth-century proverb collection of Correas reveals that this proverb originally had, or was intended to have, only an edifying religious meaning, but that already the sly, ironical insinuation had begun to spread. The proverb he gives in this form: "It is to the innocent that the Mother of God appears." And he comments:

> By the innocent we are to understand the good and the holy, although this [proverb] is commonly applied to men of little sense . . . this [meaning] must be deplored and it [the proverb] should never be so used.[22]

But because supernatural apparitions to the innocent have no edge to them, the preference for something cutting led to the change of "innocent" into "fools"; and the ambiguity allowed the irony to pass because of the new and respectable meaning of Fortune favouring fools.

Religious irreverence, I have suggested, is a way in which the common man at the bottom of the social ladder can assert a sense of his own importance: nobody is really any better than he. This points to a third form in which the basic humour of Spanish proverbs is expressed. One might be tempted to call this cynicism—a refusal to accept any form of idealism at its face value, always looking instead behind the exterior for the pleasure of finding a disreputable interior. But rather than a sneering sort of cynicism I would prefer to call it a matter-of-fact bluntness, a refusal to be impressed, to be taken in by anything that men claim to prize, because this is a way of lessening in your own eyes the superiority of other people. But however we define it, this is a humorous attitude in that the contrast between the screen of decorous drapery and what lies behind it is made laughable.

Here, I think, is the main contrast in content between the general run of international proverbs and the best and most characteristic of the Spanish ones. Proverbs tend to take themselves very seriously as guides to respectable and successful living. They moralize with a disarming naiveté as they give dispiriting advice about farthings saved being twice earned, about eating to live not living to eat, about eggs in one basket, about silver linings, half a loaf, spilt milk, and so on. Of course dull moral truisms are found in Spanish proverbs as in all others, but every collection is constantly enlivened by the regular appearance of a refusal to take anything seriously.

Qué buena cara tiene mi padre el dia que no hurta ("What a happy face my father has on the day he doesn't steal"). We say *There is no rogue like the godly rogue*, but how much more cutting it is to make your father godly on his days off from thieving, for what then becomes of filial reverence and respect?[23] If that goes, what reverence is left? And is there really such a thing as altruism? Isn't self-interest behind even the vaunted unselfishness of love? *Gana tiene de coles quien besa al hortelano* ("She has a liking for cabbages who kisses the market-gardener").

Our own proverbs do their utmost to inculcate habits of early rising, hard work, frugality and so on. The early bird catches the worm, but *No por mucho madrugar amanece más temprano* ("By always rising early in the morning you won't make the dawn come any sooner"). Why then go to all that trouble? There is not much praise in Spanish proverbs for the industrious self-made man; long hours and hard work are nothing to shout about. *Más dias hay que longanizas* ("There are more days than there are sausages"). In general this means that there is always plenty of time;[24] but I like to think it means, more particularly, that the number of sausages one can profitably consume is limited: in other words, there are certain material needs which must be satisfied, but these can be kept to the minimum; life must not be equated with the unrelenting pursuit of economic ends: one can leave oneself time to be human. *Idleness is the root of all evil* is therefore only a half truth. Unimpressed by work for its own sake a corresponding Spanish proverb says *Más vale bien holgar que mal trabajar* ("It is better to idle well than to work badly").[25] In a hot country it is really impossible to work well and supremely easy, because quite inexpensive, to idle well—and also, one must admit, supremely enjoyable. In the less civilized atmosphere of our arctic regions one must either be very rich or delude oneself about the virtue of early rising and long hours. In other words *One must make a virtue of necessity*. But even this ancient maxim is not acceptable in Spain where, with an underlying suspicion of the motives behind moral respectability, they say: *Quien más no puede, con su mujer se acuesta* ("He who can't do any better goes to bed with his own wife").

This not taking anything seriously is not only a refusal to harbour any illusions, it is also a disinclination to put oneself out, to be swept off one's feet by either enthusiasm or despair. *It is no use crying over spilt milk* is a rather trite way of expressing the need for equanimity. As we expect, the Spanish sense of humour puts it much more vigorously: *Si vieres tu casa quemar, llégate a escalentar* ("If you should find your house on fire go up and warm yourself by it"). A delightful way of saying that most disasters for which we are not responsible we can look upon as having happened for our benefit: we can face them accordingly. We are more important than what we possess. Even when life threatens to crush us, we can retain our dignity.

This makes it sound more stoical than funny; and of course it has often been pointed out that there is a strong stoic element in Spanish life and culture. But on the whole I would prefer the term fatalism. Spanish proverbs show not so much an indifference to pain and suffering as a resigned acceptance of them. You can't escape from adversity so there is no point in making a fuss and bother about it; rather than bang your head against a brick wall it is better to grin and bear it, with an emphasis on the grin. This submission to the inevitability of everything that happens is fatalism rather than stoicism, and it seems to me much more characteristic of Spain than the self-conscious search for virtue through indifference. However that may be, our proverbs do not fail to stress this attitude, and a contrast with a Romance equivalent illustrates it clearly and neatly. *In a big river one catches a big fish* say the French and Italians, which indicates that great results follow only from important undertakings: you will not get anywhere if you do not aim high. The Spaniards do not deny this, but their version of the proverb adds a rider: *En gran rio, gran pez; mas ahógase alguna vez* ("In a big river a big fish, but sometimes you'll get drowned"). This proverb, in contrast to the French and Italian form, does not overlook the possibility of disaster—aim high if you want to, but be ready for the fall.

The Spanish proverbs that express this inevitability of suffering are, like most of the others I have put before you, not devoid of humour, but it tends to be humour of a sardonic kind. For example, *No hay más chinches que la manta llena* ("You can't have more bed bugs than a blanketfull"); in other words, there is a limit to even the unpleasantnesses of life, but the limit may well be the maximum that it is possible for life to cram in.

Spanish culture is most fatalistic where the greatest adversity of all (humanly speaking) is concerned, namely death: *Al que ha de morir a oscuras, poco le importa ser cerero* ("To him who is going to die in the dark, it won't be much help being a candle-maker"). Unamuno was surely right in saying that what to the busy, materially purposeful man of short vision can appear to be laziness, may well be a wisdom beyond his ken—a wisdom that, I like to think, is enshrined in *No se me da nada, que en muriéndome yo, todo se acaba* ("I don't care about anything, because everything finishes when I die"). This is not only fatalism, but also perhaps a supreme assertion of individualism.[26] There is no question here of the individual's dying with the satisfaction of knowing that he has contributed his bit to the eventual immortality of the human race in the last stage of its optimistic evolution. On the contrary: I don't care, because as far as I am concerned everything comes to an end with me. Of course, a proud self-sufficiency such as this may be well-founded if we are all just waiting for a cosmic nuclear super-explosion; the world may indeed come to an end with each one of us. But whether it will or not makes no real difference either, for there is only one solution to the problem of how to face life. I conclude my attempt to show that the folk proverbs of Spain are more than commonplace generalities with the one that most succinctly, perhaps even most movingly, sums up this solution: *Paciencia y barajar* ("Patience, and shuffle the cards").

Notes

1. Gonzalo Correas, *Vocabulario de refranes y frases proverbiales,* where it is given in the form *En priesa me (nos) veis, y virgo me (nos) demandáis* (ed. Madrid, 1906, p. 120). The episode in *Don Quixote* occurs in Part II, cap. xli; for the meaning of *en priesa* see F. Rodríguez Marín's note on this passage and his Appendix XXXIV in his Nueva Edición Crítica of the novel (Madrid, 1947–49, vol. VI, p. 205, and vol. X, pp. 73–75). In modern Spanish the proverb means something rather different: "You see I'm in distress (or in a hurry), yet you ask me to surrender my virginity." This is still humorous—and still applicable to Sancho's predicament.

2. The most learned and indefatigable collector of Spanish proverbs in modern times, Francisco Rodríguez Marín, published four large volumes of them: the first (1926) comprising "21,000 proverbs not found in the copious collection of Correas," was followed in 1930 by "12,600 more proverbs," in 1934 by "the 6,666 proverbs from my last search," and in 1941 by "10,700 more proverbs."

3. S.G. Champion, *Racial Proverbs: A Selection of the World's Proverbs Arranged Linguistically* (London, 1938), p. xcviii.

4. ΠΑΡΟΙΜΙΟΓΡΑΦΙΑ. *Proverbs, or Old sayed Sawes and Adages in English (or the Saxon Toung) Italian, French and Spanish* . . . (London, 1659), p. 30. This collection was published at the end of his *Lexicon Tetraglotton, an English-French-Italian-Spanish Dictionary* (London, 1660).

5. An interesting example of proverb formation is furnished by another proverb that, from the similar assonance, would seem to have been fashioned on this one: *Antes moro que gallego* ("Rather a Moor than a Galician").

6. Quoted from "an old writer" (presumably anonymous) in F. Edward Hulme, *Proverb Lore* (London, 1906), pp. 100–101.

7. John Collins, *A Dictionary of Spanish Proverbs* (London, 1823), p. iii.

8. My colleague Mr. J. W. Crow tells me this is an Italian proverb, which appears in English, as early as 1573, as *Greet a red man and a bearded woman three miles off.* The seventeenth-century Spanish version (Correas, *ed. cit.,* p. 5b) has the addition "with two stones, not just with one"—*A la mujer barbuda, de lejos me la saluda, con dos piedras, que no con una*. (I am indebted to Mr. Crow's learning, which as regards proverbs is unrivalled, for the correction of some overstatements and mis-statements that I made in the lecture.)

9. Champion, *op. cit.,* p. xlvii.

10. E.g. Pleberio's condemnation of the god of Love in the *Celestina,* "Haces que feo amen y hermoso les parezca," is found as a proverb, *Quien feo ama, hermoso le parece*, in the *Cartas en refranes* (1541) of Blasco de Garay; Calderón's "los sueños sueños son" was a line from a popular *letrilla* and is listed in Correas, and Gracián's maxim "Si no eres casto, sé cauto" is a Latin proverb, *caute, si non caste.*

11. A convenient work of reference for comparing Spanish proverbs with their counterparts in other Romance languages is W. Gottschalk, *Die bildhaften Sprichwörter der Romanen* (Heidelberg, 1935–36), 2 vols.

12. See Archer Taylor, *The Proverb* (Cambridge, Mass., 1931), pp. 156–159.

13. The first form is in Correas (*ed. cit.*, p. 274): *Jurado ha el baño, de no hacer de lo prieto blanco*. Here "black" can only be an adjective. In the *Diccionario de Autoridades* (1734, vol. V, under *negro*) the proverb appears as *Jurado ha el baño, de negro no hacer blanco*; here the change of the word for "black" makes it possible to take it either as an adjective or as a noun, "the negro" (cf. the English form: *To wash the blackmoor white*). In 1823 Collins (*op. cit.*, p. 75) lists as a proverb *Callar como negra en baño*, which he translates "To be as silent as a black wench in a bath," and which he explains as follows: "The negroes are remarkably fond of bathing. They commonly contrive to get into their master's baths, and from fear of being discovered they are particularly cautious of making the least noise." The phrase *como negra en baño* ("furtively"), which is no longer common, must have helped to give our proverb its modern form, *¿Para qué va la negra al baño, si blanca no puede ser?* (F. Rodríguez Marín, *Más de 21,000 refranes castellano,* Madrid, 1926, p. 361 a).

14. The only monograph that I know of on the humour of Spanish proverbs characterizes it as irony, which it defines as meaning the opposite of what one says so that the form contradicts the content; telling lies is generally an attractive temptation, and irony, whereby one appears to lie without actually doing so, is the only proper way

of indulging in this forbidden pleasure: a humorous proverb, therefore, is one that has "alguna pinta de ingeniosa mentira" (Julio Cejador, "La ironía y el gracejo en los refranes," in *La España Moderna,* No. 207 (March, 1906), pp. 84–101). With two exceptions all my examples of humorous proverbs are different from Cejador's, most of which do not strike me as being particularly funny.

15. Cejador, giving a slightly different form of the proverb (*El lobo harto de carne métese fraile*; "The wolf whose belly is full becomes a friar"), interprets it as "Physician heal thyself" (*op. cit.*, p. 91).

16. "Falibilidad de los adagios," in *Cartas eruditas* (Madrid, 1781), vol. III, pp. 1–12. J.M. Sbarbi defends the proverb by maintaining that *rezador* means specifically a hypocrite (*El refranero general español*, vol. IX (Madrid, 1878), pp. 113–114), but this is not corroborated by dictionaries, old or modern.

17. See Archer Taylor, *op. cit.*, pp. 29–30.

18. "Eso no, Sancho—respondió don Quijote—; que el necio en su casa ni en la ajena sabe nada, a causa que sobre el cimiento de la necedad no asienta ningún discreto edificio" (*Don Quijote*, Part II, cap. 43).

19. *El criticón*, ed. M. Romera-Navarro (Philadelphia, 1938–40), vol. III, p. 202.

20. Originally this proverb was probably no jibe at sanctity or saints. Correas quotes it without comment, but Howell says of it "Palabras son del Labrador, y se entienden de los Disantos, y las fiestas de las quales ay muchas en el año" ("Words spoken by the peasant, and they refer to Holy days and feasts, of which there are many in the year." *Op. cit.*, section entitled *Refranes o Proverbios en Romance*, p. 18). There is a modern form of the proverb that, by the addition of the definite article, removes the irreverence: *Rogar a Dios por los santos, mas no por tantos* ("Pray to God through the saints, but not through so many); the explanation given of this is that it is good to ask favours for oneself but not to excess (*Refranero Español*, ed. José Bergúa, (Madrid, *Ediciones Ibéricas*, n.d.), 5th ed., pp. 466–467).

21. I remember seeing this proverb in a modern list with the misprint *lobos* for *bobos*, thus making *It is to wolves that the Mother of God appears*; the comment "although one cannot see how they deserve it" thus acquired added solemnity.

22. "A los inocentes se aparece nuestra Señora. (Entiéndese por los buenos y santos, aunque vulgarmente lo aplican a hombres de poco saber . . . y se debe reprobar y no usar en tal manera" (*ed. cit.*, p. 7a). The twelfth proverb listed after this is a variant: *A los párvulos se aparecen los santos* ("It is to little children that saints appear"). The comment here is: "Párvulos se toma aquí por las personas inocentes en santidad y niños en la inocencia, y por eso Dios los favorece. Decir a los bobos es necedad de vulgo y reprobada."

23. An earlier form of the proverb is *Buen recado tiene mi padre el día que no hurta*) "My father is well provided on the day he doesn't steal"). The "corruption" of *buen recado* into *buena cara* is a happy one.

24. Collins (*op. cit.*, p. 205) says of this proverb: "It is addressed to a person who is lavish of his money; to signify, that he may outlive his wealth."

25. As Mr. Crow has pointed out to me, this is in the *Adagia* of Erasmus: *Satius est otiosum esse quam nihil agere.* The English equivalent is *Better be idle than ill occupied.* Neither the Latin nor the English has the idea of *working* badly, which gives

the special humour to the contrast in the Spanish form.

26. Cejador (*op. cit.*, p. 85) quotes an abbreviated version that loses the fatalistic tone by suppressing the first clause: *En muriéndome yo todo se acaba.* This he instances as a noteworthy example of irony as he defines it. The longer version is wittier, more impressive and older, going back as far as Correas.

Fatalistic Traits in Finnish Proverbs

*Matti Kuusi**

The previous paper ended by suggesting that fatalism might be part of Spanish worldview as indicated by a number of Spanish proverbs reflecting this perspective. In the present essay, folklorist Matti Kuusi, one of the twentieth century's leading proverb scholars, discusses the same topic using Finnish data.

Finland has long been one of the most active countries with respect to encouraging folklore research and its collecting efforts go back at least to the founding of the Finnish Literature Society in 1831. The truly extensive amount of proverb material amassed, more than two million texts, makes the Finnish corpus almost unique in the world. Unfortunately, very few folklorists can read Finnish and so the work of Professor Kuusi is of special interest to proverb specialists.

In this paper, presented as part of an entire symposium devoted to the subject of fatalism, Kuusi tries to show that the popularity of proverbs may change over time. In short, the idea is not just that proverbs may reflect a culturally specific worldview, but that as there are historical shifts in worldview so there will be corresponding changes in proverb repertoires and usage. If this is so, then one may speculate that statistical samplings of favorite proverbs in a given era may possibly serve as reliable indices of significant differences in fundamental philosophies of life from one generation to another.

* Reprinted from Helmer Ringgren, ed., *Fatalistic Beliefs in Religion, Folklore and Literature* (Stockholm, 1967), pp. 89–96. Reprinted by permission of the author, of the Donner-Institutet, and of Almqvist & Wiksell Förlag.

For more details about the Finnish Literature Society, see Jouko Hautala, "The Folklore Archives of the Finnish Literature Society," in Jouko Hautala, Eino Nivanka, and Toivo Vuorela, Activities of the Finnish Literature Society, 1831–1956 *(Helsinki, 1957), pp. 20–53. See also Jouko Hautala,* Finnish Folklore Research 1828–1918 *(Helsinki, 1969). For more of Professor Kuusi's research on proverbs, see his* Parömiologische Betrachtungen *(Helsinki, 1957) and* Towards an International Type-System of Proverbs *(Helsinki, 1972).*

1. In his main work Oskar Loorits characterizes Fenno-Ugrian *Weltanschauung* in the following way: "Sie hat durch die Seelenwanderung ohne eine präzisierte Reinkarnation, durch den Schamanismus ohne ein berufsmässiges Priestertum, durch den Manismus ohne eine Vergöttlichung der Ahnen und durch den Fatalismus ohne eine Vorherbestimmung von höherer Seite (d.h. durch den Determinismus ohne irgendeine Prädestination) ihre Originalfärbung in der Jahrtausende währenden Waldkultur herauskristallisiert."[1]

The verb *luoda*, which in modern Finnish has the basic meaning 'to create' with a strong Christian colouring, was obviously used earlier to express fatalistic ideas. Its primary meaning appears, for instance, in a laconic proverb from Perniö (in south-western Finland): *Tam lua*, literally "The oak creates," which is given the following explanation: "It is the weather in January [*tammikuu*, month of oak] that in some way predetermines what the spring and the summer will be like."

Special attention should be given to the use of the perfect passive participle *luotu* (modern Finnish: 'created') which in Schroderus' *Lexicon Latino-Scondicum* (1637) is interpreted as: "Fatum, ödhe (i.e. destiny, fate), Gottes Schickung."

I quote some typical examples of proverbs in which the reference is marital predestination.

Jokaatten täytty luatus otta, Everyone has to take his *luotu.*

Ei luotu poika portist palaa, mut luomaton menee viel sänkystäkin, The boy who is *luotu* (for a girl) does not return from the gate, but the one who is not *luotu* for her returns even from the bed.

Luotu löytyy loukosta, aijottu tulee vaikka pystöaijan takaa, or *vaik yli yhdeksä virra*, You find (that which is) *luotu* (even) in the nook, the premeditated even comes through the fence (or, across nine rivers).

Luatu luakses vettä, Luotu draws (attracts) to itself.

Mihes luadustas mene, How could you escape your *luotu?*

Luotuunsa, suotuunsa, ei kauan katseltuunsa eikä mielen tehtyynsä, You belong to the one who is *luotu* for you, granted to you, not to the one whom you have long been looking for and desiring.

Luoja sen luodun tuo, vaan toinen sen toivotun vie, God brings the *luotu*, another (man or woman) carries away what you wish for.

The last proverb, with a Christian Creator, *Luoja*, is an exception to the general usage of the passive without an agent. In Lappish the word *luondo* has a corresponding range of meanings, e.g. *Kalle mon adtjob tab neitab jus le luondo*, "I shall certainly get that girl, if she is allotted to me."[2]

Proverbs like the above have obviously been quoted in support of the old patriarchal marriage system. "Rarely does it happen that a girl or a young man oppose their parents' will, and that she elopes with a man or allows herself to be abducted. The girl subordinates herself and prepares herself in advance to say: *Ku kelle on luotu mänemöä*, "one is *luotu* to marry someone," or: *koha se nii ol sallittu,* "if it is ordained by Fate," or: *koha se on suotuhie, luotuhie eikä mieltiet-tohie,* "if you only end up with one who is granted, *luotu* (for me), and not with my beloved."[3]

The paratactic rhyme figure *suotu—luotu* occurs also in ancient poems of wooing as a cliché employed by the girl to refuse unwanted suitors. Larin Paraske, for example, who knew 32,000 verses in Kalevala metre, sang in her variant of "Suitor from the Sea" the following refusal formula:

Ei oo suotu eikä luotu,
eik o eukko toivotantu
saunan maass ei maatessaase
olkiloill ei ollessaase
pehuloill levätessääse.[4]

"It has not been granted, nor *luotu* (that I marry you), nor has my mother wished (me for you) when she lay (in childbed) in the sauna on straw and chaff."

In some cases the difference between *suotu*, 'granted' and *luotu* is emphasized. If the wife is older than her husband it may be said: *On suatu mutte o luatu*, "it has been granted but not *luotu*." Likewise:

Vaikk moni ols sul suottu, muttei ne kaik ol su vartte luottu, "Though many a one may have been granted to you, they are not all *luotu* for you."

The reference to the wish of the mother in childbed should probably be taken as poetic license and hardly as an attempt to explain man's inborn destiny. Indeed, in ancient folk lyrics man's destiny is often associated with his time of birth.

Passivum fatale occurs in some ten Finnish proverbs which use a formula with *luotu*. Here are some examples:

Luotu on köyhä kulkemahan, vaivainen vaeltamahan, The poor man is *luotu* to walk around, the miserable one to wander.

Mies on luotu miekka vyölle, nainen värttinä kätehen, A man has been *luotu* to carry a sword in his belt, a woman to have a distaff in her hand.

Lintu on luotu lentämähän, huolellinen laulamahan, The bird is *luotu* to fly, the sorrowful to sing.

Thus certain behaviour is characterized as a natural necessity that cannot be evaded. There are also *luodut päivät*, a predestined number of days (of life): *Näkeminen luodut päivät, jos nälän nähtäköön; tekeminen luodut lapset, jos tiellä tehtäköön*, "You have to see your *luotu* days, even if it be in hunger, you have to bear your *luotu* children, even if it be on the road." The same fatalistic formula, based on the Finnish fourth infinitive, is found e.g. in the proverb: *Pitäminen päätynyttä, jystäminen jäätynyttä, saatua syliäminen,* "You have to keep that which has reached you, you have to gnaw that which has frozen, you have to embrace the one you have received."

Luotu, fatum, is not only an expression of erotic fatalism. "He that's born to be hang'd shall never be drowned" is in Finnish: *Joka hirtettäväks on luatu, ei se vetteen kuale*. When a man ventures on to unsafe ice, he says: *Ei hullummin käy kun luotu on*, "It will not go worse than what is *luotu* (for me)." The opposite of *luotu* is *luomaton*, 'uncreated,' 'not predestined.' *Ei luomaton surma tapa*, "A mortal danger that is *luomaton* does not kill," for "every man dies such a death as has been decreed for him on the *luoma*-day." The time and manner of death are predestined and cannot be altered.

2. Learned abstractions like fatalism, or destiny can only with difficulty be applied to the metaphorical thoughts of the Finnish proverbs. The word *kohtalo*, which corresponds to 'destiny' in the

modern written language, is rare in ancient folklore and has primitive shades of meaning. In a dirge in Kanteletar (II 305) the singer says: When I die in the swampy woods the ravens get *kohtaloa* and the crows warm blood from my corpse. *Kohtalo* has here retained its old meaning of "piece of meat," "the allotted share of the common booty."[5]

The only proverb that mentions *kohtalo* runs: *Osallaan mies elää, koira toisen kohtalolla*, "A man lives off his [own] share, a dog lives off another's *kohtalo*." Here the synonyms *osa* and *kohtalo* have a double sense: in the case of the dog the reference is to the piece of meat, but man's *kohtalo* is 'portion, lot, portio, sors' as Kristfrid Ganander translates the word *kohtalo* in his dictionary as early as the 1780's. The idea of this proverb is central in Finnish proverbial ideology: one should be content with one's lot and not covet the lot of others. This proverb occurs for the first time in Lönnrot (1842), but its twenty variant forms come from all parts of the country and the Kalevala metre proves that it is of considerable antiquity.

The concepts *osa*, 'lot, share,' *onni, lykky,* 'fortune, luck,' appear in Finnish proverbs sharing similar features with the old poems. In folk songs too there are references to a concrete, personified *osa* or *onni* which accompanies man, can be divided, bought, exchanged, thrown away, which sleeps or is wakeful, and receives such parallel names as *haltija* (ruler, owner), *synty* (genius) and *jumala* (god). I quote some relevant proverbs.

Onni miehen tyyrmanni, Fortune is man's pilot, or *Onni se miestä tyyrää*, It is fortune that steers man.

Osa orjana pitävi, lykky toisen lyötävänä, One's lot makes him a slave, fortune causes him to be beaten by another, or *Onni orjana pitävi, onni orjan käskijänä*, It is fortune that makes one a slave, and the other the slave's master.

Osastaan ja onnestaan ihminen ei pääse yli, ei ympäri, A man can neither skip over nor dodge around his lot and fortune.

Ei saa onnea ostamalla eikä lykkyä vaihtamalla, One does not get [good] fortune through purchase or exchange.

Ei ole osa ostettava eikä ikä jatkettava, One's lot cannot be bought, nor one's time extended.

Ei oo onnee, ei oo ossoo—kuka minunnii onnellain elänee, I have neither luck nor portion—who could it be that lives off my luck?

Mies makaa, onni valvoo, Man sleeps, fortune is awake.

Onnessa se on ihmisen elämä, It is on luck that human life depends.

Ei sua osua etsie, gu ei osa itsie etsinne, You should not seek your fortune if it does not itself seek you.

Uno Harva, V.J. Mansikka, Oskar Loorits, Martti Haavio, and Ivar Paulson have analyzed the concept of *osa* and *onni*, though without considering the proverbial tradition. They have produced Scandinavian and classical as well as Fenno-Ugrian and East Slavonic parallels. What I find especially interesting in this context is the fact that proverbs concerning lot and luck in the earlier material are common all over Finland, while in the 20th century they are found predominantly in the eastern parts of the country, to a great extent only in Karelia. Even in the East new chords are now struck, e.g. *Ei onni hyväinenkään syötä miestä syrjälleen, istuvalleen ei elätä*, "Not even good luck feeds a man who only lies and sits." This proverb was found in four parishes on the Karelian Isthmus and can be regarded as a protest against "Man sleeps, luck is awake."

We may choose as a typical example *Vaivainen varahin nousi, kova onni kohta kanssa*, "The poor man got up early in the morning, hard luck immediately after." In the earliest material there are 11 variants equally distributed in eastern and western Finland. The most recent western variant is from 1885 and the most recent one from Eastern Finland is from 1936. We are confronted with a dying tradition: destruction begins in the west and spreads gradually to the east. Conditions are the same as in old Finnish poems, marriage rites etc.: the eastern periphery keeps a vanishing tradition the longest.

3. In his book *Die altgermanische Dichtung* Andreas Heusler compared Old Nordic proverbs with more recent ones. He characterized the difference in the following way: "Der Blick auf die Welt (scil. in the old proverbs) ist männlich und kühl, wehrhaft und misstrauisch. Humor ist selten und nicht von der gutmütigen Art. Aus einem sehr grossen Bruchteil dieser Sätze vernehmen wir den herrenhaften, fatalistisch beschatteten Kriegersinn, der uns aus der Heldendichtung, auch aus den Bauern- und Fürstenfehden der Sagas bekannt ist. Die jüngere, uns geläufige Gnomenweisheit ruht mehr im friedlichen Kleinleben, sie hat oft einen gedrückten, entsagenden, oft einen gemütlich-schalkhaften Ton."[6]

Heusler's view of the basic difference between old and new proverbs came to my mind eleven years ago when I made a little experiment with old and recent favourite Finnish proverbs. The material was the twenty proverbs that recur most frequently among the 11,000 variations of proverbs published or recorded before the fire of Turku in September 1827, and twenty others which recur most often in a similarly sized collection of proverbs from the 1930's. Among the differences that emerged from the 20 old and the 20 new favourite proverbs was a noticeable decrease of fatalistic ideas.

The old group included the following proverbs: *Tulee mies merentakainen, ei tule turpehen alainen*, The man who is beyond the sea returns, but not the one who lies under the turf. *Vuosi vanhan vanhentavi, kaksi lapsen kasvattavi,* A year makes the old man aged, two years make the child grow up. *Jumalall on onnen ohjat, Luojalla lykyn avaimet, ei katehen kainalossa, vihansuovan sormenpäissä*, God has the bridles of fortune in his hand, the Creator has the keys of luck, they are not in the arm-pit of the envious, nor on the enemy's fingertips. *Tikka kirjava metsässä, ihmisen ikä kirjavampi*, The woodpecker of the forest is motley, more motley is human life.

In the most common proverbs of the 1930's there are no counterparts to the sentences and maxims about life and death and the nature of human existence quoted above. The proverb that comes closest to the first group runs: "The sniveller becomes a man, but not the one who laughs unnecessarily." The long fatalistic perspective is lacking here, and this is still more obvious in the other recent favourite proverbs.

There are still no accepted methods of measuring and demonstrating trends of development from one generation of proverb users to another. But in my opinion investigations of frequency can give new information concerning the changes that are taking place in the minds and the attitudes of people. In Helsinki we have approximately two million Finnish proverbs, 1,425,000 in the Sanakirjasäätiö in the old university building and 500,000 in the Folklore Archives. The latter have been copied and arranged according to two title-words in a big card-index which is now almost ready. The large collection of the Sanakirjasäätiö is arranged according to parishes: it is easy to find all proverbs that have been recorded in e.g. Nurmijärvi, but the variant forms of certain proverbs are very difficult to find. Nevertheless, through sufficiently numerous and comprehensive sample tests it has been possible to ascertain that humorous sayings ridiculing blind, deaf, crippled or insane people are proportionally decreasing, or that the main stress of folk humour is moving from local to social and professional conditions.

Fatalism, the belief in fate, unfortunately does not belong to the phenomena that are easily defined or statistically measured. No doubt there are fatalistic and anti-fatalistic proverbs. The common European proverb: "Everyone is the architect, or smith, of his own fortune" is known all over the Finnish area: *Jokainen on oman onnensa seppä*. But in four parishes the anti-fatalistic proverb has been turned into its opposite: in Nilsiä, Sumiainen, Jämsä and Lieto it is said: *Kukaan ei ole oman onnensa seppä*, "Nobody is the smith of his own fortune." How could statistics be made in such cases? A hundred votes against four? As a matter of fact, it is very interesting that the proverb: "Everyone is the smith of his own fortune" does not occur in Finnish tradition until the 1880's; till then this ancient proverbial idea had obviously been repudiated. In the 1880's the threshold had become lower, but opposition showed itself here and there through the antithesis "Nobody is the smith of his own fortune." If we had thousands of variants of "the smith of fortune" from various decades and provinces, we might try to measure statistically the strength and the weakening of the opposition in time and space. But we do not have this. We can only collect more individual cases, without preconceived ideas, and see whether they fit into the pattern or not.

Probably there have always been both activists and fatalists in Finland—and no pure activists or fatalists. Even in the oldest collection of Finnish proverbs, from 1702, activistic opposition asserts itself: *Niin luotu kuin tehdään,* "Such is fated as is done." In the 18th century H.G. Porthan records two sharply anti-religious proverbs: *Teko pellon jumala*, "Work is the god of the field," *Aura on arpoja parahin*, "The plough is the best diviner."

In the more recent collections of proverbs it is easily seen that the fatalistic tradition is diminishing and man's own will and enterprise are more and more unanimously emphasized as the most important causes of success. A sense of uncertainty, danger and powerlessness is—or was—close to disappearance. In the textbooks of the primary schools it is God who holds the bridles of fortune, but in the compositions for the matriculation most students believe that man is the architect of his own fortune. The study of proverbs can primarily record the changes that have taken place in people's minds many years ago, but hardly the processes that are going on at present. The question of whether fatalism is undergoing a revival in the big cities of the atomic age has to be answered by other means.

Notes

1. O. Loorits, *Grundzüge des estnischen Volksglaubens*, Uppsala 1949–57, III p. 249. It (the world view) found its true form during the forest culture which lasted several thousand years by means of the transmigration of souls without a precise reincarnation, shamanism without a professional priesthood, manism without deification of the ancestors and fatalism without a predestination from a higher source (i.e. determinism without any predestination).
2. E. Lindahl-J. Öhrling, *Lexicon Lapponicum* (1780) p. 222.
3. Iris Kähäri, in: *Räisälän historia*, 2nd ed. Turku 1952, p. 573.
4. *Suomen kansan vanhat runot* V_3 107.
5. Cf. V. Ruoppila, " 'Kohtalo' ja 'osa'," *Virittäjä* 37/1933 pp. 361 ff.
6. A. Heusler, *Die altgermanische Dichtung*, Darmstadt 1957, p. 68. The view of the world (scil. in the old proverbs) is masculine and cool, valiant and untrusting. Humor is seldom to be found and not of a good-natured type. From a very large portion of these sentences we perceive the domineering fatalistically tinged warrior spirit which is known to us from the heroic epics and also from the peasant and princely feuds of the sagas. The newer gnomic wisdom as we know it is based more on the peaceful everyday life; it often has a tone of suppression, renunciation and often a good-natured roguishness.

Irish Proverbs and Irish National Character

*F.N. Robinson**

Perhaps one of the most treacherous but yet fascinating areas of folklore scholarship concerns the potential of folklore for studies of national character. Do the proverbs of a people contain in distilled form the essence of their philosophy of life and worldview? Or is this very question merely a naive piece of wishful thinking on the part of certain scholars? Comparative folklorists are invariably wary of assuming that a proverb (normally found in more than one culture) necessarily expresses national character. Anthropologists, in contrast, are often more likely to believe that the proverbs collected from 'their' people or village do in fact reflect local ideology. Probably the truth lies somewhere in between. In the following essay, F.N. Robinson probes the controversy with reference to Irish materials. For further sources for the whole national character scholarship, see J.C.H. Duijker and N.H. Fridja, National Character and National Stereotypes *(Amsterdam, 1960).*

This paper, like some more important contributions to knowledge, had its origin in a symposium. A faculty club, devoted to the study of the history of religions, was listening to a learned discourse on the later Greek civilization in Alexandria and some of the island cities.

* Reprinted from *Modern Philology*, 43 (1945), 1–10. Reprinted by permission of The University of Chicago Press.

The lecturer remarked that if we only possessed the proverbs current among the people, we should be better able to understand their national character. He was interrupted by one of his hearers, who protested that proverbs reflect general human wisdom rather than the special traits of a particular people. There ensued a discussion, in which two or three classical scholars, an Indic philologist, an Arabist, and a medievalist exchanged opinions without coming to any positive conclusion. But all agreed that it would be well to have the theory of national character tried out in particular areas more thoroughly than it has been hitherto; and the present writer, who had been guilty of the original interruption, undertook, by way of penalty, to report on the situation in Irish. My examination of the subject has been most tentative, and the account of it here, because of limitations of time and space, is very incomplete. I hope to publish some of my material more fully at another time. But the present brief paper may at least serve some purpose in defining the problem.

The question of national character in proverbs is, of course, by no means new to paroemiologists. My original impulse in denying such a character came, not so much from my own observations—for I have not been in any systematic way an investigator of proverbial literature—as from the fact that I knew that two of my personal friends who are experts in the field, Professors Archer Taylor and B.J. Whiting, had questioned the theory, the latter in conversation and the former in his admirable book on *The Proverb*.[1] Any consultation of the literature on the subject reveals at once a great difference of opinion upon the question at issue. A priori, there seems to be no reason why races or nations should not express their character in their popular sayings, just as individuals show their personal traits by the proverbs they have constantly on their lips. It is commonly assumed that they do, I should say, by those who have not made a special study of the matter. Lord Bacon, in one of the most famous utterances on the subject, declared that "the genius, wit, and spirit of a nation are discovered in its proverbs," and Erasmus compared proverbs to wines which cannot be transported. And in this opinion they have had plenty of followers. Taylor[2] lists a whole series of studies of national traits in the proverbs of different countries, though he characterizes their results as "insignificant." In the Celtic field (which Taylor does not undertake to cover) two of the most industrious collectors have tried to show national characteristics in both Irish and Scottish Gaelic sayings.[3] In view of the existing differences of opinion, an examination of the Irish material seems worth while.

I have already said that my study of the problem has been thus far of a very tentative character. To get securely valid conclusions we need, in the first place, more nearly complete collections of the Irish gnomic material, and, what is more important, we ought to know more about the age and originality of particular sayings. Only a limited number have been dated, and nobody has attempted to make a chronological collection or to distinguish proverbs which were clearly borrowed from those which were probably composed in Ireland. The currency or vogue of individual sayings is another important consideration in determining their bearing on national character. They should be weighed as well as counted. It means little to find recorded a proverb, say, in praise of thrift, if the people never use it. I shall mention these considerations in dealing with particular proverbs, but they have never been adequately applied to the general body of material.

Of that material there is at least no reason to complain of a lack of quantity. For the modern Irish period I know of over fifty printed collections, longer or shorter, besides several in manuscript. The collectors list over eight thousand Irish proverbs (of course, with a vast number of duplicates or close variants), and more than four thousand have been published in the closely related Scottish Gaelic. For the purposes of this present study I have used O'Muirgheasa's proverbs of Ulster (over 1,900 in number), O'Siochfhradha's proverbs of Munster (about 2,150), a general collection by O'Rahilly (about 400), and several hundred that I have noted down from my own reading of Irish literature of all periods.[4]

I should add that in any thorough analysis of this material one should take into account several very early Irish compilations of proverbial morality. I have in mind particularly the *Testament of Morann*, a document probably of the eighth century, though ascribed to a legendary figure of the first, and the *Instructions of Cormac,* the *Old sayings of Fithal,* and the *Sayings of Flann Fína,* all three composed probably between 800 and 900, though they are attributed, respectively, to King Cormac of the third century; his counselor, Fithal; and King Aldfrith, the seventh-century king of Northumbria. The sayings in these old compilations are not strictly popular proverbs; at least, there is no evidence that most of them ever had general circulation. The treatises are rather literary works comparable to the Wisdom books of the Old Testament. But, like the Proverbs of Solomon, they contain moral wisdom in aphoristic form, and some of the sayings certainly did circulate and established patterns of proverbial formulas.[5]

These early collections obviously throw light on the antiquity of many individual sayings. Another means of getting at this information is by collecting proverbs from early literary texts. But this nearly all remains to be done. Mr. O'Rahilly gives early citations for a considerable number of the proverbs in his book, and a systematic collection from the sagas of the Ulster cycle was made by Miss Alice Bell (now Mrs. Robertson) in an unpublished doctoral dissertation at Radcliffe College.

After this account of the nature of the material, it will be apparent why I do not claim to have arrived at any final solution of the problem. That must await a more thorough classification of the proverbs than has yet been made. But in my tentative discussion I have approached the question in two ways.

1. First, I have taken certain traits generally supposed to be characteristic of the Irish and have examined the proverbs to see if they reflect these qualities. But I realized from the outset that in this method there is danger that one will argue in a vicious circle—first, selecting proverbs in the light of a preconceived idea of the Irish and then using the proverbs to confirm the preconception. So I decided to check myself by a second procedure.

2. I have selected a number of recent works of a representative popular character and have made a strictly objective and, to the best of my ability, complete collection of the proverbs they contain. In this way I have assembled, without exercising personal choice, several hundred sayings which I know to be current and have examined them to see what traits they reveal. Limitations of space will prevent my publishing these contemporary proverbs in this article, but I hope to print them at another time. Meanwhile, I will give here the results of the first part of my inquiry.

Of the thousands of sayings in the collections I have mentioned, it is obvious that a great many are irrelevant to our particular problem. Proverbs on weather and the seasons, medical maxims, and many sayings about trades and mechanical crafts have little bearing on individual or national character. The same is true of much animal lore, except where the animals, as in Aesopic fables, represent human qualities. Proverbs of foreign origin or of universal currency should also be used cautiously as evidence. A borrowed proverb, to be sure, may be as indicative as a native one of the character of the man who uses it. But in appraising the proverbial stock of a people, the old sayings, rooted in the national tradition, seem more significant.

Very many Irish sayings are so close in words and phrasing to English counterparts that one strongly suspects the Irish to be borrowed. Out of the hundreds that could be cited, I have room for only a few illustrations:

> *Is feárr go mall ná go bráth* (Better late than never).
>
> *An té a chomhnas a' t-slat millean sé a' mac* (He that spares the rod, spoils the child).
>
> *Cuidigheann Día leis an té a chuidigheas leis féin* (God helps him who helps himself). The idea, of course is universal: *Fortes Fortuna adjurat.*
>
> *Os amharc, os cuimhne* (Out of sight, out of mind).
>
> *Is tighe fuil ná uisge* (Blood is thicker than water).
>
> *Níor bhris focal maith fiacaíl ríamh* ('Never did a good word break a tooth'). Not so clearly from "Soft words break no bones." Irish has a word-play not in English. Moreover, both have a source in Prov. 25:15 or Eccles. 28:21.
>
> *Sguabann sguab úr go glan acht tá fios ag an t-seansguab ar na coirnéalaibh* (A new broom sweeps clean—with an addition, 'but the old broom knows the corners,' which I thought might be characteristically Irish until my friend, Dr. Sven Liljeblad, told me it is current in Swedish).

Although there is, in general, a greater probability that the modern Irish borrowed proverbs from the English than that the English borrowed from the Irish, close resemblance does not always prove that the borrowing was in that direction. The Irish *Feárr sean-fhiacha ná sean-fhala* has a counterpart in northern English (Scots), "Better auld debts than auld sairs." But the Irish proverb, in the older form *Ferr senfhiacha senfhala*, is recorded in the collections attributed[6] to Fithal and to Flann Fína. The Scots version comes doubtless from the Scottish Gaelic equivalent of the Irish. Again, the modern Irish proverb *Is feárr leath-bhairgein ná bheith gan arán* is very close to "A half loaf is better than no bread," from which it may well have been borrowed. But the idea is the same as that of the Old Irish *Ferr leth lánetech* ('Better a half than a full refusal'), and *Ferr beg éra* ('A little is better than a refusal'), both ascribed also to Flann Fína.[7] These examples show the desirability of a general chronological study of the Irish sayings.

Of the proverbs of universal, or at least of widespread, international currency, I also have space for very few examples. They form a large part of the material. In fact, there are so few Irish sayings that one cannot easily match in English or other languages, without having any special knowledge of this kind of lore, that I sometimes have wondered if any proverb can be regarded as the exclusive or original property of any people. But the same underlying idea is often presented by different figures or comparisons in different localities, and the varieties are sometimes of interest. The following are a few specimens of these sayings of wide distribution:

> *Sgéitheann fion firinne* (Wine discloses truth; *In vino veritas*).
>
> *Is olc a'breathamh ar dathaibh dall (Caecus de coloribus non indicat).*
>
> *Bi an t-súil do shior mar am-bíonn an grádh (Ubi amor, ibi oculus).* An early equivalent, *Is airdhe na sercci sirshilliuth* ('Long gazing is a sign of love') occurs in the *Tochmarc Etaine.*
>
> *Labhraidh duine, innisidh Dia* ('Man speaks, but God tells the story'). A variant of *Homo proponit, Deus disponit*, which has its remote Islamic counterpart, "The servant plans, but Allah brings to pass," and perhaps an ultimate origin in Prov. 16:9.
>
> *Mol an lá um trathnóna* ('Praise the day in the evening'). A special form of "Don't count your chickens before they are hatched," "Don't crow until you are out of the woods," etc. But the Irish phraseology has close parallels: "Schöne Tage soll man abends loben, schöne Frauen morgens," and in the *Hávamál*, "At kveldi skal dag leyfa," with succeeding lines which look like embellishments of the original proverb.[8]
>
> *Aithnightear cara i geruatan* ('A friend is known in need'), which I include because it is one of the earliest recorded Irish proverbs. It occurs in the form *Is and asgniintar in charait in tan mbither "in periculis"* in the ninth-century Milan glosses, 108*b*4.[9]

It would be easy to multiply examples like these of Irish proverbs with counterparts in other tongues. But I must devote the rest of my space to the consideration of national characteristics. What, then, are the features to look for? Three things, I think, may be expected to distinguish a body of national proverbs: (I) local color or setting; (II) local stylistic devices, formulas, and the like; and (III) national customs, traits, virtues, or vices which the proverbs may reflect.

I. Local Color

Local color we unquestionably find in the Irish proverbs. It appears most plainly in the ascription of the sayings themselves to national figures, historic or legendary. I have spoken of Cormac, Fithal, and Flann Fína. An obscure Crimthann Nia Nair also appears as authority for a proverb in an early saga. Goban Saor, the mythical artificer, is credited with many sayings, or they are introduced into anecdotes about him. Other figures are used in proverbial comparisons: *coem cách co h-Etain* ('fair is every one until [compared with] Etain'); *comh sean leis a'Chailleach Bearra* ('as old as the Old Woman of Beare'). A striking example of this kind of personal allusion appears in the Irish saying which corresponds to the English counsel that a man should have "more than one string to his bow": *Ní ar aonchois tháinig Pátraic go h-Eireann* ('Patrick did not come to Ireland on one leg').[10]

Local color may also appear in references to local customs:

> *Fál ar an ngort tar éis no foghla* ('Fencing the field after the cattle-raid'). Cf. "shutting the barn door after the horse is stolen," or "covering the well after the child is drowned." Cattle-raids were, of course, a familiar feature of Irish life.
>
> *Ní bheag nod don eolach* ('A manuscript contraction, a *compendium scribendi*, is enough for a scholar'). Cf. *Verbum sapienti*, 'A word to the wise.' The reference to the manuscript stroke may occur in the proverb outside of Ireland, but it is certainly appropriate to the scribes of the heavily abbreviated Irish writings.
>
> *Is maith an tiomanaidhe an fear bhíos ar an gcladh* ('The man on the ditch is a good hurler'—"The looker-on sees more than the gamester").

Dána gach fear go tulaig ('Bold is every man until [he reaches] the hill,' i.e., until he enters the assembly).

Ceithre neithe nach tugtha d'Eireannchaibh ionntaoibh leo . i . adharc bó, crúb chapaill, dranna madra agus gáire Sassanaigh ('Four things that Irishmen never trusted: the horn of a cow, the hoof of a horse, the growl of a dog, and the smile of an Englishman'). Oddly enough, allusions to the English, to landlords, and to agents do not seem to be common in current Irish sayings.[11]

II. Stylistic Formulas

Proverbs tend, as everybody knows, to follow certain familiar patterns, "Better *x* than *y*," for example, "Better late than never," "Better a half-loaf than no bread." Most of these forms are of wide diffusion, and it would be hard to prove their origin in any particular region. But there are local fashions in these matters. It has been pointed out that late Greek proverbs tend to use a narrative form where western Europe prefers a maxim. Compare "A man gave another an ass, and he looked at its teeth" with "Don't look a gift-horse in the mouth."[12] Taylor holds that the *Man soll* formula is characteristically Germanic, and it is certainly well established in Anglo-Saxon, Scandinavian, and German. But the Irish proverbs in *Dligid* offer a pretty close parallel. Irish has favorite patterns of its own, particularly noticeable in the old compilations of Morann, Flann Fína, and Fithal, where allowance must, of course, be made for artistic composition. Of the "Better *x* than *y*" type, there are nearly a hundred in Flann Fína. A considerable number have the form referred *to just above, beginning with Dligid* ('deserves,' 'ought to have'): *Dligid aide urraim* ('A teacher deserves respect'); *Dligid maith mórad* ('Good deserves to be magnified'). There is a similar form beginning with *Adcota* ('obtains,' 'produces'): *Adcota maith a molad* ('Good obtains its praise'); and of this type Flann Fína has over sixty examples. The same collection has a score or more in the pattern *Tosach eolais imchomarc* ('The beginning of learning is inquiry'), a form which may not have been uninfluenced by the biblical "The fear of the Lord is the beginning of wisdom." It still occurs in modern proverbs, as in *Tosach slainte codla* ('Sleep is the beginning of health') in O'Siochfhradha's Munster collection. A favorite Irish form, and perhaps the most peculiarly characteristic one, is represented by two proverbs I have already quoted: *Coém cách co h-Etain* ('Fair is everyone until [compared to] Etain'), and *Dána gách go tulaigh* ('Bold is everyone until [he reaches] the hill'). This form has persisted from the earliest sagas down to the present day. A modern example is *Ughdar gach neach go labhrann* ('Everyone is an authority until he speaks').

It would be interesting to have a careful classification of the fomulas in the whole body of the modern Gaelic proverbs, to determine to what extent the old patterns have persisted and perhaps replaced different forms in foreign proverbs of similar import.

In connection with the formal types which give local flavor to proverbs, mention should also be made of legal maxims, many of which, in Irish as in other languages, have found their way into popular use. They ought to be systematically collected. But I have space here for only two examples: *Is fiach ma gelltar* ('It is a debt if it is promised'), a close equivalent of Chaucer's *Biheste is dette*;[13] and *Is lę gach buin a laegh* ('To every cow its calf'), i.e., to the owner of every manuscript its copy—King Diarmaid mac Cearbhaill's famous announcement of the principle of copyright.[14]

I ought also to explain that I have not attempted to deal here with metrical proverbs, which, of course, exhibit the formal and stylistic traits of Irish. But they present a special problem, as being in considerable measure artistic productions. Their character is well illustrated in the charming little book *Amhráin chúige Chonnacht: an leath-rann* (Dublin, n.d.), by Dr. Douglas Hyde, former president of Eire. Dr. Hyde has published a number of complete quatrains, as repeated or recorded, and in the case of many couplets which may or may not have formed parts of quatrains he has composed lines to fill out the stanzas.[15]

III. National Traits

It might be expected that the most interesting character of a body of national proverbs would be found in its reflection of the popular character. In fact, it was the prevalence of this idea that led in the first place to this investigation. But I may say at once that the evidence afforded by Irish proverbs is very dubious.

Consider, for example, the treatment of women by the proverb-makers. Mr. O'Muirgheasa, compiler of one of the most extensive collections, the *Seanfhocla uladh*, says in the introduction to his first edition that Irish proverbs show extraordinary respect for women and priests, often sneered at in other lands.[16] But on the second page of his book I find the following gallant tribute: *Tri nídh gan riaghail: bean, muc, is muille* ('Three things without rule: a woman, a pig, and a mule'). And the same collection contains: *Is foisge do mhnaoi leithsgéal ná braisgin* ('An excuse is nearer to a woman than her apron'); *Is feárr órlach gasúir no troigh cailín* ('Better is an inch of a boy than a foot of a girl'); *An áit i mbíonn mná bíonn gab* ('Where there are women, there is gabble'); *Uabhar ban is uabhar sagart* ('Pride of women and pride of priests'—two things to be feared); and the triad, a variant of the venerable saying that goes back to Prov. 27:15,

> Sólás an fhir bhreoidhte,
> Toit 'sa toigh,
> Bean ag troid,
> Is droich-phlainneead

('The sick man's solace: smoke in his roof, a quarrelsome woman, and a bad blanket'). It is obvious that Mr. O'Muirgheasa's own collection hardly bears out his claim that the Irish proverb-makers treated women with exceptional respect, and there are plenty of other Irish sayings which reflect the common disparagement of the sex as being gossips, unable to keep secrets, extravagant, stubborn, unaccountable, or not always what they appear to be. But, on the other side, it is fair to point out that there are proverbs in praise of women, though rather less numerous than the opposite sort. Such are: *Is feárr bean ná spré* ('A woman is better than treasure'—perhaps of biblical origin); *Mairg na deineann comhairle deaghmhná* ('Woe to him who does not follow the counsel of a good woman'); and *Is leath beathadh bean mhaith tighe* ('A good housewife is half of life'). The fact is that on this subject, as on many others, the people have contradictory sayings, presenting two sides of the case. It is recognized as characteristic of popular wisdom that it often represents a "middle way."[17]

The cynical strictures of the Irish proverb-makers are not confined to women. Priests, in spite of Mr. O'Muirgheasa's contrary impression, get their fair share of abuse, and human nature in general comes under considerable condemnation. I shall not take the space to illustrate these sayings here. But there are so many comments of this nature on love and marriage that the editor of the Munster proverbs thinks it necessary to explain that they do not represent serious Irish opinion.[18]

Probably no quality of character is more commonly ascribed to the Irishman, whether justly or unjustly, than combativeness, the love of a fight. On this subject his proverbs are pretty evenly divided. On the one side are warlike counsels like these:

> *Gach sluagh nach saigh, saighfidir* ('Every troop that does not attack will be attacked,—"The best parry is a lunge").
>
> *Be theid as no ná théid, ní théid fear na h-eadargala* ('Whoever comes off or doesn't, the peacemaker will not come off').
>
> *Ní frith breithem bus fíriu cathrae* ('There has been found no juster judge than the battlefield'), recorded in the ancient text of Morann.
>
> *Is buaine bladh ná saoghal* ('Fame is more enduring than life'). An exhortation to bravery which occurs in various forms in the older sagas.[19] It is a characteristic sentiment of the heroic age and by no means peculiarly Irish (cf. *Beowulf*, 11, 1386 ff., and *Aeneid* x. 467 ff.).

Over against these we find the praise of peace:

> *Is ferr síth sochocadh* ('Peace is better than successful war'), ascribed to both Fithal and Flann Fína.
>
> *Feárr teithe maith ná droich-sheasamh* ('Better a good flight than a bad stand'), also recorded as Fithal's and Flann Fína's in the archaic form *Ferr teiched tairisium*.[20]
>
> *An té grádhas an dáinsear cailltear ann é* ('He who loves danger shall perish in it')—paralleled by the more laconic form in Morann: *Gonas gentair* ('Who wounds shall be wounded'). Compare also Matt. 26:52.
>
> *Is feárr an t-sláinte ná na táinte* ('Health is better than raids').

Again with relation to spending and saving, there are proverbs on both sides—once more the "middle way." In the case of talkativeness, a quality often attributed to Irishmen, we find little praise of it in the popular sayings. On the contrary there is frequent commendation of silence or of deeds as compared with words.

It is probably generally recognized that a conspicuous characteristic of the Irish people is its devotion to religion, its Catholic Christian piety. As might be expected, this trait finds frequent expression in popular sayings, many of them of biblical origin. They do not appear to be any more numerous than those current in other Christian lands, or in any way different in kind. But it is perhaps not without significance that the saying I have found to be most often recurrent is the familiar expression of faith in divine help in trouble: *Is foisge cabhair Dé ná an dorus* ('The help of God is nearer than the door'). Another proverb of similar import, *Níor dhún Día bearna riamh ná h-oslochadh sé ceann aile* ('God never closed one pass [gap, path], that he did not open another') has an English counterpart: "God never closes a door without opening a window."

If the Irishman's Christian faith is expressed in many current sayings, the same is not true of his supposed absorption in fairy lore. Except for two common references to the pooka—*Níl sprid ńa púca gan fios a chúise aige féin* ('There is no spirit or pooka who doesn't know his own business') and *An rud a sgríobhanñ an phúca, léigheann sé féin é* ('What the pooka writes, he reads it [or *léigheadh,* "let him read"] himself'), and occasional admonitions about the keeping of *geasa* ('taboos,' 'mysterious injunctions'), I have found very little mention of supernatural doings or beliefs.

The one quality, I suppose, which most persons look for in any product of the Irish mind is humor, and I have often been asked about it while engaged on the present study. Of course, the proverbs of all peoples, with their neat epigrammatic turns, their unexpected figures and incongruous comparisons, show a considerable element of humor, or perhaps oftener of wit. In the satirical sayings, too, we must assume that a humorous purpose often tempers the cynicism. These qualities have been sufficiently illustrated for Irish by the proverbs already cited, but I should not say that they are more conspicuous in Irish than in the sayings of other nations. And it is interesting to note that Mr. O'Muirgheasa, the enthusiastic compiler of the Ulster collection, holds the Irish proverbs to be surpassed for humor by the Scottish Gaelic. I have not attempted to follow up this comparison. Such humor as the Irish show, he thinks, is mainly that of exaggeration, a form commonly supposed to be characteristically American.

A deliberate attempt at comic effect appears chiefly in those proverbs of the type which have been labeled as "Wellerisms," because of the constant use of the device by Sam Weller in the *Pickwick Papers.*[21] They have an additional phrase or a tag, which brings in some incongruous situation. "There's nothing so refreshin' as sleep, sir, as the servant-girl said afore she drank the egg-cupful of laudanum," observed Mr. Weller, recommending a good night's rest to Mr. Pickwick. Of course, Wellerisms do not necessarily occur with proverbs, but they are very commonly attached to them.[22] " '*Virtus in medio*,' said the Devil, and sat between two priests (or two harlots)." A considerable number of Irish proverbs have tags of this sort, and in those I have collected from the conversation of Tomas O' Muirthe, reported in *Cainnt an t-sean-shaghail,*[23] I am sometimes unable to judge whether the additions are generally current or are the humorous comment of the speaker. The following are a few examples of Irish Wellerisms:

> *"Glór mór ar bheagan olna," már adubhairt an t-Aidhbheirseoir mar a bhí sé ag bearradh na muice* (' "Much talk about little wool," as the Adversary said when shearing the pig').
>
> *"Is deas an rud a' ghlaine," mar dubhairt an bhean nuair thionntaigh sí a léine in-diaidh seacht m-bliadhna* (' "Cleanliness is good thing," as the woman said when she changed her shirt after seven years').
>
> *"Is luachmar an rud an t-anam," mar adubhairt an tailleiúir, agus é ag rith on nganndal* (' "Life is precious," as the tailor said when he was running away from the gander').

And at least one of the serious proverbs of pious faith has been given a similar turn: *"Bíonn cabhair Dé ar bóthar," mar abudhairt an Goban Saor nuair a theangmhuigh sé ar an sparán* (' "The help of God is on the way," as the Goban Saor said when he chanced on the purse').

To bring the discussion now briefly to a conclusion, this review of the characteristics, real or supposed, of the Irish people has yielded very little evidence that their national proverbs have been affected by their character or temperament. The presentation of the case is, of course, unsatisfactory because it rests upon one man's canvassing of the great body of proverbial literature, and the material itself cannot be laid before the reader. Somebody else might have caught significant features that I have missed. The method itself, too, is open to criticism, as I have already pointed out, because it deals with certain preconceived notions of the Irish character. But I hope that any errors that may have arisen from this procedure will be corrected in the study to be published later, in which a considerable body of current proverbs will be collected and examined and published in full. Meanwhile, so far as the evidence now in hand goes, it seems to support Professor Taylor's opinion that the national element in proverbs is not very significant. Irish sayings, like those he has discussed in other tongues, represent, on the whole, common human experience and universal wisdom generally at a practical level. At the same time, it should be remembered that the Irish people belong to the same cultural tradition—European and Christian—as ourselves, and the proverbs with which I have compared theirs lie, with very few exceptions, within the same area. It is possible that if the comparison were extended to a remoter civilization—say that of the Islamic or eastern Asiatic peoples, with their different presuppositions in ethics and religion—national or regional characteristics might become more apparent.

Notes

1. *The Proverb* (Cambridge, Mass., 1931), p. 164. I wish to acknowledge at once my indebtedness to Professor Taylor. Although he deals very little with Celtic proverbs, I have profited at every turn by his general discussion and have drawn on him occasionally for illustrative material. The opinions of both Taylor and Whiting on national proverbs are reflected in the brief discussion in the report of the Committee on Proverbs of the Modern Language Association (see the *Modern Language Forum*, XXIV [1939], 76).

2. Pp. 164 ff. To Taylor's references may be added *Racial Proverbs* by Dr. S.G. Champion (New York, 1938), in which the subject is discussed in special prefaces by authorities in the various fields.

3. E. O'Muirgheasa and A. Nicolson.

4. A convenient account of the publications about proverbs in Irish, Scottish Gaelic, and Manx will be found in T.F. O'Rahilly, *A Miscellany of Irish Proverbs* (Dublin, 1922). The first part of the book is an edition of 231 proverbs noted by Micheál Og O'Longáin in about the year 1800, to which Mr. O'Rahilly has added nearly 200 sayings, triads, and proverbial phrases collected by himself from various sources. In his bibliography he lists over fifty collections, longer or shorter, of proverbs

from various parts of Ireland. The most extensive compilation listed by him is the *Seanfhocla uladh* (1907), containing 1,637 Ulster proverbs. A second edition, published in 1931, adds some 300 to this total. Besides this I have had access to two other collections, published since 1922: *Seanfhocail na muimhneach*, by "An Seabhac" (i.e., Padraig O'Siochfhradha), published in 1926 and containing 2,152 proverbs; and *Seanaimsireacht*, by D.A. Murchadha (Dublin, 1939), containing a shorter list. There must be an enormous number of proverbs in the manuscript materials assembled by Mr. Delargy at the Folklore Institute in Dublin. But nobody can predict how many new sayings they would add to those in print.

5. *Aùdacht Morainn* is edited by Rudolf Thurneysen in the *Zeitschrift für celtische Philologie,* XI (1916), 56 ff.; the *Tecosca Cormaic,* by Kuno Meyer in the "Todd Lecture Series" of the Royal Irish Academy, Vol. XV (Dublin, 1909); the *Senbriathra Fithail*, by Rudolf Thurneysen in *Abhandlungen der königlichen Gesellschaft der Wissenschaften zu Göttingen,* phil.-hist. Kl., N.S., Vol. XIV (1912), and by R.M. Smith in *Revue celtique*, XLV (1928), 1 ff.; and the *Briathra Flainn Fina*, by Kuno Meyer in the *Anecdota from Irish Manuscripts*, III (Halle, 1909). There is much material common to the collections of Cormac, Fithal, and Flann. The *Triads of Ireland* are edited by Kuno Meyer in the "Todd Lecture Series," of the Royal Irish Academy, Vol. III (Dublin, 1906). There is a good general account of this "instructional" literature by R.M. Smith in *Speculum*, II (1927), 411 ff.

6. See O'Rahilly, p. 1.

7. See ibid., p. 41.

8. These and other parallels, but not the Irish saying, are discussed by Taylor, pp. 178 ff.

9. See O'Rahilly, p. 80, where variant forms are given and the "literary parents" in Ecclus. 12:8, 9 and Ennius are cited.

10. Another Irish equivalent is *Bíodh dá abhrais ar do choigeal agat* ('Have two sticks on your distaff').

11. I have been more struck by slurs on landlords and officials in a very small collection of Russian proverbs called to my attention by my friend Mrs. Norman Hapgood.

12. Cited by Taylor, p. 158, from Krumbacher, *Sitzungsberichte der Münchener Akademie, phil.-hist. Kl.,* II (1893), No. 1, 23.

13. Discussed by O'Rahilly, p. 81, where the Chaucerian parallel is noted. On legal maxims in general see Taylor, pp. 86 ff.

14. See O'Rahilly, p. 94.

15. A considerable number of these metrical proverbs are printed in O'Muirgheasa's *Seanfhocla uladh,* pp. 174–208. Cf. also T.F. O'Rahilly, *Dánfhocáil: Irish Epigrams in Verse* (Dublin, 1921). The *dánfhocail,* or versified sayings, are, as O'Rahilly's subtitle indicates, really of the nature of epigrams, and they often resemble the Priamel, discussed by Taylor at pp. 179 ff.

16. Nicolson makes the same claim with regard to women for Scottish Gaelic.

17. See Taylor's comments, p. 168.

18. An Seabhac. p. 31.

19. See O'Rahilly, pp. 38–39.

20. See ibid., p. 15.

21. For further illustrations of the type, with references to earlier discussions, see Taylor, pp. 200 ff.

22. For an extensive collection of American Wellerisms, mostly of the period from 1840 to 1880, both proverbial and nonproverbial, see B. J. Whiting, *American Speech*, XX (1945), 1 ff.

23. Ed. Arland Ussher (Dublin, 1942).

Tensions in Proverbs: More Light on International Understanding

*Joseph Raymond**

Proverbs may or may not reflect national character, but all over the world, peoples have proverbs purporting to describe the character of their neighboring nations. In short, the folk apparently do believe in national character. Sometimes this proverbial invective can lead to tensions; sometimes it may serve to relax these same tensions through the socially sanctioned release of humor.

Joseph Raymond in the following essay examines proverbs as vehicles for the expression of interpersonal and international tensions. For a recent review of the question with respect to national stereotypes, see Alan Dundes, "Slurs International: Folk Comparisons of Ethnicity and National Character," Southern Folklore Quarterly, *39 (1975), 15–38. Some of the standard collections include Otto von Reinsberg-Düringsfeld,* Internationale Titulaturen. *2 vols. (Leipzig, 1863); Henri Gaidoz and Paul Sébillot,* Blason Populaire de la France *(Paris, 1884), and A.A. Roback,* A Dictionary of International Slurs (Ethnophaulisms) *(Cambridge, 1944).*

Educators in the social sciences and languages, seeking pathways to clearer international understanding, have numerous disciplines at their disposal.[1] One path leads into a fundamental part of the language and culture of a national group: the popular utterance or proverb. This vehicle of expression is often marked by tensions and crises—so often

* Reprinted from *Western Folklore*, 15 (1956), 153–158 by permission of the California Folklore Society.

that the critical mind has cause to inquire: To what extent do these utterances reflect tensions, perhaps otherwise unexpressed and hidden, in the culture itself? Are these repeated phrases not a common-denominator clue to the state of mind of a given group? Let us examine the nature of some proverbially expressed tensions and how they reflect strife or index prevalent inclinations of the group mind.

Proverbs Reflect Tensions

Sharp tension is reflected in the popular Korean proverb, "When whales fight, the shrimp's back is broken." The popularity of this folk saying, vividly analogous to the Korean tragedy, rests upon existing tensions in the people who suffered as helpless shrimps while contenders, proportionately huge as whales, fought. Violent anti-clerical sayings paradoxically abound in the language stream of traditionally devout peoples.[2] Potent antiauthoritarian proverbs reflected tensions between the Russian people and the Czar.[3] The rollickingly malicious undertone of these folk verbalizations constitutes what might be labeled a "paremiological revolt."[4] To avoid openly criticizing a given authority or cultural pattern, folk take recourse to proverbial expressions which voice *personal* tensions in a tone of *generalized* consent. Thus, personal involvement is linked with public opinion.

Proverbs in Tension Reduction

Proverbs are important verbal instruments for minimizing interpersonal friction and tensions.[5] This is partly explained by their generalized nature.[6] During tense United Nations debates, the former Soviet Union delegate, André Vishinsky, supported many arguments with proverbs:

> In these meetings proverbs sometimes are flung back and forth like verbal missiles. . . . Visitors have a field day when Moscow's Vishinsky is in action. He flings more proverbs . . . than any other delegate . . . except perhaps Peru's Belaúnde. Interpreting Vishinsky taxes the best of the United Nations Interpreters.[7]

The tension-reduction role of many proverbs may be understood in terms of their function as social safety valves for marked social restraints. The phenomenon suggests a highly stylized culture in which tradition is important. The "safety-valve" hypothesis is supported further by the fact that proverbs always have abounded in the so-called lower classes. In this group, expressions of anger, rebellion, and nonconformance are found frequently. This is the view of Ruesch, who affirms that conflicts often progress beyond the verbal level.[8] Clearly, proverbs not only express interpersonal conflicts and tensions but also function in resolving them.[9]

Proverbs and Pariahs: Some Inter-Group Relations

Folk sayings may reveal considerable tension between the in-group and social outcasts or pariahs. Derogatory statements frequently are in proverb form. In Germany under Hitler, proverbs were considered important enough to occupy the attention of political leaders. Jente describes a "purified edition" of a book of proverbial sayings which appeared in Germany during the Nazi regime. First published by L. Heinemann in Berlin (1929), it was modified by V. Tornius, a verified Aryan, in Leipzig (1936). "Modification" consisted of deleting current sayings coined by non-Aryans. Instead of these phrases, certain political leaders' utterances were substituted prescriptively, even though they were not current sayings, but simply because "they ought to become such."[10] Beyond these verbalized tensions is overt action, which at times extends to drastic group manifestations.

Roback, in *A Dictionary of International Slurs*, investigates the nature of derogatory statements, many of which are in proverb form.[11] He asserts that people show a proclivity to make disparaging rather than flattering allusions to people other than their own "kind." In defending his concentration on derogatory phrases, he states there simply are none of the flattering type, and that it might as well be asked why medicine fixes attention on disease rather than on health.[12] In English alone, he points out, there are some one thousand slurs against all nationalities, and most of the prejudices derive from the common people and the illiterate. Yet, he says, there has been no incisive attempt to interrelate historical, psychological, and sociological facts into one coherent picture. This points to the need for integrated approaches to attitude studies, as urged by many writers such as Fromm, Klineberg, Kluckhohn, and Murray.

Groups proverbially rejected for economic, ethnic, religious, regional, or other reasons constitute significant material for social study. As Sumner says, epithets condense ideas and produce summary criticisms and definitions of types by societal selection.[13] Proverbial phrases like "jealous as a Turk," "dumb as a Swede," "obscure as a Greek," "unlucky as a Negro," "to Jew down" (barter) are in themselves conclusive of nothing, but may be clues to historical tensions. Their currency, extensiveness, weighting in the culture, and contextual definition would have to be established before tentative conclusions could be drawn as to types of existing tensions. When such phrases are particularly pungent, they may outlast the circumstances which popularized them; for example, more than 450 years have passed since Jews were banished from Spain, but disparaging proverbial phrases linger in the language stream of Spain.[14]

Proverbs and National Crises

Prior to the Pearl Harbor incident, a Japanese government agency stressed the sociological function of Japanese proverbs in canalizing latent tensions. Hints of drastic events to come were inscribed on the proverbial walls. Tremendous emphasis was placed upon virtues translatable into military competencies:

> The education and training of the warriors were conducted with main emphasis on the importance of loyalty to their masters, contempt of death, and indifference to money. The class of men who were taught to deny themselves and to hold pleasures of life beneath their dignity, naturally had little to do with the making of proverbs. Nevertheless, the century of civil wars or its experience had not been lost on the minds of people. . . . This may be said also with regard to the bourgeoisie who formed the bulk of the urban population. Their minds were by no means foreign to conflicting problems of life such as duty and worldly ambition, pleasure and self-denial, pursuit of life and resignation therefrom, indulgence and self-examination . . . the section of society which was most fertile of proverbs as this period bore the impress of thoughts and experiences of the warrior class, priests and court-nobility.[15]

It is not surprising then, that from a people whose minds were regimented to self-denial, sacrifice, and stoicism, as reflected in the Japanese proverbs, such phenomena as kamikaze attacks and other manifestations of blind obedience were common Japanese war tactics. These acts were but implementations of this philosophy in a national crisis. It is Erikson's thesis that there should be more extensive study of the conscious and unconscious imageries of nations so as to be able to discern in human motivations "those archaic and infantile residues which in national crises become subject to misuse by demagogic adventurers." He also says:

> A nation's totality of basic attitudes and symbols is deeply rooted in her geographical position and her history . . . these attitudes and symbols are unavoidably recreated in every child trained and educated in the national culture area . . . they are reflected both in what a member does—and in what he fails to do.[16]

Tensions, attitudes, and symbols are embedded in the language, in what folk say, or fail to say (the "discontinuity" aspect). An anthropologist, commenting on proverbs, indicates "the very incompleteness of a distribution [goes] far to illuminate the history of a cultural trait."[17]

For proverbs and national crises, attention is called to *War Proverbs and Maxims East and West* (1945), in which "belligerent" proverbs from several prominent world languages are cited.[18] English and Russian sayings predominate.[19]

Blood, Toil, Tears and Sweat

Characterizing tensions of the British mind in World War II was Churchill's phrase, "blood, toil, tears and sweat."[20] Group tensions popularized and sanctioned Churchill's quotation; it metamorphosed into a common phrase evocative of the conditions in which it arose.[21] Often the phrase is "blood, sweat and tears," with easier rhythm and less to remember.[23]

Tensions in national crises are fertile with sayings and slogans; for example "54–40 or fight!" "Remember the Alamo!" "The Yanks are coming!" "Remember Pearl Harbor!" The alacrity with which these tension phrases spread among the masses is an index to the degree of social cohesiveness in a particular group or nation. Conversely, where there is no unity of thought, such phrases do not thrive. A case in point is the absence of any quasi-proverbial phrases for the Korean crisis initiated in 1950.[23] No single event or trend of motivations served to unify national thinking in the United States to the point that a proverb or slogan could capture its essence. Until such a time, no people are mentally prepared for drastic measures, actions, or sacrifices. In the case of Great Britain, folk anxiety, common interests, and tensions readily pinned down Churchill's words because they articulated the prevalent state of mind. This psychological phenomenon of group remembering, so implicit in the nature of proverbs, also is an integral part of rumors, slogans, fables, legends, and cartoons. Similar causes and effects are involved in each of these expressions shared in varying degrees by the masses.

Proverbs as Clues for International Understanding

International understanding depends upon knowing more about the tensions and attitudes of other peoples. Under Lewis' definition of group mind as "group behaviour mediated by group symbols," proverbs are vivid expressions of group mind, group remembering, feelings, volitions, and tensions.[24] Emphasis has been placed upon finding differences among peoples, although a certain uniformity of human nature seems to spell itself out in proverbs. Seiler in his paremiological analysis stressed differences between Romans and Germans.[25] It would have been of value to see a treatment of similarities. A mutually electing affinity *(Wahlverwandtschaft)* is the chief cause for intercultural proverb borrowing, such as occurred between the Germans and the Romans, who in turn previously had borrowed from the Greeks.

We need other links in the chain of international thinking and emotions. It is proposed here that proverbs form one link, providing countless clues to comprehending other minds. Every clue contributes to the total picture.

Whether or not a clearer understanding of proverbs as group symbolic communications in other cultures will lead to a kindlier appreciation of the people is a matter not easily resolved. Prejudiced notions and nationalistic misconceptions form an almost impenetrable barrier to international understanding. The French proverb *tout comprendre c'est tout pardonner* is, perhaps, but a warm expression of hope, since there is no such understanding unless there is a will to it.

Notes

1. For example, intuitive or impressionistic accounts of journalists, tourists, native or visiting professors; there are anthropological interpretations of child training, studies in social and vital statistics, psychiatric and psychoanalytic approaches, or analyses of psychosomatic data. There are community and attitude studies, public opinion surveys, intensive interview techniques, semantic studies, or content analyses of cultural products. For a comprehensive review of these techniques, see Otto Klineberg, *Tensions Affecting International Understanding* (Social Science Research Council Bulletin 62, New York, 1950), pp. 8–92.

2. Spanish proverbs often are anticlerical: "Show not the monk nor the swine the road"; "When you see a monk, get your back to the wall"; "Priests live off the dead"; "The devil, fed up with his lot, became a monk." See J.M. Sbarbi y Osuna, *Gran diccionario de refranes . . .*, ed. Joaquin Gil (Buenos Aires: Ateneo, 1943). See also J. Raymond, "Attitudes and Cultural Patterns in Spanish Proverbs," *The Americas*, IX (July, 1954), 74.

3. For example, "When the Czar spits into the soup dish, it fairly bursts with pride"; "If the Czar be a rhymster, woe be to the poets"; "The hen of the Czarina herself does not lay swan's eggs"; "The Czar may be the cousin of God, but he's not His brother"; or "When the Czar takes snuff the people will sneeze." See *Harper's Weekly*, XXXIX (Feb. 23, 1895), 187.

4. *Paremiology* is the technical term for the study of proverbs.

5. "Proverbs are almost the exclusive, certainly the most important verbal instrument for minimizing friction and effecting adjustment, legal, social, or intellectual" (George Herzog, *Jabo Proverbs from Liberia* [London: Oxford University Press, 1936], pp. 5–6, 14–15). Or, "It is safer to take recourse in a traditional expression to vent their feelings than to become involved in accusations and recriminations" (M.J. Herskovits and F.S. Herskovits, *Suriname Folk-Lore* [Columbia Univ. Contributions to Anthropology, Vol. 27], New York, 1936, pp. 135–136). Or, "In the form of a general truth we may give vent to the bitterest feelings without making ourselves responsible for its personal application" (J. Bigelow, *The Wit and Wisdom of the Haytians* [New York: Scribner, Armstrong, 1877], p. 13). And, "Many an angry dispute has been silenced . . . many a long, diffuse argument has been clinched by the apt quotation of one of these proverbs" (E.W. Smith, A.M. Dale, *The Ila-speaking People . . .*, quoted in J.S. Slotkin, *Social Anthropology* [New York: Macmillan, 1950], pp. 548–549). And, "A proverb is a very suitable vehicle for giving vent to one's feelings . . . it makes even . . . sarcasm less offensive by making it less

personal" (E. Westermarck, *Wit and Wisdom in Morocco* [London: Routledge, 1930], p. 57).

6. Funk-Wagnalls' *Standard Dictionary of Folklore*... (New York, 1949), I, 22.

7. F.A. White, "United Nations' 65 Interpreters," *Word Study*, 2, Vol. 26 (Newark: Merriam, December, 1950).

8. J. Ruesch, "Social Technique, Social Status, and Social Change in Illness," *Personality in Nature, Society and Culture*, p. 125, f. 30. Arne Naess, in "The Function of Ideological Convictions," *Tensions That Cause Wars*, ed. by H. Cantril (Urbana: Univ. of Illinois Press, 1950), p. 271 appeals for the investigation of "verbal stereotypes with no fairly precise meaning, but influencing controversies." This would apply to proverbs.

9. For interesting documentation, see the section, "Retorting Proverbs," in D.E. Marvin, *Curiosities in Proverbs* (New York: Putnam's, 1916), p. 4.

10. R. Jente, "A Review of Proverb Literature Since 1920," in *Corona*, by A. Schirokauer and W. Paulsen (Durham, North Carolina: Duke Univ., 1941), p. 30.

11. A.A. Roback, *A Dictionary*...(with a supplementary essay on aspects of ethnic prejudice) (Cambridge: Sci-Art, 1944). He terms these expressions "ethnophaulisms." [See also Marvin, op. cit., "contemptuous proverbs," pp. 309–321.]

12. *Ibid.*, pp. 11–12, 247, and 252.

13. W.G. Sumner, *Folkways* (Boston: Ginn, 1906, 1940), p. 646.

14. Roback enlarges upon the psychology of unflattering allusions, stating that folk locutions are almost invariably unfavorable when applied to outsiders because of two main tendencies: "self-magnification at another's expense (megalomania) and scapegoat hunting when economic conditions are bad or where mass discomfitures provoke tension in the community." The idea seems to be, he indicates, "to give a dog a bad name and hang him" (*ibid.*, pp. 302–305).

15. Otoo Huzii, *Japanese Proverbs* (Japanese Government Railways, Board of Tourist Industry, 1940), p. 5.

16. Erik Homburger Erikson, "Hitler's Imagery and German Youth," *Psychiatry*, V (1942), 493. See also p. 476. Further social interpretation of "gross slogans" and "catchwords" is found in *Tensions That Cause Wars*, pp. 258–259. More fundamental data are provided by Gordon W. Allport and Leo Postman, *The Psychology of Rumor* (New York: Holt, 1947), p. 135.

17. A.L. Kroeber, *Anthropology*... (New York: Harcourt Brace, 1948), p. 544.

18. Selwyn G. Champion, *War Proverbs*... (London: Probsthain), 1945.

19. For example, an anti-English saying from Spanish is: "When the apes die out of Gibralter the British will have to go." Other "war proverbs" are more general in nature: "Build a golden bridge for the fleeing enemy," "War with all the world... peace with England," "He who never draws the sword without cause never lays it down without honor," and "Every war ends where it should begin."

20. Winston Churchill, as prime minister of Great Britain, addressed the House on May 13, 1940: "I would say to the House, as I said to those who have joined this Government: 'I have nothing to offer but blood, toil, tears and sweat.' We have before us an ordeal of the most grievous kind. We have before us many, many long months of struggle and suffering. You ask: 'What is our policy?' I will say: 'It is to wage war by sea,

land, and air with all our might, and with all the strength that God can give us: to wage war against a monstrous tyranny never surpassed in the dark lamentable catalogue of human crime.' That is our policy. You ask: 'What is our aim?' I can answer in one word: 'Victory . . . at all costs . . . in spite of all terror . . . however long and hard the road may be . . . ' " (*Maxims and Reflections*, ed., C. Coote et. al. [Boston: Houghton Mifflin, 1949], pp. 101–102). [Note: In 1611, John Donne wrote: "Mollifie it with thy teares, or sweat, or blood" (*An Anatomy of the World*, I, 430–431); see J. Bartlett, *Familiar Quotations*, ed. by C. Morley (Boston: Little, Brown, 1949), p. 848.]

21. Precisely, this is a "quotation proverb" or *Sagwort*; for further definition, see A.H. Krappe, *The Science of Folk-Lore* (London: Methuen, 1930), p. 148.

22. There is cause to inquire why certain words in such expressions tend to drop out, while others are retained in the saying. Three psychological aspects of group remembering are involved: leveling, sharpening, and assimilation. These are lucidly treated in F.C. Bartlett, *Remembering: A Study in Experimental and Social Psychology* (New York: Macmillan, 1932), p. 31. Also, "Since a number of individuals are involved, the meaning that emerges is likely to be what is common to the group. . . . The idiosyncrasies of one respondent are apt to be omitted by the next, and thus the story [or proverb] is whittled down to a core understandable to all. Rumors are therefore usually more standardized, more acculturated, and have more of a common denominator than do individual memories. For the same reason they are more likely to acquire a moral tone characteristic of the culture" (Allport and Postman, op. cit., p. 60).

23. A possible exception: "All out or get out!"

24. M.M. Lewis, *Language in Society* (New York: Social Sciences, 1948), p. 93.

25. F. Seiler, *Deutsche Sprichwörterkunde* (München, 1922), p. 290.

Tradition and Innovation: Proverbs in Advertising

*Barbara and Wolfgang Mieder**

Lest anyone think the study of proverbs refers only to the Bible, Shakespeare, and other works of the past, he need only look around to see proverbs at work in the mass media. Modern advertising provides abundant proof that the proverb's vitality remains undiminished. While the following essay emphasizes advertising, one should realize that the proverb is similarly utilized in newspaper headlines and cartoons. For a full-fledged book-length treatment of the proverb in twentieth century modern life, see Wolfgang Mieder, Das Sprichwort in unserer Zeit *(Frauenfeld, 1975).*

A few years ago the provocative question was posed whether folklorists are doomed "to study only the disappearing, the dying, and the dead."[1] Admittedly there are certain folklore genres which are losing ground in the age of modern technology, yet one must hasten to state that other genres are actually increasing in popularity. Recent research has attempted to illustrate the continuity of traditional folklore genres by drawing attention more and more to the innovative application of old forms in the present time.[2] The goal of such research endeavors is to point to the phenomenon that Goethe in a poem of 1803 called "Dauer im Wechsel" (constancy in change). Changing times and situations require forms of expression which the traditional

* Reprinted from the *Journal of Popular Culture*, 11 (1977), 308–319 by permission of the *Journal of Popular Culture*.

forms no longer can supply. However, it often suffices to adapt an antiquated folklore item to the modern context. This process of innovation on the basis of tradition then becomes the proof of the continuity of the traditional forms.

This interplay of tradition and innovation can be found to a large extent in modern advertising, which has been the subject of regrettably few investigations by folklorists,[3] although the importance of advertising for the study of folklore is generally accepted. Advertising attempts to reach a wide spectrum of people, and it accomplishes this by using the mass media and by calling on folklore items of all modes. By drawing on verbal folklore genres such as fairy tales, legends, folksongs, tall tales, riddles, and proverbs the advertisements have a familiar ring that lures the customer into regarding the advertised product as one which has withstood the test of time.[4] Usually the folklore materials used are varied to a great degree to fit the advertisement, but the basic traditional statement is still recognizable.

The proverb is one of the folklore genres that is most alive today,[5] despite the fact that it has been stated again and again that proverbs "are not as commonly used as they were in olden times."[6] One American sociologist talked about "the virtual disappearance of the use of the proverb,"[7] and another one proclaimed "we do not need proverbs any more."[8] Although one would perhaps have to agree that proverbs are today used less frequently in their traditional way, i.e. as a didactic piece of wisdom, one glance at the advertising of any magazine or newspaper shows that proverbs have become the most popular folklore item used by Madison Avenue.

One of the reasons for this preferential treatment of proverbs lies in the basic fact that "advertising must talk to people naturally and effectively."[9] For this reason copy writers prefer to use simple and short sentences because a complicated sentence structure would interfere with the comprehensibility of the advertiser's message.[10] The proverb certainly satisfies the demand for shortness and simplicity, but even more importantly, it inspires trustworthiness in the advertised product by awakening positive traditional feelings in the consumer. After all, proverbs express apparent truths and an advertiser wants to tell the "truth" about his product. The authority of generations speaks through proverbs and the copy writers shrewdly take advantage of this very striking aspect of the proverb to give their advertisements proverbial headlines that, although often varied, make authoritative statements just as the traditional proverb does.

Advertising people generally agree that the headline is the most important single factor of an advertisement, for "on the average, five times as many people read the headline as read the body copy."[11] Much emphasis therefore, is given to the writing of these headlines which act as attention-getters, flagging down the reader to get him to read the entire advertisement copy. For this reason, and also due to the lack of space, the headline must be as clear and concise as possible; it must telegraph the message of the advertisement, and "it must telegraph it in plain language."[12] This is where the proverb is useful, often even in its original form. The proverb "Good things come in small packages"[13] certainly was an appropriate headline for advertising a 35mm camera, and the statement "To see it is to believe it"[14] quite literally invited the reader to come and take a look at another camera. The "University Year for Action" program headed its advertisements with the proverb "Actions speak louder than words"[15] and thereby pointed directly to the main aspect of the program. The old unchanged proverb "He that stays in the valley shall never get over the hill"[16] functioned as the headline for what was billed as the more responsible broadcasting of the Westinghouse Broadcasting Company. A last example from the Burlington (Vermont) Savings Bank has not just one but three proverbs as headlines: "The early bird gets the worm," "A stitch in time saves nine," and "A penny saved is a penny earned."[17] The following copy makes clear what the bank has in mind with its proverbial headlines: "These oft quoted words carry a very simple message. Act now to plan for the future and succeed. Part of planning for the future is the saving for it. . . ." This advertisement actually uses the proverbs in the old didactic fashion, attempting to convince the reader of the necessity for saving. A very effective approach indeed, for who could disagree with three such popular proverbs? In addition, quoting the three proverbs increases the "folksiness" of the ad.

The quotation of proverbs in the original wording is, however, by no means the most effective utilization of this folklore genre in advertising. Copy writers are very interested in creating striking and original headlines. As Lloyd Herrold explains, "imaginative headlines may result from the use of (1) dramatic interest. . . , (2) figures of speech—metaphors, similes, and other implied comparisons. . . , (3) alliteration. . . , (4) news headings. . . , (5) personification of the product. . . , and (6) twisted wordings of well-known quotations, proverbs, phrases and axioms. . ."[18] Copy writers seem to have a particular love for changing proverbs which Helmut Herles has called "the conscious manipulation of proverbs,"[19] for even in their altered form the proverbs retain their appeal for authority and claim of truth. In addition, a twisted proverb will serve even better than the original as an attention-getter, since the new wording increases the interest in reading the following copy. Only a small word exchange or addition to the proverb is necessary to startle the reader into further perusing the advertisement. Two airline advertisements show this effective play with proverbs very well. The German airline Lufthansa used the headline "All roads used to lead to Rome"[20] questioning the validity of the old proverb "All roads lead to Rome" by merely adding the words "used to." The copy then explains that nowadays Frankfurt, the home of Lufthansa, is the central European city to which all roads lead. In regard to European air travel it could perhaps, in fact, be stated that "All roads lead to Frankfurt." The other airline advertisement shows two businessmen aboard Japan Air Lines. To stress its truly first class food service and to emphasize also the meeting of two cultures, the copy writers changed the proverb "One man's meat is another man's poison" to "One man's *sushi* is another man's steak."[21] And Cutty Sark Scotch uses an advertisement headline that reflects its double blending process assuring maturity of the whiskey: "When it comes to maturity, two barrels are better than one."[22] Although only one word was exchanged of the original proverb "Two heads are better than one" the varied form expresses in a familiar tone the claim for maturity of Cutty Sark, and who would want to argue with such a proverbial claim?

None of the above examples has mentioned the name of the product in the proverbial headline. These headlines are primarily employed as attention-getters to encourage reading the advertising copy. Proverbs are used because their familiar sound creates a feeling of positive identification and trustworthy authority. When the product name is included in the main statement of the advertisement, the headline has usually become a slogan which "*is a message designed to be repeated over and over again, word for word!* This insistence that a slogan be quoted in its exact words distinguishes it from the headline, which can be and usually is changed from advertisement to advertisement, saying the same thing in different ways. Slogans always say the same thing the same way."[23] The key element to a successful slogan is its memorability and recognizability, thereby assuring the continuity of an advertising campaign. The linguistic tricks to make a slogan "click", i.e. memorable and recognizable, are, among others, rhythm, rhyme, alliteration, parallel structure, euphony and swing cadence,[24] all also stylistic features of the proverb! The difference between the slogan and the proverb lies therefore not in form but rather in the mode of expression. The slogan is more a narrow statement of a particular advertising theme, whereas the proverb expresses an apparent truth.[25] Naturally, however, copy writers have drawn heavily on proverbs to create slogans. By altering an existing proverb the memorability of the new slogan is literally assured. The Coca-Cola Company, known for several decades for its slogans, has often made use of proverbs and proverbial expressions as the following selection shows:[26]

All roads lead by Coca-Cola signs (1929)
Thirst come – thirst served (1932)
All trails lead to ice-cold Coca-Cola (1935)
Where there's Coca-Cola there's hospitality (1948)
A chore's best friend (1936)

By the same token slogans may become so popular and generally accepted that they take on a proverbial character in themselves without originally being formed on a proverb,[27] as for example Coca-Cola's "It's the real thing" (1942) or "Things go better with Coke" (1963).

Slogans that contain the name of the product will encourage the consumer to remember it when confronted with a purchasing choice. Seagram's V.O. Canadian Whiskey, for example, has adapted the established proverbial pattern "X is X"[28] for its slogan. Each advertisement uses the pattern in double form, the first statement (together with an exotic picture) indicating the international distribution of the whiskey and the second identifying the brand:

Only Kyoto is Koyto
Only V.O. is V.O.[29]

Only St. Moritz is St. Moritz
Only V.O. is V.O.[30]

Only Venice is Venice
Only V.O. is V.O.[31]

A similar advertisement pattern is used by the Canadian Imperial Bank of Commerce based on the proverb "One good turn deserves another." To be sure the proverb is strongly expanded, but its core is nevertheless recognizable.

> One good banking idea in Canada
> led us to another in Frankfurt.[32]
>
> One good banking idea in Canada
> led us to another in London.[33]
>
> One good banking idea in Canada
> led us to another in Paris.[34]

The name of the Canadian bank appears in each one of the examples, and although each names a different city illustrated by a typical street scene, the basic slogan pattern is there, repeated again and again to emphasize the international aspect of the Canadian Bank. Another catchy slogan, without any particular significance other than spreading the name of the company, is used by Dan River men's and women's wear fabrics, namely "Dan River runs deep."[35] The name "River" calls forth the association with water and with that the proverb "Still (smooth) waters run deep," demonstrating, perhaps, that there is more to these fabrics than meets the eye.

No list of slogan examples would be complete without a reference to the skillful advertising techniques of Volkswagen. Now that the renowned "Beetle" is only one of several models built by Volkswagen, the slogan "Different Volks for different folks"[36] is certainly appropriate. It has all the elements that make a successful slogan.[37] Based on the proverb "Different strokes for different folks," only one word needed to be exchanged with the shortened product name. The proverbial slogan has parallel structure and rhyme and gives the whole story in one short catchy phrase that is illustrated by pictures of the various Volkswagen models. This is a slogan *par excellence* in all of its simplicity, a slogan masterpiece!

The American insurance companies, like Volkswagen, also do their best to use proverbial materials as headlines for their magazine advertisements. Leo Spitzer once noted that "it would not, perhaps, be wrong to see a sermon in all advertising,"[38] drawing particular attention to the preaching and didactic note that many ads carry. The insurance companies take direct advantage of the didactic aspects of the proverb to sell their policies. Often the proverbs are quoted unchanged to stress the wisdom and truth of the offered insurance. The proverb headline attempts to create the feeling of familiarity and agreement. The Horace Mann Insurance company, for example, uses the headline "Two heads are better than one."[39] Since this is a proverbial truth, it must be correct to "put your head together with a Horace Mann agent" as the advertisement copy continues. Naturally, the accompanying picture shows a Mann agent with a customer talking over a homeowners insurance program. Equally clever is the illustration of a nice home, car, and family neatly tied together with a bow above the caption "Good things still come in small packages."[40] This is the Continental Insurance Company's way of stating that they have an insurance package that covers the entire family and their belongings. As a final example, an interesting advertisement was made by the Aetna Insurance Company showing three people sitting on the floor: a woman holding her ears shut, a man holding his eyes closed, and another man holding his mouth. The caption reads "Don't just sit there . . . .It's *your* health care, *your* auto insurance they're arguing about. Join the action. You can't afford not to. Not while State and Federal lawmakers are debating issues that are going to affect your life, your well being, and your pocket book."[41] The picture is, of course, an illustration of the well-known proverb "Audi, vide, tace," i.e. "Hear and see and say nothing."[42] With this ad Aetna wants to get customers involved in insurance politics by encouraging them to overcome the common lethargic attitude about insurance. In this advertisement as well as in all those mentioned above the didactic purpose is obvious in that the utilized proverbial material adds an aura of authority to what the insurance brokers tell the public.

The copy writers show great versatility in their proverb use for the creation of effective headlines, and yet, certain proverbs seem to reappear again and again. Volkswagen's slogan "Different Volks for different folks" has already been mentioned. The underlying proverb "Different strokes for different folks" can easily be considered as the proverbial pattern "Different X for different folks," where X can be replaced by literally anything. An advertisement for U.S.Savings Bonds, for example, used the innovative "Different hopes for different folks."[43] Another example of this type of proverbial patterning is the proverb "Where there's smoke there's fire," which can quickly become the proverbial formula "Where there's X, there's Y" or "Where there's smoke, there's X" as a lesser varied form. The Grumman Corporation employed the headline "Where there's smoke there's money"[44] to explain its discovery of recovering wasted gases for reuse. And an advertisement for Vantage cigarettes uses the provocative headline "Where there's smoke there's controversy,"[45] an excellent modern adaption of the old saying. Nothing, however, approaches in frequency the use of the biblical proverb "Man does not live by bread alone" (Mathew IV, 4) in advertising. There probably is no better way to stress authority and trustworthiness in an advertising headline than to use a biblical proverb.[46] When McDonald's came out with its "Quarterpounder" hamburger, it used a two page ad with two giant juicy hamburgers and the headline "Man does not live by bread alone."[47] In other words, more meat for your money, or, as the copy read, "it won't cost you a lot of bread to get a lot of meat." Although McDonald's used the proverb in its traditional wording, other copy writers recognized that the proverb can also be generalized into the formula "Man does not (cannot) live by X alone" without losing its effectiveness. For instance, Pierre Cardin formulated "Man cannot live by clothes alone"[48] to advertise men's cologne. Very successful is also "Man cannot live by blue jeans alone,"[49] a headline used by Wrangler, which makes jeans in 37 colors, 20 fabrics, and 21 styles. Naturally a picture with people wearing a variety of jeans illustrates the claim of the headline. But an advertisement for men's hosiery even goes so far as: "Introducing patterned Supp-hose Socks. Because feet cannot live on solid colors alone."[50] The statement is, of course, ridiculous, but it is catchy and authoritative, and therefore convincing. Once again the traditional biblical and proverbial wisdom is manipulated into a new form to increase sales of a new product.

Several times already mention has been made of the illustrations that accompany almost all of these proverbial headlines. Most copy writers consider the interplay of headline and illustration of great importance, since "the illustration, like the headline, attracts attention, selects the audience, and stimulates interest in body copy. What is more, the illustration can be invaluable in showing the product or the product's use and explaining graphically certain ideas or situations that are cumbersome to put into words. The old saying that one picture is worth a thousand words has much merit in it."[51] A recent advertisement by Four Roses Whiskey illustrates this point splendidly. The headline simply reads "In whiskey, this picture is worth a thousand words"[52] and under it is a picture of four roses. The traditional proverb together with the illustration expresses in figurative language the whole advertising idea: the proverb shows the claim of excellence of the whiskey, and the picture shows the particular brand name.

Of special interest in this regard is the practice of actually illustrating the metaphorical proverb text. Proverb illustrations have a long history in art, dating way back into the Middle Ages. Most famous of all is, of course, Peter Breughel's picture "The Netherlandic Proverbs" (1559). The tradition continued in the woodcuts and emblem books, gaining a peak in the "Bilderbogen" of the nineteenth century.[53] The practice of illustrating proverbs continues to the present day, now particularly in comic strips, political cartoons, and of course, advertising. The proverbial headline which is illustrated strengthens the advertiser's claim through word and picture, a double exposure of striking effectiveness. The Committee for Hand Gun Control, for instance, is asking for donations to its campaign to ban bullets for hand guns with the headline "We need bullets like we need a hole in the head."[54] A picture of a pretty girl with a hole in the head drastically illustrates the popular American proverbial expression "To need (it) like a hole in the head." Another advertisement by the Israel Government Coins and Medals Corporation used the proverbial expression "Don't put all your eggs in one basket"[55] as a headline with the accompanying picture of a basket with eggs and Israel commemorative coins and medals. Word and picture work hand in hand to explain each other and thus become a kind of "picture-writing."

Naturally the advertisers presume that the reader makes a positive identification with the proverbial headline, nodding his or her head in agreement. Certain advertisements even use only one half of the original proverb, assuming from the beginning the general currency of the proverb among the readers. Close to Christmas time Harveys Bristol Cream sherry was advertised with the headline "Do unto others"[56] accompanied by a picture of a man wrapping sherry bottles for Christmas gifts. And close to Mother's Day the Fabergé Fragrance Company added one letter to the above proverb remnant and made it "Do unto mothers"[57] Both headlines are shortened forms of the biblical proverb "Do unto others as you would have them do unto you" (Luke VI, 31), which almost adds a prophetic value to the ad. The implication is clear: who wouldn't like a bottle of Harveys sherry or a bottle of Fabergé cologne for himself, and since that is true, why not give these products as a gift as the proverb and bible recommend.

Finally, a few examples follow which show particular imagination on the part of advertisers and illustrators. Avis rental cars used for quite some time the clever slogan "To err is humam. That's why we invented the Wizard of Avis."[58] Only the exchange of the final "n" with an incorrect "m" makes this advertisement striking enough to get the attention of the reader. Just as simple and yet original are the ads by the clothing company Jones of New York. Each ad shows a model in a fashionable outfit and the slogan is always the same:

JONES NEW YORK
No wonder everyone is trying to keep up with us[59]

Taking the expression "Keeping up with the Joneses" and connecting it with the company's name is a shrewd way of maintaining the currency of the name of the company and implying that Jones offers the best there is. Naturally a woman must keep up her figure in order to remain fashionable, and the people selling Dole bananas have used this fact as a basis for the following advertisement. The picture shows a delicious banana with the splendid headline "If the dress no longer fits, peel it."[60] The copy explains that a medium-size Dole banana only contains about 85 calories, making it filling, but not fattening. Taking the proverb "If the shoe fits, wear it," the copy writer has changed the fitting shoe to the dress that no longer fits. The traditional proverb wording is barely extant anymore, but this innovative variation still carries the familiar ring to it. What reader would not stop for such a headline to see what it is all about? Once again the manipulated proverb text is the primary attention-gettter.

The innovation process of traditional proverbs has also reached the woman's liberation movement. Even a cursory glance at English proverbs will bring to light the anti-feminism of proverbs, "for proverbs in praise of women are in a pitiful minority."[61] This being the fact, standard proverbs need to be changed in order to fit the goals of the movement. Sears, Roebuck and Co. chose the headline "We don't separate the women from the men"[62] for a job advertisement on the first page of a *Ms.* magazine. Sears, as an equal opportunity employer, simply took the proverbial expression "To separate the men from the boys" and changed it for its sales training program, at the same time saluting International Women's Year 1975. Interesting in this regard is also an advertisement by the First National Bank of Boston showing two men and a woman in a picture with the headline "If you're disappointed with your pension plan's performance. . . . how do you think Tom, Dick, and Mary feel?"[63] Once again, an exchange of a couple letters makes all the difference. This time the old expression "Tom, Dick, and Harry" is changed to contain the name of at least one woman. But the most progressive example is the following one by Junior House fashions:

A WOMAN'S PLACE
IS IN THE HOUSE

(picture of the White House and the House of Representatives)

Even some of the die-hards are beginning to say Amen! Women have finally let their brains come out of the closet because there's an awful lot of mess that needs cleaning up: After all, isn't that what everybody said girls were born to do?[64]

The proverb itself is barely changed. The word "house" is substituted for the usual "home" for two reasons: first of all, the change allows an association with the name Junior House fashions, and secondly, it provides the basis for the thought that it is high time that a woman either occupies the White House or that more women get elected to Congress, which the picture obviously implies. Once again the interplay of proverb and illustration is evident along with the obvious wordplay. With the thought of women's lib in mind, the old proverb takes on an entirely different meaning,[65] another proof of the fact that the context in which the proverb appears is of large significance.

The preceding remarks and examples have amply illustrated that the proverb has become an often utilized and effective tool in advertising. The author of a short note on "Proverbs as Copy-Patterns" from the year 1933 found it surprising "that there has not been more copy modeled on the style of the old saws and adages."[66] Some forty years later it now can be stated that local advertising as well as the nation-wide and sophisticated ads of the fashionable Madison Avenue agencies have learned to employ proverbs very shrewdly. Although the proverbs are frequently quoted in their traditional form the majority of the ads include varied proverbs. The original wording of the proverbs is manipulated without destroying the familiar ring of the sayings, thereby increasing the sales appeal of the ad. Advertising most assuredly has become a new and vital stomping ground of the timeless and adaptable proverb, which of all the folk narrative genres has coped best with the problem of overcoming the dichotomy of tradition and innovation.

Notes

1. Alan Dundes, "The Devolutionary Premise in Folklore Theory," *Journal of the Folklore Institute,* 6 (1969), 13.

2. See the 12 theoretical essays in *Kontinuität? Geschichtlichkeit und Dauer als volkskundliches Problem,* ed. by Hermann Bausinger and Wolfgang Brückner (Berlin 1969).

3. See Otto Görner, "Reklame und Volkskunde," *Mitteldeutsche Blätter für Volkskunde,* 6 (1931), 109–127; Leo Spitzer, "American Advertising Explained as Popular Art," in L. Spitzer, *A Method of Interpreting Literature* (New York 1949), pp. 102–149; Julian Mason, "Some Uses of Folklore in Advertising," *Tennessee Folklore Society Bulletin,* 20 (1954), 58–61; Alan Dundes, "Advertising and Folklore," *New York Folklore Quarterly,* 19 (1963), 143–151; Karl Veit Riedel, "Werbung und Reklame als volkskundliches Problem," *Beitrage zur deutschen Volkskunde und Altertumskunde,* 10 (1966), 93–117.

4. Priscilla Denby speaks in this connection of "folklore as 'folklure' " in her essay "Folklore in Mass Media," *Folklore Forum,* 4 (1971), 113–125.

5. See Wolfgang Mieder, *Das Sprichwort in unserer Zeit* (Frauenfeld 1975).

6. Dwight Edwards Marvin, *The Antiquity of Proverbs* (New York 1922), p. 28.

7. William Albig, "Proverbs and Social Control," *Sociology and Social Research,* 15 (1931), 528.

8. Joyce Hertzler, "The Social Wisdom of the Primitives with Special Reference to Their Proverbs," *Social Forces,* 11 (1933), 317.

9. Alfred J. Seaman, *The Power of Words* (New York 1971), p. 4.

10. See Ruth Römer, *Die Sprache der Anzeigenwerbung* (Düsseldorf 1971), p. 164.

11. David Ogilvy, *Confessions of an Advertising Man* (New York 1963), p. 104. See also Maurice I. Mandell, *Advertising* (Englewood Cliffs, N.J. 1974), p. 450.

12. Ogilvy, p. 107.

13. *Anchorage Daily Press* (October 31, 1974), p. 17.

14. *Anchorage Daily Press* (December 30, 1974), p. 18.

15. *Catalyst Newsletter,* vol. 2, no. 1 (January 1974), p. 3.

16. *Time* (November 18, 1974), pp. 92–93.

17. *Burlington Free Press* (September 13, 1972), p. 21.

18. Lloyd Herrold, *Advertising Copy. Principles and Practice* (New York 1926), pp. 229–230.

19. Helmut Herles, "Sprichwort and Märchenmotiv in der Werbung," *Zeitschrift für Volkskunde,* 62 (1966), 71.

20. *Scala,* Nr. 12 (December 1972), p. 13.

21. *Gourmet* (September 1974), p. 69.

22. *Punch* (September 12, 1973), p. 326.

23. Otto Kleppner, "How to write a slogan," *Printers' Ink,* 222 (March 19, 1948), 40.

24. Otto Kleppner, *Advertising Procedure* (New York 1933), p. 112. See also S. Watson Dunn, *Advertising. Its Role in Modern Marketing* (New York 1961), p. 302.

25. See Volker Klotz, "Slogans," *Sprache im technischen Zeitalter,* 7 (1963), 538–546; Paul D. McGlynn, "Graffiti & Slogans: Flushing the Id," *Journal of Popular Culture,* 6 (1972), 351–356; Wolfgang Mieder, "Sprichwort und Illustriertenwerbung," *Sprachspiegel,* 30 (1974), 100–106.

26. See Cecil Munsey, *The Illustrated Guide to the Collectibles of Coca-Cola* (New York 1972), pp. 312–318.

27. See Mathilde Hain, "Das Sprichwort," *Deutschunterricht,* 15 (1963), 40. In this connection attention should be drawn to the magazine's *Printers' Ink* "Clearing House of Advertised Phrases" begun in 1919. Over 10,000 phrases are on file and judging by representative lists printed from time to time in *Printers' Ink*, slogans based on proverbs were popular at all times.

28. See Archer Taylor's study "The History of a Proverbial Pattern," in *Classical, Mediaeval and Renaissance Studies in Honor of Berthold Louis Ullman,* ed. by Charles Henderson, vol. II (Rome 1964), pp. 483–489.

29. *Gourmet* (July 1974), p. 35.

30. *Gourmet* (February 1974), p. 25.

31. *Gourment* (April 1974), p. 37.

32. *Financial Executive* (September 1974), p. 65.

33. *Financial Executive* (August 1974), p. 7.

34. *Financial Executive* (May 1974), p. 101.

35. *New York Times Magazine* (January 5, 1975), pp. 18–19. *New York Times Magazine* (August 25, 1974), pp. 8–9.

36. *Time* (December 16, 1974), p. 31.

37. See Hans Ferdinand Kropff, *Die Werbemittel und ihre psychologische, künstlerische und technische Gestaltung* (Essen 1961), p. 139. Here Kropff lists the following aspects as indicators of a good slogan: brevity, rhythm, catchiness, meaningful content, imagination and easy association with the product.

38. Spitzer, p. 127.

39. *Vermont Blackboard,* vol. 40, no. 10 (May 10, 1974), p. 3.

40. *Time* (September 9, 1974), p. 78.

41. *Time* (December 2, 1974), p. 24.

42. See Archer Taylor's discussion " 'Audi, Vide, Tace,' and the Three Monkeys," *Fabula*, 1 (1957), 26–31.

43. *Good Housekeeping* (February 1974), p. 28.

44. *Money* (January 1975), p. 2.

45. *New York* (May 12, 1975), p. 93.

46. See Jochen Möckelmann and Sönke Zander, *Form und Funktion der Werbeslogans* (Göppingen 1972), p. 85.

47. *Time* (January 21, 1974), pp. 34–35.

48. *New York Times Magazine* (December 15, 1974), p. 30.

49. *Punch* (May 1-7, 1974), pp. 724–725.

50. *Time* (April 15, 1974), p. 7.

51. Mandell, p. 451.

52. *Burlington Free Press* (April 24, 1975), p. 8.

53. See Lutz Röhrich, "Sprichwörtliche Redensarten in bildlichen Zeugnissen," *Bayerisches Jahrbuch für Volkskunde,* (1959), 67–79. Wolfgang Mieder, "Biblio-

graphischer Abriss zur bildlichen Darstellung von Sprichwörtern und Redensarten," in: *Forschungen und Berichte zur Volkskunde in Baden-Württemberg 1974–1977,* ed. by Irmgard Hampp and Peter Assion, vol. III (Stuttgart 1977), pp. 229–239.

54. *Vermont Cynic,* vol. 93, no. 13 (April 17, 1975), p. 5.

55. *New York Times Magazine* (September 22, 1974), p. 101.

56. *Punch* (November 20-27, 1973), inside of back cover.

57. *Time* (May 13, 1974), p. 8.

58. *Time* (October 22, 1973), p. 53.

59. See for example the *New York Times Magazine* (August 25, 1974), p. 114; (September 15, 1974), p. 26; (September 22, 1972), p. 24.

60. *Woman's Day* (May 1975), p. 57.

61. Archer Taylor, et al., "The Study of Proverbs," *Modern Language Forum,* 24 (1939), 70.

62. *Ms.,* vol. 3, no. 8 (February 1975), p. 1.

63. *Financial Executive* (April 1974), p. 87. See also Archer Taylor's study "Tom, Dick and Harry," *Names,* 6 (1958), 51–54.

64. *New York Times Magazine* (September 22, 1974), p. 34.

65. See Barbara Kirshenblatt-Gimblett, "Toward a Theory of Proverb Meaning," *Proverbium,* 22 (1973), 821–827.

66. Marsh K. Powers, "Proverbs as Copy-Patterns," *Printers' Ink,* 164 (August 17, 1933), p. 24.

Suggestions for Further Reading on Proverbs

For those readers interested in additional scholarship on the proverb, we have listed some representative books and articles, emphasizing English language materials. Those primarily concerned with finding collections of proverbs from particular peoples are advised to check the bibliographical works by Bonser and Stephens and by Moll where literally hundreds of collections are cited. A valuable source for numerous short contributions to proverb scholarship is the unusual periodical *Proverbium* (1965–1975). For other references to special proverb research topics, the reader is urged to consult the bibliographically oriented *Sprichwort* by Lutz Röhrich and Wolfgang Mieder.

1. Bibliographies

Bernstein, Ignacy *Catalogue des Livres Parémiologiques composant la Bibliothèque de Ignace Bernstein.* 2 vols. (Warsaw, 1900)

Bonser, Wilfrid and T.A. Stephens *Proverb Literature: A Bibliography of Works Relating to Proverbs* (London, 1930, rpt. Nendeln, 1967)

De Caro, Frank and W.K. McNeil *American Proverb Literature: A Bibliography* (Bloomington, 1971)

Duplessis, M.G. *Bibliographie parémiologique* (Paris, 1847, rpt. Nieuwkoop, 1969)

Mieder, Wolfgang *International Bibliography of Explanatory Essays on Individual Proverbs and Proverbial Expressions* (Bern, 1977)

Mieder, Wolfgang *Proverbs in Literature: An International Bibliography* (Bern, 1978)

Moll, Otto E. *Sprichwörterbibliographie* (Frankfurt, 1958)

2. General Discussions of the Proverb

Hulme, F. Edward *Proverb Lore* (London, 1902, rpt. Detroit, 1968)

Koller, Werner *Redensarten. Linguistische Aspekte, Vorkommensanalysen, Sprachspiel* (Tübingen, 1977)

Kuusi, Matti *Parömiologische Betrachtungen,* FFC 172 (Helsinki, 1957)

Marvin, Dwight Edwards *The Antiquity of Proverbs* (New York, 1922)

Mieder, Wolfgang, ed. *Ergebnisse der Sprichwörterforschung* (Bern, 1978)

Permyakov, G.L. ed. *Paremiologičeskii Sbornik* (Moscow, 1978)

Permyakov, G.L. *From Proverb to Folk-Tale. Notes on the General Theory of Cliché* (Moscow, 1979)

Pilz, Klaus Dieter *Phraseologie. Redensartenforschung* (Stuttgart, 1981)

Pineaux, Jacques *Proverbes et dictons français* (Paris, 1973)

Röhrich, Lutz and Wolfgang Mieder *Sprichwort* (Stuttgart, 1977)

Seiler, Friedrich *Deutsche Sprichwörterkunde* (Munich, 1922, rpt. Munich, 1967)

Taylor, Archer *The Proverb* (Cambridge, 1931, rpt. Hatboro, 1962)

Taylor, Archer *Selected Writings on Proverbs*, ed. by Wolfgang Mieder, FFC 216 (Helsinki, 1975)

Trench, Richard *On the Lessons in Proverbs* (London, 1853, rpt. London, 1905)

3. Some Specific Studies

Alster, Bendt *Studies in Sumerian Proverbs* (Copenhagen, 1975)

Arewa, E. Ojo and Alan Dundes "Proverbs and the Ethnography of Speaking Folklore" *American Anthropologist*, 66(6), pt. 2 (1964), 70–85.

Bond, Donald "English Legal Proverbs" *PMLA*, 51 (1936), 921–935.

Bryant, Margaret M. *Proverbs and How to Collect Them* (Greensboro, 1945)

Firth, Raymond "Proverbs in Native Life, with Special Reference to those of the Maori" *Folklore,* 37 (1926), 245–270; 38 (1927), 134–153.

Gossen, Gary H. "Chamula Tzotzil Proverbs: Neither Fish nor Fowl" in *Meaning in Mayan Languages*, ed. Munro S. Edmonson (The Hague, 1973), pp. 205–233.

Grober-Glück, Gerda *Motive und Motivationen in Redensarten und Meinungen* 2 vols. (Marburg, 1974)

Hain, Mathilde *Sprichwort und Volkssprache. Eine volkskundlich-soziologische Dorfuntersuchung* (Giessen, 1951)

Kuusi, Matti *Regen bei Sonnenschein. Zur Weltgeschichte einer Redensart,* FFC 171 (Helsinki, 1957)

Kuusi, Matti *Towards an International Type-System of Proverbs*, FFC 211 (Helsinki, 1972)

Levin, Maurice I. *The Structure of the Russian Proverb* (Cambridge, 1968)

Loukatos, Démétrios "L'emploi du proverbe aux différents âges" *Proverbium*, 2 (1965), 17–26.

McKenna, John F. "The Proverb in Humanistic Studies: Language, Literature and Culture; Theory and Classroom Practice" *The French Review*, 48 (1974), 377–391.

Mieder, Wolfgang "Bibliographischer Abriss zur bildlichen Darstellung von Sprichwörtern und Redensarten" *Forschungen und Berichte zur Volkskunde in Baden-Württemberg,* ed. Irmgard Hampp and Peter Assion (Stuttgart, 1977), pp. 229–239.

Nyembezi, C.L. Sibusiso *Zulu Proverbs* (Johannesburg, 1963)

Voigt, Vilmos "Les niveaux des variantes de proverbes" *Acta Linguistica Academiae Scientiarum Hungaricae*, 20 (1970), 357–364.

Westermarck, Edward *Wit and Wisdom in Morocco: A Study of Native Proverbs* (London, 1930)

Whiting, B.J. "The Nature of the Proverb" *Harvard Studies and Notes in Philology and Literature*, 14 (1932), 273–307.

Whiting, B.J. "The Origin of the Proverb" *Harvard Studies and Notes in Philology and Literature*, 13 (1931), 47–80.

Zolkovskij, A.K. "At the Intersection of Linguistics, Paremiology and Poetics: On the Literary Structure of Proverbs" *Poetics*, 7 (1978), 309–332.